EGYPT AND ISRAEL

Also by Howard M. Sachar

The Course of Modern Jewish History
Aliyah: The Peoples of Israel
From the Ends of the Earth: The Peoples of Israel
The Emergence of the Middle East, 1914–1924
Europe Leaves the Middle East, 1936–1954
A History of Israel: From the Rise of Zionism to Our Time
The Man on the Camel

EGYPT AND ISRAEL

Howard M. Sachar

Richard Marek Publishers
New York

Maps by Jean Paul Tremblay

Library of Congress Cataloging in Publication Data

Sachar, Howard Morley, date.
   Egypt and Israel.

   Bibliography: p.
   Includes index.
   1. Egypt—Foreign relations—Israel.
2. Israel—Foreign relations—Egypt. I. Title.
DT82.5.I7S197   327.6205694   81-8282
ISBN 0-399-90124-8   AACR2

Printed in the United States of America

For Edward and Hindy

ACKNOWLEDGMENTS

In the prefaces of earlier works on Israel and the Middle East, I expressed my gratitude for the contributions of numerous Israeli friends and colleagues. Their help, evident most particularly in my *History of Israel*, has been incorporated in this volume as well, and to them once again I express my warmest appreciation. More recently, their commentary has been supplemented by that of other respected Israeli authorities. I must note here the valuable insights provided on international affairs by the late Yigal Allon, Israel's foreign minister and deputy prime minister, and by Mr. Asher Ben-Natan, formerly Jerusalem's envoy to Bonn and Paris; on Israel's counterespionage efforts overseas by Mr. Iser Harel, formerly director of the Mossad, and by Mr. Shmuel Segev, senior correspondent of the afternoon daily, *Ma'ariv*.

Messrs. Ze'ev Schiff and Eli Eyal, military editor and former political correspondent, respectively, of the morning newspaper, *HaAretz*, Dr. Amnon Sela, senior lecturer in political science at the Hebrew University, and Mr. Zvi Tsur, former chief of staff of Israel's armed forces, supplied critical information on the October 1973 war; even as Dr. Itamar Rabinovitch, Mr. Daniel Dishon, and Mr. Aluph Hareven, all of Tel Aviv University's Shiloach Institute, significantly buttressed my knowledge of Israel's strategic posture between 1967 and 1973. I am grateful to Professor Yigael Yadin of the Hebrew University (and until recently Israel's deputy prime minister) for his shrewd appraisal of Israel's political configuration in the years after the Six-Day War; to Mr. Gideon Samet, Washington correspondent of *HaAretz*, and to Ms. Bracha Oshrat, formerly director of the Egyptian desk of Israel's foreign ministry, for reviewing my chapters dealing with the Egyptian-Israeli peace negotiations. Mr. Leonard Davis, research director of the *Near East Report*, kindly supplied me with useful documents, texts, and maps.

Dr. Ashraf Ghorbal, ambassador of Egypt in Washington, and Mr. Muhammad Hakki, director of the press office of the Embassy of Egypt, graciously facilitated my research visit to Cairo. Due largely to them, to Mr.

Nabil Osman, director of the International Press Center of the Egyptian State Information Service, to Major General Muhammad al-Qateb, director of public affairs for the Egyptian armed forces, and to Lieutenant Colonel Abd al-Hamid Ghaleb, who served as personal military liaison, my stay in the Egyptian capital proved unexpectedly valuable in meetings, interviews, and in the establishment of warm friendships.

Space does not permit an extensive listing of the scores of Egyptians in all walks of life who generously received me in their homes and offices, and who shared with me their recollections and viewpoints. But among my hosts it is indispensable that at least several be mentioned by name. For a broader understanding of Egypt's diplomatic and political problems, I owe especial thanks to Dr. Butros Butros-Ghali, minister of state for foreign affairs; to Dr. Osama al-Baz, presidential counselor and *chef de cabinet* of the vice-president's office; to Dr. Sufi Abu Thaleb, speaker of the People's Assembly; to Mr. Mahmud Riad, formerly Egyptian foreign minister and most recently secretary-general of the Arab League; to Mr. Tahsin Bashir, Egypt's ambassador to the Arab League; and to Dr. Wahid Ra'afat, professor emeritus of constitutional law at Cairo University and formerly legal adviser to his nation's foreign ministry.

Among those who provided me with a new understanding of the Egyptian military role since 1956 were Lieutenant General Muhammad al-Gamassi, formerly chief of staff and minister of war; the late Major General Ahmad Badawi, chief of staff of the Egyptian armed forces; Major General Hassan Abu Saada, director of the armed forces operations branch; and Brigadier General Adel Yusri, deputy director of the operations branch. It was a particularly gratifying experience to meet and exchange views with a constellation of Egypt's most distinguished intellects. Among these were Mr. Naguib Mahfuz, the venerated novelist; Dr. Lewis Awad, dean of Egyptian literary critics; Madam Gazbia Sirri, the eminent painter; Dr. Hassan Fathi, "architect of the masses"; Dr. Ahmad Naguib Hashem, formerly minister of education; Dr. Muhammad Anis, chairman of the department of history at Cairo University; Dr. Hussein Moneis, professor of Islamic history at the same institution; and Ms. Nawal Hassam, director of the Center for the Study of Egyptian Civilization.

Over the years I have learned well that skilled and veteran journalists represent a uniquely knowledgeable source of information for the visiting researchist. This has been no less true of Egypt than of Israel. As a consequence, my insight into Egyptian social, economic, and political developments has been immeasurably enhanced by the observations of Mr. Musa Sabri, editor-in-chief of *al-Akhbar*; of Mr. Ali Hamdi Gamal, chairman of the board of directors of *al-Ahram*; of Mr. Hamdi Fuad, *al-Ahram*'s political editor; and of Dr. Saïd Yasin, director of the *al-Ahram* Center for Palestinian and Zionist Studies. Here, too, I must offer my heartfelt thanks to Mr. Adib Andrawes, Washington director of Egypt's Middle East News Agency, whose insights, wise counsel, and unfailing friendship were largely responsible for my visit to Egypt and, indeed, for my decision to write this book in the first place. It was through Mr. Andrawes's personal intercession, not least of all, that my access to Egypt's leadership was climaxed by the opportunity for a question-and-answer session with President Anwar al-Sadat. Warmest appreciation must also be expressed here to Dr. Hassan Hassouna, political counselor of the Embassy of Egypt, for his kindness in painstakingly reviewing my chapters relating to Egyptian-Israeli peace negotiations.

As in my recent publishing endeavors, too, I have once again received an important subvention from the Faculty Research Committee of George Washington University, whose chairman, Dean Henry Solomon, has long remained one of my most patient and understanding patrons. Finally, a simple acknowledgment cannot express the debt I owe to my close friend, Dr. Lawrence Marwick, director emeritus of the Hebraica division of the Library of Congress, for his endless help in securing bibliographical material in Hebrew and Arabic, and in correcting my translations and transliterations in both languages. Nor can mere words reveal the extent to which my wife, Eliana, has been the editor of this work. Her effort has been one not merely of advice and criticism, but of collaboration in every meaning of the word.

The generosity of all these, and other, benefactors will not have been wasted if this volume ultimately offers a somewhat wider historical perspective on the dramatic Egyptian-Israeli rapprochement of the last four years. That is its single purpose.

Kensington, Maryland,
December 31, 1980

CONTENTS

LIST OF MAPS

EGYPT AND ISRAEL

I

A MUTUAL SEARCH FOR
POLITICAL IDENTITY

THE THRESHOLD OF EGYPTIAN AWAKENING

On May 27, 1979, an Egyptian military command vehicle pulled up to a movie theater in the center of al-Arish, the nondescript little "capital" of the Sinai Peninsula. From the automobile backseat, Lieutenant Colonel Ahmad Abd al-Ghani climbed out slowly. A tall man in his late forties, Colonel Ghani balanced himself on his cane and gazed curiously about the town square. The memories flooded back: of his tour of duty served here in the mid-1950s, a young captain charged with training Palestinian guerrillas to conduct raids across the enemy frontier; and of the Israeli juggernaut overrunning Egyptian positions in al-Arish during the 1956 Sinai war—Ghani had suffered his first wound in that campaign. His "blooding" had been the merest rehearsal, as events turned out, for the ordeal of the 1973 war. Then, in the first wave of infantry to cross the Suez Canal with the Egyptian Third Army, Colonel Ghani had been cruelly lacerated by enemy shrapnel. Afterward, his right leg had been amputated below the knee in a field hospital.

Was the sacrifice worth it? Enduring the recurrent pain of that phantom limb, he had asked the question many times. The banner of Israel still fluttered over the dusty town square; but, in the distance, Egyptian flags already were unfurling over the squalid warren of shops and kiosks. That may have been an answer of sorts. If the limb was gone, the Sinai at least was being restored. Ghani sighed. Al-Arish was still an unappetizing sight, and yet the locals appeared reasonably well-fed and -dressed. No doubt they had claimed their fair share of Israeli military spending during the past twelve years of alien occupation. Despite the congestion of military traffic and press vehicles, there appeared space enough to breathe, to move, to function.

It was more than the colonel could admit of Cairo. Although nearly seven years had gone by since Egypt's proud vindication, his native city had become the paradigm of the nation's economic crisis. Behind the chrome and neon, the handsome monuments to earlier epochs of liberation, beyond the elegant spire of the television tower and the graceful waterfront corniche, Cairo had metastasized over the recent decade into an agglomeration of overgrown villages, a seemingly endless transplantation of eight million Delta rustics and former Canal dwellers, all grafted onto a metropolitan organism capable at best of serving an eighth that number of inhabitants with even marginal efficiency. Extending for mile after mile into the countryside, the necklace of "suburbs" churned with men, women and children, all impacted with their dogs, sheep, and goats into huts, wall-holes, cemetery pavilions, alleys, and streets. Communications were surrealistic. Vehicular traffic inched forward in a near-hopeless effort to navigate a block, a half-block. Mail delivery and telephones worked only sporadically. For any practical purpose, mighty Cairo, the largest city in Africa and one of the ten largest cities in the world, had virtually ceased to function. And so, for the past decade and a half of "revolutionary" rule in Egypt, had the economy of the nation altogether.

The plight of the Egyptian people unquestionably would have taxed the resources even of the most progressive and peaceful regime. While the country's sheer expanse of 383,000 square miles was exceeded in the Middle East only by that of the Sudan and Saudi Arabia, a mere 13,000 square miles of its breadth were naturally cultivable. This was the Nile Valley. As late as the turn of the century, some two-thirds of Egypt's entire population were congested within the narrow ambit of the historic river, and most of these within the three estuaries that formed the Nile Delta. Substantially illiterate, the fellahin—the tenant farmers—who comprised the majority of the nation, lived with their swarming families in mud-and-water huts, subsisted on dried meal and beans, and not uncommonly were afflicted with bilharziasis, trachoma, leptospirosis, or with others of the diseases that raged through the open sewer of the Nile Valley.

In the late nineteenth century, too, yet another waterway added its dimension to Egypt's universe. It was the 110-mile Suez Canal, the vital international thoroughfare that increasingly provided the rationale for Britain's de facto rule in Egypt. This rule, begun in 1882, ostensibly to protect European nationals and European economic interests in Egypt, was fundamentally benign, and one that instituted substantial administrative, legal, and economic reforms in Egyptian public life. By 1914, nevertheless, the British presence had hardened into a frankly colonial garrison, a military enclave powerful enough to ensure Britain's maritime trade and naval routes to the Orient. Indeed, during four and a half years of World War I, that commitment provided the margin of difference between British victory and defeat. From the distant reaches of England's overseas empire, fully 700,000 troops passed through the Suez gateway en route to the European and Ottoman fronts. In 1915 and 1916, moreover, two abortive Turkish campaigns against the Canal served to magnify Egypt's value in British wartime and postwar calculations. Thus, even earlier, upon the outbreak of hostilities, London had decided to clarify its ambivalent relationship with the Cairo government. It formally declared a British protectorate over Egypt.

THE ORIGINS OF THE JEWISH NATIONAL HOME

Entering the al-Arish movie auditorium with other Israeli and Egyptian war-wounded on May 27, 1979, Sergeant Ilan Halpern, like Lieutenant Colonel al-Ghani, drew on his own store of military recollections. In Halpern's case, the bitterest memory was of the struggle for Jerusalem in 1967, and of the Arab grenade that had mutilated him irretrievably. Was the sacrifice worthwhile? The young Israeli sergeant had never doubted it for a moment, not even during the long and painful aftermath of physical rehabilitation. He had fought for more than the survival of his land and family, after all. Gazing at the squalor around him now, Halpern needed little reminder that he had forfeited an eye and an arm for a quality of life: for order, cleanliness, for economic and educational opportunity, and for the unlimited right of cultural self-expression as a Jew.

The little homeland was but an insignificant fraction of Egypt's mighty expanse, Halpern knew. His native Tel Aviv would have been dwarfed beside Cairo. Even now, with its half-million population, it was less than a sixteenth the size of the Egyptian capital, and surely boasted none of the latter's constellation of exquisite shrines and monuments. Yet, while not lacking its own slums and occasional decrepitude, Tel Aviv at least provided its inhabitants with adequate shelter. Virtually no one lacked running water or electricity. The city's streets and markets were reasonably clean by Middle Eastern standards. Its public transportation was efficient. So were its clinics and hospitals. Halpern recalled with pride that his fellow Tel Avivians earned tolerable salaries and enjoyed Western-style social insurance, that their children—his children—attended decent schools. In short, Tel Aviv, like the Republic of Israel, worked. In almost every respect, his little nation fulfilled the political and economic ambitions that had brought his grandparents from Europe to the wilderness of Palestine at the turn of the century, that had sustained his parents in their tiny Jaffa suburb during the last years before World War I, and throughout the grim years of labor strife, Arab riots, and underground conspiracy between the wars.

Indeed, the passion that animated the Jewish redemptionist effort of Halpern's forebears two generations earlier manifestly was not less visceral than the nationalism sweeping through Egypt and numerous other Ottoman provinces by the late nineteenth century. It was a folk movement that was particularly vigorous in the densely packed Jewish hinterland of Eastern Europe. There, in the last decades before World War I, some five million Jews lived entirely to themselves, speaking their own language, nurturing their own religious and folk mores, and responding to gentile contempt and tsarist persecution with a reciprocal ethnic clannishness of their own. For them, moreover, as for Greeks, Armenians, Moslem Arabs, or other religionational communities under foreign rule, no distinction existed between the ancestral religion and the ancestral hearth. In the case of the Jews, admittedly, physical connection with Zion had been tenuous and intermittent since the destruction of Jewish statehood in 70 A.D. As late as 1880, no more than 20,000 Jews managed to subsist in the ravaged and disafforested Ottoman vilayets and sanjaks of Palestine, and most of these were otherwordly pietists, content to spend their days in prayer within the shadow of Jerusalem's Western Wall, the remnant of the Jewish Temple of antiquity.

But the Zionist cultural renaissance of the 1880s and 1890s already was beginning to augment this fossilized remnant with modest infusions of secular nationalists. Intent upon reviving a self-supporting Jewish enclave in Palestine, the newcomers, by the end of the century, had established twenty-two agricultural outposts. The going was very tough. The settlers were obliged to buy their way in by baksheesh and to engage in a variety of legal fictions for every shop or agricultural colony they opened. It seemed a painfully convoluted way to establish a homeland. Theodor Herzl, in fact, denounced the technique as fruitless. A Viennese Jew, a distinguished journalist totally immersed in European culture, Herzl had arrived at the idea of Zionism exclusively as a panacea for anti-Semitism. What his people needed, he insisted, was nothing less than a sovereign political state of their own. In 1896, Herzl published his apocalyptic vision in an essay, *Der Judenstaat*, and the following year convened a Zionist Congress in Basel. His *idée fixe*, henceforth, was to negotiate a charter of Jewish settlement in Palestine with the Ottoman sultan.

The diplomatic endeavor came to nothing. The political impact of Herzl's ideas, on the other hand, and the growth of the Zionist Organization, played a crucial role in underwriting a major stream of Jewish migration to Palestine. By 1914, 85,000 Jews had settled in the Holy Land. Their rural villages numbered forty-three. Their citrus groves were earning profits. So were their shops, foundries, and printing presses in the towns. Substantial numbers of Palestine Jews spoke Hebrew as their daily vernacular by then, and not a few guarded their own farms. Even the nucleus of self-government was dimly perceptible by 1914 in the grass-roots democracy of collective settlements, the federation of Judean colonies in the south, and the organization of lower Galilee in the north.

By the early years of World War I, meanwhile, the British, well ensconced in Egypt, had their own ideas for Palestine's future. The scheme was influenced by two factors: the need to evict the Turks from an area dangerously close to the Suez Canal; and by London's obligations to its wartime allies. In the spring of 1916, the British had formulated an agreement with the French and the Russians—the Sykes-Picot-Sazonov Agreement—for truncating Palestine into postwar zones of Great Power influence. The compact anticipated essentially a French sphere in the north, a British sphere in the south, with the central area to function as a joint "condominium." Yet, as the war progressed, London became increasingly dissatisfied with this arrangement. If the empire's troops by then were carrying the heaviest burden of military operations on the Ottoman front, they were entitled to more for their efforts, surely, than the limited sphere of influence provided by the agreement. An unqualified postwar British protectorate over the Holy Land seemed a fairer arrangement. It occurred to Prime Minister Lloyd George, too, that sponsorship of a Jewish homeland in the biblical hearth would offer an ideal "moral" rationale for such a protectorate. At the least, the offer would mobilize the goodwill of ostensibly powerful Jewish elements in the United States and Russia, even in Germany and Austria.

It was with these joint aims in mind, during the second half of 1917, that the British government and the Zionist leadership in England collaborated in formulating a British statement of support for a Jewish homeland. The statement eventually was issued by the British War Cabinet on November 2, 1917. Bearing the signature of the foreign secretary, the document was known thereafter as the Balfour Declaration. Its principal clauses stated that

> His Majesty's Government view with favour the establishment in Palestine of a national home for the Jewish people, and will use their best endeavours to facilitate the achievement of this object, it being clearly understood that nothing shall be done which may prejudice the civil and religious rights of existing non-Jewish communities in Palestine. . . .

First and foremost, Britain's "best endeavours" envisaged the conquest of Palestine itself. By spring of 1918, this task was largely accomplished. General Allenby's climactic offensive sent the Turks fleeing, and British military occupation of Palestine soon became a *fait accompli*. Thereafter, it awaited only the end of the war and the Paris Peace Conference for the Allied Powers and subsequently for the League of Nations to validate Britain's tenure in the Holy Land. That tenure was, of course, qualified by the obligation of nurturing the indigenous population to self-government, and by the additional responsibility of fostering the growth of a Jewish National Home. Yet, except for these caveats, Britain's institutionalized status in Palestine by 1920, ruling over some 60,000 Jews (many had perished or had been exiled during the war) and ten times that many Arabs, was as manifest a fact of postwar life as was Britain's protectorate over Egypt.

EGYPT'S STRUGGLE TO NATIONHOOD

Much had been happening in the latter dependency, for that matter, since 1914. Indeed, nationalist unrest in Egypt had surfaced unmistakably even in earlier years. The British response to it, then, had been to concede "qualified voters" a certain degree of consultative latitude, mainly a legislative assembly

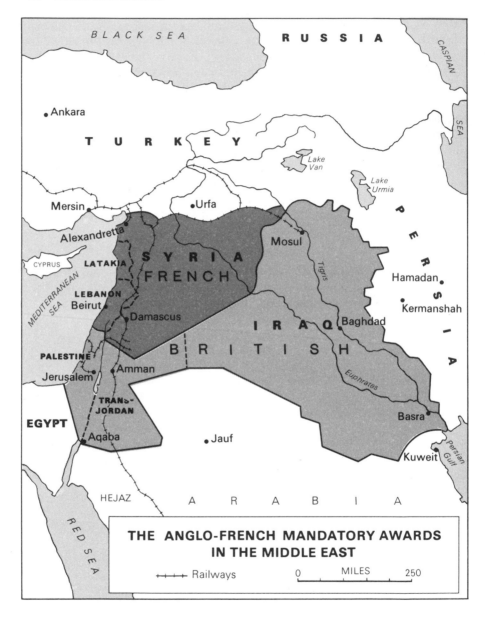

BLACK SEA

RUSSIA

CASPIAN SEA

•Ankara

T U R K E Y

Lake
Van

Lake
Urmia

Mersin•

•Urfa

Mosul

P
E
R
S
I
A

Alexandretta

CYPRUS

LATAKIA

S Y R I A
FRENCH

Tigris

Hamadan•

MEDITERRANEAN
SEA

LEBANON
Beirut•

•Damascus

I R A Q

•Baghdad

•Kermanshah

PALESTINE

B R I T I S H

Jerusalem•

•Amman

Euphrates

TRANS-
JORDAN

EGYPT

•Aqaba

•Jauf

Basra•

Kuwait•

Persian Gulf

HEJAZ

A R A B I A

RED SEA

**THE ANGLO-FRENCH MANDATORY AWARDS
IN THE MIDDLE EAST**

+-+-+ Railways

0   MILES   250

with broad advisory powers. The assembly was suspended during the war. So were Egyptian nationalist newspapers. Political suspects were exiled or imprisoned. It was only with the end of hostilities that popular discontent came raging onto the Egyptian scene with a long-suppressed vengeance; for by then the nationalist movement had found a leader. He was Sa'ad Zaghlul, a lawyer with extensive connections among the nation's commercial and professional middle classes, and a man of uncommon oratorical skills. Together with his following of businessmen and lawyers, Zaghlul had been inflamed by Wilsonian promises of self-determination and by British wartime declarations promising the Arabs self-government.

Following the Allied victory, Zaghlul requested permission of the British high commissioner to present Egypt's case for independence to London. He was refused. In the ensuing violence of public reaction, Zaghlul and other nationalists were arrested, rioting erupted in the major Egyptian cities, and Britain was obliged to ship in troop reinforcements. The demonstrations continued. At the end of 1919, a Royal Commission was dispatched from London. The following year its members recommended the establishment of Egyptian independence. It would be an independence so qualified by guarantees of British military domination, however, as to consist of little more than domestic autonomy. When, predictably, Zaghlul and his followers rejected the plan, London terminated the protectorate on its own in 1922, solemnly declaring Egypt to be an "independent sovereign state." But, of course, the British were careful to reserve for themselves control of Egypt's communications, its defenses, its foreign policy, the "protection of foreign interests and minorities," and de facto rule over the southern hinterland of the Sudan.

After some hesitation, the Cairo government grudgingly accepted this ambiguous formula. It proceeded to draft a constitution and, in March of 1923, to proclaim Sultan Fuad the King of Egypt. Whatever his mortification, Zaghlul did not hesitate to exploit the impending elections for his own political purposes. Campaigning vigorously at the head of the Wafd party, as his nationalist followers were called, he scored an overwhelming triumph at the polls and became prime minister in January 1924. Typically, he wasted no time in inciting his countrymen to renewed acts of violence against the British. Thus, in November of that year, Britain's governor-general in the Sudan was assassinated. Immediately, the high commissioner forced Zaghlul's resignation and thereafter dissolved the Egyptian parliament. A year of political chaos ensued before an uncertain calm was restored and new elections were held. Not long afterward, in 1927, Zaghlul died and tensions between the high commissioner's office and the Egyptian government finally eased. Mustafa Nahas, Zaghlul's successor as Wafdist leader, indicated a certain willingness to collaborate with the British.

One reason for this new "moderation" was the Egyptian king's growing interference in his nation's political life, his periodic dissolution of Wafdist parliaments and his replacement of constitutionally appointed cabinets with hand-picked royalist sycophants. It was this Palace-Wafdist rivalry, in turn, that diverted attention from the more traditional Anglo-Egyptian friction. So did Italian imperialism. Mussolini's invasion of Ethiopia in 1935 convinced many liberal Egyptians that a predator even more dangerous than Britain was loose in the eastern Mediterranean; even as the British, for their part, were increasingly sensitive to the need for cultivating Egyptian goodwill against the Italian menace. London accordingly intimated its willingness to discuss a new Anglo-Egyptian relationship.

Cairo's response was affirmative. The new king, Farouk, who succeeded his late father in 1936, allowed the elections that had been canceled the previous December to take place as scheduled; and once the Wafd was returned to power under Nahas, the latter wasted no time entering into serious negotiations with the British. At last, in August 1936, an Anglo-Egyptian Treaty of Alliance was signed. Under its terms, Britain formally reaffirmed Egypt's sovereign independence and agreed to be represented in Cairo henceforth by an ambassador rather than by a high commissioner. The Foreign Office similarly agreed to withdraw all its troops from the principal Egyptian cities, concentrating these forces primarily in the Canal Zone. In response, the Egyptians conceded Britain's option to resume full control of Egyptian military, air, and naval bases, and public communications, in the event of war or the threat of war.

Having reluctantly negotiated this treaty, however, the Wafd seemed to lose its usefulness as a political force. In 1937 the new ruler, Farouk, dismissed Nahas from office, and thereafter political life in Egypt ground to a halt. Although a coalition of smaller parties managed to patch cabinets together, their leaders appeared virtually powerless to legislate on any issue of public concern. Not a finger was raised subsequently to deal with the nation's continued submarginal level of subsistence, with the raw poverty of the fellahin, or with the endless rapacity of the absentee landlords. It was indeed precisely the combination of lingering anti-British resentment and governmental paralysis that rendered Egypt vulnerable to the penetration of the Axis Powers.

THE GROWTH OF JEWISH AND ARAB NATIONHOOD IN PALESTINE

During the same interwar period, by contrast, Britain's national administration in Palestine appeared to develop as competently and fair-mindedly as it had in Egypt during the apogee of British rule in that country. The legal system was organized essentially along Anglo-Saxon lines. Efficient postal, railroad, and telephone systems were installed. Sewage lines were laid, hospitals and clinics built. Public order was maintained. What did not function, or even develop, on the other hand, was a system of operative self-government. The failure was not attributable to lack of British goodwill. Determined to fulfill the premise upon which his nation had been awarded the mandate, Britain's high commissioner appointed an advisory council, hoping in this fashion to bring representatives of the Arab and Jewish communities into consultation, and eventually to give the council significant legislative authority on all purely domestic matters. It was a doomed effort, and one that was eventually abandoned in the face of a steadfast Arab refusal to participate with the Jews (pp. 28). As a result, the high commissioner was left with no alternative but to govern Palestine cen-tralistically. Negotiating with Arabs and Jews, he was obliged in the end to deal with two separate entities, each with its own communal structure.

In the case of the Jews, that structure was based upon two components. One was a national assembly, which was authorized by the British mandatory to exercise a limited jurisdiction in such matters as health, education, and religion. The second, and more important, component was established for the administration of the Jewish National Home. The terms of the mandate laid down that "an appropriate Jewish Agency shall be recognized as a public body" to cooperate with the government of Palestine in those economic, social and other matters that "may affect the establishment of the Jewish National Home." To fulfill this advisory role, a Jewish Agency was officially established in 1929, drawing its authority increasingly from the Jewish leadership of Palestine itself. Thus, the Agency gradually assumed responsibility for Jewish colonization and settlement, for selecting and training immigrants, and for determining the policy of the various Jewish national funds. Soon, in fact, the Agency evolved into a Zionist quasi-government, fostering its own corps of Jewish civil servants, a widening network of Jewish primary and secondary schools, even its own underground militia, the Haganah.

Among its various functions, the Agency regarded as its preeminent responsibility the active encouragement of Jewish settlement in the Holy Land. And here it registered its greatest success. At the end of World War I, barely 60,000 Jews remained in Palestine, most of these impoverished and demor-alized. Following the issuance of the Balfour Declaration, however, and the establishment of the mandate and the Jewish quasi-government, successive waves of immigration poured into the country. Until the mid-1930s, most of them came from Eastern Europe, and they were strongly animated by the ideals of both socialism and Zionism. Later, the rise to power of Hitler in Germany added still other Jewish newcomers. By 1939, as a result, the Jewish population of Palestine had climbed to over 500,000.

With Jewish Agency help, the immigrants drained swamps, plowed fields, enlarged citrus groves, established scores of new collective and cooperative agricultural colonies. Many others—the majority—settled in towns, dramat-ically enlarging and modernizing the Jewish communities of Jerusalem and Haifa, and the all-Jewish city of Tel Aviv. Indeed, by the eve of World War II, the Jewish National Home was becoming a civilized, even attractive, enclave in the Middle East, nurturing its own institutions of self-government, its own agricultural and industrial economy, a distinctive Hebraic culture that supported theaters, concert halls, universities, newspapers and publishing houses. It was a society animated, above all, by a fierce determination to achieve a creative, evenly-balanced, sociopolitical "normalcy." That determination was the more notable in contrast to the poverty and lethargic traditionalism of the surrounding Arab community.

By 1929, the 700,000 Arabs of Palestine were concentrated largely in the hill districts of the central and northern parts of the country. Except for enclaves of town dwellers in the coastal cities, and in Ramle, Lydda, Nazareth, and Jerusalem, most of them were farmers, and of these, fully half had come from neighboring lands, attracted essentially by the substantial new Jewish market in the Holy Land, and by a standard of living that was higher, as a result, than elsewhere in the Arab Middle East. These advantages notwithstanding, the Arab rank and file were less than enthusiastic about Zionist settlement. Like their kinsmen in Syria and Iraq, like their neighbors in Egypt, they were awakening to their identity as a people, and they resented the intrusion into their midst of an "alien" minority from the West. Well before 1914, for that matter, groups of Syrian and Palestinian Arabs had protested Ottoman laxness in tolerating Zionist settlement on Arab soil. Thus, in 1912 the "Decentralization party," formed by a group of expatriate Syrians living in Cairo, had taken an official stand against the "Zionist danger." These misgivings became far more pronounced after the war, with the establishment of the Palestine mandate. The Arab fear was genuine that the European Jews, with their superior literacy and technological skills, would someday engulf the whole of Palestine and transform the country into a Jewish state, a "dagger poised at the Arab heart."

As early as 1921, groups of Palestine Arabs began expressing their protest through violence. Riots, burnings, and killings extended from Jaffa on the coast to Zionist agricultural colonies in the interior. The outburst startled and shook the British Colonial Office no less than it did the Zionist leadership. To placate the Arabs, therefore, London decided to "redefine" the area affected by the Balfour Declaration. The "redefinition" was achieved by severing Transjordan from the area encompassed by the Jewish National Home and by issuing a White Paper to assure the Arabs of Palestine that they would not be inundated by Jewish settlement. In fact, this was the beginning of a process of attenuation that, during the next twenty-five years, systematically gutted the lingering authority of the Balfour Declaration. In 1922, the mandatory government similarly authorized the Arabs to establish a Supreme Moslem Council. Although the Council's purpose ostensibly was to coordinate the religious activities of the Palestine Moslem community, it soon took over virtually unchallenged political power among the Arab population. Its president, or Mufti, was Haj Muhammad Amin al-Husseini, a scion of Arab Palestine's wealthiest family. Haj Amin soon revealed himself, as well, to be perhaps the most intractable nationalist and anti-Zionist in the Arab world.

Rapidly building a personal, country-wide political machine, the Mufti appealed openly to the religious xenophobia of his followers, and incited them to overt violence against the Jews. In August 1929, Arab bands launched a series of nation-wide assaults against outlying Jewish farm settlements, inflicting some 500 Jewish casualties. To the consternation of the Zionists, the report of two investigating British Royal Commissions afterward tended to absolve the Mufti and his followers of guilt for the riots, and to suggest rather that it was Jewish economic domination and exclusivity that were responsible for provoking Arab unrest. Although Britain's recommended limitations against Jewish settlement and land purchases were not put into effect, the Zionists by then sensed their growing vulnerability under the less-than-precise language of the Balfour Declaration, and at a time when the rise of Arab nationalism in the Middle East threatened to effect a major shift in British imperial policy.

The Jews' misgivings were justified. In 1932, following an Arab insurrection in Iraq, London granted the Baghdad regime de jure independence. Four years later, as a direct result of Arab revolts in Syria and Lebanon, the French promised to match this British concession in the Levant mandates. In 1936, too, Britain redefined its relationship with Egypt, allowing that nation a fuller measure of authentic sovereignty. The local Arab populations had learned well by then that nationalist pressures could bring tangible results. In the 1930s, moreover, those pressures were augmented by an implicit Arab threat to gravitate into the camp of Germany; for, together with Italy, the Nazi regime was exploiting Arab unrest against Britain and France at every opportunity, mounting an effective barrage of propaganda, concentrating on the danger of Zionist "rule" in the Holy Land, and encouraging Arab protest demonstrations. In Palestine, the Arabs (and the Axis Powers) suspected that they had found Britain's Achilles' heel. The Mufti and his followers anticipated that London might be willing to throttle the Jewish National Home altogether as the quid pro quo for Arab peace and quiet.

BRITAIN REPUDIATES THE JEWISH NATIONAL HOME

To achieve that goal, Haj Amin and his followers organized a nation-wide strike in April 1936. Some months later, under the rubric of an "Arab Higher Committee," the Mufti's partisans launched a series of armed raids against Jewish settlements. The governments of Syria, Lebanon, and Iraq in turn promptly supported the guerrillas by dispatching "volunteers" of their own into Palestine. Taken aback by this new unrest, the British at first were hesitant to offer more than nominal protection for the Jewish settlers. In later months, however, as Arab guerrillas similarly began attacking British garrisons, the mandatory government allowed the Jews openly to activate their militia—the Haganah—and even provided the Zionists with a certain limited training and equipment. By late 1938, British reinforcements also reached Palestine, and within weeks the tide of battle turned against the Arab rebels.

Yet the attacks had accomplished their purpose, for they had compelled London to reevaluate the entire basis of its Palestine mandate. As early as November 1936, a Royal Commission under the chairmanship of Lord Robert Peel was dispatched to the Holy Land to make a detailed investigation of the tensions there. After several months of hearings, the Peel Commission issued a report in July 1937. Suggesting that the mandate was no longer workable, the report offered an astonishing new proposal for solving the Palestine crisis: it was to partition the country into independent Arab and Jewish states. The scheme electrified the Zionist leadership. Even though the Jewish state envisaged in the report was to be far smaller than the territory originally embraced in the Jewish National Home, the notion of sovereignty was a dazzling inducement. Indeed, because it implied open-ended Jewish immigration in future years, it won the all but official endorsement of the Zionist Organization. The Arabs, on the other hand, categorically rejected the proposal.

Intent by then upon finding common ground between the two opposing parties, Britain's Prime Minister Neville Chamberlain, in December 1938, invited representatives of the Jews, the Palestine Arabs, and the Arab states to a Round Table Conference in London. The conclave began in February 1939 and almost immediately proved to be a fiasco. The Arabs were flatly unwilling to consider anything but full sovereignty for an undivided Palestine under its current Arab majority. Faced with this obduracy, the British then terminated the conference in March. Two months later, in May, the Chamberlain government announced its own, unilateral, solution. It took the form of still another White Paper, this one signifying a near-total capitulation to the Arabs. The document set a maximum of 75,000 Jewish immigrants into Palestine during the ensuing five years. Thereafter, further Jewish immigration would depend upon Arab approval—that it, in effect, would be terminated. The White Paper similarly precluded further Jewish land acquisitions from Arabs, and for all practical purposes confined the Zionists henceforth to a territorial ghetto.

In releasing this statement of policy, with its evisceration of the Balfour Declaration, London manifestly was operating on the assumption that the Jews could not go over to the Axis camp, whatever their outrage at the mandatory power; but the Arabs could, and they would now have to be held in line at all costs. It was a not entirely unreasonable approach at a moment when Britain's Middle Eastern route of passage remained the one indispensable lifeline of imperial security. Unfortunately for the Chamberlain cabinet, the approach at once destroyed the lingering reality of Anglo-Jewish trust, even as it failed simultaneously to win Arab goodwill in Britain's emerging denouement with the Axis.

II

OVERTURE TO A
CONFRONTATION

EGYPT, EGYPTIAN JEWRY, AND THE JEWISH NATIONAL HOME

During the 1930s, the Egyptian government found itself increasingly involved in these critical Palestine developments. Egyptians and Jews were by no means strangers to each other, as it happened, nor was their relationship necessarily that of adversaries. By 1935, approximately 67,000 Jews resided in Egypt proper, many of them former inhabitants of the Ottoman Empire. With few exceptions, they regarded themselves as "Europeans" now, integral members of that privileged economic and social elite that included hundreds of thousands of Greeks, Italians, English, and French, all of them living under capitulatory (European consular) protection. Although later, as a result of the Anglo-Egyptian Treaty of 1936, this privileged extraterritoriality was withdrawn, the change created few problems at first for Egyptian Jewry. As "local subjects," if not citizens, they still enjoyed full legal protection in their personal and business activities. Indeed, they continued to achieve an impressive economic security for themselves. A middle-class community, they owned many of the largest shops and business enterprises of Cairo and Alexandria. Hundreds of Jews served as executives in Egypt's banking system and in the currency and cotton exchanges. Others were prominent lawyers and doctors. Living for the most part in their own quarters, the Harat al-Yahud, in the main cities, they spoke mainly French among themselves, educated their children in a network of Jewish schools, supported their own hospitals, and belonged to Jewish sports associations such as Maccabi or HaKoach, or to other exclusive, essentially "European," clubs.

This coveted exclusivity bespoke more than a sense of "European" clannishness. Rather, it signified a proudly conscious ethnocentrism as Jews. "In" Egypt, but not "of" Egypt, the people of Israel guarded their traditions fiercely. Central among these in the 1920s and 1930s was a sentimental Zionism that matched, without transcending, their affection for their adopted Egyptian homeland. Hebrew courses were offered in all Jewish schools. Zionist weeklies were published. In Alexandria, sizable Zionist libraries and drama groups were active. Some Jews collected money for the Jewish National Fund (a Zionist land-purchasing agency); others went to Palestine on visits, and even invested money there. Yet, until World War II, this dual cultural allegiance hardly ever involved emigration to Palestine. By the late 1930s, moreover, as Egypt identified increasingly with the Arab cause, the Jews found it useful to become more circumspect in their Zionist loyalties.

The relationship between Egypt and Palestine in modern times actually was quite well-developed. Throughout the 1830s and 1840s, the Egyptian viceroy, Mehemet Ali, governed Palestine as a de facto Egyptian province. During the British conquest of Palestine in World War I, thousands of Egyptians served as auxiliary workers, hauling equipment and digging roads for General Allenby's expeditionary force. And from 1919 on, a series of Egyptian governments maintained a distinct economic interest in the Holy Land. In the 1920s, the Egyptian pound was widely used as currency in Palestine. Egyptian ports were vital for Palestine's trade until the opening of Haifa harbor in 1931. Between 1922 and 1937, Egypt's volume of trade with Palestine exceeded that of any other Arab country.

Until the early decades of the twentieth century, however, the question of Arab-Jewish relations in Palestine did not loom large as an Egyptian political or diplomatic issue. The Egyptians were obsessed with their own problems: with their struggle for independence and, internally, with the political conflict between the Wafd and the Palace. "Our problem is an Egyptian problem, not an Arab problem," insisted Sa'ad Zaghlul at the Paris Peace Conference. The sentiment was echoed by virtually all Egyptian parties, from the Wafd to the Liberal Constitutionalists. The Zionists, in turn, did not hesitate to endorse Egypt's nationalist aspirations. As far back as 1897, Theodor Herzl, the founder of political Zionism, was visited by Mustafa Kamil, a pioneer Egyptian nationalist, and was exposed to a diatribe against the British occupation. In those days, to be sure, the Zionists were only vaguely aware of the depths of gestating Egyptian national feeling, even as the Egyptians failed to gauge the longer-range implications of Zionism.

Except for the Kamil-Herzl meeting, the first tentative interface between the two movements occurred in 1902 under the aegis of Britain's colonial secretary, Joseph Chamberlain. An ardent spokesman for the "Greater Englanders," Chamberlain was known to favor the use of client peoples as dependable instruments of British imperialism. Conceivably the Jews might play such a role. To explore that possibility, Chamberlain met with Herzl in the summer of 1902 and intimated that, if the Zionist leader could show him, Chamberlain, "a spot among the British possessions which was not yet inhabited by white settlers, then we could talk." Whereupon Herzl proceeded to outline for the colonial secretary his scheme for the colonization either of Cyprus or of al-Arish, in the northern Sinai Peninsula. Chamberlain immediately ruled out Cyprus but considered the notion of "Egypt" feasible. "No," smiled Herzl, "we will not go to Egypt. We have been there." Instead, he pressed specifically for al-Arish, a tract of Sinai Desert land that was not part of "integral" Egypt, and that also might lend itself to wide-scale cultivation. Intrigued by the proposal, Chamberlain forthwith arranged a meeting between Herzl and the foreign secretary, Lord Lansdowne. The latter was equally cordial. It was Lansdowne's suggestion that Lord Cromer, the British agent-general of Egypt, negotiate the matter directly with a Zionist mission. Herzl was delighted. Thus, after preparing memoranda and holding further discussions with government officials in London, he appointed a group consisting mainly of Zionist engineers and agronomists, and dispatched it to Egypt.

Almost at once, however, the Jews began encountering difficulties with Cromer and with the Egyptian prime minister, Butros Ghali. Both men were less than enthusiastic about the plan. Herzl himself then departed for Cairo in March of 1903. He found Cromer "the most disagreeable Englishman" he had ever met, and Butros Ghali even less amiable. Somewhat fearfully, he presented them with the interim report of the Zionist technical commission. It found al-Arish suitable for Europeans, for the cultivation of tobacco and cotton, provided irrigation were available; and irrigation from the Nile, while expensive, was not unfeasible. Two months later, nevertheless, Cromer informed the Zionists that the Egyptian government had rejected the plan on grounds of "inadequate irrigation." The argument was a fake. Cromer, and particularly the Egyptian authorities, admitted later that they simply disliked the notion of a Jewish enclave in their backyard. Herzl accepted the rebuff manfully. By then, too, he sensed that the Russian Jews, who constituted the bulk of the Zionist membership, in any case would never have accepted an alternative to the Holy Land. Moreover, the Egyptian nationalists he had encountered during his visit to Cairo were not the sort of people whom one antagonized. Herzl was much impressed by these young men. "They are the coming masters," he wrote in his diary. "It is a wonder that the English do not see this."

For their part, the Egyptians later developed a certain cautious admiration of their own for Zionism. Thus, in the mid-1920s, the Egyptian newspapers *al-Mahrusa* and *al-Muqattam* advised the Arabs to adopt a moderate stance toward the Balfour Declaration. In 1924, Colonel Frederick Kisch, director of the Zionist Organization's Palestine office, visited Cairo for friendly talks with influential Egyptians. Among these, Aziz Ali al-Misri, a distinguished nationalist leader, expressed his warm support for Zionism as a creative factor in Near Eastern revival. The following year, other prominent Egyptians, including Dr. Mahmud Azimi, editor of the Liberal Constitutional newspaper *al-Siasa*, accepted invitations to attend the inauguration of the Hebrew University in Jerusalem.

Yet there were discordant notes as early as the 1920s. Indeed, the newspapers *al-Izdam* and *al-Ahram* had adopted a pan-Arab, anti-Zionist line even in the prewar years; and in the immediate postwar period, several religious leaders of al-Azhar University detected an Islamic component in Palestine Arab unrest.

Accordingly, in May 1925, when an Islamic Congress on the caliphate assembled in Cairo, the Egyptian delegates listened with sympathy to Haj Amin al-Husseini, who led the Palestine Arab delegation. During the Palestine riots of 1929, Egyptian-Moslem opinion veered even closer to the pro-Arab viewpoint. Two years later, in 1931, the Mufti organized his own Islamic conference in Jerusalem on the issue of Palestine. Although King Fuad vetoed the dispatch of an Egyptian delegation (suspecting that the Mufti would use the occasion to undermine his, Fuad's, claim to the office of caliph), the Wafd party—the king's main political opponent—sent its own delegate. This was Abd al-Rahman Azzam Pasha, later to become a key figure in the Palestine conflict as first secretary-general of the Arab League. Other Egyptian political figures visited Palestine in the early 1930s to express growing support for the Arab cause.

While the Palestine issue was relatively quiet between 1931 and 1936, several developments in 1936 produced important changes for Egypt itself. One was the formulation of the Anglo-Egyptian Treaty. Henceforth, Egyptian governments enjoyed a new latitude for participation in international affairs. Upon the death of King Fuad, moreover, and the accession to the throne of Farouk in 1936, the pro-Arabist, Ali Maher, a wealthy landowner who had served as prime minister the year before, assumed an important advisory position as a member of the Regency Council. So, too, did Sheikh Mustafa al-Maraghi, rector of al-Azhar University and a man of strong pan-Islamic views. Others of this new "Palestine lobby" close to Farouk were Muhammad Mahmud, a Liberal Constitutionalist who became prime minister in 1939, Azzam Pasha, and Muhammad Ali Alluba, president of the Egyptian Bar Association. These men were not laggard in sensing the diversionary usefulness of the Palestine issue and of pan-Arabism as key weapons in the Crown's ongoing struggle with the Wafd.

1936: THE TURNING POINT

So long as the Wafd remained in power under Prime Minister Nahas, however, governmental discretion on the Holy Land continued. Thus, during the Palestine Arab general strike, which began in April 1936, and which led ultimately to the violence of the ensuing two years, the British sought the intercession of the Arab kings to help resolve the work stoppage. The Wafd, in turn, immediately blocked Farouk from participating in this royal intervention, and thereby from using the Palestine unrest to augment his personal prestige. Yet Nahas could hardly be indifferent to mounting student and religious criticism in Egypt of the Palestine issue. As a result, the prime minister laid his emphasis on quiet diplomacy. "Evidently the idea is growing on [Nahas]," stated the British ambassador's report to London, "that the Palestine question offers opportunities for him and Egypt to pose as leaders of the Arab world." It was certainly plain to Nahas that he could not afford to let Palestine become volatile enough to be exploited by the monarch. Again, when the Peel Report (p. 30) was issued in 1937, Nahas reacted with his original caution, expressing to the British ambassador his private reservations on a Jewish state next to Sinai, but tabling any parliamentary debate on the matter. In a statement before the League of Nations Mandates Commission, Foreign Minister Wassif Butros-Ghali (son of the 1902 prime minister) expressed his opposition to the notion of partitioning Palestine, but chose to present his case in moderate and restrained terms, to express sympathy for Jewish suffering in Europe and his warmest personal hopes for Arab-Jewish cooperation in the Holy Land. In sum, as long as the Wafd continued in office, Palestine remained an issue of secondary importance for the Cairo government.

Then, in late December 1937, Farouk dismissed the Wafd cabinet, and the Palace's supporters consolidated their grip on the government. The following June, at the initiative of the king's adviser, Ali Alluba, invitations were dispatched to a "World Interparliamentary Congress from Moslem Countries for the Defense of Palestine." Some 2,500 delegates arrived in Cairo for the gathering. As the Wafd feared, the subsequent meetings were shrewdly exploited to enhance the prestige of Farouk's royal government. Predictably, the Congress execrated the Balfour Declaration, the Peel partition scheme, and demanded an independent Arab Palestine. Whereupon Farouk and his counselors appointed three Egyptians to the ten-man delegation chosen to deliver this demand to London. On November 24, 1938, alluding to Palestine in his speech opening Parliament, the Egyptian monarch expressed sympathy for the "rights of the Arabs" in that country.

By the time, finally, the London Round Table Conference was convened in February 1939, the chief of the Egyptian royal cabinet, Ali Maher, emerged as the principal spokesman for the Arab delegation, with Azzam Pasha serving as his adviser. Yet, even then, the Zionists' relations with the Egyptians were far less envenomed than with the Arabs. Both sides, in fact, met separately and informally on several occasions during a break in the London Conference. At the first of these private meetings, on February 23, 1939, between Ali Maher and Dr. Chaim Weizmann, the Zionist spokesman, Maher gently proposed an independent state in Palestine with important minority guarantees for the Jews—a suggestion that Weizmann, with equal courtesy, rejected.

Throughout the conference sessions, too, Ali Maher played the role of the moderate, insisting that if only the British offered more concessions to the Arabs, he, Ali Maher, would invite the Mufti to Cairo and make him "toe the line." Ironically, the Egyptian prime minister extracted more from Whitehall than he expected or even demanded; for the subsequent White Paper, we recall, ensured a virtual moratorium on any further growth of the Jewish National Home. The ambivalence in Cairo continued. When the hard-line Arabs repudiated even the White Paper as a gesture of British appeasement, the Egyptians felt obliged not to break ranks in the public denunciation. But, even so, Muhammad Mahmud received Chaim Weizmann graciously afterward in Cairo. Expressing his personal admiration for Zionist accomplishments, Mahmud suggested that technical cooperation between Jews and Arabs might still bridge the gap between the two peoples.

If the Egyptian-Zionist dialogue continued discreetly, however, the most tangible impact of the government's mounting pro-Arabism was on the Jewish minority of Egypt. As late as 1936, at a time when anti-Semitic graffiti were beginning to appear on the walls of Jewish shops and homes, the prime minister could still seek medical treatment for himself and his family at Cairo's Jewish Hospital. Nevertheless, it was the militant right-wing fringe groups—the Ikhwan al-Muslemin (Moslem Brotherhood) and the Misr al-Fatat (Young Egypt), among others—that were beginning to set a new and ominous tone. In preparation for the 1938 "World Interparliamentary Congress," Ali Alluba warned Egyptian-Jewish leaders to repudiate their traditional support of Zionism. "Anything less than a complete condemnation of Zionism would brand you as foreigners in the Arab East," he insisted; and if the Egyptian government still maintained "restraint" on the Palestine issue, the Egyptian people "are not bound to follow that lead." As if to underscore the warning, in mid-1939 the Misr al-Fatat called for a boycott of Egyptian Jews, then began issuing a list of prominent Jewish merchants and communal organizations.

That same year, too, a number of Jewish communal offices were bombed. Physical disruption and occasional anti-Jewish boycotts fortunately would come to an abrupt end with the martial law of World War II. Yet it was plain by then that the barometer of toleration was falling among the Egyptians, among a people that until the 1930s had maintained a wide distance between themselves and "integral" Arabs. Indeed, for the Jews, the new climate was a decisive revelation of their vulnerability as a stateless minority not only in Hitler's Europe, but even among the most gentle and compliant of their "sister" civilizations in the Middle East.

III

A SHARED STRUGGLE
FOR FREEDOM

With the outbreak of World War II, Britain's position in Egypt appeared well secured. The Cairo government evidently intended to fulfill its treaty obligations: to build strategic roads and erect barracks under British contract; and to make available to Britain the country's extensive network of military bases and harbors. Yet London's sanguine expectations of Anglo-Egyptian cooperation were dashed within less than a year. The surrender of France and the entrance of Italy into the war in June 1940 immediately eroded Egypt's treaty loyalties. Sensing the apparent imminence of British defeat, the royal cabinet lost no opportunity thereafter to ingratiate itself with the onrushing Axis Powers. Typical was the reaction of Prime Minister Ali Maher (who had returned to office in 1940) to Italian air raids against Egyptian border posts in June 1940. Dismissing the attacks as "mere frontier incidents," Ali Maher then pulled his army back from the Libyan border and rejected persistent British demands for the confiscation of Italian assets in Egypt. Ultimately, on June 24, the British found it necessary to "advise" King Farouk to dismiss Ali Maher in favor of a less compromised politician, Hassan Sabri, and upon the latter's death in November, in favor of Hussein Sirri.

Even afterward, during Britain's 1940–41 winter offensive in Libya, further evidence was uncovered of Egyptian collusion with the enemy. Among other matters, it was learned that General Aziz Ali al-Misri, the former Egyptian chief of staff, was secretly dispatching information on British troop movements to the Italians. Whereupon General Sir Archibald Wavell, Britain's Middle East commander, ordered the Egyptian army to evacuate the battle zone forthwith and retreat to the Western Desert. "[W]e could not take this new provocation lying down," recalled a disgruntled officer, Major Muhammad Anwar Al-Sadat. "I pressed the view that . . . the army should rise up in general revolt with the support of the civilian population." At that juncture, an uprising doubtless would have been premature; but in April 1941, as Rommel's *Panzerarmee* launched the Axis counterattack toward Egypt's western frontier, Prime Minister Hussein Sirri blandly assured parliament that "the situation was not such as to cause uneasiness." By midsummer, with the German vanguard well inside Egypt, Foreign Undersecretary Sharara Pasha informed the press that "there is no need for Egypt to be on bad terms with any country."

These insipidities convinced General Wavell that a fundamental shift of Egyptian allegiances was imminent. He was right. On May 15, 1941, General Misri this time attempted to fly off to Vichy-controlled Lebanon in an Egyptian air force plane, carrying with him large quantities of additional intelligence on British troop dispositions. His plane was intercepted by the RAF and forced down. Again, Sadat recalled in chagrin: "I still think that if ill luck had not dogged our enterprise, we might have struck a quick blow at the British, joined forces with the Axis and changed the course of events." All was not lost for those who shared his hopes. Another, rather more influential, public figure similarly was in communication with the Germans. This was King Farouk. Through his ambassador in Teheran (who was also his father-in-law), the Egyptian monarch, on April 14, 1941, arranged the transmission of a personal message to Hitler. It stated that Farouk

> was filled with strong admiration for the Führer and respect for the German people, whose victory over England he desired most sincerely. He was one with his people in the wish to see victorious German troops in Egypt as soon as possible as liberators from the unbearably brutal English yoke. . . .

The German government responded two weeks later, emphasizing Hitler's personal gratification and his desire to achieve "close cooperation with King Farouk." In ensuing months, the discussions continued.

Then, on January 6, 1942, Prime Minister Sirri felt it circumspect to accede to British pressure and to "suspend" diplomatic relations with Vichy France. The move both surprised and angered Farouk. Within a few weeks, therefore, the king's supporters exploited the latest German military successes in the Western Desert by encouraging raucous street demonstrations against the cabinet. Hussein Sirri was obliged to resign on February 2. Appalled, the British were certain by then that Farouk intended to appoint a pro-Axis prime minister. To abort this danger, Ambassador Sir Miles Lampson presented the ruler with an ultimatum on February 4. It was to reinstate Nahas as premier—the Wafdist leader was pro-British—or to face enforced abdication. Farouk wilted under the threat and made the appointment. The humiliation was a bitter one for Egypt's nationalist extremists. Sadat was one of those who now redoubled his negotiations with Nazi agents in an attempt to overthrow the Wafd government and to repudiate the British connection. But in October 1942 Sadat was arrested, then convicted and imprisoned for his efforts. Soon afterward, General Sir Bernard Montgomery's Eighth Army hurled Rommel's troops from the Western Desert and Egyptian hopes for an Axis victory went glimmering.

PALESTINE AND THE ALLIES

No courtship of the Axis was more avid, however, than that carried out by the emigré Mufti of Jerusalem. Following his original departure from Palestine in 1936, Haj Amin had resided, until the outbreak of the war, first in Syria, then in Iraq, in each case fleeing only days before Allied invasion. From Baghdad in 1940, he dispatched a representative to the German embassy in Ankara to offer his collaboration. The offer was accepted, and Haj Amin left immediately for Europe in the summer of 1941. Soon afterward he was received by Mussolini in Rome, then by Hitler in Berlin. To the latter, he again professed his—and Arab—loyalty, but in return solicited Hitler's assurance of support for Arab independence. The Führer willingly acquiesced. Thereupon the Mufti set about recruiting Moslems in Axis-occupied territory to serve in the German armed forces. Broadcasting, too, on German radio, he repeatedly exhorted Moslems everywhere to rise up against the Allies. The effort was a vain one for the Holy Land itself. Intimidated by the presence of tens of thousands of British troops, even those Arab nationalists who had participated in the 1936–38 uprising were not constrained to budge this time. Neither, on the other hand, did the Palestine Arabs evince the remotest desire to support Britain's military effort. For them, as for the Egyptians and the Iraqis, the British were an unwelcome occupying power.

For the Jews, conversely, the British were allies in the common struggle against Hitler. Despite their bitter resentment of the 1939 White Paper, leaders of the Jewish Agency announced their intention of mobilizing Zionist agricultural and industrial resources for Britain's wartime needs. By 1943, not less than 63 percent of Palestine's Jewish work force was employed in meeting those needs, producing weapons components, tank engines, light naval craft, machine tools, uniforms, scientific apparatus, medical supplies and food. In the first month of the war, too, the Jewish National Assembly announced the registration of volunteers for national service. Within five days, 136,000 men and women were enrolled. By August 1942, some 18,000 Palestine Jews served in Britain's armed forces, approximately 25 percent of them in front-line positions. Two years later the British War Office authorized the formation of an official "Jewish Brigade," and its 3,400 combat troops saw action on the Italian front in the last phase of the war.

Following the Nazi conquest of France in 1940, meanwhile, Britain similarly eased its restrictions against the Jewish underground (the Haganah), allowing a certain measure of supervised training. Thus, in the Allied invasion of Vichy Syria in June 1941, two companies of Haganah volunteers reconnoitered Vichy positions, attacked enemy communications, ambushed Vichy patrols, dynamited culverts and sabotaged roads (it was in one of these actions that Moshe Dayan lost an eye). Other Haganah units served the British in espionage, working behind the German lines and in neighboring Arab lands. Once the Axis danger to the Middle East ebbed in the autumn of 1942, however, the British closed the various Haganah training bases and eventually relegated this fighting force to its original illegal status. The Haganah response, in turn, was simply to go underground again. The numbers of its troops swelled to 21,000. As a result of their earlier military collaboration with the British, the Haganah leadership also understood better the ways in which a regular army functioned. It was information that they would put to renewed use once the war ended, and against the British no less than against the Arabs.

The Zionists felt, in any case, that they had little enough reason to be grateful to the British. As the Nazi extermination program reached its highest crescendo by 1942, and millions of Jews were fed into gas chambers at Auschwitz and at other death camps, the mandatory administration in Palestine relentlessly enforced the White Paper, turning back the handful of refugee ships that managed to reach the nation's coastal waters. Several of these derelict vessels foundered on the high seas, with the loss of hundreds of lives. By 1944, as a consequence of the British blockade, Jewish frustration and despair had generated a vindictive underground campaign in the Holy Land. In large measure, the guerrilla effort was conducted by elements such as the Etzel and the Lech'i, right-wing splinter factions that repudiated the disciplined moderation of the Jewish Agency, and resorted instead to violence, even to assassination, in an effort to drive the British from Palestine. Thus, in August 1944 the dissident underground onslaught included an unsuccessful murder attempt against the British high commissioner, General Sir Harold MacMichael. Three months afterward, the Lech'i perpetrated its most audacious coup. It took place in Cairo and was directed against Lord Moyne, Britain's minister-resident in the Middle East. The Zionists considered him an enemy from his days as colonial secretary, when he had insisted upon enforcing the White Paper with undeviating rigor. On November 6, 1944, two young Lech'i members, Eliahu Bet-Zouri and Eliahu Hakim, shot Moyne fatally as he was leaving his office.

The Jewish assassins were seized and immediately imprisoned, then placed on trial in January 1945 before an Egyptian court. The trial was a fair one. The defense attorneys who were engaged by the prisoners' families included several of Egypt's most distinguished lawyers, among them a former president of the Cairo court and a former cabinet minister. At times these men waxed almost Zionist in their courtroom perorations. Describing the Jewish plight in Europe, they equated the Zionist struggle for freedom with that of Egypt. The young defendants "breathed in the atmosphere of the Holy Land," declared one attorney, "and they saw with their own eyes the realization of the four-thousand-year-old dream of a Jewish homeland." It was no less significant that the prisoners' bitter denunciations of the British White Paper evoked wide and sympathetic Egyptian press coverage. And when death sentences were handed down by the court, processions of Egyptian students marched through the streets of Cairo, chanting: "Free the Moyne slayers." The two youths were hanged. Nevertheless, during that brief, poignant moment, the sense of shared anti-British resentment transcended even the developing confrontation between the Jews and the Egyptians.

EGYPT'S BID FOR FREEDOM

Britain emerged from World War II virtually bankrupt, and with a new Labor government determined to launch a far-reaching and expensive social welfare program at home. Under tight financial restraints, Labor's foreign secretary, the veteran trade union leader Ernest Bevin, was convinced that his nation had no alternative but to reduce its elaborate colonial garrisons abroad. In the Middle East, the largest of those garrisons was in Egypt, and in the autumn of 1945 Bevin intimated his government's willingness to withdraw from that country completely, provided guarantees could be secured to protect the Suez Canal.

Cairo was interested—passionately. By the end of 1944 the wartime censorship had been relaxed, almost simultaneously with Farouk's dismissal of the Wafdist cabinet. This relaxation in turn opened the floodgates of Anglophobia. In their competitive diatribes against the British, moreover, the "respectable" parties were endlessly chivied by smaller extremist groups, particularly by the Ikhwan al-Muslemin and the Misr al-Fatat (p. 36). So fearful was the government of these quasi-terrorist organizations that cabinet ministers viewed the race to extract concessions from Britain as literally a matter of their own lives or death. In February 1945, Prime Minister Ahmad Maher was shot dead by partisans of the Misr al-Fatat for entering the war at Britain's side (simply to meet the March 1 deadline for charter membership in the United Nations). It appeared plain to Maher's successors that there was no room for compromise on the issue of British withdrawal.

Thus, on December 20, 1945, the government of Prime Minister Ismail Sidqi formally requested Britain to open negotiations with a view to revising the 1936 Anglo-Egyptian Treaty. The British concurred. Yet when delegations of both parties gathered in Cairo in April 1946, Sidqi insisted that no agreement was possible except on the basis of complete British military evacuation. Britain's Labor government eventually accepted this ultimatum, but with the caveat of its right of access to Suez in time of crisis; and on condition, too, of special status for the Anglo-Egyptian Sudan. The compromise proposal seemed a fair one, and Sidqi and his advisers responded to it favorably. After extensive negotiations throughout the autumn, a draft agreement was initialed by both sides in October 1946. Under its terms, the British committed themselves to full evacuation by September 1, 1949. The Egyptians for their part agreed that, in the event of aggression "against countries adjacent to Egypt," they would invite the British to return to their Suez bases and would offer "full cooperation." If a threat should develop to one of Egypt's neighbors, Cairo and London similarly would consult together to take all necessary measures. The issue of sovereignty over the Sudan apparently was resolved by defining the southern hinterland as "within the framework of the unity between the Sudan and Egypt under the Common Crown of Egypt."

In fact, the Sudan issue was not put to rest, and the ambiguity of the Anglo-Egyptian formula was destined in the end to sink the treaty. Returning to Cairo in late October 1946, Sidqi made a point of claiming exclusive Egyptian sovereignty over the Sudan. Learning of the prime minister's statement, Bevin in London felt obliged to challenge it on the spot. The British foreign secretary's reservations in turn provoked outrage in Egypt and forced Sidqi's resignation. Taking over as premier of a Sa'adist government, Mahmud Fahmi al-Nuqrashi thereupon officially pronounced the treaty moribund. In July 1947, moreover, Nuqrashi went so far as to appeal to the Security Council, insisting that British occupation of Egypt violated the fundamental United Nations principle of sovereignty and equality. Yet, after long and indecisive discussions, the Security Council adjourned on September 10, leaving the Egyptian question unresolved. The ensuing lacuna of defined status accordingly remained a festering provocation to the Egyptian nation, one that transcended even the explosive Palestine issue. Indeed, it was in some measure this resentment of continued British occupation that would account for Egypt's equivocal and ultimately ineffectual role in the Holy Land.

THE BIRTH OF ISRAEL . . .

Within months after the war ended, a tentative balance sheet of the European Jewish tragedy could be drawn up. Its statistics numbered over five million human beings—all liquidated by shooting, gassing, hanging, burning, starvation, or disease. By early 1946, approximately 250,000 Jewish survivors of the Holocaust had reached the Allied occupation zones of Germany, and for these displaced persons the vision of escape from the European charnel house soon became an obsession. Yet it was not simply Britain's wartime Conservative government that insisted upon maintaining the White Paper's ban against Jewish immigration into Palestine. In the postwar Labor cabinet, Foreign Secretary Bevin and his advisers regarded a "stable" Middle East as vital for the safety of Britain's oil supplies and for Britain's imperial lifeline throughout the Arab world. Arab goodwill consequently dared not be jeopardized in order to appease the Zionists. For the while, the White Paper would remain intact.

As far back as 1942, however, rumors of the Nazi death camps had impelled the Zionist leadership into a new statement of policy. If the White Paper denied Palestine Jewry the right to control immigration, even at a moment when an

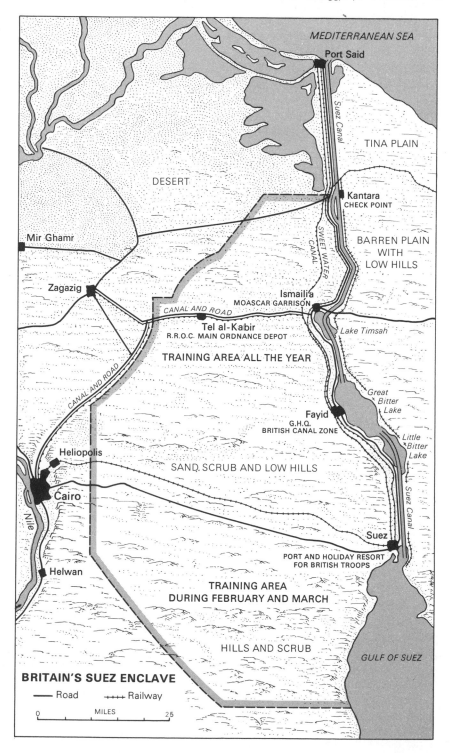

MEDITERRANEAN SEA

Port Said

Suez Canal

TINA PLAIN

DESERT

Kantara
CHECK POINT

SWEET WATER CANAL

Mir Ghamr

BARREN PLAIN
WITH
LOW HILLS

Zagazig

Ismailia
MOASCAR GARRISON

CANAL AND ROAD

Tel al-Kabir
R.R.O.C. MAIN ORDNANCE DEPOT

Lake Timsah

TRAINING AREA ALL THE YEAR

CANAL AND ROAD

*Great
Bitter
Lake*

Fayid
G.H.Q.
BRITISH CANAL ZONE

*Little
Bitter
Lake*

Heliopolis

SAND, SCRUB AND LOW HILLS

Suez Canal

Cairo

Nile

Suez
PORT AND HOLIDAY RESORT
FOR BRITISH TROOPS

Helwan

TRAINING AREA
DURING FEBRUARY AND MARCH

HILLS AND SCRUB

GULF OF SUEZ

BRITAIN'S SUEZ ENCLAVE

—— Road   +++++ Railway

0   MILES   25

open door meant life or death for the Jews of Europe, then the Balfour Declaration's initial, somewhat amorphous, conception of the Jewish National Home would have to be rejected for a sovereign Jewish commonwealth— nothing less. Thus, by war's end, London's intransigence provoked more than expressions of Zionist outrage. It provoked a renewed physical response. At the least, it lent a measure of respectability to those desperate elements who earlier had engaged in anti-British violence. Throughout 1945 and 1946, members of the Etzel and Lech'i ran wild in Palestine, attacking British military installations, shooting down British soldiers, even, in July 1946, blowing up British intelligence headquarters in Jerusalem's King David Hotel, with heavy loss of British, Arab, and Jewish life.

During the same postwar period, nevertheless, the most significant resistance to the White Paper took the form of a vast, ingeniously organized program of "illegal" Jewish immigration into Palestine. Directed by Haganah agents, thousands of Jewish displaced persons left their internment camps in West Germany each month for secret inlets on the Mediterranean. There they were loaded onto assorted Haganah-purchased vessels—many of them hardly more than fishing schooners—and were carried off toward Palestine. In fact, the majority of the refugee ships failed to reach the Holy Land. Most were intercepted by the British navy and their passengers were interned in Cyprus. But even in internment, the DPs represented a standing lien on the world's conscience and, in this fashion, an exceptionally effective political weapon in the Zionist arsenal.

Meanwhile, under intense diplomatic and financial pressure, the British government instinctively appealed to Washington for help in solving the refugee issue independently of Palestine. The effort was fruitless. Harry Truman, the new American president, sympathized with the wretched plight of the Jewish survivors. As early as the summer of 1945, he had proposed to London the immediate admission into Palestine of 100,000 Jews. It was a proposal endorsed, in May 1946, by a joint Anglo-American Committee of Inquiry. Once more, then, Truman pressed London to act on the recommendation. Bevin's grudging response was to seek Truman's cooperation in totally revising the Palestine mandate. The president immediately agreed. Indeed, he authorized the State Department to work closely with the British in formulating a new plan for what clearly had become an unworkable political arrangement in the Holy Land. Yet, as revealed in late July 1946, the Anglo-American blueprint— the "Grady-Morrison Report"—would have established separate Jewish and Arab provinces in Palestine under British control, and again would strictly have limited the number of Jewish immigrants. The Zionists rejected the scheme outright. So did Truman. At this point, exhausted by the cost of maintaining the blockade of Palestine, of supporting a large military garrison there against Jewish terrorism, and of flouting outraged world opinion, the British announced in February 1947 that they were turning over the Palestine problem in its entirety to the United Nations.

Two months later, in April 1947, the UN General Assembly appointed an eleven-nation special committee to deal with the Palestine impasse. Linking its investigation to the plight of the displaced persons, the committee visited the Holy Land in the summer of 1947 and conducted extensive hearings there. On August 31 it completed its report. The document recommended the termination of the British mandate and the partition of Palestine into sovereign Arab and Jewish states. Jewish territory would consist of eastern Galilee, the coastal plain, and the Negev Desert. Arab territory would encompass the rest of Palestine, except for Jerusalem, which would be administered by a United Nations trusteeship. This time it was the Arabs who furiously rejected the proposal. The Zionists accepted it. So did the Americans. So, unexpectedly, did the Soviets, who evidently detected in a Jewish state an opportunity to undermine Britain's presence not only in Palestine but in the entire Middle East. The combination of Great Power support was decisive. On November 29, 1947, the UN General Assembly voted in favor of partition. After a transitional period not to extend beyond October 1948, the mandate would expire.

Bevin did not accept this decision gracefully. It was his intention, rather, to avoid antagonizing the Arab nations, to offer no cooperation whatever to the emerging Jewish administration. In this fashion, Britain's puppet, King Abdullah of Transjordan, presumably would manage to occupy at least that sector of the Holy Land assigned to the Arabs, and British influence accordingly would be restored to Palestine through the "back door." By the end of 1947, too, Arab guerrillas, trained and equipped in Iraq and Syria, already were intensifying their attacks upon Jewish farm colonies. When the Jews fought back, they were disarmed by the British. This was hardly the swift, surgical resolution of the Palestine and refugee problems that the Truman administration had envisaged. As the fighting mounted, therefore, the American government began to waver in its support of partition, and in March 1948 suggested instead a "temporary" United Nations trusteeship over the Holy Land.

Among the Zionists there was no equivocation whatever. David Ben-Gurion, chairman of the Jewish Agency Executive, was determined to force the issue of sovereignty for his people. Russian-born, a pioneer agricultural worker in early-twentieth-century Palestine, Ben-Gurion had worked his way up in Labor Zionist councils and had assumed his current position as leader of the Jewish quasi-government as early as 1935. Yet, whatever his title, he remained the flinty trade unionist at heart, as plainspoken as Bevin but even more stubborn. Sixty-one years old in 1948, he looked the uncompromising role he was to play: stocky, muscular, his face hard and weatherbeaten under a corona of white hair, his voice rasping, his fists banging—the quintessential spokesman for a new generation of militant Jews. Now, on March 25, 1948, Ben-Gurion formally notified the United Nations that he and his colleagues were proceeding to establish a provisional government in the sector of Palestine assigned to the Jews.

It was a desperate act of faith. In the chaos left behind by the departing British, the railroads and mail service had stopped, the treasury had been stripped clean. Numbering only 600,000, the Jews needed money, personnel, equipment. Almost immediately, their provisional government set about raising a national loan. Civil servants were recruited from the Jewish Agency. Haganah agents were sent abroad on arms-purchasing missions. Little time remained to organize a coherent defense. London had announced that it would abandon the mandate not in October, but as early as May 15; and in the half-year between the UN Partition Resolution and the scheduled end of the mandate, thousands of Arab irregulars were pouring in from across the frontiers, ambushing Jewish convoys, seizing key heights, besieging the Jewish sector of Jerusalem and Jewish farm settlements in the Galilee and Negev. The Zionists were *in extremis* by then. Their armory consisted of a few thousand rifles and several hundred homemade mortars and grease guns.

It was trained manpower and near-fanatical commitment that made the difference. During April and May, the Haganah managed to recapture several of Palestine's key heights, to protect the littoral zone, the western and most of the eastern Galilee, and—precariously—the coastal highway to Jerusalem. On the evening of May 14, therefore, Ben-Gurion and his cabinet gathered in a reconverted art museum in Tel Aviv. There they solemnly proclaimed the independence of the Republic of Israel, and made ready to confront a full-scale invasion from the neighboring Arab states.

. . . AND THE ARAB RESPONSE

During these last years before Jewish statehood, the Egyptians were coping with their own grave internal dissensions. As noted, with the approaching end of World War II, the nation's political life entered a stage of all but uninterrupted turmoil. Public opinion was inflamed by the regime's continued failure to effect social or economic reforms. Communist agitation on the left, and Ikhwan and Misr al-Fatat pressures on the right, were becoming more violent. Seeking to defuse this unrest, King Farouk dismissed Nahas and the latter's Wafdist cabinet in October 1944 and appointed Ahmad Maher, brother of Ali Maher (p. 37), as prime minister, and Azzam Pasha as minister of state for Arab affairs. The stopgap effort did not work. Ahmad Maher was assassinated the next year, and the very survival of the Egyptian political system appeared to hang in the balance.

Facing national elections, then, and the likelihood of a Wafdist victory, the king at this point decided to exploit the Palestine issue as a diversion. By espousing the cause of the Palestine Arabs, Farouk would appear to his subjects as a visionary statesman, towering over those who opposed the royal preroga- tives. Additionally, a pro-Palestinian stance might serve as a technique to project Egyptian, and especially Farouk's, influence outward in the Arab world at large. That opportunity first surfaced at a conference in Alexandria, in March 1945, with the establishment of the Arab League. Counseled by Ali Maher and Azzam Pasha, the monarch envisaged the League as an instrument through which Egypt, as the largest and most prestigious of the Arabic-speaking nations, would lead the cause of Arab statehood in Palestine and thereby simultaneously advance the cause of its own freedom from Britain.

By no coincidence, Farouk's militant new pan-Arabism led to the rise of an authentically virulent anti-Jewish xenophobia in Egypt. In early 1945, news- paper editorials were "advising" Egyptian Jews to refrain from Zionist activities. In February of that year, Farouk's director of public security speculated publicly on the need to arrest Leon Castro, a leading Egyptian Zionist. Students at al- Azhar University and at the University of Cairo, as well as members of the Ikhwan and Misr al-Fatat, all were vocal in the agitation. In November, Truman's frequently expressed support for the admission of 100,000 Jews into Palestine led to large-scale anti-Jewish demonstrations in Cairo and Alexandria, this time spurred on by the pro-royalist newspapers. Hooligans were allowed to smash and ransack Jewish shops, to attack and loot a synagogue in Cairo. The police stood by quietly. At the palace, meanwhile, Farouk addressed a mob of 20,000, acclaiming Arab unity and denouncing Zionism. Even Mustafa Nahas, a known moderate on Palestine and a man traditionally friendly to the Jews, felt obliged to warn a delegation of concerned Jewish leaders to "repudiate" Zionism unequivocally.

By May 1946, working the anti-Zionist issue overtime, Farouk took the initiative in summoning a conference of Arab states at Inshas to discuss methods of countering the Anglo-American Committee Report, which had supported Truman's plan for admitting 100,000 Jews into Palestine. This meeting in turn was but a preliminary to a larger gathering of Arab leaders at Bludan, Syria, the following month, where the Egyptians were prominently represented. By then yet an additional reason for Farouk's militancy was his concern lest Abdullah of Transjordan, a client of the British, embark on adventures of his own in the Holy Land that would challenge the Egyptian ruler's carefully nurtured prestige and leadership in the Arab world. Indeed, as matters developed, the rise of inter-Arab territorial rivalry became the decisive catalyst propelling Egypt into the invasion of the Holy Land, and thereby into an escalating disaster of all but unimaginable military and political ramifications.

IV

THE FIRST PALESTINE WAR

A CONFUSION OF ARAB PURPOSES

Under normal circumstances, Arabs and Jews in Palestine conceivably might have lived together in a certain uneasy accommodation. If that state of affairs never developed, it was due specifically to the unwillingness of other governments to leave the two peoples alone. The possibility of armed Arab intervention had been discussed as far back as June 1946, during the conference of Arab leaders at Bludan. Abdullah of Transjordan supported the idea. So did the Iraqi prime minister, Salih Jabr, and Haj Amin al-Husseini, the Mufti of Jerusalem. Their aims were quite different, however. Abdullah's purpose was to extend his dynasty to the Arab sector of the Holy Land; he would arrange his own deal with the Jews for the rest of the country. The Syrians and Iraqis were determined simply to conquer as much as they could of northern Palestine. The Mufti's goal was the most forthright of all. It was to drive the Jews out and rule the country. Yet the rest of the Arab nations—Lebanon, Egypt, and Saudi Arabia—in fact were quite equivocal about intervention.

In Egypt's case, this ambivalence was apparent as early as the Inshas Conference, the gathering summoned by Farouk in reaction to the Anglo-American Committee Report. The Egyptian monarch ventilated his indignation on the Palestine issue, but procrastinated when it came to tangible suggestions for intervention. It was an authentic reflection of his nation's uncertainty. Still hopeful of avoiding bloodshed, Egyptian statesmen in recent years had maintained circumspect contacts with Zionist representatives. In 1945 and 1946 Eliahu Sasson, a leading Arab affairs specialist of the Jewish Agency, met privately in Cairo with Prime Ministers Ali Maher and Ismail Sidqi, then with Azzam Pasha, secretary-general of the Arab League. In the course of these discussions, Sasson assured Sidqi that, in return for Egyptian moderation on the Palestine issue, the Zionists would place their influence with friendly British Laborites at the service of the Cairo government, and would seek to persuade London that Palestine encompassed sufficient base facilities to offset any installations the British might give up in Egypt. Sidqi was not uninterested in the idea. Neither was the more militant Azzam, who explored the possibility of Zionist support for an Egyptian trusteeship over Libya. If the conversations ultimately were inconclusive, they at least made plain that the Egyptians had not foreclosed the alternatives to war. Indeed, a later meeting of Arab statesmen in Sofar, Lebanon, in September 1947 witnessed an identical equivocation. And three weeks after that, when the danger of United Nations action on partition became serious, an Arab League political committee met in Aley, Lebanon, to discuss possible military action. This time the Egyptians did not so much as participate.

By December 1947, however, Egypt faced a volatile domestic situation. Anti-British and anti-Zionist demonstrations were being mounted in such numbers that the government briefly declared a state of emergency. At this point, the Ikhwan, exasperated by the cabinet's indecision, began opening recruiting offices on its own for volunteers to fight in Palestine. Soon afterward, the Grand Ulema of al-Azhar University declared a *jihad*—a holy war—against the Zionists. Still the government hesitated. Azzam Pasha, like Prime Minister Nuqrashi, preferred to hold off armed intervention. A better approach, Azzam felt, was to train and equip the Palestine Arabs themselves for guerrilla warfare. At an Arab League meeting in Cairo in December, therefore, a compromise plan was adopted to supply the League's military committee with 10,000 rifles, to arrange for the passage of 3,000 Arab volunteers through Syria into Palestine, and to supply a million pounds sterling toward the "defense of Palestine." Even this approach was a bit much for Nuqrashi, who continued to favor a negotiated solution for the Holy Land. The prime minister had in mind a federalized cantonal Palestine, a scheme proposed by the United Nations Minority Report in November 1947, if such an alternative were still offered.

Like many of the Palace's coterie of politicians, Mahmud Fahmi al-Nuqrashi Pasha had begun his career as a militant Wafdist, then had moved to the right. Serving in the cabinets of Ali and Ahmad Maher, he had acceded to the prime ministry upon the latter's assassination early in 1945. Nicknamed the "timid sphinx," the sixty-year-old Nuqrashi was not the man, in 1947, to take decisive action in coping either with internal or with foreign issues. On the domestic scene, the prime minister blandly "guaranteed" the Jews of Egypt his "full protection," then allowed a scurrilous anti-Jewish press campaign to accuse them of smuggling gold and weapons out of Egypt, of flooding the nation with counterfeit banknotes, even of contaminating the water supplies and of plotting to destroy the country's sewage systems.

Confused and hesitant on the Palestine question, therefore, Nuqrashi was openly relieved when the United States, in March 1948, called for a temporary delay in implementing partition. He personally was willing to accept any alternative to warfare, he assured the United States ambassador. Yet it was difficult for Nuqrashi to maintain this posture of ambiguous restraint. The theological faculty of al-Azhar, and the leaders of Misr al-Fatat and the Ikhwan, were adding their pressures for action. The latter already were shipping volunteers and medical supplies to Palestine. For his part, Nuqrashi was well aware that his army was not ready, that its officer class was corrupt and incompetent. A mere four battalions of infantry were fit for battle. Worse yet, rumors were circulating of an impending Wafdist countercoup against the prime minister, and Nuqrashi would have preferred that the army remain home to ensure the government's security.

By April, however, it was evident that a mere show of inter-Arab "determination" would not suffice to block partition. The military balance in Palestine was shifting in favor of the Zionists. Even more ominously, Abdullah declared his intention that month of sending Transjordan's Arab Legion into the Holy Land, once the mandate ended. It was, in fact, this critical revelation that decided matters for the Egyptian government. For the sake of limiting Abdullah's territorial gains, not to mention his prestige in the Arab world, Farouk insisted now that Palestine must be "liberated" and returned to its "own inhabitants"— the local Arab population. The Arab League in turn agreed to the Egyptian formula; whereupon the Arab chiefs of staff hurriedly met in Damascus in late April. As their strategy was outlined, the Syrian and Lebanese armies would invade and occupy the Galilee; the Iraqi army and the Arab Legion would move west toward Haifa. In this first phase, the Egyptian role would be essentially diversionary, pinning down Jewish forces south of Tel Aviv.

But the scheme was outdated long before it could be put into operation. By the first week of May, the Jews had taken firm possession of the western Galilee and much of the eastern Galilee, and their lines of communication to Haifa were well protected. As a result, the elaborate Arab blueprint deteriorated into a loose understanding that the Syrians, the Iraqis, and the Arab Legion would enter central-eastern Palestine, while the Egyptians would be responsible for "investing" the southern half of the country. Logistics undermined even this program. The distance from Baghdad to Haifa was 700 miles. The Egyptian army's line of communication extended 250 miles, mainly across desert. Even the Arab Legion faced 90 miles of travel to the Palestine front, including first a descent and then a climb of 4,000 feet in crossing the Jordan Valley. Aware of these dangers, then, the Egyptian and Saudi governments frantically sought a last-minute compromise settlement through American intercession. What doomed further negotiations was Abdullah's determination to "solve the Palestine problem" on his own. On May 14 the Hashemite monarch appointed himself military "commander-in-chief," a title that was meaningless, for coordination among the various Arab armies proved nonexistent from the outset.

FAROUK'S TENTATIVE BID FOR PALESTINE

The Egyptians would have been less hesitant to invade Palestine had they known the actual state of Jewish defenses. As late as May 15, the Haganah mobilized barely 30,000 men and women. Its supply of weaponry was pitiably meager. The Zionist government and economy operated only in fits and starts.

If the Jews possessed a single advantage, it was to be found in the dedication and military experience of their troops. Yigael Yadin, Israel's commander of operations, represented a case in point. A graduate student of archaeology in civilian life, Yadin from his earliest youth had followed a typical Haganah career of secret operations against both Arab guerrillas and British military installations. In 1948, when he assumed acting command of the Jewish defense forces, he was thirty years old. None of his brigade commanders was older—or less experienced in underground operations. Several had fought in the wartime British army.

Yadin divided his limited forces with care, allocating three of his nine brigades to the north, two to the coastal plain to guard the Tel Aviv area, and two to the south as a counterpoise against the Egyptians. Finally, in the Judean hills, one brigade was assigned to the defense of Jerusalem, and one to the struggle for the highway in the Jerusalem Corridor. It was barely enough. On May 16 a Syrian armored column moved down along the southern tip of Lake Galilee toward the cluster of Jewish settlements in the Jordan Valley. Several of these villages were overrun. As the Arabs proceeded to attack the veteran kibbutz of Degania, however, they were stopped in their tracks by a howitzer salvo. Unnerved by the unexpected presence of Jewish artillery, the Syrian column reversed course and proceeded back up the mountain road, never to return. The Iraqis proved hardly more effective. Their combat force had been stationed in Transjordan near the Palestine frontier before May 14. It numbered only 3,500 men. Seeking to cross the Jordan River opposite Beisan the day the mandate ended, the Iraqis were halted by tough Jewish resistance. From then on the Iraqi battle commander stationed his troops in the Samarian "triangle," where they adopted an exclusively defensive position.

The most critical areas of the war proved to be in the south, along the Egyptian line of invasion up the Mediterranean coast; and in the Judean hills, where Abdullah's Arab Legion laid siege to Jerusalem. Ironically, until May 6 Egyptian army headquarters had shared the government's expectation that the United Nations somehow would resolve the Palestine issue. When the order actually came to march, therefore, Prime Minister Nuqrashi assured General Ahmad Ali al-Muawi, commander of Egypt's expeditionary force, that the UN Security Council unquestionably would order a halt before the fighting became serious. So confused were the Egyptians in their purpose even at this last moment, however, that Azzam Pasha, the Arab League secretary-general, could boast to a press conference on May 15: "This will be a war of extermination and a momentous massacre which will be spoken of like the Mongolian massacres and the Crusades."

The invading Egyptian army of 10,000 was organized into two brigades. Brigadier Muhammad Naguib commanded one of these; his principal staff officer was Major Abd al-Hakim Amer. Naguib led his troops from eastern Sinai along the coastal road extending to Gaza and Tel Aviv. The second brigade, under Lieutenant General Abd al-Aziz, moved inland toward Palestine's Hebron hills. On May 20, en route, Aziz's column entered the small Bedouin caravansary of Beersheba, then continued northward toward Bethlehem, taking over this bustling little tourist town from the Arab Legion. Naguib, meanwhile, leading 5,000 troops, proceeded cautiously up the littoral road toward the Tel Aviv urban enclave. To counter that threat, Yadin, the Israeli commander, ordered 2,000 men from the Jerusalem Corridor transferred to the coast. Exhausted and ill-equipped, these troops already had suffered heavy losses fighting the Legion. Naguib was unaware of their vulnerability, however. Rather, for the last five days half his own force had been engaged and badly mauled by two fiercely resisting kibbutz settlements, Yad Mordechai and Negba. As a result, the Egyptian commander moved with elaborate caution, slowing his drive barely sixteen miles from Tel Aviv.

Naguib's strategy was shortsighted. With a population of 250,000, Tel Aviv had become the principal concentration of Jewish settlement in the Holy Land; its fall clearly would have meant the end of the new Israeli state. On May 29, meanwhile, Yadin ordered his reinforcements to encircle Naguib's positions at night and to attack from the rear. Although its troop strength comprised less than half that of the invaders, the Jewish relief force found darkness and surprise effective weapons. Thrown into confusion by the unexpected descent upon their flank, the Egyptians pulled up short. The setback proved to be the turning point of their invasion. Tel Aviv was never again in jeopardy. The Egyptians' single accomplishment thus far was their control of the main Negev roads, and for Prime Minister Nuqrashi and his equally timorous cabinet this seemed accomplishment enough for the while.

It was the struggle against the Arab Legion that nearly did the Jews in. Abdullah had never disguised his intention of preempting for his dynasty the Arab sector of the Holy Land, and most particularly Jerusalem, with its venerated Moslem historical associations. After ten days of savage fighting in late May, however, the outnumbered Jewish troops managed to drive the Legion back from Jerusalem's northern access routes. From this point on the Legionnaires switched their offensive to the city's southern approaches. On May 29, Egyptian and Jordanian infantrymen stormed the kibbutz of Ramat Rachel, lying astride Jerusalem's southern entryway. In the most furious single encounter of the Palestine war, the little settlement changed hands five times in four days, but ultimately remained in Jewish hands. By contrast, Jerusalem's Old City, encompassing a congested Jewish warren of streets and courtyards, failed to break the Arab Legion's stranglehold. Its Haganah defenders surrendered on May 28. The loss of the Old City, and the subsequent desecration of its historic Jewish shrines, was a painful blow to religious Jews. Yet its fall was of little military importance to Israel, and the nation's secular majority learned to live quite comfortably without the Old City in future years.

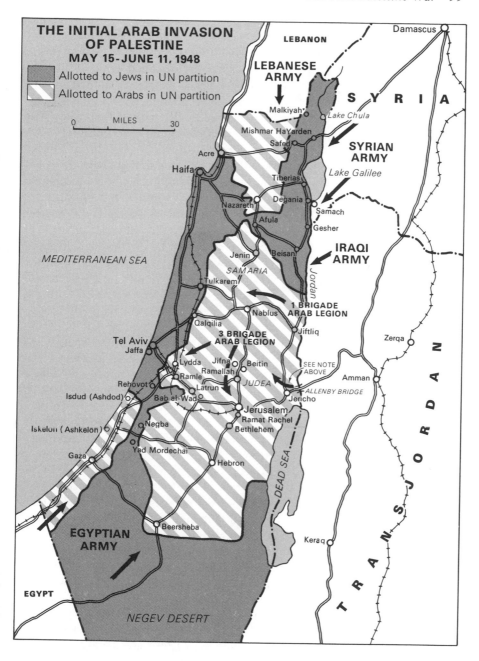

**THE INITIAL ARAB INVASION
OF PALESTINE**
MAY 15 - JUNE 11, 1948

Allotted to Jews in UN partition
Allotted to Arabs in UN partition

MILES
0   30

LEBANON

**LEBANESE
ARMY**

Malkiyah

Lake Chula

Mishmar HaYarden

Safed

Acre

Haifa

Tiberias

Lake Galilee

Nazareth

Degania

Afula

Samach

Gesher

S Y R I A

Damascus

**SYRIAN
ARMY**

MEDITERRANEAN SEA

Jenin

Beisan

SAMARIA

Tulkarem

Nablus

Qalqilia

Jiftliq

**1 BRIGADE
ARAB LEGION**

**3 BRIGADE
ARAB LEGION**

Tel Aviv

Jaffa

Lydda

Jifna

Beitin

Ramallah

Ramle

Latrun

JUDEA

SEE NOTE
ABOVE

Rehovot

Isdud (Ashdod)

Bab al-Wad

ALLENBY BRIDGE

Jericho

Jerusalem

Ramat Rachel

Iskelon (Ashkelon)

Negba

Bethlehem

Gaza

Yad Mordechai

Hebron

**EGYPTIAN
ARMY**

Beersheba

Keraq

EGYPT

NEGEV DESERT

**IRAQI
ARMY**

Zerqa

Amman

Jordan

DEAD SEA

T R A N S J O R D A N

INTERREGNUM AND REAPPRAISAL

On June 11, the Security Council finally won agreement from Arabs and Israelis for a one-month truce. Both sides were exhausted. Strategically, the Arabs had gained only minimal advantage. They were also aware that the Jews were expecting the arrival of ordnance and personnel from abroad, and doubtless would be strengthened by the end of the truce. One urgent Arab priority, therefore, would have been an immediate unification of forces. Yet, when the Iraqis offered the post of commander-in-chief to General al-Muawi, who was leading the Egyptian expeditionary force, Abdullah promptly vetoed the appointment; the Hashemite king by then had lost interest in continuing the war. So, too, had the rank and file in all the Arab armies. Indeed, once the truce came into effect, Israelis and Egyptians on the southern front emerged from their bunkers, even met and occasionally chatted with each other. The decision to continue the war actually was made not by the Egyptian and Arab army commanders, but rather by their political leaders, who expected in this fashion to sustain their reputation as patriots. Nuqrashi in Egypt frankly doubted that his cabinet would survive if the cease-fire were extended. Thus, by the first week in July, the Arabs had augmented their troop strength in Palestine from 32,000 to 45,000 men.

For the Jews, on the other hand, the issue of continuing the struggle was much simpler. Although the invading enemy armies had been contained, the Negev was largely in Egyptian hands; the Iraqis were ensconced only eleven miles from the Mediterranean, and the narrow highway from the coast to Jerusalem remained in grave jeopardy. During the cease-fire, convoys of food and medicine were rushed to the Holy City. Mobilization was dramatically increased. With the arrival of new immigrants and of Jewish military volunteers from abroad, Israeli troops numbered 60,000 by mid-July. Thousands of tons of military equipment had been unloaded by then, much of it from Communist Czechoslovakia, which was dutifully following Moscow's lead in supporting Israel against Arab "reaction" (and the British imperial presence) in the Middle East. Accordingly, by the time the fighting resumed, the Israeli army was well embarked on its transformation into a modern fighting force.

On July 8, even before the truce expired, General Naguib renewed his attack against Negba, the linchpin of the Israeli defense system in the south. His troops were hurled back. Thereafter the Jews themselves began a limited offensive and succeeded in reoccupying the northwestern corner of the Negev. It was, in fact, the ease of the reconquest that convinced Yadin and his staff that the Egyptians no longer posed a major threat, that they could be dealt with later. The presence of 2,000 Arab irregulars in the lower Galilee was a somewhat more serious danger, but the Jews disposed of it in a week-long campaign, overrunning Nazareth and clearing other neighboring Arab communities. In a sledgehammer operation commanded by Lieutenant Colonel Moshe Dayan, the Israelis also managed to seize control of the Legion-occupied Lydda-Ramle area, thus widening the neck of the Jerusalem Corridor.

The shift in the momentum of the war similarly effected a critical alteration in the demography of Palestine. In the chaos of British departure and of mounting hostilities, some 175,000 Arabs fled the country during the last weeks of the mandate. After May 15, the invasion of organized Arab armies transformed the entire Holy Land into a battleground. Terrified by the cacophony of gunfire about them, and by not infrequent acts of Jewish intimidation, the local Palestine Arabs fled in even greater numbers. By the time the war ended in January 1949, approximately 650,000 of them had departed, more than two-thirds of the entire Arab population of the country. Not all those who fled their homes departed Palestine itself. Approximately 240,000 Arabs simply crossed into the Legion-occupied eastern sector of the country. Another 60,000 traversed the Jordan River and entered the Hashemite kingdom proper. An additional 180,000 fled toward Gaza, within Palestinian territory, but on the edge of the Sinai Peninsula. The rest found sanctuary in other, neighboring Arab states. At first this Arab departure served Israel's security and economic purposes by reducing the threat of a fifth column, and by making homes and farmland available for new Jewish immigrants. With the passage of the years, however, as the refugees vegetated in the squalor of refugee camps, they came to fulfill an equally useful political purpose for the Arab governments themselves (p. 67).

THE EGYPTIAN BID FAILS

The UN Security Council and its appointed mediator for Palestine, Count Folke Bernadotte, moved with dispatch in negotiating a second cease-fire on July 18. Unlike the earlier truce of June, the new cease-fire was intended to remain in force without time limit. In his report to the Security Council on September 16, the Swedish count genially offered his own blueprint for peace in the Holy Land. It envisaged the award of the Negev Desert (allocated to the Jews under the UN Partition Resolution) to the Arabs, with the lower Galilee (initially assigned to the Arabs) to be awarded to Israel as compensation, and Jerusalem (now effectively partitioned between Transjordan and Israel) to be internationalized. The mediator's report was contemptuously rejected by both sides. The day after it was submitted, in fact, Bernadotte himself was assassinated in Jerusalem by Jewish terrorists. Yet by then it was evident to Israel's Prime Minister Ben-Gurion that the scheme for the Negev and Jerusalem gave the United Nations a handle for applying pressure on the Jews, that Israel's bargaining position would have to be strengthened by new and decisive military realities. He agreed with Yadin, then, that priority henceforth should be given to a full-scale offensive in the Negev.

In this southern desert region, the Egyptians loosely controlled three long strips. The first was the coastal region from Rafah to Gaza. The second was an inland strip running from al-Auja north through Beersheba to Bethlehem. Linking the two enclaves was a third, a cross-country strip along a road extending from Majdal through al-Faluja to Beit Gubrin (see map, p. 59). Tactically, these holdings were extremely vulnerable, although the Egyptians had reinforced them with 15,000 new troops and large quantities of heavy weapons. During the same period, the flow of overseas supplies to Israel continued uninterruptedly. Thus, in preparation for the new offensive, Israeli transport planes carried a full brigade of men and matériel to an airstrip in the northern Negev. Under cover of darkness, the troops were infiltrated behind Egyptian lines. Throughout early October, two additional brigades were moved southward, until the Israelis had concentrated 30,000 men on the southern front. The attack began on October 14. Sweeping low behind enemy lines, the fledgling Israeli air force struck Egyptian bases and supply lines in the Sinai. At the same time, the secret—infiltrated—Negev brigade now thrust ahead up the coastal road toward Beit Hanun.

It was all a feint. Yadin's actual goal was the al-Faluja crossroads, the junction controlling the highway net into the Negev Desert. Throughout October 15, other detachments of Israeli infantry launched a major attack against Egyptian fortifications at Iraq al-Manshiyyah. The battle was a savage one, with heavy losses on both sides, but the Jews finally took the fortress. On October 20, in another frontal assault lasting a day and a night, the Israelis invested Huleiqat, the heavily defended stockade anchoring the Egyptian line in the upper Negev. That line was now breached, and the major concentration of Egyptian troops in Palestine, some 30,000 men, faced the possibility of entrapment near al-Faluja. Hereupon, Colonel Yigal Allon, the Israeli southern front commander, sent his three brigades racing toward Beersheba, the Bedouin "capital" of the Negev. The Egyptian garrison there was caught off guard and surrendered after only brief resistance. Two days later the neighboring Lachish area was occupied by fast-moving Jewish motorized columns.

During the last week of October, as yet a third United Nations truce gradually settled on the desert, the Egyptians began evacuating their units from the western Negev, loading troops on naval craft anchored off the coast. Even here they suffered painful losses. Two of their frigates were sunk by Israeli underwater demolition teams. One of the vessels, *Emir Farouk*, flagship of the Egyptian navy, went down with 700 soldiers aboard. Finally, 3,000 of Egypt's elite troops, the Fourth Brigade, were encircled and immobilized in the northwestern Faluja "pocket." Both sides chose to ignore the truce in this isolated sector. Under the command of a resourceful Sudanese brigadier, Taha Bey, the Fourth Brigade steadfastly resisted the tightening Israeli siege. On his own, then, Allon arranged a parley with Taha Bey. The two officers met at Kibbutz Gat, two miles east of al-Faluja. Taha Bey was a stocky, good-natured

Negro. He congratulated Allon on the latter's "admirable" military victories, but insisted that "I shall fight to my last bullet and my last man."

The one consequence of the discussion was to establish a rapport between Major Yerucham Cohen, Allon's aide-de-camp, and Major Gamal Abd al-Nasser, Taha Bey's adjutant. Nasser was fascinated by the kibbutz settlements and by the evidence he saw around him of Jewish social democracy. For him, the contrast was vivid between Israeli "progressivism" and the venality and absentee landlordism of his own country. Yet his angriest diatribes were reserved for the British. "They maneuvered us into this war," he insisted. "What is Palestine to us? It was all a British trick to divert our attention from their occupation of Egypt." The Arab "allies" were equally the target of Nasser's wrath, particularly Abdullah, who evinced not the slightest willingness to help the trapped Egyptians. Someday the Hashemite ruler would pay for his "betrayal," Nasser declared.

The young major's contumely well reflected the suspicion festering between his government and Transjordan's. Determined to block a Hashemite annexation of Arab Palestine, Nuqrashi and the Egyptian cabinet invoked the "rights of the Palestinian people" and announced plans for a separate, quasi-independent government for the Holy Land. To that end, in September 1948, Cairo organized an "all-Palestinian government," with its seat in Gaza, and on October 1 an Egyptian-sponsored "National Palestinian Council" dutifully met in Gaza to elect as its president Haj Amin al-Husseini, the Mufti of Jerusalem. Within two weeks this puppet regime was extended formal recognition by Syria, Lebanon, and Iraq. Abdullah did not sit by quietly, however. Rather, the Transjordanian monarch organized his own handpicked conference of Palestinian delegates, and in late October this gathering solemnly repudiated the Gaza regime. On December 1, finally, Abdullah graciously "accepted" the appeal of a second conference to unite Palestine and Transjordan into an indivisible "Arab Hashemite Kingdom of Jordan." Abdullah's countermaneuver provoked an infuriated response from Cairo. In ensuing days, Farouk anathematized the Palestinians who had attended the conference, and the Grand Ulema of al-Azhar University formally denounced the Hashemite regime for "nefarious interference threatening to destroy Arab unity."

Even as the Egyptians and Hashemites reviled each other, the Jews were preparing to eradicate the Egyptian army's last garrison on Israeli territory. Their troops were ready, totaling nearly 100,000 by December 1948, and by then their accumulated armory included heavy artillery, even a scattering of tanks. The Egyptians were deployed slightly to the north of the Sinai frontier between their own country and Israel, and formed two prongs. The northern force, consisting of two brigades flanking Rafah and Gaza, was supported by the great Sinai staging base of al-Arish. The southern prong, also of two-brigade strength, extended from al-Auja to Bir Asluj and aimed upward toward Beersheba. Additionally, the Egyptian Fourth Brigade, locked into the Faluja pocket, tied down a Jewish unit of comparable size. The Egyptians defended well-fortified positions. The Israelis enjoyed the advantages of initiative and surprise. These were assets that Yadin now intended to exploit. The Egyptians presumably would expect the attack to be launched against their northern line, the detachments threatening the heavily populated coastal area. Without hesitation, then, the Israeli command agreed to thrust southward, toward al-Auja, the anchor of the Egyptian position in the Negev.

The offensive began the night of December 22. According to plan, Allon sent an armored column rolling ominously toward Gaza. Another brigade of infantrymen charged in the direction of the main highway between Bir Asluj and al-Auja. Both attacks were feints, and both convinced the Egyptians that the Israeli offensive was unfolding according to orthodox pattern. During the next few days, therefore, as the Egyptians braced themselves against repeated frontal assaults on their main fortifications, an Israeli armored column already was moving slowly along their flank on an ancient Roman road, a thoroughfare discovered by Yadin in the course of his earlier archaeological research. Without warning, the vanguard of the Israeli army battered into the defenders' rear at al-Auja, careening into the square. After a full day and night of close-quarter fighting, the Egyptian garrison capitulated.

The Israelis forged ahead without pause. In the enveloping movement, their columns overran Abu Agheila, ten miles inside Egypt's Sinai territory. From there they pressed on toward the Mediterranean coast in the direction of al-Arish itself. It was plain by then that the Jews had come farther in seven months of war than the limited distance of mere geographic advance. In May their ill-armed little militia had faced Egyptian tanks only sixteen miles from Tel Aviv. In December their battle-seasoned troops, supported by armor and fighter planes, were driving into the territory of their Egyptian enemies.

Virtually bereft of support from its allies at this point, the Egyptian government soon was confronted with equally painful repercussions at home. By entering the Palestine war, Farouk had intended to divert public attention from his country's economic chaos and to upstage his rival, the Wafd party. For a while he appeared to have succeeded. Real and imaginary victories filled the press; the king had even ordered his "triumph" inscribed on postage stamps. With the onset of Israel's final December offensive, however, Cairo found it necessary to dissemble. Ultimately the army's failures in Palestine became known. They coincided with a cholera epidemic, with lower-middle-class unrest, and with violent Ikhwan-instigated demonstrations against Jewish businesses. Riots erupted in the streets of Cairo and Alexandria. Nationalist slogans were intermingled with epithets against Nuqrashi's government. The prime minister reacted by outlawing the Ikhwan. Yet, before the order could be carried out, Nuqrashi himself, the genial "sphinx," was murdered on December 28 by an Ikhwan gunman. Some political observers believed that Egypt was on the verge of civil war.

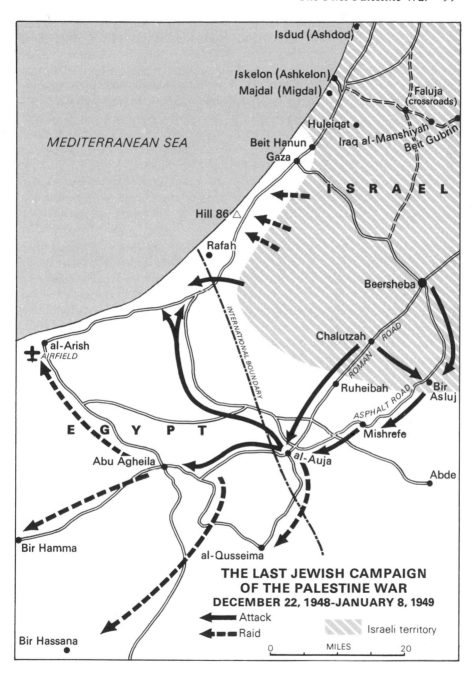

MEDITERRANEAN SEA

Isdud (Ashdod)

Iskelon (Ashkelon)

Majdal (Migdal)

Faluja (crossroads)

Huleiqat

Beit Hanun
Gaza

Iraq al-Manshiyah

Beit Gubrin

I S R A E L

Hill 86 △

Rafah

Beersheba

al-Arish
AIRFIELD

Chalutzah

ROMAN ROAD

INTERNATIONAL BOUNDARY

Ruheibah

Bir Asluj

ASPHALT ROAD

E G Y P T

Mishrefe

Abu Agheila

al-Auja

Abde

Bir Hamma

al-Qusseima

**THE LAST JEWISH CAMPAIGN
OF THE PALESTINE WAR**
DECEMBER 22, 1948-JANUARY 8, 1949

Attack

Raid

Israeli territory

Bir Hassana

0   MILES   20

Help for the distraught nation came from another quarter. Under the terms of the 1936 Anglo-Egyptian Treaty, Britain was obliged to assist Egypt against attack from an outside party; and on December 29 the Security Council ordered an immediate cease-fire in Palestine. This directive was regarded by Foreign Secretary Bevin as a unique opportunity to strengthen Britain's tenuous presence in Egypt, and conceivably to revive it in Palestine. Unless Israel obeyed the United Nations resolution, Bevin insisted, Whitehall would honor its "treaty obligations." The ultimatum was a chilling one. Accordingly, on January 2, 1949, unwilling to risk a confrontation with a Great Power, Ben-Gurion ordered Yadin to withdraw his troops from Sinai.

At Yadin's insistence, however, the Israeli prime minister authorized seizure of the heights above the border town of Rafah, thereby sealing the escape route of the entire Egyptian expeditionary force. Cairo's response in turn was to declare its willingness to enter armistice negotiations, provided the Israelis halted their operation. The British sought now to add an "inducement" of their own, by increasing the number of RAF sorties along the Egyptian-Israeli frontier. But on January 7, four of their Spitfires were shot down by a patrol of Israeli Messerschmitts. Enraged by this development, Bevin issued a sharp warning that his government took an "extremely serious" view of Jewish military operations. Cairo then promptly exploited the threat of British intervention against Israel by declaring, on January 12, that the Egyptian government under no circumstances would enter into armistice negotiations unless the Jews first evacuated the Rafah heights. Once more the decision was Ben-Gurion's to make. The Israeli prime minister hesitated only briefly. He was aware that the other Arab nations had indicated their willingness to follow Egypt to the armistice table. It appeared, then, that the wiser course would be to allow the Egyptians—and the British—to save face. Over the heated objections of his military commanders, Ben-Gurion gave the order to pull out.

Ten days later, the remnants of Taha Bey's brigade were also permitted to depart al-Faluja. Yerucham Cohen, Allon's aide, watched the evacuation from a hillside. Suddenly he caught sight of Major Nasser. Cohen shouted a greeting, and the two men ran toward each other, warmly shaking hands for the last time. The Egyptians then drove off in personnel carriers toward their encampment at al-Arish. It was a bitter moment for the giant of Middle Eastern nations. In May 1948 its army had posed an apparently unsurmountable danger to the little Zionist enclave to the north. A half-year later that same army was coming home, soundly thrashed; while the Cairo government, by agreeing to enter into armistice negotiations with the Jews, was virtually admitting its helplessness against even the feeblest of its enemies. The unanticipated climax to the Palestine adventure sent shock waves throughout Egypt, and indeed throughout the Arab world at large. As shall be seen, the impact of that defeat would not be dissipated for more than a generation to come.

V

A LETHARGIC HOSTILITY

THE RHODES ARMISTICES

On December 29, 1948, the UN Security Council, which for a half-year had confined itself to orders for cease-fire and truce in Palestine, issued a call for a permanent armistice. Exhausted, the Egyptians and the Arab nations accepted. Yet none agreed to negotiate "directly" with Israel—that is, without benefit of mediation. Thus, when initial discussions opened between Egypt and Israel on the island of Rhodes early in January 1949, the talks were defined as United Nations negotiations. It was a formula that occasionally produced ludicrous complications. The United Nations mediator, Dr. Ralph Bunche, an American Negro who had served as Bernadotte's deputy until the latter's assassination, was obliged to hold his opening conversations separately with each delegation. After several days, however, Bunche's persistence was rewarded. The Egyptians and Israelis finally were gathered together in his hotel suite. At the outset, the Egyptians still insisted on addressing all their remarks to Bunche, as if the Jews were not in the room. But this artificiality could not be maintained for long, and soon the two groups were arguing with each other directly.

As a first step, the armistice agreement was drawn on the basis of the existing military lines. The Negev would remain in Israel under this format, with the exceptions of the Gaza coastal strip, occupied by Egyptian troops, and the town of al-Auja and its vicinity, which would be demilitarized under United Nations supervision. The exceptions represented a face-saving gesture to the Egyptian government, which could then boast that it continued to exert influence in at least a sector of Palestine, even as the Hashemites did. Each side assumed, too, that the armistice would be supplanted in the near future by a permanent peace treaty. Indeed, the document itself began auspiciously: "With a view to promoting the return of permanent peace in Palestine . . . the following principles . . . are hereby affirmed. . . ." The agreement between Egypt and Israel finally was signed on February 24, 1949, in a ceremony of such mutual cordiality that delicacies were flown in from Cairo by special plane. And once Egypt, the greatest of the Arab powers, consented to negotiate with the Jews, it was a much simpler matter for the others to follow. Ultimately, Iraq was the only Arab belligerent unwilling to sign an armistice directly with Israel.

The agreements left the Jewish state in possession of approximately 8,000 square miles of Palestine, 21 percent more than had been allotted under the UN

Partition Resolution. It was assumed, nevertheless, that the frontiers were tentative and that they would be adjusted in final peace negotiations. If they were not, the accords represented hardly less than a built-in time bomb. Israel's demarcation line with Jordan, for example, separating many Arab farmers from their land, became a perennial magnet for infiltrators and a source of endemic border violence between the two countries. The convoluted nature of the Jerusalem settlement, with its precarious Jewish easements to the Hebrew University on Mount Scopus, was too dependent on Arab goodwill to be workable. So were the arrangements negotiated with Syria. The territory adjacent to Israel's demilitarized zones along the Syrian frontier was populated by Jewish farmers. Expecting to plough near the border region, the Jews cited the clause in the Syrian-Israeli armistice agreement that recognized as a basic aim of the document "the gradual restoration of normal civilian life in the area of the Demilitarized Zone." The Syrians rejected this interpretation. Rather, ensconced on the Golan Heights, their troops blocked Israel's original plan for tapping the Jordan River, and periodically fired on Jewish farmers cultivating the land below. The zones thereafter remained a critical focus of potential warfare, one that ultimately threatened to suck Egypt, too, into confrontation with Israel.

So, even more directly, did the Gaza Strip, where the Egyptians continued to maintain armed forces within Palestinian territory. All the armistice settlements spoke of a moratorium on "aggressive action" by either party against the other. But one provision in the agreements with Jordan, Syria, and Lebanon was not incorporated into the Israeli-Egyptian covenant (at the time, possibly by inadvertence). It was: "[N]o warlike act or act of hostility shall be conducted from territory controlled by one of the Parties to this Agreement against the other Party." The Egyptian government subsequently construed this lacuna as legal justification for encouraging guerrilla activity against Israel from the refugee-packed Gaza enclave, and also for proclaiming its right to bar Israel's use of the Strait of Tiran. Here, too, was a lethal delayed-action bomb.

But so remote did these dangers appear in 1949 that, even before the final armistice documents were signed in the summer of that year, a newly appointed United Nations body, the Palestine Conciliation Commission, began to take over and enlarge upon the mediator's functions. By the terms of the UN General Assembly resolution of December 11, 1948, the PCC's announced intention was to arrange nothing less than "a final settlement of all questions outstanding between [Israel and the Arabs]." This matter-of-fact statement appeared sufficiently pregnant with hope to compensate the Jews for all they had recently endured in their struggle for independence: for the loss of 6,000 lives and five times that many wounded, an appreciable number for a nation of barely 600,000; for the destruction of the country's citrus groves, once the basis of the Palestine Jewish economy; indeed, for economic ruination of such magnitude as to constitute virtual national bankruptcy. Yet, these wounds

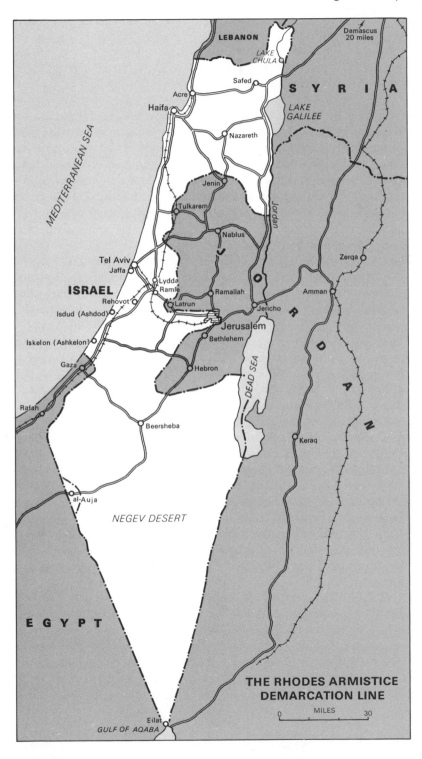

LEBANON

Damascus
20 miles

*LAKE
CHULA*

Safed

S Y R I A

Acre

Haifa

*LAKE
GALILEE*

MEDITERRANEAN SEA

Nazareth

Jenin

Tulkarem

Nablus

Jordan

Zerqa

Tel Aviv
Jaffa

J

Lydda
Ramle

Ramallah

Amman

ISRAEL

Rehovot

Latrun

Isdud (Ashdod)

Jericho

Jerusalem

J O R D A N

Iskelon (Ashkelon)

Bethlehem

Gaza

Hebron

DEAD SEA

Rafah

Beersheba

Keraq

al-Auja

NEGEV DESERT

E G Y P T

THE RHODES ARMISTICE
DEMARCATION LINE

Eilat
GULF OF AQABA

MILES

0   30

notwithstanding, the little Israeli republic at least had survived its grim birth ordeal physically intact.

THE "SHAME OF PALESTINE"

For Egypt, on the other hand, the Palestine war doomed a government, a monarchy, and ultimately a potentially hopeful connection with the Western liberal tradition. Constitutionalism was abandoned at the very outset of the Palestine invasion of May 15, 1948. Declaring a state of martial law, the Nuqrashi cabinet assumed power to censor mail and the press, to requisition property, and to arrest and imprison arbitrarily. Paid informers and torture were used as instruments to extort information. These draconian measures in any case proved useless. News of defeat filtered through, together with accounts of graft and misappropriation in high places.

The Jews, of course, could be blamed for every misfortune. On November 25, 1947, at a time when the United Nations was still debating partition, Muhammad Husseinein Heykal, the journalist who led Egypt's delegation to the General Assembly, warned that "[t]he lives of a million Jews in Moslem countries would be jeopardized by partition. . . . If Arab blood is shed in Palestine, Jewish blood will necessarily be shed elsewhere in the world despite all the sincere efforts of the governments concerned to prevent reprisals." The words were as prophetic for Egyptian Jewry as for Jews in other Arabic-speaking lands. Retribution began slowly. In 1947 the Companies Law was instituted, obliging at least 75 percent of all employees in private business to be Egyptian citizens. Inasmuch as few Egyptian Jews belonged in this category, Jewish enterprises were severely crippled by the new enactment. On May 15, 1948, the day Egypt launched its invasion of Palestine, hundreds of Egyptian Jews were arrested and more than a thousand had their property confiscated, ostensibly for "Zionist plotting." Throughout the summer of 1948, Jewish businesses were looted. Bombs were planted in Jewish neighborhoods, killing or wounding some 250 individuals.

Although the Ikhwan played a central role in arousing this frenzy of "anti-Zionist" brutality, the fanatical brotherhood was equally responsible for the murders of Ahmad Maher, the Sa'adist prime minister; of Aman Uthman, the Wafdist ex-minister of finance; of the Cairo police chief; and, in December 1948, of Prime Minister Nuqrashi himself. Plainly, terrorism had gone out of control. The assassinated Nuqrashi was succeeded in office by the respected, nonpolitical Ibrahim Abd al-Hadi. With the Palace and a majority in the parliament behind him, the new prime minister immediately and courageously emptied the prisons of Zionist suspects and filled them with members of the Ikhwan. Hassan al-Banna, the Ikhwan's leader, was mysteriously killed in February 1949. Extremist groups of every coloration were intimidated into silence. After a half-year of ruthless police activity, the nation appeared safe again for the traditional intrigues and maneuverings of Egyptian parliamentary democracy.

For a while, too, the circumstances of Egyptian Jewry seemed to ease. In July 1949 the government released a substantial portion of confiscated Jewish assets. Permission was also granted for "non-Moslems" to leave the country. Thus, between 1949 and 1951, 30,000 Egyptian Jews sold their homes and businesses, transferred their holdings to European banks, and summarily departed for France and Italy. A third of these in turn went on to Israel. Yet nearly three-fifths of the Egyptian-Jewish community remained, cautiously optimistic that stability and security were being restored at last. As if to buttress that hope, the governor of Cairo once again began paying his routine courtesy visit to Chief Rabbi Chaim Nahum on the eve of the Jewish New Year.

The illusion of normalcy was destined to be short-lived. If Egyptian resentment was burning more quietly now, the flame was hardly extinguished. For many of the nation's intellectuals, it was all but impossible to accept the shame of defeat at the hands of "Zionist gangs." This reaction was not yet universal. Thus, in 1950, Salama Musa, writing for *Saud al-Uma*, the organ of the Wafd, called for "an end to the cold war between Israel and the Arab states," and urged both sides "to wind up the war by honorable means." It was the contention of Hafez Ramadan, leader of the National party, that Britain was deliberately fanning the Arab-Israel dispute to guard its own power in the region. The identical charge was repeated against the United States by Fiqri Abaza, editor of the popular weekly, *al-Mussawar*.

Otherwise, hostility to the Jewish state appeared implacable. Zionism was described as an invidious virus, even was traced back (in classically anti-Semitic fashion) to the alleged *Protocols of the Elders of Zion*. In an article for *Ikhtarna Lak* ("Chosen for You," a series), Abbas Mahmud al-Aqqad, a respected essayist, defined Zionism as "the odious characteristic which, in ancient times, struck root among a group of Hebrews and made them hated and despised in every place where they lived or to which they came. . . . We refer to the characteristic[s] of aggressiveness, unjust demands, and selfishness. This is an ancient disease of this people, which has never left them." For Aqqad and other Egyptian writers, Zionism was not simply a manifestation of Western imperialism, but of Judaism itself. Muhammad Darwash, one of Egypt's most eminent authors, elaborated upon this theme for the *Ikhtarna Lak* series, insisting that the Jews traditionally had been steeped in "cruelty, malice, treachery and selfishness, horrible to other nations. . . . The vices pass on from fathers to sons."

An equally typical reaction to the Palestine debacle was the tendency to extol Arab honor and to attribute defeat to those perennial *bêtes noires*, the British. "The enemy knew all about our arms," complained Muhammad al-Khattab. "The colonial power supplied the Jews with this information." The charge rarely varied. As early as July 1948, Azzam Pasha stated publicly that "England and America followed every Arab effort to obtain arms and opposed it with all their power, while at the same time they worked resolutely . . . to assure the flow of war matériel and troops to the Jews by sea and air and every direction." "We were not defeated in Palestine," insisted Gamal Abd al-Nasser, writing for *Ikhtarna Lak* in 1955, "inasmuch as the Egyptian army did not fight in 1948." And Anwar al-Sadat added, in his *Revolt on the Nile*: "The British mandate did not allow the [Arab] inhabitants to take up arms. . . . The creation of a State of Israel was a strategic move by the West, designed to weaken the Arab world." As Sadat regarded it, Britain and the United States sponsored Israel in the Middle East as an outpost from which the Western Powers might "keep an eye" on the Soviet Union.

LAUSANNE AND POST-ARMISTICE DEADLOCK

A weathervane of practical Egyptian-Israeli relations, meanwhile, could be discerned in the fate of negotiations between the two countries during the aftermath of the armistice. In December 1948, the Palestine Conciliation Commission, appointed by the UN General Assembly, was charged with three major tasks. These were: the accomplishment of a binding settlement between Israel and its Arab enemies; the repatriation and resettlement of the Palestine refugees; and the organization of a permanent international regime in Jerusalem. As matters developed, the PCC failed to achieve any of these goals. Rather, by its ineptitude, the commission undermined whatever chances for peace still existed. It would have been useful, for example, had the Israelis and representatives of the individual Arab states been chivied into direct negotiations immediately, along the Rhodes format. Instead, the three members of the PCC, appointees of Turkey, France, and the United States, spent three months in a leisurely, disorganized tour of Middle Eastern nations, not reaching the permanent site of their discussions, Lausanne, until April 1949. Once there, the PCC made the egregious error of allowing the various Arab representatives to participate in discussions as a bloc, rather than separately. As a consequence, no individual Arab or Egyptian dared take the initiative in expressing moderation. During the rare occasions when efforts were made to bring the two sides together, the Arabs repudiated the pattern of the Rhodes armistice negotiations and declined to sit in the same room with the Jews.

There were serious enough differences to be resolved even without procedural complications. The PCC regarded it as its function to devise a permanent trusteeship regime for Jerusalem, as envisaged in the original 1947 Partition Resolution. Yet, well before the Palestine war ended, Abdullah's Arab Legion had occupied the Old City, while most of New Jerusalem remained in Jewish hands. On March 1, 1949, therefore, the Hashemites and Israelis signed an agreement recognizing the de facto partition of the Holy City. The other Arab governments in turn were horrified by this tacit acceptance of a Jewish presence in Islam's third holiest city. Intent upon counteracting it, they informed the United Nations of their belated willingness to accept internationalization for Jerusalem. Thus, on December 9, 1949, a majority of the General Assembly voted for the entire city to be transformed into a *corpus separatum.* Israel's reaction to the vote was swift and emphatic. On January 1, 1950, the government transferred itself from Tel Aviv to Jerusalem's New City, except for the ministries of defense, police, and foreign affairs (the latter two were shifted later). That same day, across the border, Abdullah issued a decree conferring Transjordanian citizenship on the population of the West Bank, including the inhabitants of Arab Jerusalem (the following April, he renamed his kingdom Jordan).

Other issues similarly bedeviled the PCC negotiations. The General Assembly resolution of December 11, 1949, called upon Israel and the Arab states not only to begin peace negotiations but also to allow the Palestinian refugees to return to their homes "at the earliest practicable date." Yet the Arabs insisted that they expected the refugee question to be fully resolved before they would so much as consider peace negotiations. The Israelis, for their part, warned that a "fundamental solution" of the refugee issue would have to be based upon the settlement of emigré Palestinians in neighboring Arab countries. Throughout the summer months of 1949, as tens of thousands of Jewish displaced persons flooded into Israel, and as peace negotiations failed to make progress in Lausanne, the Ben-Gurion cabinet further limited its already minimal category of eligible Arab returnees to wives and minor children of "Arab breadwinners lawfully resident in Israel" and to occasional other "compassionate cases. . . ." The practical effects of the concession were negligible.

In their turn, the Arab governments were equally unwilling to contemplate alternative plans for integrating the Palestine Arabs in their own lands. The refugee issue served them, rather, as a useful pretext to block future discussions with Israel. Accordingly, by the end of 1950, between 650,000 and 700,000 Palestinian emigrés were confined to the tents and ration lines established by the United Nations Refugee Works Administration. If there was a redeeming feature in their plight, it was Abdullah's decision to confer Hashemite citizenship on the approximately 200,000 refugees impacted on the west bank of the Jordan. Of these, however, only half found employment. The rest continued to subsist in camps on the UNRWA dole. Elsewhere, the Gaza refugees were confined by the Egyptians virtually as prisoners in the tiny coastal zone abutting the Israeli frontier. Denied employment in Egypt itself, they vegetated in misery and bitterness.

THE FAILED PEACE

This seething refugee presence made its impact not only on the throttled pace of the PCC negotiations in Lausanne, but directly along the Arab-Israeli borders. Indeed, it activated one of the most critical provisions of the four armistice agreements. These accords were intended to offer a transitional interregnum until permanent peace was assured. To that end, machinery was established to reduce the danger of border violence. Its principal element was the Mixed Armistice Commissions (MACs). Each MAC (one for each of Israel's four frontiers) was composed of an equivalent number of Israeli and Arab delegates, presided over by a United Nations officer, and charged with the responsibility of investigating armistice violations, of assessing blame, then of encouraging the parties themselves to resolve the dispute. With further UN Security Council action envisaged only as a last resort, the successful operation of this machinery plainly depended upon the willingness of Arabs and Israelis themselves to cooperate for peace.

Conceivably, at the outset, it was a not altogether unrealistic expectation. The initial meetings of the Israeli-Egyptian MAC were reasonably cordial. The first Israeli representatives, Colonels Yitzchak Rabin and Amos Horev, established good rapport with their Egyptian counterparts, Brigadier Mahmud Riad and Colonel Salah Gahar Riad. In September 1949 Mahmud Riad even accepted an invitation from Yerucham Cohen, the friend of Nasser (p. 57), to visit the Israeli kibbutz of Givat Brenner. In February 1950 Nasser and Cohen met again in the Israeli-controlled al-Faluja region, where the Egyptian helped identify the burial sites of Israeli soldiers killed in the 1948 fighting. Except for these intermittent episodes of cooperation, however, productive contacts between Israelis and Egyptians were minimal. Once the momentum toward peace generated at Rhodes failed to be sustained at Lausanne, the rot set in immediately. The armistice machinery simply was not equipped to function as a permanent substitute for peace.

Moreover, the configuration of the Rhodes boundaries was guaranteed to bedevil even the most accommodating of joint commissions. Intended at best as temporary lines, the frontiers made no concessions to civilian needs. From the very outset, Arab refugees on the Hashemite side began crossing over to reclaim their possessions in Israel. Some even attempted to harvest their old fields. The MAC at first dutifully sought to cope with the pilferage of crops and chattels. Yet by 1952 vandalism of Israeli farm property became acute, and the Israeli border police responded increasingly with shooting. In that year alone, 621 Arabs were killed or wounded and 2,595 captured.

The demilitarized zones represented yet another focus of violence. The armistice agreements established four such zones: one (divided into two sections) in the north, on the former Palestine-Syria border; a second encircling the Hebrew University and Hadassah Hospital buildings on Mount Scopus in

Jerusalem; a third on Jebel al-Mukhabbir in Jerusalem; and a fourth around al-Auja on the Egyptian border. Ultimately, the Syrian DMZ would prove to be the most explosive. In the 1950s, however, it was the southern line of confrontation that became the most volatile. The al-Auja DMZ, evacuated by the Egyptians in return for assurance of tactical sterilization, lay diamond-shaped for a distance of 22 miles along the Palestine-Egypt Sinai border. From late 1949 onward, the Israelis repeatedly attempted to establish a military camp in this zone under the guise of a kibbutz. By September 1953, evicting some 6,000 Bedouin who lived in the area, the Jews finally established their settlement. Then, soon afterward, an Egyptian checkpoint was also discovered within the DMZ. Neither side was prepared to budge, and clashes eventually erupted during late 1954 and early 1955, with mounting casualties on both sides. Finally, on November 2, 1955, Israeli troops moved in force against the Egyptian position. Some fifty Egyptians were killed and over forty captured in the attack. Although the UN Security Council censured Israel for this action, the Jews did not relinquish their hold on al-Auja.

Israel's determination to emplace its troops in the al-Auja DMZ was influenced by more than a perverse need to assert its sovereign independence. The zone was a vital buffer against rising Arab infiltration from the Gaza Strip. Allotted to Egypt by the Rhodes Armistice, this modest wedge of Palestine coastal land, 4 miles wide and 30 miles long, became the focal area of approximately 120,000 Arab refugees. Tightly circumscribed as they were under Egyptian military rule, denied the right of employment in Egypt proper, the Gaza refugees generated a hatred against Israel more unremitting than that of any other emigré concentration on Israel's borders. Between 1949 and 1952, the Egyptian authorities did little to encourage refugee infiltration. The armistice agreement worked reasonably well here. Rather, it was the advent of the Nasser regime and the subsequent deterioration of Egyptian-Israeli relations that eroded the initial restraint.

As noted, little of this militancy could have been prophesied from the armistice agreements themselves. For that matter, the Arab governments no less than Israel were assumed to have vested interests in a policy of mutual recognition. They had urgent problems of their own that required solution, after all, among them the need for an outlet on the Israeli Mediterranean coast, for Egyptian-Hashemite land access through the Negev, and for a defined status in Jerusalem. Abdullah, in fact, was so eager for a compromise agreement that his emissaries quietly formulated a treaty with the Israelis in 1950. The document resolved all conflicting issues of boundaries, of access to Jerusalem, and of land links between Jordan and Haifa. Yet, tragically, the fate of Abdullah was the fate of peace itself. Rumors of his negotiations leaked to other Arab countries. On July 30, 1951, returning from prayer in Jerusalem's Mosque of Omar, the Hashemite king was shot dead by a gunman in the pay of the Egyptian Ikhwan. Elsewhere, as punishment both for losing the war and for signing the armistice accord, the Syrian regime was overthrown by a military coup. Prime Minister Riad al-Suhl of Lebanon was assassinated for displaying moderation. And in Egypt, as we have seen, Prime Minister Nuqrashi was murdered simply for having agreed to a ccase-fire. Whenever inter-Arab relations reached a point of crisis after 1949, moreover, expressions of anti-Israel hostility proved to be the one dependable integument among contending factions in the Arab world.

For the while, except for limited border clashes, the techniques of Arab revenge against Israel remained essentially nonmilitary. Their purpose in the early 1950s was to isolate, harass, and eventually to strangle the Zionist republic through political pressure, boycott, and blockade. One of the most effective maneuvers here was diplomatic quarantine. All borders with Israel were closed. No person whose passport bore an Israeli visa was allowed entry into an Arab state. The Arab governments were relentless, too, in their attempts to dissuade other nations from establishing diplomatic ties with Israel. It was a campaign that was particularly effective among the newly liberated states of Asia. Either Moslem or partly Moslem, most of these nations accepted the Arab contention that Israel was a puppet of the imperialist West. Although Turkey, Iran, and India established consular links with Israel, they rejected all subsequent Israeli overtures for diplomatic relations. Ironically, during their first years after independence, the Israelis had anticipated that their socialism and recent colonial servitude under the British somehow would establish a common interest and bond with the Asian nations. That hope now appeared dashed.

The Arab economic boycott was another, even more effective, tactic against the fledgling Zionist republic. In January 1950, the Arab League drew up a far-reaching plan to deter other nations and companies from entering into business relations with Israel. Coordinated by a central office in Damascus, the Arab states enacted stiff penalties against firms in Europe, in the United States, or elsewhere that maintained branch factories, plants, or agencies in Israel. These measures were not wholly successful. Nevertheless, the major American and British oil corporations halted the flow of petroleum from Iraq to Haifa in 1948. Under the terms of the boycott, foreign vessels found it impossible to call at Israeli and Arab ports on the same run. No commercial airliner touching down in Israel could so much as fly over Arab territory. As a result, Israel soon became a minor side-stop of world tourism rather than a crossroads.

Even more painful for the Jews was the Egyptian blockade of Israel's international waterways. When the Rhodes Armistice was signed, the likelihood of a blockade had not so much as occurred either to the Israelis or to Dr. Bunche, the United Nations mediator. Because each of the documents contained a flat injunction against "aggressive action" by either party, it was taken for granted that the wartime maritime blockade of the Suez Canal and of the Gulf of Aqaba would end. Yet the Egyptians dashed this assumption, too, by refusing Israeli shipping passage through both thoroughfares. Although Cairo at first moved somewhat obliquely against neutral shipping bound for Israel through Suez, in February 1950 the Egyptian government published an extended list of "strategic" goods that might not be transported to Israeli ports. The banned items included oil, pharmaceuticals, chemicals, ships and automobiles, and subsequently the list was enlarged to include foodstuffs and similar consumer goods. Outraged, the Israelis repeatedly protested these measures to the Security Council, and in September 1951 they apparently won recourse. The United Nations body issued a stern warning to Egypt to end its restrictions on the passage of international shipping. Thus, for several months afterward, the Egyptians deemed it expedient to relax their blockade. But in 1952, Cairo gradually reimposed the ban. As a consequence of a shift in the Soviet diplomatic position, moreover (p. 78), the UN Security Council was helpless to act this time. Few shipping companies subsequently would agree to test the closure against Israel.

The second of Israel's prospective routes to Africa and Asia, the Red Sea outlet, was similarly interdicted by the Egyptians. The Gulf of Aqaba's 230-mile coastline in fact was shared by four nations: Saudi Arabia, Jordan, Egypt, and Israel. Two uninhabited Saudi islands, Tiran and Sanafir, located at the southern end of the Gulf, limited the navigable area between the Gulf itself and the main body of the Red Sea to a three-mile channel, the Strait of Tiran. In late 1949, by agreement with the Saudi government, Egypt installed coastal artillery on Tiran and Sanafir, as well as on Ras Nasrani, at the tip of the Sinai coast facing the two islands. Thereafter, the Egyptians closed the Strait of Tiran to all shipping bound to or from the Israeli port of Eilat. The move represented a contravention not only of the armistice agreement, but of international legal precedents for gulfs and bays flanked by the territories of more than one littoral state. The issue of the Strait of Tiran was particularly urgent to Israel. Closure of this waterway imperiled the Jewish state's future trade with the Orient and with East Africa. With both the Canal and the Red Sea cut off, Israel was blocked from all its potential Eastern markets.

To be sure, the confluence of these Arab pressures—boycott, blockade, diplomatic isolation, border violence—had not yet strangled Israel's capacity to survive. By the mid-1950s, nevertheless, as the Zionist republic gradually absorbed its first waves of immigration, its government leaders recognized that the nation's opportunities for economic growth were being painfully, even intolerably, constricted. Peaceful or otherwise, a remedy would have to be found—and doubtless sooner rather than later.

VI

REVOLUTION AND REEVALUATION

CHAUVINISM AND PARALYSIS

The asassination of Prime Minister Mahmud Fahmi al-Nuqrashi in December 1948 launched yet another cycle in Egypt's traditionally oscillating political pendulum. Nuqrashi's successor, Ibrahim Abd al-Hadi, immediately set about restoring public order and a reasonable measure of civic equilibrium. By the end of 1949, as a consequence of Hadi's efforts, the nation had resumed the normal, lethargic tempo of its daily social and economic affairs. Only the deeper-rooted causes of Egyptian unrest remained. The gap between rich and poor steadily widened. The corruption in government, the nepotism and political patronage, flourished unchecked. No party appeared willing to address these issues. When the January elections of 1950 returned a Wafdist majority, Prime Minister Mustafa Nahas routinely offered a number of unexceptionable reformist proposals, including a collective work-contract law, a sickness compensation act, a high cost of living allowance law. It was all sham. Dependent upon its own retinue of wealthy property owners and sycophantic attorneys, the Wafd was entirely unprepared to grapple with absentee landlordism, with illiteracy or widespread disease in the countryside. In the end, Nahas found it a simpler matter to divert public unrest by capitalizing upon native chauvinism, an emotion kindled by the ignominy of defeat in Palestine and by failure to achieve British withdrawal at home.

It was the latter grievance that Nahas determined now to exploit to the limit. In March 1950 the Wafdist cabinet demanded the resumption of talks with the British government. London's response was to stand fast on its earlier conditions for renegotiating the 1936 Anglo-Egyptian Treaty; that is, Egypt would have to accept Britain's option of returning to Suez in the event of war, and agree, as well, to the special status of the Sudan as an Anglo-Egyptian condominium. Thus, in October 1951, as popular dissatisfaction with his administration became increasingly vocal, Nahas decided to terminate the indignity of foreign occupation by risking direct confrontation with Britain. He formally notified the British ambassador of "the cession of the alliance between Egypt and Great Britain and of the authorization of the latter to station certain forces in the vicinity of the Suez Canal. . . ." Hereupon, at the government's instigation, Egyptian railroad workers refused any longer to transport British equipment and personnel to Suez. Egyptian suppliers of British troops broke their contracts. Soon afterward, again with less than veiled government encouragement, squads of irregulars were organized, and early in 1952 their attacks on British troops and installations in the Canal Zone grew in scale and intensity.

So did British retaliation. Aware that the guerrilla campaign was officially sponsored, the British army soon trespassed its delimited areas of concentration and began seizing control of large numbers of towns and villages in eastern Egypt. The "Battle of the Canal" reached its climax in January 1952 when British troops attacked Egyptian auxiliary police headquarters in Ismailia, killing some fifty personnel and wounding more than a hundred. The public response was an orgy of violence. Anti-British demonstrations exploded in Cairo. Students, police, and soldiers mingled indiscriminately to set fire to British homes and businesses, and to raze the exclusive British Turf Club, in the process incinerating twelve British citizens. Afterward, hundreds of Jewish shops similarly were put to the torch. Before order was finally restored, E£23 million in damage was inflicted, 400 buildings were destroyed, 12,000 families were deprived of shelter, and business was all but paralyzed. The crisis was well described by the newspaper *al-Ahram* as an act of collective suicide by a population "driven to despair by its defaulting leaders."

Immobilized by terror and by its own corruption, the Wafd at this point was entirely incapable of filling the vacuum of leadership. On January 26, therefore, the same day rioting was taking place, Farouk dismissed Nahas and called upon Ali Maher to save a nation teetering on the brink of anarchy. Although an experienced political veteran, the new prime minister barely succeeded in restoring a minimal degree of order. Two months later, the king replaced Ali Maher with Naguib Hilali Pasha, a well-regarded lawyer of unchallengeable probity. Hilali promptly set about bringing arraignment proceedings against officials and former ministers who had waxed fat on graft in earlier governments. But here, not surprisingly, he ran afoul of the Wafd. The party's leaders managed to distribute enough baksheesh among court circles to engineer Hilali's resignation. As it turned out, this Wafdist act of desperation also marked the beginning of their own, and King Farouk's, downfall.

By then, the monarch's dissipations had already thoroughly exasperated the Egyptian people. It was notorious that ministerial portfolios and titles of pasha were bought at huge prices, and that no important deal went through without the king taking his share. It was known also that Farouk had blocked inquiry into the scandal of arms profiteering during the Palestine war. Already discredited, then, the Palace entourage compounded its malodorous reputation by entrusting the task of forming a new government to Hussein Sirri. Although a political veteran who had held the prime ministry briefly in 1940, his administration was a cabal of underlings and unknowns. Any further efforts to root out corruption were palpably doomed. If hope for reform still lingered, it was dissipated on July 1, when Hussein Sirri sought to persuade Farouk to reappoint General Muhammad Naguib as president of the influential Officers Club. The king demurred, fearing the popularity Naguib had won in the Palestine war. On July 19, rather, Farouk ordered the prime minister simply to dissolve the Officers Club outright. Afterward, in an incredible act of obtuseness, the monarch foisted his brother-in-law on the government as minister of war. This gaucherie was too much even for Hussein Sirri. He resigned on July 21. The obscure rivalry between Muhammad Naguib and the Palace accordingly made the former an unwitting symbol of revolt, and the king's resistance to the popular general helped to ignite a climactic uprising.

THE COLONELS' REVOLUTION

Dissatisfaction with ineffectual civilian government was hardly a recent phenomenon in the Egyptian officers' corps. It was an emotion that had provoked the Urabi uprising of 1881, the act of violence that had brought British troops to Egypt in the first place. Although contained in later decades, nationalist unrest among the military became particularly mutinous during the collapse of public order between 1950 and 1952. Only a small minority of the younger officers had a vested interest in the regime. As far back as 1936, after the promulgation of the Anglo-Egyptian Treaty, the Wafd government had enlarged the reservoir of army leadership by opening the military academy to all qualified young men, regardless of class or wealth. The decision exerted a far-reaching influence on the nation's subsequent history. The cadets graduating in 1938 were the first to come mainly from the lower middle class, and a large number of them were sons of small provincial landowners or of salaried government employees. The latter was the element in which both social and nationalist dissatisfaction was uniquely inflamed.

The leanings of this new group of middle-ranking officers became evident during World War II. Some, like Anwar al-Sadat, were closely associated with General Aziz Ali al-Misri, and were linked with Misri's pro-German activities. A few were influenced by the Ikhwan. Others, like Gamal Abd al-Nasser, even toyed with the neo-Nazism of the Misr al-Fatat. All were deeply frustrated by the government's obsequiousness to the British. Their chagrin became all but insupportable in the aftermath of the Palestine war. Soundly trounced by an opponent inferior both in manpower and in equipment, the returning veterans preferred to blame the king and his regime for the fiasco. At the end of 1949, several of these majors and lieutenant colonels clandestinely organized themselves into a Free Officers Committee. Their founding members included Nasser, Sadat, Abd al-Hakim Amr, Salah Salm, and Zakarriyya Muhyi al-Din. Early in 1950, Nasser was elected the group's chairman.

A tall, hawk-faced lieutenant colonel, thirty-two years old at the time, Nasser was the son of a post office employee in upper Egypt. Since his public-school days, he had been active in anti-British causes. Early in World War II, he had also participated in General Misri's effort to collaborate with the Germans. For him, as for Sadat and for other junior officers, the indignity of British rule was exacerbated in 1948 by military defeat in Palestine. Nasser recounted afterward: "I thought about [the corruption in Egypt] a good deal while in the trenches and foxholes of [Palestine]. . . . We were sorely pressed, but the political climate in the capital, when we received our orders, created a siege there—a tighter and more crippling siege than anything we experienced while dug in at the Faluja Pocket."

Returning to Egypt, Nasser and his fellow conspirators broadened their activities throughout the officers' corps. Yet even as late as 1951 they had formulated no coherent political program other than resisting the king's abuses in the military. Their views ranged from Islamist-fundamentalist and Fascist to left-wing radical Socialist and Communist. In their hostility to the Farouk-dominated government, nevertheless, the members of the group won moral support from General Misri, whom they considered their spiritual leader, and from Major General Muhammad Naguib. By 1952 endorsement came also from other quarters. One of these was Kermit Roosevelt, a member of the United States Central Intelligence Agency; he had been put in touch with the Free Officers and liked what he conceived to be their progressivism and pro-Westernism. Thus encouraged, Nasser and his associates laid their plans for an uprising.

Prime Minister Hussein Sirri's resignation on July 20, 1952, was the signal the plotters had awaited. Forty-eight hours later, on the night of July 22–23, several thousand troops seized control of the nation's army headquarters, its ports, radio stations, and communications centers. At the last moment, Naguib was invited to assume titular leadership of the coup and the genial commander's popularity all but guaranteed the uprising's success. On the twenty-sixth, finally, the Free Officers ordered Farouk to abdicate in favor of the heir apparent, Prince Ahmad Fuad. Without venturing a murmur of further protest, the corpulent monarch thereupon sailed away on the royal yacht. The party leaders in turn now rushed forward to swear undying loyalty to the revolution.

Still lacking a political philosophy, however, or even an organizational framework, the Free Officers took to improvisation based on a rather fragmentary understanding of technocratic ideas and ideals. Naguib, who had operated for several months behind the front of a civilian cabinet, now assumed the premiership, and he and his younger associates immediately launched into a self-proclaimed, but somewhat confused, "social revolution." The titles of "bey" and "pasha" were abolished. Corrupt officials were purged. Yet most of the arrested politicians and members of the Palace entourage later were released. Although landed estates of more than 200 acres were declared expropriated, the decree was honored more on paper than in fact. It was only in subsequent weeks that the officers embarked on a more radical break with the past.

Thus, in January 1953 the nation's parties were formally dissolved and a military "directorate" was announced for the ensuing three years. On February 10, the Free Officers issued a manifesto outlining the aims of the revolution. Among these were the professed intention of "driving the British from the Nile Valley unconditionally," and of launching a "total national and social reconstruction." By then, too, Nasser had emerged as the undisputed spokesman of the Free Officers on matters of basic policy. When, soon afterward, the monarchy was dissolved and a republic officially proclaimed in June 1953, Nasser acceded to the title of deputy prime minister and minister of the interior. The following year, challenged by the more temperate Naguib, he maneuvered the older man into the honorific office of president and assumed the premiership for himself. From then on, until the moment of his death, Nasser did not relinquish the reins of power.

ISRAEL'S STRUGGLE FOR SURVIVAL. BEN-GURION OFFERS AN ACCOMMODATION

In the half-decade following its declaration of independence, meanwhile, the State of Israel was undergoing a traumatic ordeal of its own. More than 600,000 immigrants arrived in the Zionist republic. By July 1953, the Jewish population of the country had doubled, to 1,200,000. Exhausted and economically desolated by the war, the fledgling nation was ill-equipped to cope with this avalanche of refugees. Soon every abandoned Arab village and neighborhood was packed with newcomers from the farthest reaches of the Jewish Diaspora.

As early as 1951, 97,000 immigrants, a tenth of the population of Israel, were reduced to living in makeshift tent villages. During the same period, tens of thousands of other Jews, newcomers and veterans alike, suffered from a critical shortage of gainful employment. Israel's economy in the early years of statehood remained woefully undeveloped. The Arab market, representing 15 percent of Palestine's export trade before 1948, was sealed off by boycott. With many of the best groves laid waste during the war, citrus output, formerly Palestine's major source of hard currency, remained far below its prewar level. It was the subsequent lack of foreign exchange, in turn, that dictated rigorous governmental austerity measures. Thus, all essential foodstuffs, all clothing and other consumer goods, were placed under tight rationing; and in February 1953 Prime Minister Ben-Gurion was obliged to announce a forced loan of 10 percent on all bank deposits. In short, the nation was teetering on the verge of bankruptcy. Had it not been for contributions from overseas—United States government loans and grants, remittances from Jewish communities abroad, and, later, West German reparations—Israel would have been altogether incapable of supporting the unprecedented burden of feeding, housing, and employing its refugee population and simultaneously of defending its frontiers.

Indeed, the crisis of economic survival was equaled, if not surpassed, by the awesome challenge of military defense. Nor was that challenge mitigated even by an important Western initiative to restore Middle Eastern stability. In May 1950, with the Lausanne peace conference a shambles, the United States, Britain, and France issued a Tripartite Declaration. "Should the three Governments," it warned, "find that any one of these states [Israel or its Arab neighbors] contemplates violating the frontiers of the armistice lines, they will . . . act both within and without the framework of the United Nations in order to prevent such a violation." Weapons would be rationed out to the Middle Eastern nations only for legitimate purposes of self-defense and to "permit them to play their part in the defense of the area as a whole." Although this gesture reflected Western determination to block Soviet penetration into the Middle East, it was nevertheless gratefully welcomed by most Israelis.

Yet the illusion was soon punctured that the Tripartite Declaration offered Israel any genuine security. By 1951 Britain's new Conservative government was actively pressing its scheme for a Middle East defense system. Egypt was invited to join the projected organization. By contrast, Israel was asked to stand aside—at least until the other Arab states agreed to participate. Ben-Gurion and his colleagues were appalled. In the event the Arab nations, and particularly Egypt, joined the defense pact, Israel's enemies would have access once more to Western arms, to equipment that might be used later against the Jewish state. One of Israel's most critical problems during the 1950s, in fact, was the acquisition of its own supply of modern weapons. Fearful of antagonizing the Arabs, the Western Powers were unwilling to sell the Israelis more than niggardly quantities of obsolescent arms.

Nor, after issuing the 1950 Tripartite Declaration, were the Western allies constrained to offer Israel the alternative of a formal security guarantee. Intent, rather, upon encircling the Soviet Union with Middle Eastern bases, American Secretary of State John Foster Dulles and British Prime Minister Anthony Eden in 1955 persuaded Turkey, Iran, Pakistan, and Iraq to join a "Baghdad Pact," a mutual defense treaty ultimately signed in the Iraqi capital. Again, the Israeli government was chagrined. As in their earlier courtship of Egypt, the Western democracies seemed willing this time to broaden their military assistance to Iraq, yet another enemy nation. Ben-Gurion's instinctive reaction, at that point, was to seek an identical treaty relationship for Israel, either through NATO, or, bilaterally, with Washington itself. It was a hopeless quest. The Eisenhower administration was uninterested in jeopardizing its relations with the Arabs. For the while, the Jewish republic had to satisfy itself essentially with American financial largesse.

Here, too, it was of significance that Israel's diplomatic, no less than its economic, dependence on the United States was growing with each passing, near-bankrupt, month. With his nation barely surviving on American transfusions, Ben-Gurion and his cabinet felt obliged to follow Washington's lead in condemning North Korean aggression in June 1950. The decision was a landmark one, for it was destined to forfeit Soviet friendship—the friendship of a government whose political and military support had all but saved Israel in the 1948 war. Notwithstanding Ben-Gurion's assurances in Moscow that his country under no circumstances would serve as a Western base against the USSR, Israel was hopelessly compromised afterward in Soviet eyes. From June 1950 on, the Russians adopted an increasingly anti-Israel line. In 1952, the Kremlin actually placed a group of eminent Soviet Jews on trial for alleged pro-Israeli "espionage."

There were several reasons for Moscow's unanticipated and virulent anti-Jewish and anti-Israeli campaign. One related to the fear of heterodoxy that had plagued Stalin since his rupture with Yugoslav Marshal Tito in 1948. As a minority group with extensive connections abroad, particularly in the West, the Jews, like the Titoists, appeared to present a "deviationist" threat to the Soviet ruler. And now, after the June 1950 vote condemning North Korea, Israel appeared to be offering itself to the West as an ally in the Cold War. It could not have escaped Russian intelligence sources, too, that Israel was repeatedly demanding admission either into NATO or into a bilateral treaty relationship with the United States. From the Soviet viewpoint, in any case, political change in the Arab world between 1952 and 1955 would itself have justified a diplomatic shift against Israel. Left-wing regimes were consolidating their power in Egypt and Syria, after all, and were adopting a strenuously anticolonialist line. Moscow could not be indifferent to the value of these "liberationist" movements for its own purposes. Thus it was that Israel, in turn, confronted by a chain of Western-sponsored, potentially pro-Arab alliances in the Middle East, and by the rising truculence of the Soviet bloc, sensed a new dimension of vulnerability; indeed, the Jewish state was being driven now into an isolation as ominous as any it had faced in its short history.

A brief interlude of optimism, ironically, was provided by the Egyptian revolution of July 1952. For some months afterward, it seemed possible to the Israelis that a new government in Cairo, eager for friendship in its campaign against Britain, uninterested in Western plans for a Middle East defense organization, and sharing Israel's vision of social and economic reform, might be willing to depart from Farouk's rejectionist line and come to terms with the Zionist republic. For his part, Ben-Gurion had long been of the opinion that Egypt was the one state powerful and resourceful enough to break the Arab front. The Israeli prime minister accordingly extended his hand in welcome to the colonel's regime, declaring before the Knesset that "there was not any time, nor is there now, reason for strife between Egypt and Israel." His statement represented more than a pious hope. The Egyptian revolutionaries appeared to be moderate and progressive men. Both Naguib and Nasser were personally known to the Israelis. Thus, Ben-Gurion went so far as to intimate his endorsement of Egypt's campaign for British withdrawal. His delegates to the Mixed Armistice Commission even stated frankly that Egypt might now feel free to withdraw its troops from Gaza to maintain order in Egypt proper; Israel would not exploit the situation. In a symbolic effort to revive an earlier friendship, too, Yerucham Cohen (p. 57) sent a gold pen and a letter of congratulation to his old counterpart, Nasser, and included another present for Nasser's son.

At first the new junta in Cairo appeared to respond favorably to these overtures. In March 1953, through the intercession of British members of Parliament traveling between the two Middle Eastern countries, a set of Egyptian proposals was dispatched to Israel. These raised the possibility of an Israeli payment of 120 million pounds sterling as refugee compensation, as well as Israel's support in obtaining Western economic aid for resettling the Palestine refugees. Certain adjustments of the border were outlined, too, including a land link to Jordan through the southern Negev. The Israelis promptly agreed to negotiate. But then the months went by and no tangible progress followed. Rather, the opposite was the case. By the summer of 1954, Arab guerrillas, trained this time by the Egyptian army, were beginning to increase their forays out of the Gaza Strip. As matters later developed, it was yet another of Nasser's political achievements—this one against Britain—that offered the Egyptians a new and wider freedom of military action against their Israeli neighbor.

THE ANGLO-EGYPTIAN TREATY OF 1954

In anticipation of levering the British out of Egypt, the Free Officers were determined not to be bound by years of Wafdist brainwashing on the issue of "Unity of the Nile Valley [the Sudan and Egypt] under the Egyptian Crown." Their objective now was simply to accelerate British departure. Thus, in October 1952, the revolutionary regime signed an informal agreement with the Sudanese leadership, acknowledging the Sudan's right to independence. In England, meanwhile, the newly-elected Conservatives were not less eager than the Egyptian colonels for a fresh start on the Anglo-Egyptian imbroglio. Encouraged by evidence of a new Egyptian moderation, the British succeeded in reaching agreement with Cairo in February 1953 to liquidate the Anglo-Egyptian Condominium in the Sudan. It was this breakthrough, in turn, that revived hopes for a new approach on the Suez issue. The Anglo-Egyptian Treaty was due to expire in 1956, and London recognized the importance of securing a workable agreement before then. For their part, the Egyptian colonels appreciated that Britain remained their nation's most important customer and supplier, and that friction over the Suez Canal Zone already had severely injured Egypt's foreign trade and balance of payments.

On July 10, 1954, therefore, with conciliation the mood on both sides, official negotiations were resumed in Cairo. And, almost miraculously, agreement was reached a bare seventeen days later. The Cairo government acknowledged Britain's right to maintain RAF landing and servicing facilities in the immediate Canal Zone, as well as several additional installations to be maintained exclusively by a British civilian caretaker force. Britain matched these concessions by agreeing that its option of return to the Suez facilities would be limited to a "direct [enemy] attack" on Egypt. A mere "threat of attack" obliged Egypt only to "immediate consultation" with London. Similarly, the British abandoned their insistence on a twenty-year term of agreement, and compromised instead on seven years; while the Egyptians yielded to Britain's view that twenty months was the minimum time required to withdraw men and matériel. Signatures on the final document were exchanged in Cairo on October 19, 1954, and mutual ratifications were completed on December 6. The Egyptians thereupon fell heir to ten airfields, a flying-boat station, thirty-four military camps, and a vast network of auxiliary military installations. They came into their own as a sovereign nation as well. For all practical purposes, the treaty represented the end of seventy-two years of British military occupation in Egypt. Among the Egyptian people, therefore, the agreement was received with a jubilation bordering on euphoria.

The Jews did not share this reaction—once Cairo turned a deaf ear to Israeli peace overtures. The Jerusalem government was appalled at the prospect of a vast network of Suez depots and installations falling into Egyptian hands. In Egypt itself, meanwhile, the local Jewish population experienced even graver misgivings as it contemplated the imminence of British departure. Ironically, the Egyptian-Jewish community had welcomed the 1952 revolution no less enthusiastically than had Israel. Like the Israelis, they were convinced that the fall of the monarchy signified a distinct trend toward reform and moderation. For a while, too, that hope appeared justified. So long as the easygoing General Naguib remained in power, the Zionist issue at least was not beaten to death; the Jews of Cairo and Alexandria were left essentially alone. It was only after Gamal Abd al-Nasser emerged as his government's undisputed leader in 1954 that matters took a turn for the worse. Amidst the rising mood of anti-British and anti-Israeli xenophobia, the military regime turned with increasing harshness against the European "monopoly" of Egyptian economic life. By government decree, Arabic was recognized henceforth as the exclusive language of use in the schools (a disaster for the Jewish school system), in the courts, and in the cotton and stock exchanges. Greek, French, Italian, and Jewish entrepreneurs now were arbitrarily denied access to the national markets.

Even as Nasser set about training and equipping his "Palestine liberation" forces, moreover (p. 90), he singled out the Egyptian-Jewish community for denunciation as a fifth column. Thus, in the winter of 1954–55, a "cold pogrom" was launched against Egypt's remaining 40,000 Jews. Jewish shops were boycotted. Jewish importers were deprived of their licenses. Underwriting houses severed their connections with Jewish stock- and cotton-brokers. With growing frequency, mobs swarmed through Jewish neighborhoods, protesting Jewish "treason," occasionally smashing the windows of Jewish shops and homes. Far from intervening, the police themselves were being indoctrinated now by experts in Jew-hatred. These were former Nazi officers, imported from Germany and Austria to organize Nasser's "State Security Cadre."

By the spring of 1954, therefore, even before the signing of the new Anglo-Egyptian Treaty, it was clear to Egyptian Jewry that their only hope was emigration. Yet it was not a simple matter to leave the country, even if exit visas occasionally were available. There were businesses and homes to be disposed of, and the market for Jewish properties had collapsed. There were savings to be transferred abroad, and the government blocked that. Those few hundred Jews who did succeed each month in departing for Europe took with them the barest residue of their former estate. Those who remained behind—still the majority—searched vainly for methods of salvaging the remnants of their businesses and careers. One tentative alternative proved a disaster for them—and very nearly for Israel.

THE ''SPY MISHAP''

Aware that it had been effectively cut off from its traditional information sources in Egypt, Israeli intelligence decided to plant an agent in Cairo with the goal of establishing a "base" there. The man chosen for the mission was Avraham Dar, a former kibbutz member who had carried out a number of intelligence missions during the 1948 war. In the summer of 1951 Dar arrived in the Egyptian capital from Europe. His British passport listed him as John Darling, a traveling salesman for a British electric apparatus firm. The following day, Dar met with Dr. Victor Sa'adi, an Egyptian Jew known to Israel as a fervent Zionist and as the leader of a small underground organization dedicated to Jewish emigration. Dar explained to the young doctor that the purpose of his, Dar's, mission was to establish a network for special intelligence operations in Egypt. Sa'adi in turn immediately put himself at Dar's disposal and began recruiting other Jews as collaborators. Nevertheless, the group remained largely inactive for the ensuing year and a half.

In 1953, then, as the change in Egypt's political climate became increasingly ominous, several young members of the network followed Dar's instructions and departed for France "on vacation." Once in Marseilles, the group boarded an Israeli ship and sailed for Haifa; and upon arrival in Israel, they were sent to an intelligence school and trained in the use of explosives, codes, invisible inks and photography. Returning to Egypt several months later (via France again), the young conspirators received their first assignment. Under Dar's supervision, they were ordered to fabricate explosive devices in preparation for sabotaging a carefully selected group of public buildings. The operation was not to take place immediately. Rather, it awaited a subsequent "development" between Egypt and Israel.

The "development" was the signature of the Anglo-Egyptian Treaty. As has been seen, the imminence of British departure from Suez gravely alarmed the Israeli government. Not only was a vast collection of military bases to be made available to Egypt, but, emancipated from British restraint, Nasser and his group conceivably might then feel free to launch new military action against the Jewish state. The question was what steps could be taken to abort this danger. At that juncture, the Israelis were not prepared to act decisively. Ben-Gurion had recently retired, and his successor as prime minister in late 1953 was Moshe Sharett. A moderate, Sharett had never been in sympathy with Ben-Gurion's policy of border raids as retaliation against Arab infiltration. Yet the new premier inherited as his defense minister Pinchas Lavon, a man who was a dedicated Ben-Gurionite and a believer in the tough line against the Arabs. Lavon also had established close ties with the director of military intelligence, Colonel Benyamin Gibli, and Gibli had recently cooked up a fascinating scheme for inducing the British to remain in Egypt. It anticipated acts of destruction against American and British office buildings in Egypt, thus endangering Western lives, exposing the alleged irresponsibility of the Egyptian government, and thereby persuading the British to remain. The project was now "refined" by Gibli's staff—without being revealed to Prime Minister Sharett. The question of Lavon's personal knowledge similarly remains unclear. It was doubtless a criminally stupid plan; but in Egypt itself, nevertheless, the Jewish spy ring was ordered to execute it.

By early 1954 this network had a new director. He was Avraham Seidenberg, a veteran Israeli intelligence agent who had been sent to Egypt under the alias of "Paul Frank." Blundering from the very outset, Seidenberg pointlessly involved many of the network's members with each other, even those having little to do with acts of sabotage. Those who did, however, set about touching off fires and explosions at several British and American buildings in Cairo and Alexandria. It was in the latter city, in mid-July 1954, that one of the plotters, Philip Natanson, inadvertently detonated his explosive prematurely. Natanson was arrested, his premises were searched by the Egyptian police, and the names of the entire ring soon were discovered. One after another, eleven of the participants were arrested. Only Seidenberg managed to escape to Europe. It developed later that he may well have been a double agent, and had alerted the police himself.

After the captive Jews were brutally interrogated in prison, the Nasser government released news of the "Zionist" network on October 25, 1954, and its ostensible purpose of "creating chaos" among the Egyptian people. In Israel, Prime Minister Sharett was horrified; he had known nothing of the plot. Investigating the authorship of the fiasco, he found Defense Minister Lavon and Intelligence Director Gibli blaming each other. Whoever was responsible, the damage to Israel was far-reaching. Thus, the trial of the Jewish conspirators, which began in Cairo on December 11, 1954, was shrewdly used by the Nasser regime to solidify national support for the revolutionary government. Each day's courtroom proceedings were described by press and radio in an ominous and inflammatory tone, conjuring up hair-raising visions of Jewish treachery and Israeli cunning. Nor was the accusation of guilt limited to the prisoners. The entire Egyptian-Jewish population was branded as a fifth column, undeserving of the nation's "hospitality." By January 1955, with government encouragement, Egyptian businessmen dropped their last Jewish employees.

The trial ended after three weeks. Twenty-seven days passed before the verdicts were issued. In the meanwhile, Israel's Prime Minister Sharett acted vigorously, dispatching emissaries to France and England, seeking influential intermediaries to persuade the Egyptian regime to stay its hand. During secret conversations in Paris between Yosef Tekoa, an Israeli foreign office official, and Mahmud Riad, the Egyptian officer-diplomat, the latter was warned that death sentences imposed on the Jewish defendants would abort any future peace negotiations. Israel's former chief of staff, Yigael Yadin, similarly traveled to London, expecting to be invited to Cairo for a private meeting with Nasser. The invitation never came. None of these, and other, frantic efforts bore fruit. Rather, the verdicts and sentences were announced in Cairo on February 2, 1955 (by then, one of the prisoners had committed suicide). Two of the defendants were condemned to death, two others to life imprisonment, four others to long prison terms. Only two were acquitted and released. Israel was stunned by the harshness of the sentences. Despite appeals for clemency from influential personalities throughout the world—Eisenhower, Nehru, Pope Pius XII, among others—the sentences were carried out. Immediately, then, all secret meetings between Tekoa and Riad were suspended. The suspicion and animus generated between Egypt and Israel henceforth became virtually irreversible.

Not least of all, the "spy mishap" produced far-reaching domestic consequences in Israel itself. It began with an embittered internecine struggle between Defense Minister Lavon and his colleagues. The former angrily disclaimed any advance knowledge of the operation. Gibli doggedly contradicted the defense minister. Sharett at this point selected a commission of inquiry. But after extensive interrogation, the commission members were unable to produce conclusive findings. In the interval, Lavon sought to dismiss Shimon Peres, director-general of the ministry, and Gibli, who had issued the order for the Egyptian operation. Yet if Sharett had agreed to uphold the defense minister in these dismissals, he would have lost several of the army's highest-ranking officers, including Chief of Staff Moshe Dayan. He chose to support Peres, and Lavon promptly resigned in February 1955. Unanticipated at the time, Lavon's sense of grievance was destined years later to effect a tumultuous upheaval in Israel's political life. For the immediate future, however, the most decisive consequence of the ruined spy operation was to be found in the wreckage of a briefly promising dialogue toward Egytian-Israeli peace.

VII

THE RISE OF NASSERIST IMPERIALISM

The tradition of authoritarianism in Egyptian history extended as far back as antiquity. The nation's struggle to subsist within the confines of a single effluvial valley, to ensure a proper distribution of the Nile's waters, virtually dictated the establishment of a centralized, omnicompetent administration. By the same token, developments in the economic and political sphere exerted their impact on ideology. To the master of the Nile was attributed divinely ordained, all-encompassing temporal power. With few exceptions, passive acceptance of autocracy survived as a norm of public behavior from the time of the pharaohs down to Mehemet Ali, and thereafter through the British agents-general and high commissioners of the nineteenth and early twentieth centuries. Never was this tradition manifested more vividly, however, than under Gamal Abd al-Nasser.

In the aftermath of Nasser's stupendous coup in engineering the Anglo-Egyptian Treaty of 1954, with its promise of forthcoming British evacuation, the young colonel easily silenced the few remaining opposition journalists by the simple device of closing down their newspapers and summarily arresting and trying their editors. When an Ikhwan fanatic bungled an assassination attempt on him in October 1954, Nasser organized a trial of all "implicated" conspirators. Seven were executed, and the Ikhwan itself was dissolved (for the second time after the murder of Prime Minister Nuqrashi) by "emergency" edict. General Naguib, meanwhile, was quietly removed from the office of president of the republic (Nasser himself assumed this title) and consigned to house arrest. In ensuing years, within the Free Officers group, personal loyalty to Nasser became the single immutable criterion for political longevity. In short, national leadership was reverting once again to its classic profile of autocracy, even of functional dictatorship.

Under these circumstances, the "representative committee," which had been appointed in 1952 to draft a constitution, was replaced in January 1956 by a new body, this one more congenial to Nasser. Its completed draft was adopted "by plebiscite" on June 23 of the same year. The principles enunciated by the document seemed unexceptionable. They included: the abolition of "imperialism"; the destruction of "feudalism"; the achievement of "social justice" in a "democratic Socialist cooperative" society. Yet, not incidentally, Article 192 of the new constitution provided for the establishment of a "National Union," an elite body dominated by the Free Officers and their selectees, to replace the nation's former political parties. From then on, all candidates for the People's Assembly (an organ similarly created by the new constitution) required approval by the National Union Executive. Since 1957 the rubber-stamp People's Assembly met twice-yearly, essentially to hear, and compliantly to approve, lengthy policy statements submitted by Nasser and by members of his cabinet.

The initial "consolidation" stage of the military regime, from 1952 to 1956, was devoted ostensibly to the establishment of a modern industrialized society. To launch this ambitious program, Nasser replaced the conventional political leadership with technocrats—officers, economists, and engineers. These were the men who now were charged with the task of breaking the power of the landowning capitalists, of increasing the number of small landowners, and of redirecting capital investment to industry. It was an unworkable program. Although the Land Reform Act managed to cut down to size dozens of notoriously engorged pashas, landlords otherwise were allowed to keep more than enough of their estates to ensure a handsome absentee income. Worse yet, local capital, invested mainly in land until then, either remained in land or went into real-estate development and housing speculation. Only marginal sums remained for industrial investment.

The failure equally of constitutional democracy and of any significant industrial progress was a cruel blow for the liberals, and particularly for the intelligentsia, who had welcomed the 1952 revolution with eager expectations. Somewhat naively, the latter had anticipated that the new regime would achieve a rapid, far-reaching success in instituting both political democracy and economic reform. Their disappointment was profound. At first, in their writings, they marked time, devoting themselves to subjects connected with social change but not immediately related to political events, such as the "crisis of the intellectuals." Naguib Mahfuz, Egypt's most respected novelist, followed this course. Others, like Yusuf Idris, abandoned realism for a more conventional romanticism. The government encouraged this trend. Yet the Free Officers hardly were blind to the potential dangers of middle-class disenchantment and unrest. Thus, Nasser and his colleagues were not unwilling to exploit diversionary techniques. The expulsion of the British was one of these. A militant new program of pan-Arabist leadership conceivably would prove even more useful.

PAN-ARABISM AND THE ISRAELI CATALYST

By the mid-1950s, a dynamic effort to assert Egypt's leadership in the Arab world appeared to be as functional as it was potentially diversionary. Even earlier, during Farouk's time, the value of Arab economic strength to Egypt was well appreciated. As Abd al-Rahman Azzam Pasha of the Arab League stated in 1950: "On the economic level, we need the Arab states, which . . . possess the richest resources in the raw materials essential to our future industry. . . ." Nasser appreciated, too, that if a program of large-scale industrialization were ever to be feasible, his burgeoning population somehow would have to gain access to the markets of other Arab lands. This would be no simple matter. A major effort to achieve Egyptian hegemony in the Arab Middle East would hardly leave room for competition by other nations.

The Baghdad Pact of 1955 represented precisely this kind of unacceptable competition. The new Middle East defense organization outraged Nasser. By promoting Iraq as the West's major Arab intermediary, it seemed to imperil the young colonel's hopes for Egyptian leadership (and his own) in an all-Arab alliance. Worse yet, Britain, having departed Egypt, appeared now to be returning to primacy in the Middle East through a northeastern—Iraqi—access route. Other obstacles to Nasserist pan-Arabist ambitions were latent within Egypt itself. Few Egyptians considered themselves to be Arabs—people whom they regarded as culturally much inferior. Intellectuals such as Taha Hussein, Muhammad Heykal, and Salama Musa had always insisted that Egypt was a Mediterranean nation, not an Arab nation. Indeed, Egypt's struggle for freedom traditionally had been introverted; between the two world wars its nationalist ideology was almost exclusively Egypt-oriented. In the early years of the Colonels' Revolution, too, this ethnocentrism remained the accepted approach among intellectuals and political leaders alike.

It was, rather, the confluence of the Baghdad Pact, Egypt's economic requirements, and the new regime's need to transcend domestic failures that impelled Nasser to launch his calculated excursion in pan-Arabism. Accordingly, from 1955 on, all the resources of Egyptian bribery, diplomacy, subversion, and Nasser's not inconsiderable personal magnetism were thrown into the campaign to rally Arab nationalist sentiment against the new Middle East defense organization. In the course of this battle, moreover, the Egyptian president made every effort to buttress his pan-Arabist leadership by securing arms, by concluding a series of treaties with other Arab nations, and by undermining Western influence in the Mediterranean through propaganda and military adventurism. It was to that end also that Israel, even more than the traditional *bête noire* of Great Britain, proved to be a vital catalyst.

In the early 1950s, the little Zionist republic appeared a likely prey for pan-Arabist adventurism. By the time Moshe Dayan was appointed military chief of

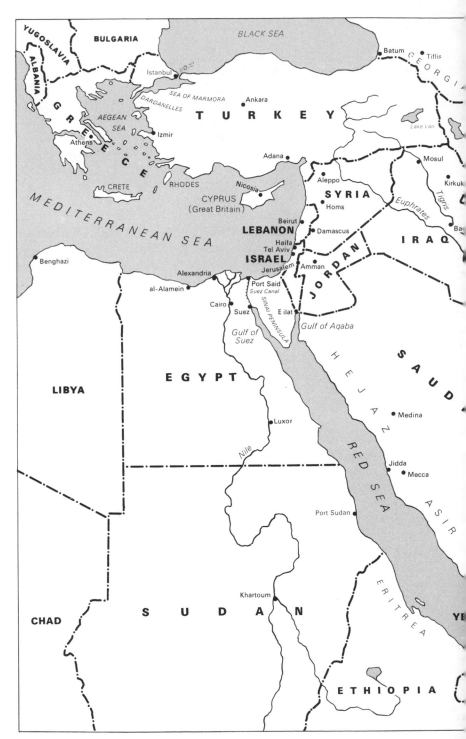

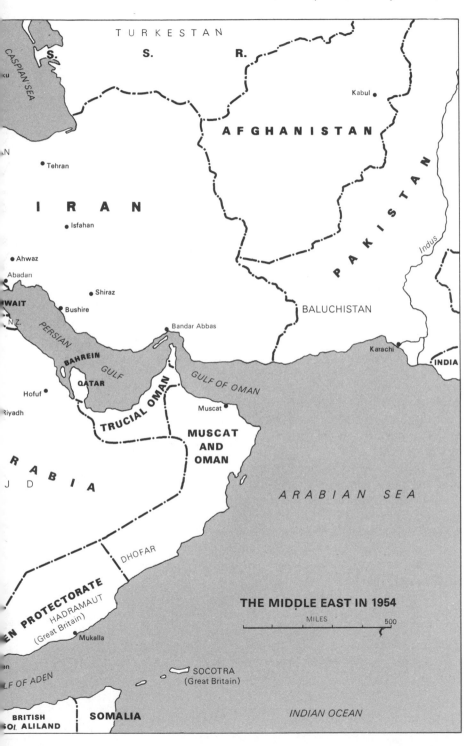

TURKESTAN

S. S. R.

Kabul

AFGHANISTAN

Tehran

CASPIAN SEA

I R A N

Isfahan

Ahwaz

Abadan

PAKISTAN

Indus

Shiraz

WAIT

N.Z.

Bushire

PERSIAN

BANDAR ABBAS

BALUCHISTAN

Bandar Abbas

BAHREIN

GULF

QATAR

GULF OF OMAN

Karachi

INDIA

Hofuf

TRUCIAL OMAN

Muscat

Riyadh

MUSCAT
AND
OMAN

R A B I A

J D

ARABIAN SEA

DHOFAR

THE MIDDLE EAST IN 1954

MILES

500

EN PROTECTORATE

HADRAMAUT
(Great Britain)

Mukalla

SOCOTRA
(Great Britain)

INDIAN OCEAN

LF OF ADEN

BRITISH
SOMALILAND

SOMALIA

staff in December 1953, the Israeli army, like the Israeli economy, had lapsed into the doldrums. Appraising this deterioration, the vigorous, one-eyed commander decided promptly to "blood" his troops in counteractions against Arab infiltrators. Thereafter, Dayan launched the army on a series of trip-hammer punitive expeditions against those Arab villages known to be harboring guerrillas, and occasionally against Arab military strong points. Until late 1954, Hashemite Jordan had served as the principal base for marauding attacks over Israel's frontiers, and Dayan's counterassaults as a result were aimed mainly at Hashemite targets.

Then, afterward, as an expression of Nasser's decision to flex his muscles in the pan-Arabist cause, leadership in the guerrilla campaign passed to Egypt. By late 1954, fedayun (suicide) squads of Palestinian refugees operating from Gaza, most of them trained and equipped by Egyptian army units, were penetrating deep into Israel, attacking roads, bridges, water pipes, carrying off large quantities of equipment and livestock, and soon threatening the entire development program in Israel's southern desert. During the next two years some 11,650 "incidents" occurred along Israel's frontiers. Approximately 3,000 of them originated from Egypt directly, but even the attacks mounted from Hashemite territory were increasingly masterminded by Egypt. Israel's casualties had risen by then to 434 killed and 942 wounded—a not inconsiderable total for a small nation. Neither Ben-Gurion nor Dayan was prepared to accept supinely these repeated acts of Egyptian belligerence. On February 28, 1955, therefore, the Israeli army launched a reprisal of brigade strength against Egyptian military headquarters in Gaza, blowing up a number of buildings, killing 38 Egyptian troops, and wounding 24 others. Although the raid was described as a response to a succession of major Egyptian provocations, it may also have been intended as retaliation for the recent hanging of Egyptian Jews in the wake of the Cairo spy trial (p. 83).

From the viewpoint of the Egyptian government, on the other hand, the Gaza raid was a shattering provocation. "This disaster was the warning bell," Nasser insisted later. "We at once started to examine the significance of peace and the balance of power in the area." The decisive impact of the Gaza raid was accepted by non-Egyptian observers, among them General E. L. M. Burns, chief of staff of the United Nations Truce Organization in the Middle East. In Israel, too, the leftist Mapam party bitterly criticized the raid, as did Abba Eban, Israel's ambassador to the United Nations. "I don't believe [Gaza] was the only reason but at least the excuse was there," Eban wrote later. It was only the excuse. The policy of blockade and of organized fedayun operations had considerably predated the Gaza raid. So had Nasser's decision to acquire a major arsenal for undermining the incipient Baghdad Pact, and for enhancing his own leadership of the pan-Arab cause.

SOVIET PATRONAGE AND THE COLLAPSE OF MIDDLE EASTERN EQUILIBRIUM

If ordnance was needed for this grand design, however, Nasser failed initially to acquire modern weapons either from the United States, Britain, or France; the three Western Powers still were bent on maintaining the Middle East arms freeze. Opportunity surfaced elsewhere. In April 1955 the Egyptian president attended the Bandung Conference of Afro-Asian Nations. It was during the conclave in this Indonesian city that Nasser first sensed the possibility of achieving diplomatic leverage by bargaining as a spokesman for the emergent "neutralist" world. At the suggestion, then, of China's Prime Minister Chou En-lai, Nasser explored the possibilities of obtaining military equipment from the Soviet bloc.

Moscow was entirely receptive. Challenged by the Baghdad Pact, the Soviets were prepared to exploit any opening to sap Western influence in the Middle East. Indeed, one of the cardinal objectives of the post-Stalin leadership was to break the vise of American and British treaty containment. To that end, Moscow in recent years had evinced a new interest in the Third World. Since 1953, it had significantly expanded its economic and military aid to Afghanistan, then had concluded an arms deal with Syria, and finally had agreed to construct a giant steel plant in India. During 1955, too, regarding the Baghdad Pact and the presence of the United States Sixth Fleet in the Mediterranean as threats to their emergent aerospace industry in the Ukraine and Central Asia, the Soviets went a good deal further in their preemptive efforts. They made known their intention of pursuing a more active policy directly in the Arab world itself. These were the circumstances, therefore, in the summer of that year, under which Moscow responded favorably to Nasser's appeal for weapons. The Egyptian president was hostile to the British, after all. Adopting a vaguely Socialist line, he seemed a likelier bet than did any other Middle Eastern leader for Communist support.

In August 1955, as a result, a historic arms transaction was consummated. Nasser was allowed to purchase some $320 million worth of modern weapons from Czechoslovakia. The terms were exceptionally favorable to Cairo; payment on an interest-free basis would be spaced out over twelve years in shipments of Egyptian cotton. The quantity of war matériel made available to Egypt, too, was altogether unprecedented by Middle Eastern standards. It included 120 jet fighters, 50 jet bombers, 200 tanks, 150 artillery pieces, 2 destroyers, 2 submarines, as well as hundreds of vehicles and tens of thousands of modern rifles and machine guns. In a parallel treaty, Syria contracted with the Soviet bloc to purchase an additional 100 tanks, 100 jet fighters, and hundreds of artillery pieces and armored vehicles. Soviet and Czech instructors would be provided to train the Egyptian and Syrian armed forces in the use of this weaponry.

Vastly reinforced in power and prestige, Nasser moved forward rapidly in his pan-Arabist campaign. During the next half-year he concluded a series of mutual defense treaties with Syria, Saudi Arabia, and Yemen. What he could not accomplish by treaty, moreover, he achieved through subversion. Thus, when Jordan's young King Hussein appeared willing to sign the Baghdad Pact, pro-Nasserist rioters forced the resignation of the Hashemite cabinet in December 1955. Intent also upon eroding British influence in Black Africa, the Egyptian government embarked upon intensified propaganda broadcasts to the Mau Mau rebels in Kenya and to the Islamic minorities of Eritrea and Ethiopian Somalia. Nor was the French Maghreb empire neglected in this campaign of incitement. By late 1955 Egyptian funds and transshipments of Soviet bloc weapons were being disbursed to the FLN nationalists in Algeria.

Not least of all, Israel was singled out as a critical target of Nasser's ambitions. Until 1954, we recall, Jordan had served as the principal base for marauding attacks over Israel's frontier. But in 1954 leadership in the guerrilla campaign passed to Egypt, and fedayun squads, trained and equipped in Egypt, soon were wreaking extensive destruction among Israel's southern development communities. Occasionally, raiding bands penetrated to the outskirts of Tel Aviv, inflicting dozens of civilian casualties each month. General Burns, the UNTSO chief of staff, traveled between Cairo and Tel Aviv, urgently seeking methods of improving border controls. After Nasser's massive arms coup, however, Burns's exertions were wasted. Instead, following Israel's Gaza raid, Mixed Armistice Committee meetings between the two nations terminated entirely.

Even before 1955, for that matter, the talk in Egypt once again was of eradicating Israel. The Jewish state was equated with imperialism, with the West's traditional "hatred" of Arabs and Islam. In an article for the April 1954 issue of *Ikhtarna Lak,* Nasser emphasized that the purpose of Zionism was "to degrade us and to acquire what was in our hands and under our feet, to exploit our wealth and our markets . . . to take our lands . . . destroy our buildings . . . liquidate the foundations of our nationality . . . deaden our hearts . . . and steal away our minds and this world of ours." Throughout 1955 the drumbeats of anti-Zionism reached a crescendo, and were ventilated in Egyptian schools, in newspapers, on radio and television.

Yet, to the Israelis, the Communist arms transaction appeared far more ominous even than the rising Egyptian propaganda and guerrilla campaigns. They understood now that, for Egypt and its allies, the new military disequilibrium in the Middle East offered a unique opportunity. It signified that Arab hostility no longer need be confined to economic or diplomatic measures, or even to an increase in border crossings and killings. To the Arab world, rather, a military "second round" against Israel now appeared to be a distinct possibility for the first time since 1948. It was the opinion of the Israeli general staff that Egypt's armed forces would require no more than nine months to absorb the new weaponry. "We therefore had to expect an Egyptian attack at any time from late spring [1956] to late summer," Dayan wrote later. To abort that possibility, the Israeli commander, on November 10, 1955, recommended to Ben-Gurion the immediate launching of a preemptive offensive. Its goals would be the capture of the Gaza Strip, the likely staging base of an Egyptian invasion; and of Sharm es-Sheikh, the key to free passage through the Gulf of Agaba. Ben-Gurion did not cavil. Nevertheless, before deciding on this critical venture, the prime minister summoned General Burns to his office on December 5 and requested the UNTSO officer to query Nasser: Were the Egyptians prepared to issue orders for a complete cease-fire along the Gaza Strip? Burns departed immediately for Cairo. Six days later, disappointed, he returned to inform Ben-Gurion that he had received a negative response. Nasser plainly was luxuriating in his new arsenal, and he was not about to be restricted any longer in determining its future use.

THE UNITED STATES SEEKS TO MEDIATE

Hardly less than the Israelis, the American government viewed the escalation of Middle Eastern border violence with mounting concern. It was assumed in Washington that the Soviets would eagerly exploit a new round of Arab-Israeli war to project their influence in the Middle East. In late 1955, therefore, following General Burns's unsuccessful mission, Kermit Roosevelt, the American CIA chief in Cairo, devised a scheme known as "Gamma Project." The plan envisaged the dispatch of Robert Anderson, a former American undersecretary of defense and a confidant of President Eisenhower, to the Middle East on a new effort of mediation. In the event Anderson managed to narrow the differences between Egypt and Israel, it was anticipated that Nasser and Ben-Gurion would meet secretly afterward to bridge the remaining gap. Eisenhower liked the idea, and Secretary of State Dulles promptly attempted to sell it to Cairo. As a sweetener, Dulles intimated that progress in the contemplated discussions would influence Washington's response to an Egyptian financial aid request. Nasser thereupon agreed to receive Anderson.

After a two-day visit in Cairo, the American emissary reached Jerusalem on January 23, 1956. There he reported to Ben-Gurion the substance of his conversation with Nasser. The Egyptian president agreed with Anderson that his nation was unable simultaneously to maintain a large army and to embark on a major program of economic development. But although he, Nasser, was "ready and willing" to make peace with Israel, no progress could be achieved toward that goal until the Palestine refugees were offered the opportunity of repatriation. He personally was not interested in numbers on this issue as much as in the principle of free choice. Territorial matters were also of secondary importance, although they too would have to be resolved. In any case, Nasser made clear that he was ready study Israel's proposals for peace, on strict condition that they were kept secret.

Listening to this report, Ben-Gurion reminded Anderson that two months earlier, he, the prime minister, had asked General Burns to elicit Nasser's commitment to a cease-fire, but Nasser had refused. "I understand Nasser's difficulties in undertaking to observe the whole of the armistice agreement," remarked Ben-Gurion, "such as freedom of navigation in the Suez Canal, and so forth. But why does he not agree to a cease-fire?" Anderson was sympathetic, and at this point offered his own compromise formula. It was for both sides to commit themselves to a cease-fire. The pledge would be made not to each other, however, but to Eisenhower. For Nasser, such a face-saving alternative would then open the door for secret meetings with Ben-Gurion. Anderson inquired: Would Ben-Gurion accept this formula? The prime minister's answer was a categorical yes. But he reiterated that a cease-fire was the indispensable first step, with a personal meeting between the two leaders the logical sequence. The refugee question was a difficult one for Israel, Ben-Gurion admitted, mainly due to absorption problems, but even here some give-and-take was possible—if there were a direct meeting.

The American emissary then returned to Cairo on January 25. Six days later he traveled back to Jerusalem. Nasser understood Ben-Gurion's concern on the refugee issue, Anderson assured his Israeli host. Indeed, the Egyptian president was willing to discuss the problem in search of a compromise solution. Regarding the question of border incidents, too, Nasser had assured Anderson that he would issue orders to stop the violence, although it was difficult to "control" the refugees. He also had denied any hostile intentions with his new Czech weapons. As for a personal meeting, however, Nasser's difficulty (said Anderson) was "that his Intelligence and Police did not know about the matter. . . . He said he did not want what happened to Abdullah [the late Hashemite king, assassinated in 1951] to happen to him. [And] the only charge against Abdullah had been that he had held negotiations with Israel."

Ben-Gurion listened carefully to this account, and with evident disappointment. It was clear now, he said, that even such fundamental issues as violence on the border could not be resolved secondhand—or through commitments to Eisenhower. Only a face-to-face meeting would suffice. As for the refugee problem, "I may have some ideas for [Nasser]. I will propose things that he does not even think about." These included territorial matters. Anderson interjected then: "Haifa for the use of Jordan?" Ben-Gurion replied: "And Eilat, too—and Alexandria, as well, for our use." Immediately, then, Anderson embarked once more for Cairo. Two subsequent meetings with Nasser followed. When the American emissary returned to Jerusalem on March 9, he reported this time with some frustration that Nasser apparently had lost all interest in a face-to-face meeting. Alluding repeatedly to the murder of Abdullah, the Egyptian president had declared his willingness to speak to the United States, and the United States could then talk to Israel; but he, Nasser, simply could not take the risk of direct contacts. On the issue of refugees, too, Nasser had proved suddenly obdurate. The most he would promise now was to refrain from engaging in an aggressive war against Israel. The Israelis said nothing. Their silence was as eloquent as Anderson's embarrassment. It was plain to them, if not to him, that Nasser had been dissembling from the very beginning, probably to avoid offending Eisenhower.

Yet one secret meeting did occur two weeks later. It took place between Moshe Sasson, Israel's veteran foreign ministry adviser on Arab affairs, and Egypt's former prime minister, Ali Maher. The two conferred in Montreux, and the discussions were entirely unproductive. Ali Maher engaged in generalities, listened politely to Sasson, and promised simply to convey the latter's (i.e., Ben-Gurion's) views to Nasser. Then, in late March, Egyptian forces in the Gaza Strip suddenly launched an artillery bombardment of Israeli kibbutz settlements. The Jewish counterreaction of April 5 was a particularly savage shelling of the Gaza marketplace. Sixty Arabs were killed and 100 others wounded. Within days afterward, fedayun violence from Gaza erupted on a scale unprecedented since the 1948 Palestine war. Both Egypt and Israel appeared now to be on the verge of full-scale hostilities. At this point the United Nations secretary-general, Dag Hammarskjöld, flew off to the Middle East in a last-minute effort to reduce border tensions. His mission was given a new urgency by Ben-Gurion's stern warning, on April 10, that he would wait only two days for Nasser's solemn promise to observe the cease-fire. Otherwise, Israel would "reserve its freedom of action."

Apparently the Egyptians were impressed by the ultimatum. On the eleventh, Radio Cairo announced that the fedayun raids had been conducted in retaliation for the shelling of Gaza, but that now they were over. Ben-Gurion was less than satisfied. Through Hammarskjöld, he sought Nasser's commitment not merely to a cease-fire but also to the full spectrum of assurances implicit in the Rhodes Armistice—that is, an end to boycott, blockade, and hostile propaganda. No commitment was forthcoming; the Egyptian response was a glacial silence. The disappointment in Jerusalem was profound, even bitter. Repeatedly, for three and a half years, Ben-Gurion and his colleagues had extended their peace overtures to the revolutionary regime in Cairo by every imaginable direct and indirect route. But now it was all too plain that the door to negotiations was tightly sealed again, that nothing substantial would be forthcoming after all from Egypt's "progressive, Socialist" government of colonels.

VIII

THE FIRST SINAI WAR

As if the growing weapons imbalance and their own treaty isolation were not cause enough for apprehension to the Israelis, Washington and London decided now to press the Jerusalem government for a commitment to territorial concessions. This, it was insisted, was the one sure method of forestalling tensions with Egypt. In a major policy speech of August 1955, American Secretary of State Dulles stressed that the Rhodes Armistice lines of 1949 were not designed to be permanent frontiers. It was a less than veiled allusion to Israel's claim to the entire Negev Desert. On November 9, in language even more plainspoken than Dulles's, Britain's Prime Minister Eden appealed for a "compromise" between the boundaries of the United Nations Partition Resolution and the 1949 armistice lines, under which Israel had augmented its territory by over twenty percent. Soon afterward, in April 1956, the tripartite commitment (p. 77) received its coup de grace. In the event of a new Arab-Israeli war, stated Dulles, Washington would place its major emphasis on action through the United Nations. The approach manifestly would have exposed future enforcement measures to a Soviet veto in the Security Council. Indeed, the Jewish state's unsettled relations with Britain and the United States were occurring at the identical period when Moscow was enlarging its military and diplomatic support of Egypt and Syria, repeatedly condemning Israel in the Security Council, and accusing the "Ben-Gurion clique" of preparing war against the Arabs.

Under these bleak circumstances, the Israelis were reminded that their nation's security depended ultimately upon its own resources. Here the role of the military was to prove crucial. Fortunately for the Zionist republic, political disarray in the Arab world after 1948 allowed Israel eight precious years in which to strengthen its defenses. The nation's military forces were divided into a regular service and a reserve. The former was structured around a nucleus of commissioned and noncommissioned officers, and of young conscripts undergoing training. The trainees included all men and women who had reached the age of eighteen. Upon completion of their term—twenty-six months for men, twenty for women—the draftees entered the reserves. From this pool, men under forty were called up for a month of refresher training each year, as well as one day a month of further duty. It was a program incomparably tougher than any equivalent system in the Arab world, where conscription was essentially unrelated to future reserve service.

From the outset of Israel's independence, the defense ministry was in the hands of Ben-Gurion himself (except for one brief interruption in 1953–54 when Pinchas Lavon held this portfolio), and it was uniquely the stamp of "B.G.'s" forceful character that was imprinted upon the development of the military establishment. Under his leadership, the army, navy, and air force were transformed into a citizens' academy, the inculcator of public spirit. Theoretically, this was also true in Egypt after the revolution. But the gulf that had separated officers and men in Farouk's day continued under the Nasser regime, and military training tended to be routinized. In Israel, by contrast, increasingly heavier weight was placed upon officers' leadership in active combat. After Dayan became chief of staff in 1953, moreover, striking power became the key to strategy. The weakness of Israel's economy and the nation's limited size precluded any alternative approach. As a result, planning henceforth was geared to the preemptive blow, the hard-driving, even reckless, offensive aimed at breaking the enemy's morale. It was a strategy no less suited to Dayan's personal temperament. A native-born "sabra," a veteran of the Haganah and of the British invasion of Vichy Syria in 1941, the dynamic young general had only confidence in the unique spirit and quality of troops that had been trained in the intensely self-reliant, service-oriented Zionist school system. He knew, as well, that officers and men shared the same rations, the same privations, the same well-inculcated ideals. Morale was high.

Nevertheless, in view of the massive Soviet-Egyptian arms deal, Dayan feared that training and spirit alone might prove inadequate. Late in 1955, as has been seen, he had warned Ben-Gurion that the balance of forces was shifting, that the time remaining for Israel to attack was diminishing rapidly. By then the Egyptian-directed guerrilla campaign had moved into high gear, and clashes along the Gaza Strip were mounting in intensity. The blockade of the Gulf of Aqaba, too, was becoming increasingly painful to Israel's economy—even more critical to the nation's future than the escalating guerrilla campaign. Since 1953, Egypt's coast guard units at Ras Nasrani and Sharm es-Sheikh had closed off all Israeli shipping through the Strait of Tiran, and in September 1955 the Egyptians similarly turned back the vessels of other nations bound for Israel's port of Eilat. In recognition of these facts, Ben-Gurion, on October 22, 1955, ordered Dayan to make immediate preparations for capturing Sharm es-Sheikh, Ras Nasrani, and the islands of Tiran and Sanafir. Only one vital ingredient was missing for the preemptive blow, and this was adequate equipment.

As the first shipments of Czech and other Soviet-bloc arms began to reach Egypt in late 1955, the astonishing scale of this weaponry evoked a "backs-to-the-wall" psychology in Israel. Tens of thousands of volunteers took up picks and shovels and set about digging trenches and preparing fieldworks. Citizens contributed money, even jewelry, to the weapons fund. The spontaneous public reaction was only the most tangible expression of a defense effort that, between 1950 and 1956, had averaged 7 percent of Israel's GNP, a far higher proportion than that of any Arab state. Yet the results of this effort remained inadequate. Even as the Soviet arms deal threatened to give Egypt and Syria a weapons superiority of six to one, the Jewish state's quest for modern arms was hardly more productive than its search for territorial guarantees. The United States had no intention of matching the Communist supplies pouring into Egypt. In February 1956, Dulles informed a group of congressmen that Israel would invariably lose an arms race against the Arabs. Israel's population was less than two million, he explained, and its security would more appropriately be assured by reliance on the United Nations. Endorsing this view, President Eisenhower remarked to French Prime Minister Guy Mollet that there was no logic in selling arms to Israel inasmuch as 1,700,000 Jews could not possibly defend themselves against 40 million Arabs.

Whatever Mollet's response to Eisenhower's observation, it was in France, nevertheless, that Israel's search for weapons at last began to produce results. The French Left maintained a pro-Jewish sympathy extending back to the Dreyfus Affair and forward to the Socialist regimes that governed both in Paris and in Jerusalem. The French Right, too, shared with Israel a common fear of rising pan-Arab nationalism, most notably in Algeria. By autumn of 1954, as Radio Cairo broadcast assurances of support to the rebel Algerian FLN, relations between France and Egypt deteriorated alarmingly. Thus, in December, the French government approved a modest Israeli purchase order for twelve Ouragan jet fighters. It was at this point that Ben-Gurion, returning to the defense ministry in February 1955 after his brief retirement, accepted the contention of Shimon Peres, the ministry's director-general, that all efforts now should be exerted to developing a relationship with Paris, rather than with Washington.

Polish-born, only thirty-two years old, Peres was significantly enlarging Israel's defense ministry, expanding its production of local weapons, fostering nuclear research and development. The young director-general exhibited uncommon skill, as well, in negotiating on Israel's behalf with French defense officials. Indeed, Peres—and later Dayan and other Israeli officers—found a growing understanding among their French counterparts. Several of these latter had fought in the French wartime underground and evinced a sympathetic interest in the Zionist cause that considerably predated their common antipathy to Nasser. Then, in January 1956, the French elections returned a new Socialist government under the leadership of Guy Mollet, a protege of Léon Blum and an ardent admirer of Socialist Israel. One of the incoming premier's first policy decisions was to accept the contention of his military advisers that French influence in the Middle East could be sustained most effectively through help to the Israelis. Intent upon resisting Nasser's burgeoning power, Mollet decided then to make available to Israel sizable quantities of France's latest Mystère jet fighter, as well as other military equipment. On July 4, 1956, Foreign Minister Christian Pineau informed Israel's Ambassador Ya'akov Tsur that all former limitations on weapons delivery to Israel were now ended, irrespective of American or British policy. Paris would reserve its own liberty of action in supplying France's "true friends."

NASSER SEIZES THE CANAL

On March 1, 1956, British Foreign Secretary Selwyn Lloyd flew to Cairo in the hope of persuading Nasser to end Egypt's subversionary campaign in Hashemite Jordan. Instead, Nasser archly informed his visitor that Jordan's King Hussein had that very day exiled General John Glubb, the British commander of the Arab Legion. Lloyd returned to England in a trembling rage. Two weeks later, French Foreign Minister Pineau visited Cairo in a similar bid to end Egyptian subversion in Algeria. This effort, too, foundered as Egyptian vessels continued to transport Soviet-bloc weapons to the Algerian rebels.

Ironically, the West's final break with Cairo was precipitated by a matter relating not to foreign policy but rather to internal Egyptian economic development. Nasser's most cherished domestic project for his nation was the construction of a vast new high dam at Aswan, on the Nile. The cost of the undertaking was estimated at nearly $1 billion. In February 1956, the World Bank agreed to lend Egypt $200 million of the sum, contingent upon an American loan of $56 million and a British loan of $14 million. Egypt itself would provide the balance. Yet by then Washington had moved close to participation in the Baghdad Pact; and, in response, Nasser mortgaged another $200 million of unplanted cotton for additional Soviet-bloc arms. The West was shocked. Nasser's total budget for 1956–57 had been announced as 326 million Egyptian pounds (about $90 million), and of this, no less than 78 million pounds was for direct military expenditures—amounting to 28 percent of Egypt's total budget. Against this unprecedented sum for armaments, Nasser was spending 36,600,000 pounds for education, 23,600,000 pounds on every form of social welfare, and 45,800,000 pounds for industrial expansion. It was an appalling imbalance for a "progressive" regime that was committed ostensibly to social reform and to the economic rejuvenation of a nation suffering from 82 percent illiteracy, and from a per capita annual income of $97.

Additionally, on May 5, 1956, Nasser reached agreement to "coordinate" the armies of Egypt and Jordan. With the polarization of the Middle East well dramatized by then, and with the pro-Western governments of Jordan and Iraq partially outflanked, Washington and London took an increasingly jaundiced view of Nasser and of his Aswan project. Their suspicions were compounded on

May 16, when Cairo announced its recognition of Communist China. On July 19, therefore, Dulles formally notified the Egyptian ambassador that the United States was withdrawing its offer of funds. Two days later, Britain similarly withdrew its own offer, and the World Bank loan automatically was dropped.

As it happened. Nasser was fully prepared with a countermove, one he had been contemplating since 1954. At that time, the Egyptian government had appointed a young economist, Mustafa al-Hafnawi, to the Egyptian section of the secretariat of the Suez Canal Company. Hafnawi had earned his doctorate at the Sorbonne with his dissertation on the company, a work that later was expanded into a four-volume book. It was Hafnawi's contention that the Canal should be nationalized, in this fashion enabling the government to raise tolls at its own discretion, or even to deny freedom of passage to ships of any nation unsympathetic to Egyptian policy. Nasser was profoundly impressed by this work. It was not until June 1956, however, with the evacuation from Egypt of the last British troops, that the opportunity arose to carry out Hafnawi's proposal. Then, on July 26, during an anniversary celebration of the Colonels' Revolution, the president dropped his bombshell. The Canal was being nationalized, he announced, and its future revenues henceforth would be applied to the construction of the Aswan Dam. That night the Egyptian people erupted in mass demonstrations of renewed pride and joy. Once again, as on the signing of the Anglo-Egyptian Treaty two years earlier, Nasser was hailed as a national hero.

Of all the Western nations, it was Britain that was most directly affected by Nasser's riposte. Its government owned a controlling interest in the Suez Canal Company's shares. A third of the ships using the waterway were British, and nearly all of Britain's imported oil similarly passed through Suez. At stake, too, no less than Britain's economic and security interests, was British prestige in the Arab world. Vividly recalling the consequences of appeasing the Axis rulers in the 1930s, Prime Minister Eden was unprepared to accept this latest affront from a "tin pot Egyptian dictator." Neither was French Premier Mollet, whose "anti-Munich" reflex was as strong as Eden's. At this point, both Western leaders ordered their nations' civilians out of Egypt, then turned to Washington in the hope of formulating a joint policy.

Here they were to be disappointed, however. American dependence on Suez hardly matched that of the Western European nations. Rather, the vindictive temper of London and Paris astonished Eisenhower and Dulles. Discerning no legal or moral justification for the use of armed force, Dulles hurriedly flew off to London on August 15 to convene an emergency conference of maritime powers. A week later the participants issued a declaration recognizing Egypt's sovereign right to a fair return on the use of the Canal, but insisting on the principle of international control for the waterway. Nasser was not impressed. On September 9, he rejected the declaration.

Thereafter, Anglo-French military preparations swiftly gained momentum.

Indeed, as early as August 5, a joint team of staff officers had begun work in London on a plan for landings in Egypt. The impending operation, dubbed "Musketeer," envisaged a British contribution of several bomber squadrons, as well as 50,000 troops, to a joint expeditionary force. The French in turn would supply a number of fighter squadrons and 30,000 troops. A combined naval armada would encompass fully 100 British ships, 30 French vessels, hundreds of landing craft, and 20,000 vehicles. The Allied command estimated that the bulk of the expeditionary force would reach Egypt by sea on September 15. There, following thirty-six hours of air bombardment, troops would disembark, capture Alexandria, and advance on the main Egyptian army and on Cairo itself. As matters turned out, planning for the vast operation was almost as intricate as that undertaken for the invasion of southern France in 1944.

News soon reached Washington of what was happening. Shocked, and determined under all circumstances to forestall the invasion, Dulles on September 11 transmitted to the Allies his own hastily devised scheme for a Suez Canal Users' Association to "manage" the waterway. Somewhat grudgingly, then, London and Paris agreed to postpone the dispatch of their armada. Yet it soon became clear that Dulles had no intention of forcing Egypt to accept the "Users' Association." He suggested instead that Eden and Mollet put their case before the UN Security Council. This they did on September 23, and the Soviets promptly vetoed any meaningful resolution of censure against Egypt. As far as the two Western prime ministers were concerned, all peaceful recourse was exhausted. D-Day was now set tentatively for October 8. The one change in Allied strategy was to abandon the plan for capturing Alexandria, and to shift the objective to seizure of the Canal itself. It was specifically this alteration, in turn, that provided the opportunity for collaboration with Israel.

THE TREATY OF SÈVRES

Nasser's self-assurance in dealing with the British and French was fully equaled in his intensified campaign against Israel. It is recalled that, as far back as March 1956, another cycle of infiltration and retaliation had begun along the Gaza demarcation zone. Two months after the Israeli shelling of Gaza on April 5, and despite Cairo's promises to halt further violence, a new series of fedayun raids occurred, and within the week a dozen Israeli civilians had been killed and twice that many injured. Nasser left no doubt of his intentions toward the Jewish republic. "We must be strong in order to regain the rights of the Palestinians by force," he declared in a speech of June 19. Addressing his troops on July 5, General Abd al-Hakim Amer, commander of the Egyptian armed forces, insisted that the "hour is approaching when [we] . . . will stand in the front ranks of the battle against imperialism and its Zionist ally." Between July 29 and September 25, Egyptian-trained fedayeen assaulted Israel from bases in

Gaza, Jordan, and Syria, killing another nineteen Jews and wounding twenty-eight. By then, too, Ben-Gurion had replaced Moshe Sharett, his moderate and cautious foreign minister, with Mrs. Golda Meir, who shared the premier's conviction that forthright military action was urgently needed. Ben-Gurion now searched only for the decisive moment to act.

France supplied the opportunity. In early August, Maurice Bourgès-Maunoury, the French minister of defense, sent for Shimon Peres, who had been shuttling on supply missions between Tel Aviv and Paris. "If we make war on Egypt," asked Bourgès-Maunoury, "would Israel be prepared to fight alongside us?" Peres's response was an immediate yes—in principle. Nothing further was said for the time being, but the conversation was the young director-general's first intimation that extraordinary new possibilities were developing. Once more, then, early in September, Bourgès-Maunoury asked Peres straight out if Israel would attack Egypt on October 20, in conjunction with the French and British. At this point it was evident that the French were interested both in a pretext for Allied invasion, and in a two-pronged offensive against Nasser. An Israeli ground attack through Sinai would enable the Western allies to shift their emphasis from a broad amphibious operation to more limited paratroop assaults on the Canal Zone. Rushing back to Israel several days later, Peres and Chief of Staff Dayan discussed the matter with Ben-Gurion personally. Even as these urgent conversations went on, Bourgès-Maunoury and his staff began to press Israel's ambassador in Paris, warning that the price of additional French military support was full Israeli collaboration. Finally, on September 23, Ben-Gurion sent off a coded wire to Peres, who had meanwhile returned to Paris: "Tell them that their date suits us," the cable said. The commitment was made.

Yet Israel's acquiescence was coupled with a demand for immediate and much larger shipments of French equipment. On September 29, Dayan and Foreign Minister Golda Meir flew off to Paris in a French bomber, bringing with them a detailed shopping inventory. The list included 100 tanks, 300 half-tracks, 50 tank transporters, 300 trucks, 1,000 recoilless rifles, and a squadron of Nord-Atlas transport planes. Within the week the French high command approved the request. Thereupon an accelerated supply program to Israel was organized in total secrecy. On October 2, Dayan flew back to Tel Aviv and revealed to his senior staff what was afoot. The purpose of the impending campaign, he explained, was to destroy the Egyptian divisions facing Israel in Sinai, to liquidate the fedayun bases in Gaza, and to force open the Strait of Tiran. Only eighteen days were left before the target date of October 20.

The question preying on Ben-Gurion's mind now was London's attitude to the forthcoming operation. His concern was justified. When news of the emergent Franco-Israeli collaboration was transmitted from Paris to London on September 24, Anthony Eden was incredulous. The prime minister disliked the scheme, fearing that it would strain Britain's relations with other Arab countries. Until this moment, too, relations between Britain and Israel had been less than encouraging (p. 96). Nor did they appear likely to improve as Israel launched an increasingly ferocious series of military attacks against Jordan, Britain's treaty partner, in reprisal for fedayun raids mounted from Hashemite territory. The cycle of violence reached its apogee on October 11, when Israel conducted a particularly heavy retaliation against the Jordanian police fortress of Qalqilia. Tanks, artillery, and eventually planes were used in a savage battle that approached full-scale warfare.

On October 12, therefore, Britain's ambassador in Tel Aviv informed Foreign Minister Meir that, if the attacks continued, his government might soon be obliged to come to Jordan's aid under both the Anglo-Jordanian Treaty of 1948 and the Tripartite Declaration of 1950. Ben-Gurion was appalled; the warning had been issued at a moment when Israel, with French assistance, was preparing an offensive against Britain's enemy, Nasser. Then, on October 16, virtually at the last moment, Eden and Foreign Secretary Lloyd met with Mollet and Pineau in Paris and reached a belated understanding on the need for Israeli military collaboration. Hereupon the British finally shifted gears and withdrew their ultimatum. Yet it was at this juncture that Ben-Gurion chose suddenly to postpone the October 20 date of attack.

The Israeli prime minister was obsessed, first of all, with the need for air cover. An offensive in Sinai would risk heavy Egyptian bombing attacks against Israel's cities. Indeed, Operation Musketeer might never begin at all, leaving Israel's troops exposed in Sinai with Egypt controlling the skies. Moreover, the new role Britain was proposing for Israel (via Paris) was unacceptable to Ben-Gurion and Dayan. It was for the Israeli army to advance in strength and on a broad front in Sinai and to mount a heavy attack that would threaten Suez. What was envisaged, apparently, was a real war, one that would permit Allied forces afterward to intervene not in a broad amphibious invasion, but in a more limited paratroop landing "to save the Canal." For the Israelis, the scheme was out of the question. Their aim was simply to clear the Egyptians from eastern Sinai, from the Gaza Strip, and to break Egypt's blockade of the Strait of Tiran. Clarifications were urgently necessary.

On October 21, shortly before dawn, a French air force plane carrying Ben-Gurion, Dayan, and Peres touched down on a little-used airstrip southwest of Paris. The Israeli visitors were immediately driven to nearby Sèvres, where a small house had been placed at their disposal. The following morning, Mollet, Pineau, Bourgès-Maunoury and Abel Thomas—the latter, director-general of the French defense ministry—arrived for consultations with the Israelis. In an emotion-packed soliloquy, Ben-Gurion outlined for the Frenchmen the mortal danger facing his country, the importance of destroying the fedayun bases, and of breaking Nasser's stranglehold on Israel's economy. If Israel were to run the fearful risk of invading Sinai, Ben-Gurion insisted, then its cities would have to be protected. Deeply moved by this appeal, Mollet in turn reassured the Israeli prime minister that French planes would provide the necessary cover and that

French warships would guard the Israeli coast. By noon, further agreement was reached. Israel would mobilize on October 25, a mere three and a half days away. French Mystère squadrons would arrive in Israel throughout October 27 and October 28, and French destroyers would reach their positions off the Sinai coast by October 29, the date Ben-Gurion now set for the offensive in Sinai. Subsequently, French transport planes, operating from Cyprus, would drop supplies to the attacking Israeli columns.

Ben-Gurion required yet additional assurances, however. These were a guarantee of British involvement, and a rather more modest scheme contrived for Israel. The prime minister rejected outright Britain's proposal that his forces drive straight for the Canal; Israel would not serve as an aggressor before world opinion. Dayan explained then that Israel was prepared to launch a more limited "retaliatory" action. This envisaged the drop of a paratroop unit near the Mitla Pass, in the general vicinity of the Canal. An overland attack might join the paratroops later to put Israel's forces in the direction of their ultimate goal, Sharm es-Sheikh. The plan, in Dayan's words, would be "more than a raid, less than a war"—an operation that would be interpreted as posing just enough of a threat to the Canal to justify Allied intervention. The proposal interested the French. After some discussion, they accepted it and sold it afterward to Selwyn Lloyd when the British foreign secretary arrived at Sèvres the next afternoon.

By the evening of the twenty-third, the main lines of action had been agreed upon. Once Dayan loosed his forces in Sinai, Britain and France would address a joint ultimatum both to Israel and to Egypt to cease their military activity within twelve hours. Israel would accept, but would not be obliged actually to observe the cease-fire until its troops advanced to a line ten miles east of the Canal. Egypt meanwhile assuredly would reject the discriminatory Allied conditions. At that point British and French bombers would attack Egyptian airfields, destroying Nasser's planes on the ground, thus enabling Allied troops to land along the Canal and seize the waterway. The political features of this tripartite "Treaty of Sèvres," which was completed the next day, anticipated that France and Britain would defend Israel's interests at the United Nations and would support Israel's territorial claims in any final peace settlement. With this scenario firmly agreed upon, the participants then dispersed.

Returning to Tel Aviv on October 25, Dayan ordered his staff to make ready for "Operation Kadesh." Two days later, French LSTs began discharging additional heavy equipment at Israeli ports, and a French naval flotilla approached Israeli waters. That evening, too, a squadron of French transport planes arrived from Cyprus with equipment and technicians. Finally, two squadrons of French-piloted jet fighters landed at Israeli military airfields to assure protection for Israel's cities. In fact, Israel's own Mystère squadrons were never fully operational; only sixteen of the planes were flown during the war. "Had it not been for the Anglo-French operation," Dayan admitted later, "it is doubtful whether Israel would have launched her campaign." At most, an offensive would have been limited to Sharm es-Sheikh.

OPERATION KADESH

Until the last moment, the Israeli government skillfully disguised its intentions. Its heaviest reprisal actions were taking place along the eastern boundary with Jordan. On October 3, the foreign ministry announced that it was withdrawing its representatives from the Israeli-Jordanian Mixed Armistice Commission. Eight days later, the massive retaliatory raid against Qalqilia seemed to portend even more far-reaching hostilities (p. 103). Additionally, in late October, Israeli intelligence circulated rumors of impending war against Jordan. The accounts were given credibility on October 24, when a tripartite military agreement was signed between Egypt, Syria, and Jordan. With the chain tightening around Israel, there appeared a certain logic in a preemptive Zionist attack against the Arab enemy's weakest link. Indeed, fearing this possibility, Eisenhower cabled Ben-Gurion on October 27, and again on October 29, pleading for restraint against Jordan. Yet by then the outbreak of the Hungarian revolution, and its suppression by invading Soviet forces, had claimed world attention. As a result, Ben-Gurion was convinced that the tumultuous events in Hungary would totally absorb the diplomatic efforts both of Washington and of the UN Security Council. There would never be a better moment for Israel to attack.

Meanwhile, even as Dayan prepared to fulfill his obligations under the Treaty of Sèvres by creating a "threat" to the Suez Canal, he knew that he would have to act circumspectly, lest the Egyptians commit their air force and the bulk of their armor. Accordingly, he and his staff formulated a deliberately fluid operational plan, gambling that speed and daring would compensate for tactical obstacles. Those obstacles surely existed. One was the awesome expanse of the Sinai Peninsula itself, encompassing some 24,000 square miles of desolation. Virtually bereft of communications, the terrain in the north was pure desert; in the south, almost impassable mountain ranges. Taking this wilderness into account, Dayan's scheme for the first night, October 29, was the one he had proposed at Sèvres: to drop a battalion of paratroops near the Mitla Pass, 40 miles from the Canal and 180 miles overland from the Israeli border; other battalions would move along the southern axis of Sinai to link up with the paratroops some thirty-six hours later. At one stroke, then, the Israelis would "threaten" the Canal, triggering the Anglo-French expedition to eliminate the Egyptian air force, and at the same time confusing the Egyptians.

With an enemy brigade loose in central Sinai, and with paratroops at Mitla, Cairo would have to decide whether or not the Israelis were serious. Dayan anticipated that the Egyptian reaction would be sluggish. If things went badly for Israel, however, its entire brigade could be pulled back and Operation Kadesh passed off as a retaliatory raid. The remaining stages of the offensive were only slightly more orthodox. After a pause of twenty-four hours, a second, larger Israeli brigade would move out of the Negev and push toward the Canal; a third force would hook into Rafah to amputate the Egyptian coastal strip; simultaneously, yet another brigade would move down the eastern shore of Sinai toward Sharm es-Sheikh, at the tip of the Gulf of Aqaba.

The second major obstacle beyond the terrain of the Sinai itself was the newly equipped Egyptian armed forces. In fact, Dayan was not inclined to overrate this threat. The poor quality of Egyptian pilots and maintenance staffs was notorious. Israeli intelligence had learned, too, that of the 100 new MIG fighters in Egypt, only 30 were operational; and of the 50 Ilyushin bombers, only about 12. Of 200 new Soviet tanks in Egyptian hands, barely 50 were thus far in service. Most of the pilots and tank crews scheduled to man the new weapons were still in training school—in the Soviet Union. To be sure, the mobilized strength of the regular Egyptian army had grown to nearly 100,000 men by 1956. Its command structure, nevertheless, was regarded as hardly less unwieldly than in the Farouk era. Moreover, earlier border clashes in the Gaza area had revealed that the typical fellah recruit still tended to panic and run if caught by surprise.

Additionally, the Egyptian army's deployment in Sinai was vulnerable. Nasser's German military advisers had urged a defensive position along the north-south line in the middle of the peninsula. But the Egyptian president was uninterested in defense. He intended for his glittering panoply of troops and new equipment to loom impressively on the Israeli frontier, and to be positioned to supply the fedayun bases in the Gaza Strip. Rather than secure a line farther back in the desert, therefore, the Egyptians arrayed the bulk of their Sinai army along the al-Arish-Rafah-Gaza area on the coast, and around Abu Agheila close to the border farther south. For defense against a surprise attack, these dispositions were shockingly inadequate. Worse yet, once the Suez crisis broke in July 1955, the Egyptian high command pulled its best divisions out of Sinai to guard the Canal against Anglo-French invasion. What remained in the peninsula were two understrength infantry divisions and a number of specialized Palestinian brigades, not exceeding 40,000 men.

Upon first appraisal, Israel's own manpower resources seemed even less impressive. The standing army was hardly more than skeletal, and in wartime virtually the entire nation had to be mobilized out of its civilian routine. Even so, the system worked. When the emergency code was used on October 25, fully 90 percent of the 100,000 civilians designated for mobilization turned up. This was actually a far greater number than could be equipped; there were insufficient helmets or boots even for the 32,000 troops assigned to the Sinai offensive. Upon reaching their units, moreover, the reservists spent the next three days undergoing a "crash" training in the new French equipment. Until the last moment, preparations were nip-and-tuck.

Yet Dayan's gamble on speed and daring made the difference. Two hours before the scheduled offensive, four Israeli Mustangs flew over Sinai, cutting the overhead telephone lines with their propellers and wings. At 3:30 P.M. that same October 29, a squadron of Israeli transport planes crossed the Negev frontier and skimmed at near-deck altitude under the Egyptian radar screen. They climbed to 1,500 feet at "Parker's Monument," an identification point six miles from Mitla, and there the paratroop battalion jumped. By 7:30 that evening the Israelis had reached their positions a mile from the eastern approaches to the pass. They dug in. Meanwhile, the greater body of the 202nd Paratroop Brigade under Colonel Ariel Sharon had crossed into Sinai, intending to link up overland with the units near Mitla. Many of the brigade's vehicles and most of its artillery became bogged in the sand. Sharon left them behind. He was determined to reach Mitla within his thirty-six-hour time limit.

Even by midnight of October 29–30, General Abd al-Hakim Amer, the Egyptian armed forces commander, failed to gauge the situation. Puzzled by the Israeli air drop some forty miles from the Canal, Amer and his intelligence staff were inclined to regard it at first merely as a long-distance sabotage raid. Only when the attack developed in depth, following Sharon's crossing into Sinai, did Amer begin to sense what was happening. Without further delay, he ordered reinforcements moved across the Canal. By midnight an armored brigade had traversed the water and was headed directly for Mitla. At the same time Nasser called upon his Arab treaty partners to make war on Israel. It was wasted effort; Syria and Jordan protested their inability to mobilize on such short notice.

Despite the uncertainty of Egyptian and Arab reaction, time was becoming increasingly vital to the Israelis. Sharon raced on toward Mitla. His column finally reached the pass at 10:30 P.M. of the thirtieth, linking up with the awaiting battalion. Hours later, French transport planes reprovisioned Sharon's men by parachute. As Operation Kadesh unfolded, meanwhile, Ben-Gurion was obliged to lift the veil of secrecy. His cryptic announcement early on October 30 stated only that, in response to repeated Egyptian assaults on Israeli civilians, Israeli forces had seized positions "in the vicinity of the Suez Canal." Just enough had been revealed to enable the British and French now to fulfill their part of the scenario.

OPERATION MUSKETEER

Immediately following the Israeli statement, Mollet and Eden issued their joint ultimatum to Egypt and Israel, ordering the two Middle Eastern nations to withdraw their forces, respectively, to points ten miles west and east of the Canal; to accept the "temporary" occupation of key positions along the Canal by

Anglo-French forces; and to indicate their intention of responding favorably to this demand within twelve hours. Failing to receive appropriate replies, London and Paris warned, their forces would "intervene in whatever strength may be necessary to secure compliance." The ultimatum plainly was a fake in its alleged purpose of separating the combatants, for the Western governments were ordering the victim (Egypt) to withdraw from Sinai to the west bank of the Canal, and allowing the invader (Israel) to advance to a distance ten miles east of the Canal.

At midnight of October 30, Foreign Minister Golda Meir punctiliously transmitted Israel's reply to London and Paris. She accepted the Anglo-French deadline, but on the assumption "that a positive response will have been forthcoming from the Egyptian side." The assumption could not have been serious. From Cairo, the reply was precisely the one Israel and the Western allies had anticipated. Nasser immediately summoned his cabinet. In a panic, Amer and Salah Salem urged the president to announce his acquiescence to the British government. Nasser's reaction, in turn, took the form of a dramatic gesture. Distributing potassium cyanide capsules to every member of the cabinet, he declared his intention to commit suicide rather than surrender. Then he informed Britain's ambassador that Egypt rejected the ultimatum.

Throughout the thirtieth, meanwhile, Egyptian air action against Israeli advance units was negligible. For the time being, Israeli planes were able to concentrate on ground support, strafing Egyptian armored columns approaching from the west. Yet there could be no assurance that the Egyptian air force might not at any moment intervene in strength. During the late afternoon, the Israeli command tensely awaited the promised Anglo-French air bombardment against Egyptian fields. When the twelve-hour deadline passed and the Allies still did not bomb the Canal zone, Israeli forces in Sinai were obliged to fight their heavy battles throughout the entire day of October 31 under the threat of massive enemy air attack. Ben-Gurion was sufficiently distraught by then to consider pulling his army back. Dayan dissuaded him. Nevertheless, as the hours passed, Egypt moved additional armor and infantry units into Sinai, and ferried reinforcements by sea to Sharm es-Sheikh. For Dayan, the principal concern now was the paratroop brigade at Mitla. In an exploratory—and gratuitous—"reconnaissance" of the pass the day before, this unit already had taken heavy casualties to an Egyptian ambush. Afterward, chastened, the mauled paratroopers pulled back, awaiting orders to move south to the key Israeli objective of Sharm es-Sheikh. It was a southern advance that was facilitated almost at the last moment by Anglo-French operations against the Canal.

At 5:00 P.M. on October 31, a day and a half behind schedule, British and French jet squadrons finally launched their long-awaited bombardment of Egyptian air fields near Suez. Sweeping over the fields along the Canal and in the Delta, the Allied fighter bombers destroyed the larger part of the Egyptian air force on the ground. Even as Nasser was contemplating the wreckage of his expensive fleet of Soviet planes, a message arrived from Moscow, bluntly warning him that the Soviet Union, already heavily involved in Hungary, would not risk a possible third world war for the sake of the Canal; except for Russian diplomatic support, the Egyptians would be on their own. Accordingly, in the early evening of October 31, the sobered Egyptian president authorized a general withdrawal from Sinai. Further air operations were canceled, and pilots were ordered to make their escape to bases up the Nile. All defenses were to be concentrated henceforth on the impending Allied invasion. For the Israelis, the switch in Egyptian priorities now opened up a unique opportunity to fulfill Dayan's maximum plan of operations.

THE EGYPTIAN ARMY IN FLIGHT

On the afternoon of October 30, Israel's Seventh Armored Brigade moved against Abu Agheila, the fortified Egyptian hedgehog dominating Sinai's central access route to Mitla and the Canal. The brigade was thrown back by heavy Egyptian resistance at the Um Cataf fortress guarding the approach to Abu Agheila. After only a brief hesitation, the Israelis decided to risk bypassing the fortress and to push on directly into the desert. The gamble paid off. By this time Nasser had ordered a general withdrawal from Sinai, and Israel's hard-driving tanks subsequently invested the central Sinai bases of Bir Hassana and Bir Gafgafa. Afterward, Dayan's forces engaged in a high-speed, hit-and-run battle to gobble up the "tail" of the Egyptian column fleeing Bir Gafgafa. Eventually the Israeli brigade halted only ten miles short of the Canal. In the interval, the 3,000 outflanked Egyptian troops at Abu Agheila simply fled, attempting to make their way on foot across the sand sea to al-Arish, fifty-two miles away. It was a tragic error. Collapsing from thirst, the luckless infantrymen fell prey to Bedouin knives.

Throughout the night of October 30, meanwhile, another column of Israeli armor attacked Rafah, key to the northern al-Arish highway supplying the Gaza Strip. Rafah was manned by the crack Fifth Egyptian Brigade. Heavy losses were sustained by both sides. Eventually a French naval bombardment was required to help overcome Egyptian resistance, but by early afternoon of October 31 the Gaza Strip was sealed off and the al-Arish road was open. The next day, Cairo's general withdrawal order was in effect everywhere. Thus, as yet another Israeli tank column moved along the coastal road to Suez, it encountered a rich windfall of 385 Egyptian vehicles, including 40 heavy tanks that had been abandoned intact under Israeli air strafing. Thousands of Egyptian troops, forlornly seeking their captors and food and water, also were picked up and sent back to internment camps. By nightfall of November 2, the Israeli army was in full possession of the three lines of communication extending through Sinai from east and west, and was systematically destroying the fedayun bases.

For Ben-Gurion and Dayan, however, the most crucial phase of the Sinai offensive was directed at the southeastern tip of the peninsula, controlling the Gulf of Aqaba. The overland march from the east to the bottom of the Sinai wedge was assigned to the 1,800 farmer-reservists of Colonel Avraham Yoffe's Ninth Brigade, and began at dawn of October 31. It was an uncommonly difficult expedition, for the southern region of the peninsula was a lunar surface of jagged peaks, impassable ridges, and rock-strewn slopes. Trucks and command cars were literally manhandled over part of the route, and boulders frequently had to be dynamited. With Yoffe falling behind his three-day timetable, Dayan ordered a company of paratroops dropped at al-Tur, two-thirds of the stretch from Mitla down the western coast of Sinai. From there the paratroops thrust overland toward Sharm es-Sheikh, reinforcing Yoffe's brigade moving along the eastern Sinai slope. On November 4, the brigade approached Ras Nasrani, the heavily fortified Egyptian base commanding the narrow channel between the Sinai coast and Tiran Island. It was abandoned. The Egyptian commander had pulled his troops back to Sharm es-Sheikh. And there they resisted. Yoffe halted, awaited air cover, then advanced again. By midevening all Egyptian resistance collapsed. Immediately afterward, then, Yoffe's men were demobilized and returned home. Within the space of a week, they had traversed 1,400 miles to Sharm es-Sheikh and back.

The Sinai war was over. Initially, the opposing forces had been of roughly equal size. But the quality of Israeli manpower on all levels was far higher. At a cost of 180 men killed and 4 captured, of 20 planes and some 2,000 worn-out vehicles, Israel in a four-day campaign had occupied the whole of the Sinai Peninsula and the Gaza Strip, had shattered three Egyptian divisions, killed 2,000 of their enemy, and taken nearly 6,000 prisoners (a number that could have been far higher). Additionally, Dayan's troops had captured 7,000 tons of ammunition, half a million gallons of fuel, 100 Bren carriers, 200 artillery pieces, 100 tanks, 1,000 other vehicles, and an Egyptian frigate that had been trapped off Haifa by a French destroyer, then rocketed into surrender by Israeli planes. The 100-hour campaign was a blitzkrieg unprecedented equally for its scope and its pulverizing brevity, and it was destined afterward to be studied as a classic in the annals of military tactics. Not the least of its consequences, moreover, was the decisive coup de main it gave to the fading stereotype of the Jew as hapless martyr.

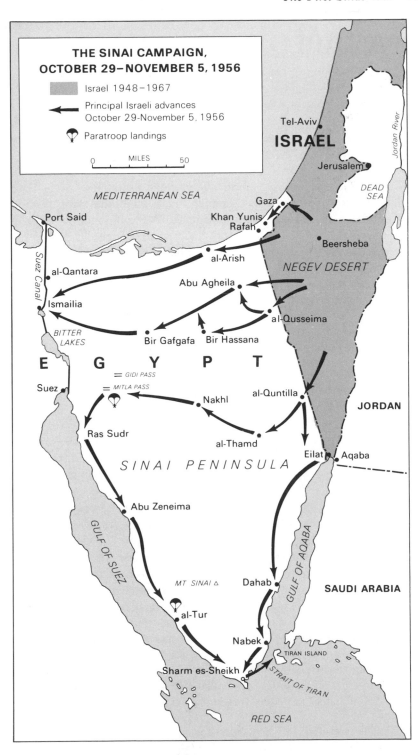

**THE SINAI CAMPAIGN,
OCTOBER 29–NOVEMBER 5, 1956**

Israel 1948–1967

Principal Israeli advances
October 29–November 5, 1956

Paratroop landings

0   MILES   50

MEDITERRANEAN SEA

Tel-Aviv

ISRAEL

Jerusalem

DEAD
SEA

Jordan River

Gaza

Port Said

Khan Yunis
Rafah

Beersheba

al-Arish

Suez Canal

al-Qantara

NEGEV DESERT

Abu Agheila

Ismailia

al-Qusseima

BITTER
LAKES

Bir Gafgafa   Bir Hassana

E   G   Y   P   T

GIDI PASS

MITLA PASS

Suez

Nakhl

al-Quntilla

JORDAN

Ras Sudr

al-Thamd

Eilat   Aqaba

S I N A I   P E N I N S U L A

Abu Zeneima

GULF OF SUEZ

MT SINAI

Dahab

SAUDI ARABIA

GULF OF AQABA

al-Tur

Nabek

TIRAN ISLAND

Sharm es-Sheikh

STRAIT OF TIRAN

RED SEA

IX

A DIPLOMATIC EPILOGUE

Whatever the Israeli people's thrilled relief at the annihilation of the Egyptian army, the reaction elsewhere, even among Israel's traditional sympathizers, was markedly different. From the viewpoint of the Western nations and the Third World alike, Israel, Britain, and France had committed acts of aggression, plain and simple. In New York, the angered members of the United Nations bypassed Anglo-French vetoes in the Security Council by transferring discussion on the Middle East crisis to the General Assembly. In Washington, Eisenhower was furious at having been "double-crossed" by his two oldest NATO partners only a week before the American elections, and outraged by the Israeli "blitzkrieg." To Israel's Ambassador Abba Eban, Dulles expressed the American attitude in more restrained tones:

> Look, I'm terribly torn. No one could be happier than I am that Nasser has been beaten. Since spring I've had only too good cause to detest him. . . . Yet, can we accept the good end when it is achieved by means that violate the Charter? . . . [I]f we did that, the United Nations would collapse. So I am forced to turn back to support international law and the Charter.

Accordingly, on November 2, the General Assembly overwhelmingly approved a United States resolution for an immediate cease-fire and the withdrawal of all occupying forces from Egyptian territory. Yet, if the situation was awkward for the Israelis, it was far more so for the British and French. By the following day, Israel's army had all but cleared Sinai; but Operation Musketeer was still hanging fire, with a naval armada still 500 miles off the Egyptian coast and airborne troops waiting in Cyprus. In the United Nations, urgent efforts were being mounted to devise a solution before the Western Allies landed troops along the Canal. Subsequently, on November 4, the General Assembly voted to create a UN Emergency Force that would anticipate Britain and France in "separating the combatants along the Suez Canal and elsewhere in Sinai."

For its part, the Israeli government that same day announced its willingness to accept a cease-fire resolution "provided a similar answer is forthcoming from Egypt." Immediately the Allies protested to Jerusalem. What rationale existed for their intervention at the Canal, they asked, if a cease-fire came into effect? The French then implored the Israeli government to retract the announcement. Privately, Ben-Gurion was fuming. It was the Allies' sluggishness in launching their own expedition that had placed him in this awkward position. Nevertheless, he agreed to help. At his instructions, Eban informed the General Assembly later that afternoon that his nation's acceptance in fact was conditional on Egypt's declared willingness to accept a cease-fire, to end its state of war with Israel, to enter into immediate peace negotiations with Israel, and to cease its economic boycott and lift its blockade against Israeli shipping. The conditions were unlikely to be fulfilled.

Finally, at dawn on November 5, a wave of British and French paratroops dropped outside Port Saïd. A second wave descended in the afternoon, successfully overcoming Egyptian resistance. Hours later Allied commandos landed amphibiously without incident. Immediately afterward an armored column forged ahead toward the southern exit of the Canal. British patrols were only twenty-five miles short of their destination when, at 6:00 P.M., London suddenly announced that it was accepting the United Nations demand for a cease-fire.

By its unexpected halt at the very threshold of success, London was reacting in part to a threat issued by the Soviet Union. At that moment, the Russians had their hands full with the Hungarian uprising. In ensuing days, therefore, the enraged Soviet press and radio campaign against Israel—and later against Britain and France—became a useful smoke screen for the humiliating developments in Budapest. On the evening of November 5, as Allied paratroops descended on Port Saïd, Soviet Prime Minister Nikolai Bulganin dispatched notes of unusual severity to Eden and Mollet, emphasizing that the USSR was prepared to crush the "warmongers" by using "every kind of modern destructive weapon." Both the Soviet Union and Red China were said to be registering "volunteers" for service in the Middle East. NATO sources reported, too, that the volume of military electronic communications traffic across the Warsaw Pact nations had tripled.

It was not the Soviet warning alone that cracked Eden's nerve. On November 6, Washington informed the prime minister that Britain's application for $1 billion from the International Monetary Fund, an appeal that had been pending for several months, and well before the Suez crisis, was contingent on a cease-fire. Additionally, domestic outrage in England itself had burgeoned out to a degree Eden had not faintly anticipated. A very sick man by then, he wilted under the confluence of these pressures. Telephoning Mollet, Eden protested that he was being deserted by his cabinet and by members of the Commonwealth. "I can't go it alone without the United States," he insisted. ". . . No, it is not possible." Mollet in turn pleaded for only a little more time to complete the seizure of the Canal. But it soon became evident that the French were incapable of salvaging the operation on their own. Frustrated and bitter, they agreed then to act jointly with the British. The Suez adventure would end at midnight, November 6.

The Israelis were unshaken. They had accomplished *their* purpose, at least. The blockade of the Strait of Tiran was broken. For the time being, the Gaza area no longer would be a launching ground for fedayeen; nor would the Egyptian army in Sinai, with its accumulation of Soviet-bloc arms, remain a threat to Israel's security. The idea of a United Nations buffer force, originated by the State Department and floated by neutral Canada, was approved by the General Assembly as early as November 5. Yet, impressive as the UNEF proposal appeared as a peacekeeper for a chronically volatile frontier region, it was initially rejected by Ben-Gurion. "On no account will Israel agree to the stationing of a foreign force . . . in her territory," he declared to the Knesset on November 7, "or in any of the areas occupied by her." The flush of military triumph plainly had had its effect on the Israeli leader. Indeed, Ben-Gurion hinted that he was even giving thought to annexing Sinai. "After all, Sinai has never been part of Egypt," he mused. The UN General Assembly gave these territorial illusions short shrift. That same November 7 it voted overwhelmingly for a cease-fire and for immediate Israeli withdrawal from Sinai. Almost at the same time, a letter from Eisenhower was delivered to Ben-Gurion, referring ominously to a possible cessation of "friendly cooperation between our two countries." In a second dispatch, the president warned that there should be no expectations of American help in the event of a Soviet-assisted attack on Israel.

To Ben-Gurion's chagrin, Britain also now chose to back away. On November 8, Foreign Secretary Lloyd privately urged an Israeli withdrawal in return for certain "assurances." These included a peace treaty and defensible frontiers guaranteed by the Allies, and free Israeli passage through the Suez Canal and the Gulf of Aqaba. It was London's way of salvaging the already shaken partnership of the Baghdad Pact. Even France now appeared to be less than reliable in its support, endorsing Lloyd's appeal for Israeli withdrawal. The Jews enjoyed a certain degree of leeway, nevertheless, in their army's new Sinai emplacement. During November and early December, the principal United Nations efforts were concentrated on replacing British and French troops along the Canal with a UN force. During the interval, there was time for the Israelis to carry off their booty of Soviet weapons. On December 22, however, the last Allied soldiers finally left Port Saïd. The Suez phase of the episode was over and Israel now confronted alone the obloquy of the international community.

THE AMERICAN-ISRAELI WAR OF NERVES

Although the UN General Assembly had included Israel among the aggressors, the Western countries were not oblivious to the provocations the Jewish state had endured in recent years. In turn, counting on this residue of sympathy and understanding, Ben-Gurion expected that his nation's case gradually would elicit world support as panic subsided over the danger of Soviet-Western confrontation. He later recalled:

> The longer the time at our disposal, the longer the time we were in effective control of the western shore of the Strait [of Tiran], and the greater the number of ships that sailed through the Red Sea and the planes that flew over it, the better our chance for demonstrating to the world the value and importance of the Strait. If we could only lay a pipeline from Eilat to Haifa . . . our case would be strengthened. Only if we succeeded in convincing the nations that this was vital for them as well as for us was there any prospect that we might have free navigation through the Strait.

Yet the prime minister faced a continuing wall of opposition. Dag Hammarskjöld, the United Nations secretary-general, refused so much as to discuss Israel's demands for security guarantees until its forces withdrew from Sinai and Gaza. This approach was endorsed by the Communist and Afro-Asian blocs. It was supported, as well, by most of the Western nations. Their economies were critically dependent upon the passage of oil through Suez. At the beginning of the Allied landings, Nasser had scuttled vessels anchored in the Canal, and now he refused to allow clearing operations in the blocked waterway until the Israelis departed. Accordingly, a new General Assembly resolution of January 7, 1957, again demanded prompt and unconditional Israeli evacuation.

The Israelis pulled back grudgingly. On December 3, 1956, their forces withdrew a distance of thirty miles from the Canal. The UNEF immediately took up positions in the evacuated terrain. On January 8, 1957, the invading army retired still farther, this time to the al-Arish line in eastern Sinai. On January 15, 1957, Ben-Gurion finally announced his government's decision to evacuate Sinai completely by January 22, with the crucial exception of the Sharm es-Sheikh area. The Gaza Strip, an integral part of Palestine, similarly would remain under Israeli control. Although Ben-Gurion had no wish to annex this enclave, with its vast and embittered refugee population, he was adamant that Gaza should not be returned to Egyptian rule. "It is inconceivable," declared Foreign Minister Meir to the General Assembly, "that the nightmare of the previous eight years should be reestablished in Gaza with international sanction. Shall Egypt be allowed once more to organize murder and sabotage in this Strip?"

The Israeli foreign minister was equally graphic in her description of years of Egyptian blockade from Sharm es-Sheikh, Ras Nasrani, and the neighboring islands of the Tiran Strait. "The mere entry into this area of the United Nations Emergency Force, even with the specific aim of preventing belligerency, would not in itself by a solution," she insisted; more effective international guarantees of free navigation were required. To that end, in Washington, Israel's Ambassador Eban concentrated his efforts henceforth on the blockade issue. Eban was aware that the United States had a greater capacity to satisfy Israel's claims of free passage in the Gulf than to change the situation in Gaza, where Egypt enjoyed a contractual position under the armistice agreement. Thus, in his memoranda, the ambassador went beyond the juridical aspect of illegal closure to a larger vision of "a new artery of maritime communication, linking the continents of the old world, depriving Suez of its monopoly and reducing Europe's explosive dependence on a single oil route which Egypt could open and close at will."

These arguments did not fail to register on the American leadership. Nevertheless, the Eisenhower administration at first evinced little flexibility. There were long-term American interests in the Arab world that could not be forfeited. One of these was the great air base in Dharan, Saudi Arabia. The Saudi monarch was prepared to allow the United States continued use of this facility for another five years, but his condition was successful American pressure on Israel to evacuate the remaining territory in Gaza and Sinai. By late December 1956, therefore, Washington's frustration with Israeli intransigence boiled over. Dulles warned again in an open press conference that Israel must withdraw "forthwith" or American-Israeli relations would have to be "seriously reexamined." Eisenhower himself was altogether hostile to Israel's stance, intimating in a letter to Ben-Gurion the possibility of economic sanctions against the Jewish state.

Yet, by January 1957, both the press and congressional friends of Israel were drawing attention to a double standard of international morality: the Soviet Union had not been punished for Hungary; but Israel, with its legitimate security grievances, was to be punished for Sinai. Lyndon Johnson, Democratic leader in the Senate, telephoned Eban periodically to express indignation at the administration's tactics. Other political leaders were equally understanding of Israel's position. Aware, then, of the need for congressional support, Dulles hinted in February at a possible accommodation. On the eleventh of the month, he and Eban formulated a compromise aide-mémoire on Gaza and the Gulf of Aqaba. Eban then flew off to Israel, discussed the compromise with Ben-Gurion and the cabinet, and returned to Washington on February 23 with a list of questions for Dulles. By the next day a consensus was reached between the two men and their advisers. In writing, a series of American answers had been given to Israel's questions:

1. Will the United States send a ship through Aqaba and will you react if stopped?
   Answer: Yes.
2. Will you support the idea that the UNEF should stay at Sharm es-Sheikh for a long time?
   Answer: Yes.
3. Will you send a ship with the UNEF flag through the Gulf of Aqaba?

Answer: This depends on [Secretary-General] Hammarskjöld's assent.

4. Will you open an oil route for us from Iran—that is, through the Red Sea and the Gulf of Aqaba?
Answer: Yes.

5. Will Gaza be a UN-administered enclave?
Answer: We will try our hardest to persuade the UN and Hammarskjöld to make such an arrangement.

In fact, the obstacle to a final understanding was no longer Dulles, but rather Hammarskjöld. The secretary-general was unwilling to send a ship through Aqaba bearing the United Nations flag; this was not the agent provocateur role he envisaged for the world body. He made clear, too, that he opposed the notion of a specifically UN regime in the Gaza Strip, for the United Nations was a peacekeeper, not a sovereign government. Both Dulles and Eban reacted in exasperation to Hammarskjöld's refusal. "Not a single spark of political imagination illuminated the arid wastes of his legalism," Eban wrote later. In an effort to break the impasse, however, Lester Pearson, Canada's ambassador to the United Nations, now offered a compromise proposal. By its provisions, the United States, Britain, France, and other maritime nations would assert every country's right to freedom of navigation in the Strait of Tiran, and the right specifically of Israel to safeguard this freedom against any aggression. Thus, while Israel's right could not be safeguarded *by* a two-thirds majority of the UN General Assembly (given the stance of the Communist and Afro-Asian blocs), it could be asserted meaningfully *within* the General Assembly by that forum's most influential maritime members.

The solution for Gaza was even more complex, but not less hopeful. Its key feature, a United Nations buffer force, actually had been submitted to Pearson by the State Department two months earlier (p. 114). Lately, the Canadian ambassador had refined the plan and elaborated upon it in discussions with French Foreign Minister Pineau and with Hammarskjöld himself. Indeed, at Pearson's suggestion, Hammarskjöld, in mid-February, had already discussed it privately with Egyptian Foreign Minister Mahmud Fawzi. An experienced diplomat, Fawzi instantly discerned in Pearson's formula a possible face-saving blueprint for his country. It was agreed, first of all, that the Gaza Strip provided an ideal location for UNEF command headquarters and for UNEF units assigned to patrol the demarcation line. Inasmuch as the enclave was desperately overcrowded with refugees, hardly enough space existed within it for both the Egyptian army and the UNEF. On the other hand, if the UNEF actually established its bases inside the Strip, no further necessity would exist for Egyptian forces to take up positions there. It was an imaginative tradeoff. Rather than being formalized by written agreement, the formula should be allowed simply to develop on a pragmatic basis.

Sharm es-Sheikh, too, could now be added to the plan, for the solution there, as in Gaza, avoided any public derogation of Egyptian authority. "If they [the Israelis] would keep their mouths shut," Mahmud Fawzi told Hammarskjöld, "we would keep our eyes shut." Immediately, then, Dulles set about presenting the formula to Eban as the best one available for Israeli evacuation. Eban reacted favorably. Upon his recommendation, the Israeli cabinet similarly accepted the plan. Within the next few days, as other members were also consulted, it became clear that Hammarskjöld had a General Assembly consensus, rather than a formal "resolution," for sending the UNEF into Gaza and Sharm es-Sheikh.

Yet the Israelis still were concerned that the UNEF might be precipitously withdrawn, that shipping might again be obstructed and hostilities renewed. Thus, they sought Hammarskjöld's commitment that any future proposal to evacuate the UNEF from Sharm es-Sheikh or Gaza must first be submitted to a special committee of the General Assembly; the procedure would ensure that no hasty steps were taken that might lead to war. Hammarskjöld confirmed the understanding on February 26 in a memorandum, and Dulles too endorsed it in writing. Thereafter, in the UN General Assembly on March 1, Foreign Minister Meir reiterated these conditions in her announcement of Israeli withdrawal from Gaza and Sharm es-Sheikh. Mrs. Meir's speech emphasized Israel's understanding that the UNEF would remain at those two sites for whatever length of time was needed to achieve a permanent settlement between Egypt and Israel; and that if conditions arose in the Gaza Strip indicating a repetition of disturbances, or in the Strait of Tiran threatening freedom of passage to Israeli shipping, Jerusalem would reserve its freedom to act in defense of its rights.

By prearrangement, Mrs. Meir's interpretation of Israel's conditions for withdrawal was endorsed in the next few days by the principal maritime members of the General Assembly—sixteen nations in all—and including, most importantly, the United States. In consequence, on March 4, as Israeli soldiers pulled out of their encampments, six battalions of blue-helmeted United Nations troops moved into Gaza and Sharm es-Sheikh. At this point, too, in gratitude to Israel for having ended an intolerable diplomatic impasse, Washington immediately approved a generous loan from the World Bank, and other loans soon followed. On April 7 an American tanker anchored in Israel's southern port of Eilat.

Had Operation Kadesh ultimately been worthwhile for Israel, then? Reporting to the Knesset on March 7, Ben-Gurion admitted that there could be no certainty that the Egyptians might not return to the Gaza Strip. In fact, the prime minister's misgivings were confirmed even sooner than he had feared. Only two days after the departure of Israeli troops from Gaza and the arrival of UNEF soldiers, local Palestinians in the Strip issued vehement "demands" for the return of an Egyptian administration. To sustain his image as champion of the Palestine, and other, Arabs, Nasser decided to take the risk of Israeli retaliation and to meet these "demands." He appointed and dispatched a civil governor to the Gaza Strip with an appropriate staff. No troops accompanied them, however. Jerusalem immediately protested, but agreed with Washington that Nasser's act was not worth another military confrontation. By then it was evident in any case that one of Israel's most cherished hopes for Operation Kadesh would remain unrealized. This was the fall of Nasser himself.

Almost miraculously, the Egyptian dictator had emerged from his battlefield disaster with his prestige intact. He had managed to camouflage the brutal shellacking his army had suffered at Israeli hands under the palpable evidence of Anglo-French bombardment and landings. By diplomatic, if not by military, means, he had secured the evacuation of every invading soldier. Neither had he been compelled to give a permanent assurance that his government might not someday choose to return armed units to Gaza or even interdict Israeli shipping to and from Eilat. On the contrary, asserting the rights of a belligerent in deed as well as in theory, he maintained the ban on Israeli shipping through the Suez Canal, once that waterway was reopened several months later.

Notwithstanding these disappointments, Israel's hundred-hour campaign unquestionably fulfilled its principal goal of advancing the Jewish nation's security. It profoundly enhanced the morale of the Israeli people. It offered important military lessons, most notably the advantages of preemptive attack. The stubbornness, too, with which Israel resisted evacuation deprived of guarantees, ended all further efforts by the Powers, especially by Britain and the United States, to attenuate Israeli territory. Admittedly, the Sinai Campaign had not brought Israel formal peace. Yet, in his Knesset speech of March 7, Ben-Gurion reminded his listeners that an enduring peace for the Gaza Strip in any case was unlikely as long as tens of thousands of unsettled refugees were impacted there. While the arrangements that had been worked out for Gaza and Sharm es-Sheikh were essentially makeshift, they were the best that could be achieved for the time being, and Ben-Gurion regarded their value as considerable.

The prime minister was not wrong. Fedayun activity from Gaza virtually ended. Israelis in their nation's outlying border settlements could now work and sleep in peace for the first time in seven years. The Gulf of Aqaba was open and remained open for eleven years. Unquestionably, this accomplishment was less than the officially recognized freedom of passage Ben-Gurion had sought for his country. But those eleven years were all that were needed to establish Israel's trade relationships with the Orient, to inaugurate a series of pipelines that transformed the little Zionist republic into one of the major oil entrepôts between Iran and Europe, and to develop an industrial infrastructure that launched Israel on the period of its most impressive economic growth and diplomatic influence. Indeed, from November 1956 on, by universal recognition, the Jewish state achieved its "takeoff" and established itself as a sovereign entity to be treated with circumspection and respect in the councils of nations.

X

A DECADE OF
OBLIQUE CONFRONTATION

ISRAEL'S "TAKEOFF"

For Israel, one of the most palpable consequences of the Sinai victory was a sudden and dramatic upsurge of immigration. Jews living in extremis abroad no longer feared for the continued existence of the Zionist state; they were prepared now to take the risk of settlement there. The figures of the influx for 1956 and 1957 alone were 55,000 and 70,000, mainly from North Africa and Eastern Europe. Between 1958 and 1960 an additional 43,000 immigrants arrived, this time from Rumania. Between 1961 and 1964, another infusion of North African and Iranian Jews added 194,000 new citizens to the nation. In sum, Israel's Jewish population rose from 1,667,000 in 1956 to 2,384,000 by the end of 1967. The dispersion of settlement also improved significantly. In 1948, not less than 43 percent of Israel's Jews had been concentrated in the three major cities of Tel Aviv, Jerusalem, and Haifa. Fifteen years later, the growth of agricultural and development communities reduced this urban imbalance by a third. In the aftermath of Operation Kadesh, then, Israel "fleshed out" its demographic lineaments as effectively as it had defended its territorial integrity and built its political institutions.

The Jews broadened their grip on the soil, as well, in their second decade of independence. By 1967 their rural population had grown to 340,000. Their farms were meeting Israel's staple food needs, even producing a surplus in vegetables and dairy products. Much of this growth could be attributed to increased water supplies. Completed in 1964 at a cost of $175 million, an elaborate irrigation network, tapping the resources of the Jordan River as well as of natural ground sources, provided the little nation with an additional 320 million cubic meters of water annually. It was a 25 percent increase in supply (and 75 percent for the Negev Desert) that revolutionized the possibilities for agricultural and industrial development, particularly in the south.

Indeed, the growth of Israel's southern hinterland was traceable directly to the Sinai victory. Once Operation Kadesh ended the blockade of the Gulf of Aqaba, the importance of an opened maritime route soon became almost mathematically discernible. In the first year after the war, thirty ships arrived at the port of Eilat. By 1967, with the improvement of Eilat's anchorage facilities and the growth of Negev-based industries, the number of arriving freighters doubled. So did the number of vessels embarking from Eilat loaded with Israeli products for Africa and the Orient. Within the Negev itself, road and rail communications were dramatically improved, offering access opportunity to quarry and market the desert's wealth. It was true that the products of Israel's southern wilderness—potash, kaolin, phosphates—supplied barely 7 percent of the country's total income, but the Negev's usefulness was augmented in other ways. With the completion of a network of pipelines from Eilat on the Red Sea to Ashkelon on the Mediterranean, the desert became an alternative overland oil route to the Suez Canal. The Negev similarly provided the vast, spacious terrain on which a quarter-million new immigrants were settled and a wide complex of industrial projects was established to employ them. Thus, by the opening of the 1960s, an impressive necklace of expanding industrial towns— Beersheba, Kiryat Gat, Ashkelon, Ashdod, among others—had arisen along the fringes of the southern hinterland.

For that matter, in the decade after Sinai, industry throughout Israel absorbed a total labor force of 260,000. The figure represented 25 percent of Israel's working population, and would continue to rise. Between 1950 and 1969, the country's industrial output quintupled. Its gross foreign currency earnings jumped from a paltry $18 million to $552 million, an increase of 20 percent a year. With the critical and decisive infusion of German reparations—over $800 million in goods and services—the Israeli maritime fleet swelled by the end of 1967 to 105 vessels of various sizes and types, with a gross tonnage of 1.4 million. The fourth largest commercial fleet among the Mediterranean nations, these freighters and transports carried 45 percent of Israel's seaborne trade and 73 percent of its Mediterranean trade. By 1967, too, the nation's annual exports in all fields—transportation, tourism, agricultural and industrial shipments— exceeded $1 billion. Plainly, Israel was moving out of its early austerity to an era of comparative abundance. By 1965 its GNP had increased two and a half times since 1953. Its average per capita increase for the same period was 6.3 percent, midway among the world's thirty most affluent states. This was substantial progress for a beleaguered, arid little republic.

EGYPT IN THE AFTERMATH OF THE SINAI WAR

In Egypt, by contrast, the mood after Sinai was one of frustration. Although the government managed at least partially to disguise the enormity of its defeat, the secret of Israel's military conquests was poorly kept. One convenient target of retaliation, of course, was the remnant Jewish minority of Egypt. Of 28,000 Jews still remaining in Cairo and Alexandria, some 3,000 were promptly interned without charges in four detention camps. By executive edict, an additional 8,000 were ordered out of the country on four days' notice. Deprived of any chance to sell their property or to take capital with them, additional thousands of Jews were encouraged to leave "voluntarily." In all, some 25,000 Jewish men, women, and children departed within the ensuing four years. By 1967, scarcely 3,000 of their kinsmen remained in Egypt.

It was small consolation to this broken and destitute community that its fate was shared by other "non-Egyptian" minorities. As in the case of the Jews, these wholesale expulsions were dictated in some measure by Egyptian economic, as well as psychological, needs. Until the Sinai-Suez War, the nation had undergone a political revolution, even a certain land revolution. What it required now was an industrial revolution. Yet, of the E£55 million released from the land by agrarian reform, only E£6 million had found its way into industry by 1956. As has been noted, the rest went to feed a luxury apartment building boom in Cairo and Alexandria. As it happened, much of the remaining, nonlanded capital was in the hands of non-Egyptians. The banks, the insurance companies, the stock and cotton exchanges, and the larger mercantile houses were heavily British or French. Most of the department stores were Jewish. The middle-sized stores were Armenian, Greek, or Lebanese. It was precisely this European, Jewish, and Levantine capital that provided the Nasser regime with its access to instant investment funds.

In January 1957, therefore, an "Egyptianization" decree sequestered the nation's foreign enterprises and shortly afterward organized an "Economic Development Organization" to direct them. By 1960 the Organization's assets totaled some E£200 million, and its "affiliated" (i.e., confiscated) firms produced a third of the country's industrialized output. The nationalized Suez Canal Company added other millions, as did the Anglo-Egyptian Oil Company and the Misr Group of insurance companies. Yet the confiscation of these businesses represented the Egyptianization of foreign assets, not their socialization. As late as 1958, when the union with Syria was launched (p. 124), Egypt's economy remained basically capitalist. Although the government repeated its appeal for Egyptian investors to take up shares in the various sequestered foreign companies, the effort was unsuccessful. Only then, when the "natives" failed to cooperate in sufficient numbers, was the decision taken for the state to fill the vacuum. The Egyptian revolution accordingly evolved on a pragmatic basis, working out its theory as circumstances required. Those circumstances now dictated the nationalization of the press in 1960, of the stock exchange and the main cotton exporting houses in 1961, of the banks and insurance companies, and of the forty-four largest industrial and transport firms in 1961 and 1962. A sharply progressive income tax and a wide series of confiscatory rental taxes were similarly introduced. In this stuttering, belated manner, then, Egypt was moving finally toward a posture of functional socialism.

Nasser's principal domestic goal for his wretched nation in fact was essentially rapid economic development without undue social pain, at least for "authentic" Egyptians, and particularly for the impoverished urban proletarian and peasant classes. These latter were now at long last to be offered major advantages in education, free welfare services, agricultural research stations, new dispensaries and birth control clinics. Nor were the government's accomplishments here unimpressive. In its first fifteen years, the regime ensured that 70 percent of Egypt's primary age children were attending school. The number of students in technical schools multiplied in the same period from 21,000 in 1954 to 161,000 in 1967. By then, too, free tuition ensured that registration had tripled in the universities, to 140,000. The quality of this education, without doubt, was generally inferior. In the universities, classes often grew to the size of 500 or more students, while laboratory and library facilities remained pitiably inadequate. Moreover, if 50 percent of the nation's secondary school graduates went on to university, less than 10 percent of primary school children achieved high school. As late as 1967, fully half the population of Cairo remained illiterate, and the proportion was far higher in rural Egypt. Of the country's 36 million inhabitants, for that matter, not less than half were under sixteen, and the Wellesian race between education and catastrophe had become a grim one. And yet, these lacunae notwithstanding, significant inroads unquestionably had been made in the nation's basic illiteracy rate, and in the production of a new technological elite. Perhaps even more impressive was the government's accomplishment in the field of health, where the scourges of trachoma, bilharziasis, and, increasingly, of infant mortality were finally lifted.

On the other hand, Nasser's larger goal of developing an industrial infrastructure to support this vast welfare program failed woefully. The nation's first Five Year Plan, launched in 1960, managed to achieve a respectable annual GNP growth rate of 6 percent; but in the vital area of export capacity the plan was entirely unsuccessful. The expensive military expedition to Yemen (p. 125, below), the uncontrolled growth of staple imports, the cost of American wheat shipments (no longer purchasable in local Egyptian currency after 1965), led in 1966 to a critical balance of payments deficit of E£152 million. As the government prepared for its second Five Year Plan, therefore, it was obliged to generate new sources of hard currency to pay for grains, capital equipment, foreign expertise, and military hardware. Nasser never found a way out of this dilemma, and from 1966 onward his economy swooned into the doldrums. Without funds for renewal, the nation's incipient industry slid hopelessly toward obsolescence. Numerous factories simply could not be completed; while others, lacking equipment, remained underutilized. Indeed, those goods that were produced tended to be overpriced, inferior in quality, and almost entirely noncompetitive in hard currency areas.

Despite the priority given to manufacturing, then, industry contributed no more to the national income by the mid-1960s than it had on the threshold of the first Five Year Plan. As in the prerevolutionary era, agricultural products, mainly cotton, made up the bulk of Egypt's exports. Speculation in foreign products was rampant. Shops in the cities, stocked essentially with Egyptian-made goods, were reduced to drab austerity. Propped up by loans from the Soviet Union, by confiscation and nationalization, the quality of Egyptian life once again began to deteriorate. For that matter, the entire economy was operating only in fits and starts, and it soon became evident to Nasser that his one remaining alternative was to turn elsewhere for new markets, new resources, new population outlets—new diversions. A revived policy of imperialism seemed likely to achieve these goals.

THE RISE AND FALL OF EGYPTIAN IMPERIALISM

Nasser's role as champion of pan-Arabism appeared to be virtually foreordained. He had successfully "repelled" the British and French, after all. He had grandly announced a new program of "Socialist" modernization. He enjoyed the support of Moscow and the friendship of Third World leaders. Admittedly, it was a self-proclaimed role that did not go unchallenged; in April 1957 the governments of Hashemite Jordan and Saudi Arabia reaffirmed their friendship with the West. Yet the Nasserist brand of socialism waxed increasingly popular in Syria. In neighboring Lebanon, too, a pro-Nasserist rebellion in May 1958 threatened that little commercial nation's traditionally moderate stance in Arab affairs; even as a parallel danger suddenly emerged again in Jordan. It required the intervention of an American marine expeditionary force in Beirut, and a British airlift of troops to Amman, to stabilize the governments in both these countries. As it was, Western help did not arrive in time to spare Iraq a coup that overthrew the monarchy and replaced it with a junta led by the "Socialist" Abd al-Qarem al-Qassem; and the advent of the Qassem government, in turn, appeared to signify yet another triumph for Nasserist pan-Arabism.

The most dramatic of the Egyptian president's erratic achievements seemingly occurred in Syria. Fearful of losing control of their Socialist administration to the Communists, the Syrian Ba'ath party offered Nasser a plan for linking the two nations in a federal union. The scheme appealed to the Egyptian leader, and in February 1958 Damascus and Cairo jointly proclaimed a "United Arab Republic." A united parliament and a united military command were established, and joint economic projects were formulated. The federation was a curious political hybrid, however, and one that survived less than four years. With the economic and military needs of Syria almost totally subordinated to those of Egypt, the military clique in Damascus ultimately found the arrangement unsupportable. In September 1961 the Ba'athists announced their country's withdrawal from the United Arab Republic. Once again it appeared as if Nasser's halo was tarnished. Indeed, it was all but knocked askew when, in Iraq, Prime Minister Qassem decided to offer his nation the "true" route to Arab socialism—in opposition to Nasser's "faulty and egotistical" path. Soon Cairo and Baghdad were exchanging broadsides in open ideological battle.

The Egyptian ruler's pan-Arabist fortunes continued to gyrate wildly. In September 1962 the Yemeni monarchy was overthrown in favor of a "progressive" republic. Sensing yet a fresh opportunity for aggrandizement, Nasser immediately dispatched military support to the new Yemeni regime—and thus unwittingly set foot into a meat grinder of Egyptian resources. By the end of the year, Egypt's military commitment to Yemen jumped to 20,000 troops, and the number would double a year after that. The incipient lesion was partially disguised by favorable developments elsewhere: the overthrow of Iraq's Qassem regime in February 1963 by a rival Socialist faction; and, a month later, an upheaval in the Syrian Ba'athist party that similarly returned pro-Nasserist elements. Indeed, both the Iraqi and Syrian Ba'athist parties favored immediate unity with Egypt. In April, therefore, after extensive tripartite meetings in Cairo, the union was proclaimed. And, as in the earlier United Arab Republic, the honeymoon was destined to be short-lived. By May an internecine Ba'athist propaganda war against the Syrian Nasserists was in full crescendo. Iraq joined the attack. One month later the tripartite "union" was dead.

It was against this hectic oscillation of Nasser's pan-Arabist campaign, which in turn provided an uncertain camouflage for his domestic failures, that the diabolization of Israel assumed renewed importance. As long as Egypt's confrontation with Israel remained fundamentally emotional, it could have found satisfaction in minor acts of vindictiveness and spite. But once the hostility assumed deeper importance for Nasser's imperial ambitions, more purposeful action was required. Thus, prior to the original union with Syria, Nasser generally had endorsed various United Nations resolutions on partition and on the return of the Palestine refugees—measures that, if enacted, would faintly have intimated the right of Israel at least to exist. After the collapse of the union, however, this line was abandoned for one that was unequivocal in its demand for the liquidation of the Zionist state.

The shift in emphasis reflected a broader awareness of the obstacle Israel represented to pan-Arab unity. It stood in the way, for example, of any far-reaching movement of people and goods between the Egyptian and Syrian "regions" of the United Arab Republic, an exchange that might have permitted the consolidation of the union. By the same token, Israel's presence unwittingly encouraged the secessionists in Syria to launch their coup in 1961; it shielded them against any effective Egyptian military action to restore unity. Israel similarly prevented the occupation of the West Bank by any Arab state other than Jordan. The great moment of hope for Arab unity, too, following the Ba'athist coups in Iraq and Syria during the spring of 1963, was effectively forfeited. Isolated from the Fertile Crescent by Israel, Egypt was blocked from the direct communications necessary to send help. It was Nasser's sober recognition of this obstacle that persuaded him to intervene in Yemen. A wide flanking movement might have achieved Arab unity by advancing from a base at the corner of the Arabian Peninsula, continuing through Saudi territory, through Iraq and Syria, before confronting Israel from the east. Thus, even as Israel's existence papered over inter-Arab hostilities and kept pan-Arabism alive, so the Jewish republic's continued viability and growth simultaneously thwarted the fulfillment of Nasser's pan-Arabist program in its broadest contours.

"It is not our intention to restore half our honor or half the [Palestinian] homeland," declared Nasser in *al-Ahram* in May 1962, "but the whole of our honor and the whole of our homeland." The imprecation was repeated endlessly, and with mounting virulence, in the early 1960s. "Israel is the cancer, the malignant wound, in the body of Arabism," insisted a commentator on Radio Cairo in April 1963, "for which there is no cure but eradication. . . ." He was speaking in the president's name. A month later, Nasser again emphasized personally: "We shall not agree to a peace of *fait accompli* no matter what the circumstances may be, for such a peace would not be a true one, but tantamount to aggression." Muhammad Husseinein Heykal, editor of *al-Ahram*, added his own, less than pacific, interpretation in September 1964: "Imperialism's drive to establish Israel came from the aspiration that it should serve as a geographical barrier to Arab unity . . . to serve as a leech which would suck the marrow and exhaust the efforts of the Arab revolutionary force." "Arab unity," explained Nasser, summarizing the issue with decisive clarity in February 1964, "means the liquidation of Israel." That was that. No compromise was possible. Remorselessly building his Soviet armory, forging and reforging his chain of alliances, projecting his nation's vision outward and away from the crumbling foundations of Egypt's domestic economy, the president discerned in Israel a provocation and a menace that sooner or later would have to be confronted head-on.

ISRAEL'S OVERT AND SUBTERRANEAN ALLIANCES

The Israelis were not about to mark time, supinely awaiting Nasser's initiative in choosing the moment and place for Egypt's "third round." In addition to developing their economy and building their armed forces, they cultivated friends and allies wherever these were available. Thus, in the immediate aftermath of the 1956 Sinai Campaign, Israel and France remained linked in a tight and mutually supportive partnership. With few exceptions, Israel accepted French guidance in its other international relations, particularly in its willingness to accept a more European, rather than a purely American, diplomatic orientation. The French in turn appeared no less committed to maintaining their recent battlefield alliance with "gallant little Israel." So long as the Algerian insurrection continued, French defense and foreign ministry officials regarded Israel as the key to Middle Eastern stability. After 1956, a joint

French-Israeli strategic planning committee met regularly to explore ways of protecting both nations' interests in the Mediterranean. French naval and air forces at Djibouti maintained patrols against Egyptian interference with Israeli shipping in the Red Sea. In 1958, the French government invited Israel to participate in combined naval maneuvers. The French and Israeli air forces shared in joint training programs, even as the French and Israeli secret services worked closely together, sharing vital information on Middle Eastern developments.

Not least of all, France remained the principal source of military equipment for Israel; and one branch of Israel's defense forces, the air arm, was almost entirely dependent on the new generation of French Mirage jet fighters. The usefulness of these shipments was by no means one-sided. Except for the French air force itself, Israel was the single most important market for France's aircraft industry. It served, too, as a proving ground for French jets, the only one in the world where French equipment was being tested, and improved, in combat against Soviet-made planes. As early as 1957, Israel similarly was allowed to produce French jet trainers under license, and two years later to invest in the Dassault Aircraft Company, where its engineers assisted in research projects of special value to Israeli defense needs. The development of the French Matra air-to-air missile was essentially a joint French-Israeli project. So was the production, in 1961, of the two-stage "meteorological" rocket, Shavit II, which received its first secret launching tests in the French Sahara. Joint research extended to the nuclear field, as well. In 1957, Paris allowed French private industry to assist Israel in constructing a nuclear reactor in Dimona. At a cost of $75 million, the installation plainly was intended for more than civilian research.

A rapidly developing relationship between Israel and West Germany, meanwhile, traced back to the Reparations Agreement of 1952, under the terms of which Bonn had agreed to provide Israel with $820 million in goods and services as partial compensation for the Holocaust. At Ben-Gurion's initiative, feelers subsequently were extended to raise financial contacts to the level of diplomatic relations. But here the Germans demurred, fearing that the Arabs would retaliate by extending recognition to Communist East Germany. Accepting the rebuff, the Israeli prime minister then directed his efforts instead toward "practical" cooperation with Germany, notably in the economic sphere, where German strength already was much greater than that of France. He sensed the residue of conscience-stricken goodwill among the German people, and notably on the part of Chancellor Konrad Adenauer. Thus, in March 1960, Ben-Gurion persuaded Adenauer to extend Israel a $357 million low-interest loan. The infusion soon would dramatically accelerate the growth of the Negev development communities. With German governmental encouragement, too, individual German corporations and institutions similarly invested in a wide spectrum of Israeli economic projects.

It was in the sphere of German weaponry, however, that Israel achieved a major coup in its efforts to match Egypt's vast Soviet-equipped arsenal. Shimon Peres, who continued as director-general of Israel's defense ministry, appreciated that his nation's armed forces dared not rely exclusively upon French or American sources of supply. Accordingly, he reminded the West German political leadership that a defensible Israel would continue as an effective bulwark against Soviet penetration in the Middle East. After only the briefest hesitation, the Adenauer government accepted Peres's contention and agreed to supply Israel with extensive quantities of military hardware, either gratis or near-gratis—provided that the arrangement remained secret. On this basis, then, German weapons began flowing to Israel early in 1959. By the end of 1961 the shipments included fifty planes, among them transports and trainers, as well as trucks, ambulances, antiaircraft guns, howitzers, and antitank rockets. Occasionally weapons were purchased by Israel in other countries—for example, helicopters in France, antiaircraft guns in Sweden, even two submarines in Britain—with the invoices sent on to Bonn. In 1964, 150 tanks were dispatched in this circuitous fashion to Israel. Although Germany's opposition parties learned of the secret arms pact, they tacitly acquiesced in it. The survival of the Jewish state was a matter that transcended politics in the new Germany.

Then, in October 1964, news of the shipments suddenly broke in two German newspapers. Chagrined at having been kept in the dark for the past years on the arms transactions, the press all but unanimously condemned military (as distinguished from economic) aid to Israel. Shipments of this magnitude would gratuitously jeopardize West Germany's trade relations with the Arab world, the editorials warned. Whereupon Chancellor Ludwig Erhard, who had succeeded Adenauer two years earlier, promptly terminated all further weapons deliveries to "countries outside of NATO." The blow was a grave one for Israel.

Neither, on the other hand, did it succeed in appeasing Nasser. Two weeks later, the Egyptian president ceremoniously greeted Walter Ulbricht, the East German Communist leader, who arrived in Cairo at the head of a large mission. Witnessing this spectacle, the outraged Bonn government in turn agreed to extend a "moral" gesture to Israel as compensation for the terminated arms shipments. The gesture included the long-awaited offer to enter into diplomatic relations with the Zionist republic.

Chancellor Erhard picked a close friend, Dr. Kurt Birrenbach, to fly to Jerusalem and negotiate with Prime Minister Levi Eshkol, who had succeeded Ben-Gurion the year before. Birrenbach informed the Israelis at the outset that there would be no compromise on the matter of weapons deliveries; under no circumstances would the shipments be resumed. Although discussions on this issue were blunt, even harsh, a formula eventually was devised. The United States would be asked to provide the matériel that Israel had expected to receive from Germany; Bonn would pay for it. Birrenbach also hinted of future long-term loans to Israel. He assured Eshkol, too, that all German scientists would soon be out of Egypt and that legal action would be taken against any person who sought to recruit Germans for military purposes abroad (see p. 131, below). On March 9, 1965, the Israeli cabinet voted to accept this package. Two months later, ambassadors were exchanged between Jerusalem and Bonn. That same day of May 12, too, Cairo severed diplomatic relations with the German Federal Republic, and the rest of the Arab governments promptly followed Egypt's lead.

THE SPY GAME AND THE FALL OF BEN-GURION

It was an earlier Israeli defense "mishap" that suddenly unsettled the politics of the Jewish state, and at precisely the moment that these far-reaching new military and diplomatic relationships were being forged with Germany. The life of the 1959 Knesset was destined to be suddenly and unexpectedly foreshortened. As events developed, it was Ben-Gurion himself who cut it short. The instrument of this unwilling act was Pinchas Lavon, the former minister of defense who, we recall, had resigned under a shadow at the time of the Cairo spy debacle. Lavon himself had been obliged to turn to a different career, as secretary-general of Israel's labor federation. With the passing of the years, he watched helplessly as the most influential government ministries faded beyond his reach. It was apparent that Ben-Gurion was grooming a number of younger protégés as his successors, especially Dayan and Peres, the men Lavon had cause to remember with undiminished bitterness.

Then, in April 1960, a crucial piece of information unexpectedly offered Lavon a revived claim on his political future. An intelligence officer was examining the minutes of the 1954–55 special committee hearings on the Egyptian spy mishap when he noticed several incongruities in the testimony of Colonel Benyamin Gibli, the former intelligence chief. He called them to Lavon's attention. The most important of the disclosures was a copy of Gibli's letter to Dayan insisting that the Cairo and Alexandria bombings had been carried out "according to the order of the minister of defense." The original of the letter was now in the files, and it did not include this vital clause; apparently the copy that had been presented to the special committee was a forgery. Elated by these revelations, Lavon brought them to the attention of Ben-Gurion the following month and demanded full exoneration for the Egyptian debacle. The prime minister's reaction was to appoint a new committee of inquiry under the chairmanship of a supreme court justice.

Soon after this body began its deliberations, it was presented with other, even more astonishing, information. Half a year earlier, in November 1959, Avraham Seidenberg, alias Paul Frank, the intelligence bureau's former liaison in Egypt (p. 82), had been placed on trial in Jerusalem. The charge, heard *in camera*, was treason. Evidently Seidenberg had been a double agent, escaping detention in Egypt by betraying his comrades there. In the course of his testimony before the district court, Seidenberg warned that he would not go down alone. He revealed that he had been coached by his superiors to commit perjury before the original committee of inquiry. At the time, Seidenberg had followed instructions. Now, in Jerusalem, facing a sentence of twelve years (he was convicted), he was taking his revenge. The evidence of this perjury reached Lavon and astounded him. In September 1960 he demanded, and received, a special meeting with the Knesset foreign affairs and security committee.

Throughout the next few weeks a dramatic series of hearings ensued. Although they were held in closed sessions, extracts of each day's testimony somehow found their way into the press. The public was mystified. The spy events of 1954 and their aftermath were still top-secret. As late as 1960, the government censor permitted only the vague information to appear that years before an "unfortunate" mishap had occurred in the defense ministry; that Lavon had been held responsible for it and had left office under puzzling circumstances; that now, five years after the fact, new evidence had surfaced that Lavon was resolved to exploit; and that a major schism was opening between distinguished officials of the government and of the Labor party. A feeling of inchoate restiveness swept through the nation. Was Lavon another Dreyfus?

In October 1960 the new investigating committee issued its report. It concluded that perjury had indeed taken place in the original 1955 hearings, enough to render them invalid. It was the committee's suggestion, nevertheless, that subsequent prosecution would be counterproductive, in view of the long period of time that had since elapsed. Armed with this document, the party leadership in turn devised a compromise formula intended to resolve the impasse. Moshe Sharett, who had been prime minister in 1955, released a statement in mid-October declaring that if he had known then of the evidence now available, he would have regarded it as a "weighty confirmation" of Lavon's version of the facts, although he would still not have accepted Lavon's demand that Peres be dismissed. With this statement, it was hoped, both Lavon and his rivals, Peres and Dayan, would be placated. They were. The "Lavon Affair" apparently had come to an end.

It had not. Ben-Gurion was infuriated by the Sharett statement. Regarding it as a slander against his beloved army and as a threat leveled by Lavon and the Labor Old Guard against his younger protégés, the prime minister insisted upon a legal commission to reevaluate the case. Somewhat reluctantly, the cabinet appointed yet another investigative committee under the chairmanship of the minister of justice. On December 21 the ministerial committee pronounced its unanimous decision: Lavon had not given the order for the "security mishap." Whereupon, all but apoplectic at this point, the prime minister tendered his resignation. After weeks of protracted interparty discussions failed, a new election was scheduled for the following August. The results proved a further setback to the Labor party; a loss of five seats, from forty-seven to forty-two. Two additional months went by until a patchwork coalition could be formed. Ben-Gurion eventually returned as prime minister, but this time his government partnership was much narrower; his liberty of action was far more seriously restricted than in earlier cabinets. In truth, he never completely recovered from the acrimony and spleen of the Lavon Affair.

There were other security issues that by then were also undermining Ben-Gurion's endurance. As far back as 1950, German engineers and technicians, many of them former Wehrmacht officers, had been hired to serve as instructors for the Eyptian army and to organize an Egyptian weapons industry. Willi Messershmitt, the famous pioneer of Hitler's aviation program, had sold Egypt manufacturing rights to his supersonic jet fighter, the HA-200, developed in Spain. Eventually several hundred Germans and Austrians were supervising the construction of airplane assembly plants in Helwan, while German factories provided spare parts. Much of this personnel, and even more of the equipment, were obtained through the efforts of one Hassan Saïd Kamal, an Egyptian engineer living in Zurich. Moreover, in 1960, a "National Research Center" was established in Cairo, ostensibly to develop a "space research rocket for meteorological purposes." Among the scientists recruited by Kamal was Germany's leading rocket expert, Dr. Eugen Sänger, and Sänger's deputy, Professor Wolfgang Pilz, both of whom had been active in the Nazi V-rocket program during the war. Their staff included several colleagues from Germany's postwar Stuttgart Rocket Institute.

Israeli intelligence learned of these developments almost immediately. One of the agents who infiltrated the program to discern its extent was Wolfgang Lutz. Arriving in Egypt (via Europe) in 1961 as a "German businessman," Lutz spent the next three and a half years ferreting out and transmitting to Israel data on the Egyptian rocket program (eventually he was caught and imprisoned). The Israeli government in turn did not hesitate to call Bonn's attention to the role of German scientists in Egypt. The embarrassed West German cabinet promptly ensured that these men were dismissed from the Stuttgart Institute. Sänger himself returned to Germany. But Wolfgang Pilz and the others remained in Egypt. Finally, in July 1962, Egypt's first locally manufactured missiles were paraded through the boulevards of Cairo, to the cheers of hundreds of thousands of spectators. Israel, it was known, lay well within the range of these weapons. Horrified, Jerusalem registered its protest with the German government. Yet the latter had no notion what steps could be taken in a democracy to prevent its citizens from working wherever they chose. Bonn was hardly willing to revert to Nazi police-state methods.

At this point the Israeli secret service took its own initiative. In July 1962, Hassan Saïd Kamal's German wife was killed by a bomb that exploded in her plane over Germany (Kamal himself had postponed his trip at the last moment).

In September of that year, Dr. Heinz Krug, director of Kamal's procurement firm, disappeared under mysterious circumstances. In November an airmail parcel addressed to Wolfgang Pilz exploded upon being opened in his Cairo office, blinding and mutilating his German secretary. The series of "accidents" continued, reaching their climax in March 1963 when Israeli agents in Switzerland contacted the daughter of Professor Paul Görcke, yet another of the German scientists employed in the rocket program, and "suggested" that she persuade her father to abandon his work in Cairo. Instead, the young woman alerted the Swiss police, who immediately arrested the Israeli agents on charges of attempted coercion. During their widely publicized trial (they were found guilty), the defendants exhibited documents proving that Egypt was embarked upon the construction of missile warheads armed with cobalt 60, a lethally radioactive nuclear waste by-product. In Israel, bitterness against West Germany now became as intense as in the postwar era. The Knesset passed a resolution insisting that "it is the duty of the German government to put a stop to these activities immediately. . . ." Once again, however, Bonn insisted that it possessed no legal recourse.

The furor gravely embarrassed Ben-Gurion. He had received private word from Bonn that the violence of Israel's anti-German campaign might endanger the secret arms deal between the two governments. He was informed, too, that the Egyptian rockets were overrated, that they were all but unguidable. Accordingly, in March 1963, the prime minister instructed his security chief, Isser Harel, to terminate all further secret service activities against the German scientists. Harel resigned instead. Ben-Gurion was similarly rebuffed by the Knesset, whose members erupted angrily at his appeal to withdraw their resolution of protest to Bonn. Worn out by these recriminations, no less than by the acrimony touched off by the Lavon Affair, the prime minister himself resigned on June 16, never to return to office. The repercussions of the Israeli-Egyptian confrontation plainly were reaching to the innermost recesses of both nations' domestic life.

THE STRUGGLE FOR AFRICA

Nasser had his own techniques, meanwhile, for outflanking his enemies, Arab and Israeli alike. The Third World offered ideal terrain for this effort. With Soviet backing and guidance, the Egyptian president authorized the establishment of an Afro-Asian Peoples' Solidarity Organization, an Egyptian front. Directed from Cairo by its secretary-general, Yusel es-Sabal, this body arranged conferences in neutralist capitals to mobilize professional groups, student organizations, and other opinion-makers in support of the Egyptian line in international affairs. With Fidel Castro, Nasser similarly formed the Three Continent Organization, its joint secretariats in Havana and Cairo maintaining ties to Latin American leftists. A leader, too, with Tito and Indira Gandhi, of the "non-aligned" nations, Nasser was endlessly calling summit conferences to publicize the group's unique brand of "neutralism" and "anti-imperialism." Moreover, by the 1960s Radio Cairo was beaming its propaganda broadcasts in thirty-two languages against Israel and against such "Arab reactionaries" as Hussein of Jordan, Feisal of Saudi Arabia, and Bourguiba of Tunisia.

Yet it was in Black Africa, more than any other sphere, that Nasser found his likeliest opportunity for Egyptian leadership. Many of these countries encompassed substantial Moslem populations. Thus, in whichever African capital an Egyptian embassy was established, it became the headquarters for well-financed efforts to organize Moslem minorities into dissident factions, to split the host country, and to encourage a leftist takeover. Ethiopia was a particularly attractive target for Egypt; a quarter of this vast nation's twenty-two million inhabitants were Moslem. Thus, the Egyptian military attaché in Addis Ababa, Lieutenant Colonel Ahmad Abd al-Aziz Hilmi, founded a Moslem League, and under its aegis set about inciting Ethiopia's Moslem (largely Eritrean) tribes to rise against the emperor. In Ghana, during the same period of the early 1960s, the Egyptian Cultural Center served as a rallying ground for that country's equally substantial Moslem minority. In Malawi, the Egyptian embassy went so far as to organize an airlift from Cairo to arm leftist and Moslem enemies of the government. As it happened, none of these efforts succeeded, and some thirty Egyptian diplomats ultimately were expelled from various African nations between 1956 and 1966. The Egyptians persisted, however. If they failed to establish client governments in their target countries, they still anticipated transforming Black Africa into a bastion of support for their anti-Israel policy.

The Israelis, in turn, well understood their pariah status in the eyes of nations with large Moslem factions. Yet they were not without resources of their own in thwarting efforts to outflank them in the vast African terra incognita. The most important of these were their demonstrated abilities and achievements in self-development. The Africans discerned in Israel an economy that had reached the "takeoff" point within less than a generation, and that had gained valuable experience in absorbing and "productivizing" immigrants from all cultural levels, including hundreds of thousands of relatively backward Orientals. Additionally, the scale of Israel's agricultural and industrial enterprises was regarded as better suited for many African countries than programs dependent upon the ample resources and large plants available to the Western Powers. Suspicious of their former European masters, the Africans felt reassured by Israel's small size, and perhaps also by the Jews' common history of racial suffering.

Nowhere, in fact, were the exertions and rewards of Israel's gamble in the Third World initially as dramatic as in Black Africa. The emergence of these former protectorates to independence coincided with the aftermath of Israel's

1956 victory. Inasmuch as the end of the Egyptian blockade in the Red Sea freed the maritime outlet from Eilat to East Africa, Israel's trade routes with the African nations were the first to be opened. Very soon, too, direct communications overcame lingering African suspicions of Israel's role in the Suez-Sinai episode. The earliest contacts were with Ghana. When the two nations exchanged ambassadors in 1957, the man chosen for the Accra post was Ehud Avriel, one of Israel's most respected public servants. Through Avriel's initiative, a broad series of Israeli technological and economic projects were launched. These included agricultural, medical, economic, and educational advisers to the Ghanian government, joint shipping and construction ventures, and the organization of Ghanian military and aviation training programs. News of Israel's accomplishments in Ghana spread rapidly throughout the African continent. Soon Israel was receiving a flow of emissaries from other African lands, each of these visitors intent upon observing the young nation's economic progress. It was to accommodate that interest that the Israel Federation of Labor organized its first Afro-Asian Seminar in 1958. The program's success, in turn, led to the expansion of Israel's foreign training activities both in trade unionism and in economic cooperatives. By 1960 the Afro-Asian Institute for Labor Studies and Cooperation was accepting hundreds of African students annually for four- and eight-week training programs.

Among Israel's leaders, it was Golda Meir who laid greatest emphasis on cultivating relations with the African nations. During Mrs. Meir's tenure as foreign minister, from the late 1950s to the mid-1960s, Israel's effort in this former colonial terrain was vigorously enlarged. Of 3,948 Israeli experts serving abroad from 1958 to 1970, 3,483 were in Africa. Of 13,790 foreigners studying in Israel during the same period, half were African. Projects carried out in Africa under Israeli supervision were extensive and diverse. They included a pilot venture for the irrigation of cotton in Tanzania; a training school for rural social workers in Kenya; a Histadrut (labor federation) advisory team to develop the Kenyan Federation of Labor; medical teams sent out to Burundi, Liberia, Malawi, Mali, the Republic of Congo (Brazzaville), Ruwundi, Tanzania, Upper Volta, and Ethiopia. In Ethiopia, moreover, Israelis occupied key positions in the medical sector as hospital directors and as chairmen of hospital departments.

Israel's Nachal—farmer-soldier—movement was particularly attractive to African countries. Most of these backward realms were in urgent need of training and employment opportunities for their youth. To meet that need, the Israelis rapidly improvised Nachal-style national service units in the Ivory Coast, in the Central African Republic, in Dahomey, Cameroun, Senegal, and Togo. The paramilitary function performed by these youth groups turned out to be equally valuable. Thus, in January 1964, when Tanzania's regular army disintegrated after barely suppressing an insurrection, the national service units, led and trained by Israelis, remained disciplined and loyal. Impressed, President

Julius Nyerere asked the Israeli government to train a thousand picked men on an emergency basis to serve as the core of a national army. Even earlier, other African nations displayed interest in Israel's military prowess. Shortly after winning independence, Ghana requested Israel's help in establishing a flying school, as did Uganda some years later.

Israeli military aid was rarely publicized, for Jerusalem was determined that its approach be as oblique and restrained as Egypt's was frontal and interventionist. Yet it was known that Israeli instructors played a vital role in Ethiopian officers' schools, that Zaire, Uganda, Ghana and other nations were frequent recipients of Israeli military instruction and equipment. The future presidents of Congo and Uganda, Joseph Mobutu and Idi Amin, won their paratroopers' wings in Israel. Ugandan pilots flew Israeli-manufactured Fouga trainers. It was significant, moreover, that Nasser got his bloodiest nose in Africa almost directly at Israeli hands. In 1963 the Egyptian embassy in the former Belgian Congo, the largest and richest new state in Black Africa, was distributing arms clandestinely to rebel forces led by the pro-Communist Antoine Gizenga; and in Cairo, expatriate followers of Gizenga announced the creation of a "People's Republic of the Congo." To deal with this incipient civil war, General Joseph Mobutu, commander of the Congolese army (and later his nation's president), sought help from the Israeli embassy, which in turn summoned a panel of Israeli military advisers. The latter recommended the creation of an elite corps of paratroopers as a mobile force. Thereupon Mobutu picked 250 officers and men for an intensive course in paratroop training and tactics in Israel itself. On its return to the Congo, the general dispatched other trainees to Israel, until in 1964 he had accumulated a crack brigade of 2,000. At that point, Mobutu's army, spearheaded by the Israeli-trained paratroops and commanded by white mercenaries, effectively put the rebels to flight.

The political consequences of this elaborate technological-military interchange were far-reaching. By 1963, Israel had established diplomatic relations with all but one of the African countries south of the Sahara. In 1961 President Maurice Yaméogo of Upper Volta opened the long list of African heads of state who, after years of participating in the Afro-Asian diplomatic quarantine, agreed to set foot officially on Israeli territory. Thereafter, hardly a month passed without the visit of a senior African minister. Israeli leaders, as well—President Ben-Zvi, Prime Minister Eshkol, Foreign Ministers Meir and Eban, and various other individual ministers—toured Africa in the 1960s. It was rare, too, before 1973, that African nations allowed Egyptian pressure to obstruct their bilateral relations with the Jewish state. President Nyerere of Tanzania spoke for the majority of them. "We are not going to let our friends determine who our enemies shall be," he declared. The Egyptians persisted in their efforts to "chase Israel out of Africa" (Nasser's words). Yet, except for Somalia and Mauritania, with their large Moslem populations, the campaign failed for many years.

Israel continued to suffer occasional rebuffs in the Black Continent. As early as 1958 there was evidence of Egyptian influence on Ghana. A communiqué issued by Presidents Nasser and Kwame Nkruma in Cairo urged a "just resolution" of the Palestine problem and expressed anti-Israel sentiments. A year later, Israel was the only country not invited to the "Africa Day" celebration at the United Nations. Plainly, a gap existed between the relationships individual African governments expected to forge with the Jewish state and their collective dealings with Israel as an African bloc (or as an Afro-Asian bloc). This dichotomy was emphasized by the Casablanca Declaration of January 1961, in which the presidents of Egypt, Ghana, Guinea, and Mali branded Israel as "an instrument of imperialism and neocolonialism." Often the very governments maintaining strong bilateral and technical cooperation links with Israel were those voting, under Egyptian and Arab influence, for anti-Israel resolutions.

Yet when the Africans chose to vote against Israel in the UN General Assembly or to adopt anti-Israel positions in other international settings, their governments after the fact advised the Israelis to disregard the vote. And, by and large, Jerusalem accepted the formula as a palatable one. Had it not been for its far-reaching program of cooperation in the Third World, Israel unquestionably would have suffered a far more extensive and painful diplomatic isolation. In its circuitous political and economic confrontation with Egypt, then, the Jewish state assuredly remained vulnerable to enemy boycott and diplomatic quarantine. But if it had not won that struggle, the auguries for the future were increasingly optimistic.

XI

THE SECOND SINAI CRISIS

THE SOVIETIZATION OF EGYPTIAN POLICY

By 1967 Egypt's revolutionary government had been in power fifteen years. Its accomplishments were by no means unimpressive. These included the repudiation of the country's semicolonial dependency, the liquidation of the effete old political parties and the old economic squirearchy, the movement toward an industrial economy, and the beginnings of a welfare state. But the costs were high: the constrictive domestic autocracy, the malaise of the nation's intelligentsia, the deterioration of educational quality (notwithstanding the completion of a new school virtually every second day), the brutal persecution of Jews and Europeans, the suffocating weight of a rapidly expanding military apparatus, and, most ominously, the projection of a subversive and dynamic imperialism—only thinly disguised as "pan-Arabism" and "Socialist modernism"—throughout the Middle East and Africa.

It was unlikely that this adventurism would have emerged as a feature of revolutionary policy had it not been for a wide-ranging new Soviet presence in Egypt. Yet, once having became the arms provisioner of Nasser's regime in 1955, and thereafter Egypt's principal diplomatic patron during and after the Suez-Sinai War, Moscow also dramatically enlarged the scale of its economic aid. Indeed, between 1955 and 1970, Egypt received not less than $1 billion in loans and grants from the Soviet bloc. Representing 14 percent of the totality of Soviet economic support to the Third World, the figure was second only to Soviet aid to India. Funds were made available for some 106 major industrial enterprises, including steel foundries and dockyards, textile factories and food combines, and chemical and petroleum complexes. In substantial measures, these infusions compensated for the relative unavailability of private capital, even for the inadequacy of sequestered foreign and Jewish assets.

For the Egyptian nation, however, the sudden largesse of Communist funds and technology produced an unanticipated consequence. It was a growing, and ultimately a near-total, economic dependence on the Soviet Union. Among developing countries, Egypt headed the list of importers of Soviet-bloc spare parts. Additionally, by contract with Moscow, the new enterprises were devoted to the production of goods intended for export first and foremost to Communist Eastern Europe—thereby repaying the Soviets for having fabricated the industrial plant in the first place. It was a dependence further augmented by the emergence of an Egyptian industrial proletariat. Increasing from 400,000 to approximately a million by 1970, this new class played its role in Moscow's larger political purpose of fostering Egypt's "non-capitalist" orientation both in domestic policy and—increasingly—in world affairs.

In the latter arena, the new Soviet-Egyptian relationship strengthened Nasser's resistance to Western pressures. By providing him with Communist-bloc funds, with technology, markets, weapons, and diplomatic patronage, it ensured that "nonalignment" remained an appealing option for his government. Not least of all, the dependency relationship allowed the Kremlin to seek military privileges in Egypt. This was a critical objective for the Russians. In 1961 the Sino-Soviet rift had cost them their naval base in Vone, Albania. Intent, afterward, upon offsetting United States air and ballistic power in the East Mediterranean, the Soviet government solicited Egypt and Syria for alternative naval and air facilities. Nasser, in turn, was willing at least partially to acquiesce in the request. Thus, on the eve of Prime Minister Nikita Khrushchev's visit to Cairo in May 1964, the Egyptian president allowed Soviet naval vessels to increase the number of their visits to the port of Alexandria—without committing Egypt to a permanent Soviet naval presence.

The Russians would not be put off. The economic aid continued. High-ranking Soviet and Egyptian officials exchanged visits more frequently, including (after the displacement of Khrushchev) Prime Minister Alexei Kosygin to Cairo and Nasser to Moscow. Important arms agreements were concluded in November 1964 and again a year later. Assured, then, of substantial funds and weapons, Cairo doubled its military expenditures from 1955 through 1970. The defense budget rose from 7 percent of the GNP in 1960 to 13 percent in 1966. Whereupon the Soviets in 1965 again sought full and unrestricted naval access to Egyptian ports. Acknowledging these requests sympathetically, Nasser still preferred to withhold a final answer.

Yet the noncommittal posture became more difficult to maintain as Egyptian reliance on Soviet economic and military assistance became all but total. By 1964 Nasser had dispatched 60,000 of his troops to the quagmire of the Yemeni civil war, still without achieving tangible results. He experienced additional setbacks when Iraq's post-Qassem regime declined to gravitate into the Egyptian orbit. Moreover, the governments of Jordan and Saudi Arabia, as well as those of Tunisia and Morocco, were firmly resisting Nasser's imperialist designs on their lands. With Israel's help, the nations of Black Africa were also stiffening against Egyptian intimidation. Finally, despite the ongoing infusion of Soviet funds, Egypt's economy ceaselessly teetered on the verge of insolvency. The purchase of vast quantities of industrial equipment and the costs of the debilitating war in Yemen continued to drain the nation's foreign reserves, and unemployment was rising.

The liquidation of Israel manifestly would have gone far both to salvage Nasser's pan-Arabist ambitions and to placate gestating nationalist unrest.

Nevertheless, the Jewish state apparently remained too formidable to tackle head-on. It was with a realistic appraisal, then, of his own weakness and of his enemy's strength that Nasser ignored Hashemite taunts to renew the blockade of the Strait of Tiran, and Syrian appeals for Egyptian help in obstructing Israel's irrigation project at the headwaters of the Jordan. On the other hand, it was equally clear to the Egyptian president that he could not indefinitely cope with his problems, internal or external, in complete disregard of Moscow's long-range ambition for a Socialist "presence" in the East Mediterranean.

MOSCOW RIDES THE SYRIAN TIGER

Despite Nasser's pained admission of his inability to offer military support, the Syrian regime by 1965 had allowed its forty-seven-mile frontier with Israel to become the Middle East's single most explosive boundary. There were a number of ingredients in the Syrian-Israeli confrontation. One was Israel's Jordan Valley irrigation project. In 1963, the Syrian and Lebanese governments prepared to divert the Jordan River tributaries arising on the Arab side of the line, and thus to prevent their waters from reaching Israeli territory. They did not get far; Israeli artillery and aircraft promptly destroyed the Arab bulldozers. A second, even more incendiary, factor in Israeli-Syrian relations was the acute state of tension along the demilitarized zones. Nowhere were Israeli citizens more vulnerable to attack. Adjacent to the main DMZ area, Syrian gun positions ensconced in the Golan Heights dominated the Chula stretch of the frontier. Whenever Israeli farmers sought to cultivate this terrain, they were fired upon from above. Exchanges of fire in 1962 and 1963 escalated into prolonged artillery duels, even aerial dogfights.

The violence no longer could be related simply to territorial claims and counterclaims. Much of it reflected the unique nature of the Syrian Ba'ath regime. Advocating a curious mélange of Leninism and pan-Arabism (although with increasing emphasis upon the latter), the junta of Syrian officers who had seized power in 1962 soon revealed themselves as the most grimly chauvinist government in the Middle East. Their diatribes on behalf of the Viet Cong, the Maoists, and the Guevarists, and against the United States and Israel were splenetic and at times psychotic. The truth was that the Damascus cabal enjoyed little popular support, and barely survived two armed revolts in September 1966 and February 1967. It was this very weakness that propelled the regime's strongman, Colonel Salah Jadid, and his colleagues into an uncompromising stance on the one issue that was universally popular—a war of liberation against Israel.

In its anti-Israel campaign, the Syrian government was prepared to make active use of the Palestine refugees. Among the latter, the most militant of the paramilitary organizations was al-Fatah, a group that had been organized in

1964 by veterans of the Mufti's former Arab Higher Committee (p. 29). In ensuing years, it was the Fatah that gravitated increasingly into the orbit of Syria's radical Ba'ath regime. Striking occasionally at Israel from the DMZ area, the guerrillas received their principal military training and weapons from the Syrian army. Indeed, from 1966 on, Damascus agreed to support a much larger scale of Fatah operations. The Palestinians' raids into Israel subsequently became more ambitious. Even as Syrian troops on the Golan shelled and mortared Israeli farm settlements in the Chula Valley below, the Fatah's irregulars laid repeated ambushes of Israeli army patrols and inflicted numerous casualties. Nurredin al-Atassi, the Syrian president, left no doubt of his government's sponsorship. Appealing for a "people's war" of resistance, sabotage, and terror, he declared flatly: "We want a policy of scorched earth for Palestine."

Nasser, by contrast, regarded the mounting campaign of Ba'athist and Fatah violence with distinct misgivings. Not having extricated himself entirely from the Yemeni war, the Egyptian president was less than certain of his ability to defeat Israel if he were sucked into a full-scale confrontation. As a result, his 1964 defense treaty with Syria was proven a dead letter on April 7, 1967, when an incident on the Israeli-Syrian frontier developed into a major air battle. A flight of Israeli jets penetrated Syrian air space and downed six MiGs before circling freely over Damascus. The Egyptian army did not budge. Rather, Cairo issued a frank warning to the Ba'athist government that "our agreement for mutual defense will apply only in the event of a general attack on Syria by Israel. No local incident will cause us to intervene."

It was the initiative not of Syria, but of the Soviet Union, that forced Nasser's hand. In the aftermath of the Suez-Sinai War, the Kremlin's approach to the Middle East had remained essentially unchanged. Soviet newspaper and radio propaganda was unceasing in its campaign against Israel as an "outpost of American imperialism." By the same token, the Russians continued to provide unlimited diplomatic support for Egypt's Suez blockade against Israeli shipping, for Syrian efforts to divert the headwaters of the Jordan, and for Syrian attacks along the DMZ. To some degree, the intensification of this Soviet pro-Arabism reflected Moscow's acute concern for the demise of Socialist regimes elsewhere. It was in the 1960s that the downfall of Ben Bella in Algeria was followed by the overthrow of Sukarno in Indonesia and of Nkruma in Ghana. In the Congo, rightist elements had maintained power (with the help of Israel). In Greece the military regime was stamping out leftist opposition. In Syria, unrest was mounting against the Ba'athist government. From the Soviet viewpoint, then, it appeared that Washington was manipulating events behind the scene. Worse yet, Communist Chinese representatives were descending upon Arab capitals with offers of weapons, technical specialists, and economic aid. Caught between these two fires, the Russians envisaged only one solution. It was to continue to outbid all other rivals in support of the Arab "national liberation" movement. No alternative front offered as likely a vehicle for Soviet penetration into the Middle East.

Nasser was prepared to encourage this hope. Grateful for Soviet military and financial patronage, he signed a new defense agreement with Marshal Andrei Gretchko in 1966, extending limited naval facilities to the Russians at the Mediterranean ports of Mersa Matruh and Sidi Barani, as well as at the Red Sea port of Quseir and at three Red Sea fishing villages. Three airports similarly were placed at the Soviets' disposal. In return, Moscow undertook to increase its shipments of arms and technicians. On May 15, 1966, Prime Minister Kosygin arrived in Cairo to pledge his government's support for the Egyptian "struggle against imperialism."

That year, too, a series of windfalls appeared likely to transform the USSR's cautious infiltration of the Middle East into a galloping conquest. The first was London's announcement that Britain intended to withdraw its military forces from Aden by 1968. With the Egyptians already entrenched in southern Yemen, the way now appeared open for a Soviet move into the Persian Gulf following British departure. The second decisive shift occurred in February 1966 when the Jadid faction of the Ba'ath party seized office in Damascus. Prodded by its Soviet benefactors, the new Syrian regime included two Communists in its cabinet. Thereafter it proceeded to nationalize many of the country's larger businesses, to dispatch its younger protégés to Moscow for training in "leadership," and eventually to allow the Soviets to operate their military electronic and monitoring equipment on Syrian territory. With Syria now apparently on the threshold of becoming the first Communist state in the Arab world, the Soviets were certain that they had access to a Mediterranean base at least as dependable as Egypt.

It was a foothold they were determined at all costs to preserve. Accordingly, the Kremlin began loosing a tough series of warnings to Israel about the "possible consequences" of further military action against Syria. On April 31, 1967, two weeks after the Israeli-Syrian air battle, Moscow bluntly informed the Israelis that they were endangering "the very fate of their state." It was the most ominous threat since the Sinai Campaign of 1956. And, in fact, the deteriorating border situation was electric with danger. As early as January 1967, after a particularly violent series of firefights along the DMZ, Prime Minister Levi Eshkol issued an open warning to the Syrians. "I cannot exclude the possibility that we may have no other recourse but deterrent measures," he declared. The air action of April 7 seemed an omen of even graver retaliatory moves. In a panic, the Syrians trundled heavy artillery directly into the DMZ, and the Israelis responded with a concentration of their own troops and weapons. On May 11, finally, the Jerusalem government notified the UN Security Council that, unless Syrian provocations ended, it would regard itself "as fully entitled to act in self-defense." At this point, deeply alarmed for the security of their favored Arab protégé, the Russians took the most calamitous misstep since the beginning of their penetration into the Near East. They turned to Nasser as their instrument for "protecting" Syria.

NASSER RETURNS TO GAZA AND SHARM ES-SHEIKH

A month earlier, in mid-April, Leonid Chuvakhin, the Soviet ambassador in Tel Aviv, had complained to Prime Minister Eshkol about "heavy concentrations of Israeli forces on the Syrian border." Eshkol promptly offered to drive Chuvakhin to the border, to enable the Russian to see for himself that his information was false. It was questionable that Chuvakhin seriously believed that the Jews intended to attack Syria's formidable topographical defenses. But to the Soviets the very accusation of Israeli troop movements would make the Jerusalem cabinet think twice about reacting to future violence along the northern frontier. On May 18, moreover, Soviet President Nikolai Podgorny repeated the charge of Israeli military concentrations in his talk with Egypt's Vice-President Anwar al-Sadat, who was visiting Moscow. Podgorny added that Israel's purpose evidently was to invade Syria. For its part, the Soviet Union stood ready to help Syria and Egypt in their war with Israel, and Egypt should be ready for action. "You must not be taken by surprise," he cautioned.

Somewhat resignedly, then, Nasser agreed to dispatch a military mission to Syria. Yet, upon being taken to the southern frontier line with Israel, the Egyptian visitors found the charges of Israeli troop concentrations to be "without foundation," as Shams Badran, the Egyptian minister of war, admitted later. If Nasser subsequently allowed the crisis to escalate, he was influenced by factors other than putative Israeli aggression. Ironically, one of these was his country's increasingly urgent financial plight—the food shortages and growing unemployment that were exacerbating public unrest. A diversion against Israel once more might serve as a useful palliative. It would put an end, as well, to repeated taunts by the Hashemite and Saudi governments, mocking Nasser for his "cowardice" in reducing border friction with Israel, and in tolerating United Nations forces on Egyptian soil. Not least of all, the Egyptian president appreciated the extent of his economic and military dependence on the Soviet Union. If the Russians asked him to make a gesture to shore up the Ba'athist cabal in Syria, he could hardly ignore their request.

On May 15, therefore, Nasser suddenly dispatched two armored divisions over the Suez into Sinai. By no coincidence, May 15 was Israel's independence day. News of the Egyptian deployment was brought to Israel's chief of staff, General Yitzchak Rabin, at the very moment the latter was reviewing his own troops along the Jerusalem route of parade. Although Rabin immediately ordered a tank brigade shifted toward the Gaza Strip, he regarded the Egyptian maneuver as essentially bluff. That assumption was rudely shaken the following evening, however, when Nasser issued orders for the 3,400-man UNEF contingent near Gaza to redeploy within the Strip itself. At this point, U Thant, the Burmese secretary-general of the United Nations, summoned the Egyptian delegate at the world body, Muhammad al-Koni, and informed the latter that the United Nations would accept no "half-measures." Either the UNEF accomplished its mission without reservation, or it would be withdrawn from Egypt altogether. The secretary-general was convinced that Nasser was uninterested in having these troops evacuated and that he would back down. Yet, unwittingly, U Thant had just dislodged the stone that loosed the avalanche. For on the afternoon of May 17, after a series of lengthy cabinet meetings, the Egyptian government called the secretary-general's hand. It ordered a complete UNEF evacuation from Egyptian territory and from the Gaza Strip.

In the aftermath of the 1956 Sinai Campaign, we recall, the United States, Britain, France, and many other Western nations had specifically interpreted the General Assembly Resolution of November 4, 1956, as a bar to UNEF evacuation without the specific consent of the General Assembly itself. This interpretation had been verified in February 1957 by Dag Hammarskjöld. On May 18, 1967, therefore, U Thant met urgently with delegates of the seven countries, including India and Yugoslavia, whose troops served in the United Nations force. It was then that the secretary-general was informed that these governments were unwilling to risk the lives of their troops in the Middle East, and were now recalling them. Shaken by this reaction, U Thant immediately capitulated to Nasser's demand. Late that day the UNEF garrison evacuated its position in the Gaza Strip; Egyptian troops and heavy equipment immediately moved in. Whereupon Cairo similarly ordered the evacuation of the tiny UNEF company at Sharm es-Sheikh, guarding the Strait of Tiran. As a result, then, of U Thant's unwillingness to invoke the full range of delaying procedures at his disposal, the UNEF, the world body's most impressive peacekeeping achievement, ignominiously collapsed.

Three Egyptian armored divisions began fanning out through the Sinai Peninsula. At the same time, Damascus mobilized fifty cadet battalions, and two Iraqi brigades moved toward the frontier of Jordan. The governments of Kuwait, Yemen, and Algeria announced their readiness to dispatch troops and planes to Syria and Egypt. As it developed, May 17 was the turning point of the Middle Eastern crisis. Until then, Nasser could have ordered his divisions back to Cairo, having mounted a show of strength and having left the impression that he had forestalled a Zionist attack. But U Thant's instant capitulation signified the moment of no return. To his own astonishment, Nasser had won a brilliant diplomatic and propaganda victory scarcely by raising his finger. On the threshold of unchallenged leadership again in the Arab world, he would now have to act the part.

By May 19 Egyptian units were reinforcing their former garrisons in Sharm es-Sheikh; while in Gaza, Palestine refugee units made ready to occupy the former UNEF border encampments. At the same time, Radio Cairo announced military preparations for "retaliatory" attacks on key Israeli cities. Other Arab governments were openly broadcasting their intention "to cut the Jews' throats." Ironically, until this point, Jerusalem had interpreted Nasser's move as a technique to deter Israel from attacking Syria. No longer. On May 20 a general Israeli mobilization was put into effect. Yet even at this late date, the government preferred to rely on diplomacy. It requested France's intercession with the Soviets. No response was forthcoming from Paris. In Washington, Israeli officials entreated the State Department to give teeth to Eisenhower's declaration of March 1, 1957—stating that the American government endorsed the right of "free and innocent passage through the Strait of Tiran"—by dispatching an American warship through the Gulf of Aqaba to Eilat. But here also the Americans, mired in Vietnam, preferred to act within the framework of the United Nations. So, too, did the British. Thereupon, stunned by the equivocation of the Western Powers, Prime Minister Eshkol appealed to the Arab governments in words that were conciliatory to the point of timidity:

> I wish to repeat . . . especially to Egypt and Syria, that we do not contemplate any military action. . . . We have contemplated no intervention in their internal affairs. We ask only from these states the application of these same principles toward us as an act of reciprocity.

There was little in these developments to give Nasser pause.

On the night of May 21 the Egyptian president made yet another fateful decision. He dispatched a destroyer, two submarines, and four missile-launcher boats through the Suez Canal to the Red Sea, and the next day followed this move with a chilling announcement: "The Strait of Tiran is part of our territorial waters. No Israeli ship will ever navigate it again. We also forbid the shipment of strategic materials to Israel on non-Israeli vessels." It was possible, as Sadat wrote of this act later, that "Nasser was carried away by his own impetuosity." Whatever the president's motives, the threat implicit in his announcement was lethal to Israel. Eilat and the Strait of Tiran represented the Jewish state's gateway to Africa and Asia. By 1966, Eilat had accommodated over a million tons of cargo, fully 30 percent of Israel's mineral exports, and had become the nation's principal oil port. Foreclosure of access to this harbor would have represented at least a partial economic strangulation. Nasser's challenge to Israel's sovereignty and economic security, as a result, was now altogether irretrievable.

DIPLOMATIC PARALYSIS, MILITARY TENSION

By noon of May 23, mobilization in Israel had become total. Bus transportation was halted as all available vehicles were commandeered for military transport. Private citizens began hurriedly digging shelters. Civil defense authorities published instructions on methods of stocking food supplies, preparing first-aid kits, and handling fire equipment. Foreign ambassadors requested their nationals to leave, and airlines dispatched special planes to Israel for the hurried evacuation of thousands of tourists. In Jerusalem, meanwhile, the cabinet was holding round-the-clock sessions. Abba Eban, formerly Israel's ambassador to Washington and now Golda Meir's successor as foreign minister, warned his colleagues that the government under no circumstances dared repeat the mistakes of 1956, when the Sinai offensive left Israel in a state of diplomatic near-quarantine. It was critical, Eban insisted, that Israel now present its case systematically to the major Western Powers. To that end, he proposed a swift diplomatic tour of Paris, London, and Washington. The cabinet agreed, and the foreign minister departed for Europe within hours.

By the time Eban landed in Paris the following morning of May 24, an emergency weapons airlift already was under way from France to Israel. Among the French military leadership and civilian population alike, the outpouring of sympathy for Israel exceeded even the community of interest of 1956. Each request for vital military supplies was immediately approved by telephone. Yet this initial show of public and popular warmth no longer reflected government policy. By the mid-1960s, in the aftermath of French withdrawal from Algeria, President Charles de Gaulle was increasingly preoccupied with his country's need to regain the friendship of the Moslem world. Even before 1967, therefore, ministers in the cabinet were instructed to sever their ties with the Alliance France-Israël. France's delegate to the UN General Assembly supported a formula calling for the repatriation of Arab refugees to Israel. Except for weapons acquisition, trade between Israel and France remained minimal. Nor, unlike Germany, was France inclined to offer Israel meaningful help in securing access to the European Common Market. While no dramatic shift thus far had occurred in de Gaulle's posture of benevolence toward Israel, until 1967 no crisis had arisen to test it.

Now, however, de Gaulle and his foreign ministry officials decided that Egypt's blockade of the Strait of Tiran povided France with an opportunity to convene a Four-Power conference, rather than a purely Soviet-American summit; in this fashion the United States and the Soviet Union would be denied a monopoly of influence in the Near East. Receiving Eban at noon on May 24, the French president began the interview with a warning: "Do not make war! Do not make war! In any event, do not be the first to fire!" Eban in turn sought to remind de Gaulle of France's 1957 pledge on freedom of navigation, but the latter interrupted: "True, but that was in 1957, and this is 1967. It is up to the four Great Powers." De Gaulle then went on to propose that the Big Four should also discuss a possible repatriation of the refugees and the "rights of the Palestinians." Soon afterward, too, the president ordered that the flow of military assistance to Israel be halted, and suggested, through his minister of information, that the appearance of an Israeli vessel in the Strait of Tiran would be a provocative act. The experience was a bitter one for Eban.

It was at least partly mitigated that same afternoon when the Israeli diplomat reached London and met with Prime Minister Harold Wilson. Here Eban found greater understanding. Wilson assured his visitor that he would support fully any international action to uphold the right of unrestricted passage in the Strait of Tiran. Indeed, he had already sent his representatives to Washington to discuss "nuts and bolts" methods of opening the waterway. Encouraged by the prime minister's stance, Eban flew on to New York the next morning.

Yet by then Israel's evident powerlessness had influenced even Hussein of Jordan. On May 25 the Hashemite king revealed that he was authorizing Iraqi troops to enter his territory and to adopt positions along the Israeli frontier. Others of Nasser's former enemies, including Feisal of Saudi Arabia, agreed at this point to revive the long-moribund Arab United Command under Egyptian leadership. These were the circumstances under which Nasser received U Thant that same May 25, and informed the secretary-general that he would not back down an inch. "The closing of the Strait," he observed with satisfaction, "wipes out the last smears of the triple aggression of 1956." In a gesture of "conciliation," nevertheless, the Egyptian president observed that he would allow ships through the Strait to Israel so long as they were not Israeli vessels and were not carrying "strategic" matériel—essentially a reversion to the status of pre-1956 (U Thant, in fact, was impressed by Nasser's "concession").

Meanwhile, British Foreign Office and Admiralty officials were holding talks with their counterparts in Washington. The visitors proposed the establishment of an international maritime flotilla to run the blockade under naval escort. The State Department and the White House initially accepted the plan. However, the Senate Foreign Relations Committee preferred to leave all decisions exclusively to the United Nations—and thereby presumably to the mercy of a Soviet veto. Indeed, three "nonaligned" members of the Security Council already had declared that they would oppose even placing the blockade issue on the agenda. These were the circumstances under which President Lyndon Johnson received Eban on the evening of May 25. Once again the foreign minister reminded the president of Eisenhower's 1957 commitment to freedom of navigation in the Strait of Tiran. Johnson in turn agreed that the basic problem was one of inducing Egypt to end its blockade. He thought that this was possible, but insisted that he could not move without authority from Congress at a time when the United States was heavily involved in Vietnam. "I must emphasize the necessity for Israel not to make itself responsible for the initiation of hostilities," Johnson warned. "Israel will not be alone unless it decides to go alone."

Flying back to Israel on the night of the twenty-sixth, Eban hurried directly to a cabinet meeting in Tel Aviv the next morning. He found the military leadership advocating an immediate preemptive strike. Alarmed, the foreign minister stressed the importance of waiting at least until American political understanding could be secured. He was buttressed in this argument by a cable that had just arrived from Johnson, assuring Eshkol that the United States and

Britain were consulting urgently on an international naval escort plan and "other nations are responding vigorously to the idea." On the basis of this assurance, the cabinet voted to postpone military action.

One source to which none of the ministers looked with even the faintest of illusions was the United Nations. From May 29 to June 4, Israel and Egypt dominated the Security Council's proceedings with argument and counterargument. On May 31 the Council entertained an American proposal that the Israelis and the Egyptians use "international diplomacy" to resolve their dispute. Even this pallid appeal was rejected by the Soviet Union and India, who were convinced that Israel was altogether helpless by then. Johnson's promise of decisive American action on a multinational flotilla was soon revealed as equally hollow. On June 2, Britain's Prime Minister Wilson flew to Washington and admitted, not without embarrassment, that his government would be unable to join such a venture if force were contemplated. The Canadians, originally friendly to the idea, now also backed away. In a cordial but regretful letter, therefore, Johnson now repeated to Eshkol that Washington was unable to act without congressional approval, and that in any case "our leadership is unanimous that the United States should not act alone." Nothing more could be secured from the United States. The American assurance of 1957 had been proved worthless in its first test, only ten years later.

The Israelis, meanwhile, were preparing for war. The armed forces were completing their military preparations. The highways were all but empty of civilian traffic. The towns were silent at night. Families cemented the windows of their children's rooms as protection against shrapnel. Parks were consigned as emergency cemeteries. Corpse identification and burial instructions were mimeographed by civil defense offices. Yet, if a grim mood had enveloped the country, it was one not of despair but of frustration. An apparent crisis of leadership had developed in the government. Ben-Gurion's hand-picked successor, Levi Eshkol, had assumed the prime ministry in 1963. Russian-born, settling in Palestine as a pioneer-farmer in 1914, Eshkol early on had displayed a unique organizational ability. In the 1930s he was a founder-member both of the Jewish labor federation and of the Haganah underground, and later became secretary-general of the Tel Aviv labor council. Upon the establishment of the state, he was immediately coopted by Ben-Gurion as director-general of the ministry of defense. Eshkol's most fulfilling role after independence, however, was as director of the Jewish Agency's land settlement department, and simultaneously, in the early 1950s, as minister of agriculture. In that dual capacity he brilliantly coordinated the massive absorption of immigrants. Afterward, until 1963, he held the key portfolio of minister of finance, where his talents as negotiator ranged over the entire field of government. As a result, no one challenged his credentials as Ben-Gurion's logical replacement upon the latter's resignation.

A huskily-built, broad-featured man of practical interests, Eshkol possessed neither the charisma nor the intellectual depth of Ben-Gurion. Rather, he was the born committee member, tireless in discussion, who won over his colleagues by solid and patient persuasion. Yet decisiveness and charisma were precisely the qualities that were needed now, and in late May it appeared to the Israeli people that Eshkol was all but helpless to resolve perhaps the gravest crisis of their nation's existence. Under the circumstances, a fierce public demand was launched during the last week of May to introduce changes in the cabinet. The need was universally acknowledged for a "Government of National Unity," including members of the opposition parties; and for Moshe Dayan, hero of the 1956 Sinai Campaign, to assume the ministry of defense (Eshkol currently held this portfolio). Deeply offended, suspicious of Dayan as a leader of the nondoctrinaire "pragmatic" wing of the Labor movement, Eshkol resisted this pressure for several days. On June 1, however, entreated by his closest Labor colleagues, Eshkol wearily gave in. Thereupon the Government of National Unity coalesced (including Menachem Begin of the right-wing Cherut party), and Dayan became minister of defense. Popular trust in the famed, one-eyed general was overwhelming. News of his appointment immediately restored the confidence of the armed forces and of the nation at large.

A MASSING OF ARAB STRENGTH

The chain of troops and armor was tightening around Israel. Egypt's armed forces were joined now by military elements from other Arab states. Jordan was one of these. Ironically, as late as May 28, Radio Cairo had denounced Hussein as a "Hashemite whore," and had exhorted the Jordanian people to assassinate him. The Syrian press had echoed this denunciation. And then, astonishingly, on May 30, Hussein flew off to Cairo to sign a mutual defense pact with Egypt, linking his country to a treaty that already had been negotiated between Egypt and Syria. It was plain that the little Hashemite monarch dared not abstain from an undertaking that was sweeping the entire Arab world into its vortex. On May 31, Egyptian General Abd al-Moneim Riad flew to Amman to devise a common strategy with Hussein. The ensuing plan anticipated a joint Hashem-ite-Iraqi-Saudi offensive to be launched toward Jerusalem and toward several key Israeli air bases.

In preparation for this expedition, Iraq joined the military pact on June 3, and the following night an Iraqi brigade crossed into Jordan. Syria meanwhile deployed four infantry brigades along the Israeli border. King Hassan II of Morocco, known until then for his restraint on the Arab-Israel issue, similarly deemed it expedient to offer Nasser assistance. So did Tunisia's equally moderate President Habib Bourguiba, who now invited the Algerian army to use his nation's communications en route to the Israeli front. Feisal of Saudi Arabia promised troops, observing that "any Arab who does not participate in this conflict will seal his fate." By then Nasser and the Arab leaders no longer were speaking of a blockade of Israeli shipping, or of defensive positions in the event of Israeli military action. "The problem currently before the Arab countries," declared Nasser exultantly before the Egyptian People's Assembly on May 25, "is not whether the port of Eilat should be blockaded or how to blockade it—but how totally to exterminate the State of Israel for all time." On June 2, Iraq's President Aref exhorted the officers of his air force: "Brothers and sons, this is the day of the battle to avenge . . . 1948. . . . We shall, God willing, meet in Tel Aviv and Haifa."

There appeared a certain justification for Arab confidence this time. The sheer extent of Egyptian manpower was impressive. Seven divisions were tucked into the sands of Sinai awaiting the Jews. These 120,000 troops—twice the number of Israel's mobilized forces on the southern front—disposed of fully 1,000 guns, 9,000 antitank guns, and 2,000 tanks. As Nasser taunted Israel's generals to strike out of the constricting Arab vise, moreover, he was waiting not merely with a heavy preponderance of troops but with an elaborate network of trenches, pillboxes, mine fields, and machine gun nests. In the decade since the 1956 war, the Egyptians had transformed the northeastern corner of Sinai into a military barrier capable both of resisting the heaviest attack and of serving as the launching base for a powerful offensive. A vast Egyptian Maginot Line, the Abu Agheila network of defenses, blocked the key Nitzana-Ismailia highway, the single narrow opening through which Israeli armor could move preemptively into the heartland of Sinai.

Um Cataf, the linchpin of the Abu Agheila network, was itself an interlocked system of fortresses, trenches, and natural ridges, and was surrounded by mine fields and guarded by tanks. Deep inside this mighty enclave, the Egyptians had distributed scores of heavy guns. Intending essentially to use the Um Cataf position as an anvil on which to smash Israeli armor, they had also concentrated a tank division just south of Abu Agheila, and another not far behind. If, as anticipated, Israeli forces battered themselves fruitlessly against the Um Cataf redoubt, both Egyptian divisions would then swing north toward the Negev, maneuver behind Israeli forces there, and annihilate them. Afterward, the Egyptian tank columns would be in a position to advance north along the coastal road toward an undefended Tel Aviv. It was a grim picture for Israel. The skull and crossbones on Cairo's unfurled flags seemed an augury of what the Jewish republic could expect before this avalanche of Arab, and particularly of Egyptian, strength. More acutely than at any time since 1948, the Israeli people sensed that their life as a nation was hanging in the balance.

XII

THE THIRD

ARAB-ISRAELI WAR

On June 1, Foreign Minister Eban informed the Israeli cabinet that there no longer appeared a foreseeable possibility that Washington could resolve the crisis. It followed, he conceded, that no additional diplomatic purpose would be served in delaying military action. With this joyless assessment in hand, the cabinet met again the next morning to hear a military intelligence report. It described the widening scale of Arab troop movements, the unmistakable evidence of Egyptian preparations for a counteroffensive in the event Israel sought to crack Nasser's blockade. Dayan and General Rabin insisted, therefore, that the logical alternative was to strike first, if only to minimize casualties. The argument was accepted by Eshkol and by the rest of the cabinet. The prime minister declared then that he would leave the timing of a preemptive offensive to Dayan and the military leadership.

As minister of defense, however, Dayan was no longer the audacious, headstrong warrior he had been as chief of staff in 1956. This time he displayed a new sensitivity to world opinion and an uncharacteristic caution in all his military moves. Conferring with Rabin and the latter's staff now, he imposed a firm set of guidelines: troops on the Jordanian and Syrian fronts were to maintain an exclusively defensive posture, even if the Arabs attacked first; the strategy Rabin had devised for the Egyptian front was unacceptable, and would have to be altered. Initially, the general staff had intended to bypass the heavily fortified Egyptian strong points in the Sinai and to concentrate instead on investing the Gaza Strip. By this limited move, Israel presumably would gain a valuable bargaining card that it could trade off later for open shipping through the Strait of Tiran. Moreover, Nasser's prestige would be tarnished and Egyptian forces, rushed to Gaza, would be vulnerable to Israeli attack there under conditions favorable to Israel.

Dayan rejected this approach. The Strip was packed with a quarter-million refugees, he argued, and Nasser would not consider it important enough for use in a trade. "But the more decisive reason [for a change] was a military one," Dayan wrote later. ". . . The real gravity of [Nasser] closing the Strait of Tiran lay not simply in the blockade itself, but in his attempt to demonstrate that Israel was incapable of standing up to the Arabs." From this premise, it followed that Israel's aim should be armed confrontation with Egypt—indeed, a confrontation sufficiently decisive to break the back of Egypt's military power. "Therefore, I said . . . we had no choice but to go out to the very center of [Nasser's] armed might." This meant crushing the Egyptians at their line of greatest strength, the northeastern Sinai salient.

Rabin and his staff had long since worked out contingency operational plans for such an offensive. Facing seven Egyptian divisions in the Sinai were three Israeli brigades under the command of General Yeshayahu Gavish. A seasoned professional, Gavish was convinced that he had found the right strategy for "blowing the locks" off the Sinai. It was to crack through Egyptian defenses at Rafah and Abu Agheila; then to send an armored division leaping forward to the Mitla Pass, blocking the Egyptian escape route; and finally to destroy the entire trapped Egyptian army. It was an ambitious scheme, one that depended upon a pulverizing blow at the first impact. To that end, air superiority would first have to be achieved.

Accordingly, at 7:10 A.M. on June 5, the attack order went out from the operations room of the defense ministry in Tel Aviv. An exceptionally skilled air arm was thereupon launched into action. Israeli pilots and ground crews were considered the equal of any in the world. Thanks also to superb intelligence, their command had pinpointed the location of virtually all Egyptian planes, all antiaircraft batteries, even wooden dummy planes. The first Israeli Mirages took off at staggered intervals for Egypt's key bases in the Sinai Peninsula, the Suez Rectangle, and the Nile Valley. Crossing the Mediterranean coast, they hooked back over Egypt at near-ground level to avoid enemy radar. Reaching their eleven separate targets at the appointed time, they embarked on their scheduled four passes, destroying the parked Egyptian planes, then rocket-bombing the fields. Three waves completed the immolation before streaking for home. In 170 minutes, Israel's pilots had smashed Egypt's best-equipped bases and had turned 300 of Nasser's 340 combat planes into flaming wrecks. Another 20 Egyptian planes were shot down in the air. The largest air force in the Middle East was now in ruins.

The Israelis were free henceforth to concentrate on the Egyptian ground armies. Throughout the next few days, their air force roamed at will over Sinai, destroying entire convoys of armor and other vehicles fleeing to the Canal. During the first day, too, as Egypt's allies began probing offensives (p. 157), Israeli planes were released to attack Hashemite and Syrian airfields, even the great Habaniyya base in Iraq. In the course of these attacks, the entire Jordanian air force of twenty Hunter jets was wiped out, as well as fifty Syrian MiGs—two-thirds of the Syrian combat air force. By nightfall of June 6, Israel had destroyed 416 planes, 393 on the ground. It had lost 26 planes during that time, all to antiaircraft fire.

Meanwhile, at 8:12 A.M. on June 5, Israeli ground forces attacked. Against heavy resistance, General Israel Tal's First Armored Brigade reached the Palestinian defenses outside Khan Yunis and overwhelmed them, then burst into the village itself. Swinging behind Egyptian entrenchments south of Rafah, a second column of Tal's armor invested the little desert town from the rear. The fall of Rafah, in turn, opened the way to al-Arish, administrative capital of Sinai and northeastern gateway to the entire Egyptian defense network in the peninsula. Tal's armor pushed on, reaching al-Arish itself by midnight of June 6. A brutal slugging match then developed against Egyptian tanks and artillery. Yet, with strafing and bombing support from Israel's air force, enemy resistance was overcome. The last phase of the operation at al-Arish consisted of liquidating the remnants of the Egyptian Seventh Division. A by-product of success here was Chief of Staff Rabin's order to occupy the Gaza Strip.

A second Israeli brigade under General Ariel Sharon meanwhile confronted the formidable task of blasting open the other "lock" to Sinai—the powerful Abu Agheila network of defenses across the Nitzana-Ismailia axis. At the western extremity of this gateway lay the death trap of Um Cataf. Sharon's single undersized infantry brigade and his one brigade of armor hardly matched the Egyptians' two-division numerical strength. Planning a night attack, moreover, Sharon would be deprived of vital air support. But, in fact, the cocky, barrel-chested paratroop veteran had no intention of mounting a frontal assault. Rather, he launched his attack on June 5 with a long, painful infantry march behind Um Cataf through the sand. At the same time a battalion of paratroops was lifted by helicopters to another point in the desert three miles behind the fortifications. The infantry slogged through the dunes, appearing at the Egyptian flanks just as darkness fell. Running along the lip of the trenchworks, they cut down the Egyptian defenders with their automatic weapons. The paratroopers, who also had made their way through the desert, now simultaneously attacked Egyptian gun batteries from the rear. After several minutes of close-quarter combat, an Israeli artillery barrage descended on the Egyptian positions. Additional infantry and tanks then began enfilading the trenches. The fighting was heavy, but the entire complicated operation went like clockwork. By 3:00 A.M. on June 6, Um Cataf was in Sharon's hands. Three hours later, Israeli armor moved through the rear of this defense ganglion to encircle and destroy isolated Egyptian tank resistance.

Even as the "locks" were being blown off the gates to the Sinai, a third Israeli brigade under General Avraham Yoffe, the veteran trekker of Operation Kadesh, confounded the Egyptians on the afternoon of June 5 by moving through an "impassable" sector, the wastes lying between the two gateways. At the road junction of Bir Lahfan, Yoffe's tanks fought a thirteen-hour battle against Egyptian armor. By noon of June 6 Egyptian reinforcements were turned back. Yoffe's brigade then raced on toward Jebel Libni, a key military installation astride the central axis. Here the Egyptians had concentrated a full infantry division supported by tanks. But this force, too, now crumpled under Yoffe's battering ram. Thus, by the end of the second day of war, after thirty-five hours of uninterrupted battle, the critical phase of the Israeli operational plan had been fulfilled. Egyptian fortifications had been penetrated and Sinai was opened wide before Israeli armor.

THE SECOND CONQUEST OF SINAI

When news of the outbreak of hostilities reached the Egyptian public, crowds in Cairo and Alexandria went wild with joy. They were certain that Israel was finished. Nasser was informed otherwise. In the late afternoon of June 5, a headquarters officer arrived at the president's office with devastating information: "I have come to tell you that we no longer have an air force." Maintaining his composure, Nasser devised an ingenious explanation for the air disaster. At 7:30 A.M. of June 6, Radio Cairo, and then other Arab stations, began releasing the "information" that carrier-based American and British planes were supplying air cover for Israel's ground forces. It was a bald "political cover-up for domestic consumption," as Sadat admitted later, and its only effect was to set off a vindictive chain-reaction of Egyptian and other Arab diplomatic ruptures with the United States.

In Washington, meanwhile, Lyndon Johnson was awakened at 3:00 A.M. on June 5 and informed of the hostilities. Immediately he cabled Moscow, appealing for restraint on both sides. The Soviets agreed: the Great Powers should stay out of the fighting. Shortly afterward, however, the Egyptian ambassador in Moscow, Muhammad Gourad Ghaleb, informed Prime Minister Kosygin of the true military situation. Shocked by the unfolding disaster to this favored client nation, Kosygin immediately promised Ghaleb that the Soviet government would replace all lost weapons and exert its full diplomatic influence to impel Israeli evacuation of the captured territory. But the prime minister warned, too, that the USSR would not intervene militarily. Whatever his disappointment at this answer, the Egyptian ambassador received some encouragement at least from Moscow's tough diplomatic stance, for Kosygin was as good as his word. Shortly before noon, Washington time, the Soviet prime minister dispatched a message to Johnson, emphasizing that he and his colleagues could not remain indifferent to Israel's "criminal aggression," and that the Soviet armed forces were prepared to use appropriate means to end the "Zionist adventure."

Yet by then Johnson and his advisers had learned of Israel's spectacular victories. Gratified that the Jews themselves were successfully liquidating a grave international crisis, and simultaneously inflicting a major diplomatic defeat on the Soviets, the President was not inclined to countenance Soviet bullying. Accordingly, he ordered the Sixth Fleet to proceed toward the fighting zone.

Within minutes the huge armada was moving in the direction of the Sinai coast. Johnson followed this gesture with another message to Kosygin, reminding the Soviet leader of numerous American commitments to safeguard the independence of Israel. Backing off at this point, the Soviets came up instead with a proposed Security Council resolution calling for all belligerents to withdraw from occupied territories.

It was wasted effort. The American delegation promptly countered with a resolution of its own, urging a straightforward cease-fire without reference to evacuation. To outraged Arab and Soviet objections, the Americans observed blandly that if a status quo ante were desired, then it must be restored to the circumstances obtaining before the crisis developed: namely, to freedom of navigation in the Gulf of Aqaba and a return of the UNEF to Gaza and Sharm es-Sheikh. Visibly confused, Nikolai Federenko, the Soviet delegate, finally suggested that the Council postpone further deliberations until the next day, June 6. This was a serious blunder, for every passing hour added to Israel's military victories. The other Security Council delegations unhesitatingly endorsed the American approach. Unlike 1956, moreover, the diplomatic climate this time was markedly favorable to Israel.

On the morning of June 7, Israel's military command launched a coordinated attack against the remaining Egyptian secondary defenses in Sinai. Tal's brigade struck at the positions near Bir Hamma, ten miles to the west, even as Yoffe's troops simultaneously engaged the Egyptians in Bir Hassana. In the ensuing armored battles on this flat terrain, the hard-driving Israeli tankers all but annihilated their Egyptian enemy. By nightfall, the invading vanguard had reached its objectives. In the north it had overrun Rumani on the coastal road, about ten miles from Ismailia. In the south the Israelis blocked the passageway through Mitla. Three of their brigades were moving in now for climactic battle. Tal and Yoffe blocked the passes; Sharon was driving the fleeing Egyptians into the trap. A continuous stream of Egyptian troops and vehicles poured headlong from eastern and central Sinai toward Yoffe's force at Mitla, even as Israeli planes mercilessly strafed and bombed this retreating host. Yoffe's brigade completed the slaughter. In the end, more than 800 Egyptian tanks were knocked out.

On that same June 7, meanwhile, the coastal fortress of Sharm es-Sheikh fell to the Israelis without resistance; the Egyptian defenders fled hours before Israeli paratroops could be dropped. The paratroop units were flown instead to al-Tur, continuing northward from there along the Gulf of Suez, then linking up with other contingents of paratroops moving down the Gulf coast by land. The entire Sinai was ringed by Israeli forces. With the greater part of the Egyptian army smashed in the desert, Tal and Joffe ordered their columns to press ahead to the Canal. In fact, only the day before, Dayan had informed a press conference that Israel had achieved its political and military objective. This was, essentially, the reopening of the Strait of Tiran to international navigation. "The Israeli army

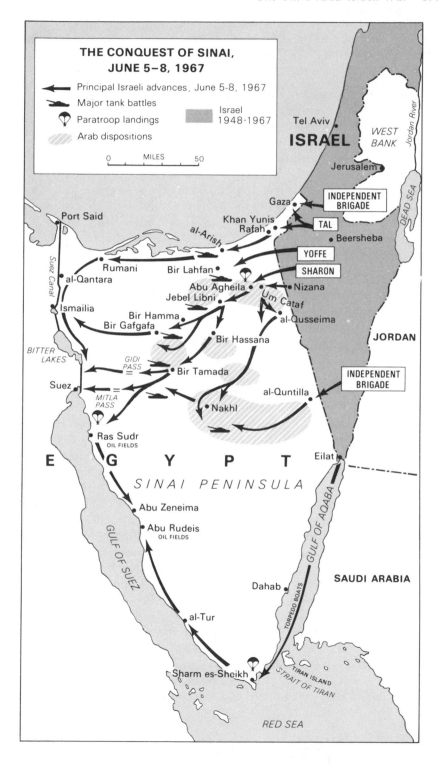

THE CONQUEST OF SINAI,
JUNE 5–8, 1967

Principal Israeli advances, June 5-8, 1967
Major tank battles
Paratroop landings
Israel 1948-1967
Arab dispositions

0   MILES   50

ISRAEL

Tel Aviv

WEST BANK

Jordan River

Jerusalem

DEAD SEA

Port Said

Gaza

INDEPENDENT BRIGADE

Khan Yunis
Rafah

TAL

al-Arish

Beersheba

Rumani

Bir Lahfan

YOFFE

al-Qantara

SHARON

Abu Agheila

Nizana

Suez Canal

Ismailia

Jebel Libni

Um Cataf

JORDAN

Bir Hamma
Bir Gafgafa

al-Qusseima

BITTER LAKES

Bir Hassana

GIDI PASS

Bir Tamada

INDEPENDENT BRIGADE

Suez

al-Quntilla

MITLA PASS

Nakhl

Ras Sudr
OIL FIELDS

Eilat

E   G   Y   P   T

SINAI PENINSULA

GULF OF AQABA

Abu Zeneima

Abu Rudeis
OIL FIELDS

SAUDI ARABIA

GULF OF SUEZ

Dahab

TORPEDO BOATS

al-Tur

Sharm es-Sheikh

TIRAN ISLAND

STRAIT OF TIRAN

RED SEA

can reach the Canal without difficulty," he said, "but that is not our objective. . . . [W]hy should we push onto Suez and get ourselves involved in international problems?" As Dayan wrote later, however:

> After we had captured Kantara East, I had requested a consultation with the prime minister and the chief of staff, and we decided that our forces would halt twelve and a half miles from the Canal. But there were now new developments. First, despite Egypt's acceptance of the cease-fire (below), remnants of her forces continued to harass our units east of the Canal. Second, America was about to submit a resolution to the Security Council calling on each side to remove its armed forces to six miles from the Canal, and we thought it well to have an area from which to withdraw. Our General Staff was accordingly issued a correction to its previous order. . . .

Dayan's initial reservations about moving to the Canal would be confirmed in the years ahead. For the moment, nevertheless, Israel's victory was a staggering one. Seven Egyptian divisions, virtually the entire Egyptian regular army, had been crushed in less than four days.

Despite the anguish and rage with which Moscow contemplated this havoc, and the loss of at least $2 billion in Soviet equipment, it was evident from the first day of the war that the Russians were not prepared to intervene in the fighting. Nor were they capable even of mobilizing support for a resolution demanding Israeli withdrawal. Both Cairo and Moscow understood now that, under all circumstances, the Jews at least had to be stopped from crossing the Canal into integral Egypt. A cease-fire was the one, rather forlorn, alternative left. Whereupon, at 1:00 P.M. on June 8, Federenko submitted his proposal for a cease-fire in the Security Council. This time he no longer attached to it the condition of evacuation, but demanded simply an 8:00 P.M. time limit for the cessation of hostilities. The proposal was accepted by the Security Council, then by the Israeli and Egyptian representatives.

Yet, in Egypt itself, the cease-fire was not announced until 11:30 P.M., when most of the population was asleep. Throughout the night, the issue of responsibility for the catastrophe was bitterly disputed by Nasser and his colleagues. Abd al-Hakim Amer and Shams Badran, representing the military, offered Nasser the choice of personally resigning, taking all blame alone, or of sharing the guilt and resigning collectively with the army commanders. Shaken by this ultimatum, the Egyptian president agreed to the first alternative. Thus, in a television speech to the nation the night of June 10, Nasser declared his willingness to "bear the whole responsibility," and summarily tendered his resignation. It was a shattering moment for the Egyptian people. Exultant only four days earlier, they were reduced now to stunned consternation. Cairo, a city of eight million people, and the very nerve center of Islamic power and culture, lay open to the Israeli enemy. Army soldiers were stationed throughout the capital to protect its main institutions.

After several hours of near-catatonia, however, the nation awakened, then erupted. Two million people—perhaps more—suddenly flooded the streets of Cairo. Much of the population of Tantah, the "eye" of the Delta, began marching on the capital. Elsewhere, from the larger cities, from hundreds of towns and villages, from Alexandria to Aswan, from the Western Desert to Suez, a whole country marched, shouting the revolutionary battle hymn, "B'ladi, b'ladi, fidaki dami—My Fatherland, O Fatherland, Yours is My Blood." In defeat or victory, Nasser apparently remained synonymous with that fatherland. Demonstrations of support for the beleaguered *sayyid*, appeals for him to remain, exploded like a thunderstorm. Three hours later, as a result, much to Israel's chagrin and bemusement, Nasser announced that he had "reconsidered" and would stay on. Amer and the military commanders had lost their bid. They would pay.

THE DIMENSIONS OF THE WAR

Meanwhile, Israel's official silence during the early hours of the war, and Egypt's contrasting boasts of far-reaching victories, influenced the precipitous decisions of Syria, Jordan, and Iraq to enter the fighting. The Syrians forfeited their best opportunity for an offensive, however. Before June, their military staff had formulated plans to move down from the Golan in strength, to capture eastern Galilee, then to proceed on toward Haifa. Yet, when hostilities began on June 5, the Syrians at the last minute adopted a wait-and-see attitude and preferred simply to shell the Galilee town of Rosh Pina, and the next day to venture a limited, unsuccessful move against several Israeli border kibbutz settlements. The Ba'athist government, too, would pay bitterly for this miscalculation.

The Jordanian blunder was even more catastrophic. On the morning of June 5, Cairo informed Amman that 75 percent of Israel's planes had been destroyed and that Egyptian forces were deep inside Israeli territory. With rare candor, Hussein admitted later that "we were misinformed about what had happened in Egypt when the Israelis attacked the UAR bases. . . . These reports—fantastic to say the least—had much to do with our confusion and false interpretation of the situation." Hussein thereafter acceded to the request of General Riad, the Egyptian liaison officer in Amman, for Jordanian troops to launch an attack against Israeli Jerusalem and to shell Israeli towns and bases. "Throughout the first day," Hussein wrote later, "our batteries . . . kept pounding at the outskirts of Tel Aviv, its concentration of military targets, and the airport at Lydda."

But it was Israeli—New—Jerusalem that was Hussein's most compelling target. The city's Jewish population of 190,000 was immediately exposed to Arab attack from the surrounding mountain ridges. Particularly vulnerable, too, was the tiny Israeli enclave on Mount Scopus on the Jordanian side of the city. Shooting from the Arab positions broke out at midmorning on June 5. Firing soon intensified, and Arab shells began hitting populated areas. In response, the Israeli air force launched its bombing runs on the Amman and Mafraq airfields, liquidating the entire Hashemite fighter fleet. At 1:˄ ˆ P.M., either by prearrangement or in a counterretaliatory spasm, Arab Legionᵢₗ crossed the Jerusalem armistice line and occupied the United Nations Supervision Headquarters on the demilitarized Hill of Evil Counsel.

At this point, with Dayan's approval, Rabin finally issued the orders to his Jerusalem area commander: "Retake Government [United Nations] House, link up with [Mount] Scopus, and protect the Jerusalem high ground by any means." Simultaneously, an Israeli armored brigade was dispatched from its encampment in the Jerusalem Corridor and ordered to push through to the ridges between Jerusalem and Ramallah. The brigade accomplished this feat with the help of devastating tactical air support. By the morning of June 6, Israeli armor controlled the Jerusalem mountain ridges. This strategic advantage in turn determined the future of the entire Hashemite West Bank, for the mountain range looked down on the region's most important towns: Jenin, Nablus, Ramallah, Bethlehem, Hebron, and Jericho, as well as Jerusalem itself. By late morning of June 7, ravaged by aerial strafing and bombing, Jordan's last brigades collapsed as fighting units. All the major cities of the West Bank were in Israel's hands.

That same morning, finally, a battalion of Israeli paratroops moved against the Lion's Gate, a major entrance to the walled Old City of Jerusalem that had been captured by the Arabs in the 1948 war. Rolling through the narrow Via Dolorosa, the column made directly for the ancient Temple Mount and reached it after a last, bitter firefight. The Wall, the Moslem holy places—the Dome of the Rock and the al-Aqsa Mosque—all were in Jewish hands. Arab resistance then ceased. For his impulsive gamble, Hussein had been stripped of half his kingdom, as well as the last Hashemite claim on Islam's holy places in Jerusalem.

The final decision awaiting the Israeli government was the action to be taken against Syria. It seemed intolerable to the cabinet and to the army command that a nation whose border incendiarism in large measure had precipitated the current war should now be allowed to keep the strategic advantage of the Golan Heights. All the more so, as Syrian gunners on the plateau continued to rain shells upon Galilee's northern settlements. On the evening of June 8, therefore, as the war ended on other fronts, the government agreed to shift its manpower for a "punitive" campaign against the Syrians. Early the next day Dayan gave General David Elazar, the northern front commander, final approval for an offensive.

The attack began at noon of June 9, as the Israelis set out to ascend the Golan, with bulldozers clearing the rocks, followed by tanks, then infantrymen bringing up the rear. Confounded by Elazar's frontal route of attack in broad daylight, the Syrians initially regarded it as a feint. They were unable in any case to summon reinforcements; for two days the Israeli air force had been savagely bombing the Golan ridges. Eventually the first wave of Israeli infantry managed to ascend to the Syrian positions, and by darkness the Jews had achieved two bridgeheads on the heights. At this juncture, with the main Golan fortifications cracked, the Arabs panicked; their troops began fleeing. As the Israeli pincers closed on the plateau during the afternoon of June 10, Damascus agreed to a cease-fire. The Six-Day War ended officially at 6:30 P.M., Israel time, that same day.

Israel had lost 759 troops killed in the fighting, and approximately three times that many wounded. The nation's equipment losses were 50 planes, 80 tanks, and some thousand personnel carriers of all types. The Arabs suffered up to 30,000 casualties (the Egyptians, two-thirds of these), and at least 450 planes and 1,000 tanks, as well as vast quantities of supplementary equipment, were destroyed. More important, a new military-geographic reality had been created in the Middle East. Before the war, Tel Aviv had lain within four minutes' flying time of the nearest Sinai air base. Much of Israel's narrow waistline had fallen within Arab artillery range, as had Jewish Jerusalem and the northern Galilee settlements. Now, after the war, the situation was reversed. Israeli planes and troops were within close striking distance of Amman, Damascus, and Cairo itself. No Israeli population center was on the firing line any longer. In the north, the heights overlooking the Chula and Jordan valleys lay in Jewish hands. In the east, Israel had pushed its long and involuted border with Jordan to the comparatively straight north-south line of the River Jordan and the Dead Sea. In the south, the 200-mile frontier between the Negev and Sinai deserts, with its threatening spike of the Gaza Strip into Israel, was replaced by the 110-mile barrier of the Suez Canal. Any future Israeli-Egyptian war would affect the heavily populated Canal cities.

RESOLUTION 242

On the afternoon of June 13, following confirmation of the cease-fires, Soviet Ambassador Federenko in the Security Council demanded that Israel be condemned and instructed unconditionally to withdraw to the 1949 armistice lines. Only four delegations supported this proposal. Federenko then asked Secretary-General U Thant to order the General Assembly into special session. The United Nations body accordingly convened on June 19. As a gesture of support to Cairo, Prime Minister Kosygin himself arrived to deliver his government's first statement. Accusing the United States and Britain of moral complicity in Israeli aggression, Kosygin asked once again for a condemnation of Israel, for Israeli withdrawal from occupied Arab territory, and for financial restitution to the Arab countries. The proposal won the swift endorsement of the Arab-Moslem-Communist blocs.

It failed to impress the United States. Once more the American delegation argued that a stable and durable peace could be achieved only through negotiated arrangements. As the Israelis gratefully noted, too, the American formulation declined to assert that withdrawal necessarily required an evacuation of Israeli forces to the 1949 armistice lines. In the end, neither the Soviet nor the American resolutions seemed likely to achieve two-thirds majority approval. Thus, during a week's reprieve in the General Assembly session, between July 5 and July 12, the search for a compromise formula went on. It foundered against entrenched Arab hostility to an accommodation with Israel, and against an equally intransigent Israeli refusal to contemplate even partial withdrawal except through direct peace negotiations with the Arabs.

Three months later, however, events in the Middle East itself took a critical new turn. On October 21, Egyptian missile boats sank an Israeli destroyer, and three days after that the Israelis retaliated by shelling oil installations in the Egyptian port town of Suez. Immediately the Security Council intensified its peace-seeking efforts. In mid-November, as a consequence largely of strenuous intermediary diplomacy by Britain's delegate, Lord Caradon, negotiations at last began to bear fruit. A formula was hammered out acceptable to a majority of the Security Council delegations, and on November 22 it was accepted unanimously as Security Council Resolution 242. On several points the document's text was deliberately ambiguous. It stated:

> The Security Council . . . [e]mphasizing the inadmissibility of the acquisition of territory by war and the need to work for a just and lasting peace in which every State in the area can live in security. . . .
> 1. Affirms that the fulfilment of Charter principles requires the establishment of a just and lasting peace in the Middle East which should include the application of both the following principles:
>> i. Withdrawal of Israeli armed forces from territories occupied in the recent conflict;
>> ii. Termination of all claims or states of belligerency and respect for and acknowledgment of the sovereignty, territorial integrity and political independence of every State in the area and their right to live in peace within secure and recognized boundaries free from threats or acts of force;
>
> 2. Affirms further the necessity
>> i. For guaranteeing freedom of navigation through international waterways in the area;
>> ii. For achieving a just settlement of the refugee problem;

GREATER ISRAEL
AFTER JUNE 10, 1967

Israeli territory 1949–June 10, 1967

Israeli conquests June 5–11, 1967

New Israeli settlements
in the Sinai Peninsula

0   MILES   50

Beirut

LEBANON

Damascus

SYRIA

al-Quneitra

GOLAN
HEIGHTS

Haifa   L. GALILEE

Nazareth

Netania   Jenin
Tulkarem

Nablus

Jordan River

Tel Aviv-Jaffa   WEST
BANK   Amman

Ashdod   Jerusalem   Jericho

Ashkelon   Bethlehem

Nachal Nezarim   Hebron

Nachal Samiri   Gaza

Nachal Morag   DEAD SEA

Nachal D'kalim   Kfar Darom

Sadot (Rafah)   Beersheba

Port Saîd   Minyam

al-Arish

Nachal Yam   Yamit   Nachal Sinai

Abu Agheila   NEGEV
DESERT   JORDAN

Ismailia

Suez Canal

Bir Gafgafa (Refidim)

GIDI PASS

MITLA PASS

Suez   al-Quntilla

SINAI PENINSULA

Eilat   Aqaba

E   G   Y   P   T

MEDITERRANEAN SEA

Abu Rudeis   Moshav N'viot

GULF OF SUEZ

GULF OF AQABA

SAUDI ARABIA

MT. SINAI   Di-Zahav

al-Tur

TIRAN I.

STRAIT OF TIRAN

Sharm es-Sheikh (Ophira)

RED SEA

iii. For guaranteeing the territorial inviolability and political independence of every State in the area, through measures including the establishment of demilitarized zones;

3. Requests of the Security Council to designate a Special Representative to proceed to the Middle East to . . . promote agreement and assist efforts to achieve a peaceful and accepted settlement in accordance with the provisions and principles in this resolution. . . .

The Arabs put their own interpretation on Resolution 242: the inadmissibility of acquiring territory by war, and settlement of the refugee question. Israel, conversely, placed its emphasis on the absence of the article "the" before "territories," implying, in its view (and in that of the United States), a commitment to less than full withdrawal; on the recognition of sovereign integrity and renunciation of force in the Middle East; on guaranteed freedom of passage through international waters; and on a special representative to "promote agreement and assist efforts to achieve a peaceful and accepted settlement"—meaning (as Israel saw it) a final negotiated settlement. It appeared to be a not unencouraging valedictory to what was, after all, an offensive military campaign, and a resolution that contrasted dramatically with the universal censure that had greeted Israel's Sinai victory in 1956. This time, too, a majority of the United Nations representatives shared the new atmosphere of mild but purposeful optimism. At long last, they speculated, a rational and peaceful solution appeared within sight for the envenomed Arab-Israeli confrontation. To professional diplomats, it was an eventuality that only months earlier would have appeared hardly less than miraculous.

XIII

THE AFTERMATH OF
TRAUMA,
THE WAR OF ATTRITION

ISRAEL CONSOLIDATES ITS VICTORY

The breadth of Israel's achievement in the Six-Day War was to be measured not alone in the nation's overpowering sense of collective deliverance, or in the wreckage of the Egyptian and other Arab armies. Fully 28,000 square miles of terrain (and not less than a million Arab subjects) had fallen unexpectedly into Jewish possession. For the first time in its history, the Israeli republic had won a meaningful defense in geographical depth. On June 13 Prime Minister Eshkol addressed the Knesset and made plain that his country's enemies no longer were dealing with the straitened little Israel of June 5:

> Let this be said—there should be no illusions that Israel is prepared to return to the conditions that existed a week ago. . . . We have fought alone for our existence and our security, and we are therefore justified in deciding for ourselves what are the genuine and indispensable interests of our state, and how to guarantee its future.

The Eshkol cabinet was determined, too, not simply to achieve direct negotiations with the Egyptians and Arabs, to hold fast to land it had conquered until peace was guaranteed, but to inform the world at large that certain territories lay beyond the realm of negotiation. Thus, on June 27, the Knesset passed three laws designed in effect to annex Arab Jerusalem. Elsewhere, on the west bank of the Jordan, lay the biblical heartland of the Children of Israel— Samaria and Sh'chem (Nablus), Hebron and Jericho—and the Israeli government warned that these historical associations, like those with Jerusalem, had now to be "taken into account."

The conqueror's initial occupation of the West Bank was entirely benign, however. Dayan, responsible as defense minister for territories under army rule, ordered the various command centers to be located discreetly away from principal thoroughfares. The cabinet in turn agreed that Hashemite laws would remain operative throughout the West Bank, and would continue to be enforced largely by the prewar Arab administration. In the Gaza enclave, civil government similarly would be directed by resident Arab officials. In August 1967, too, all prohibitions on Israeli travel to the occupied areas were canceled; free crossing was allowed from Jewish territory to the West Bank and Gaza. Several months later the process became two-way, as West Bank and Gaza Arabs were allowed to cross into integral Israel, and then afterward even to accept employment opportunities in Israel. As a result, the number of commuting Arab laborers reached 15,000 daily by June 1968, and within the year would climb to nearly 100,000.

Yet it was freedom of travel in another direction, between the West Bank and the Hashemite East Bank, that ultimately ensured the viability of the "administered" territories. To allow West Bank farmers access to the Hashemite market, Dayan within weeks of the occupation authorized a full two-way movement of people and produce. This decision not only salvaged the economy of the West Bank, but also protected the Arab inhabitants there from any sense of cultural or social isolation. Manifestly, there were psychological hardships to be endured under Israeli administration. But if the largest numbers of West Bank and Gaza inhabitants eventually came to accept their altered status as dependants of the Jews, it was because the emerging material advantages of cooperation—including, for the first time, full employment for hundreds of thousands of encamped refugees—were far greater than the Arab population had ever experienced or imagined.

THE DIPLOMACY OF REJECTION

After the June war, the Israeli government publicly and repeatedly made known its minimal conditions for peace. These included direct negotiations and a formal treaty, free passage of Israeli ships through the Suez Canal as well as through the Strait of Tiran, and a solution of the refugee problem within the framework of a de jure treaty compact. On this basis, too, the Eshkol cabinet agreed to enter into discussions with Dr. Gunnar Jarring, the envoy appointed by the United Nations under the mandate of Security Council Resolution 242. A stocky, middle-aged career diplomat, until recently Sweden's ambassador to Moscow, Jarring began his mission in November 1967 with visits to Lebanon, Israel, Jordan, and Egypt.

Of all the belligerents, Jordan had suffered by far the most grievous territorial losses, and presumably would have been the likeliest of the Arab candidates for Jarring's intermediary efforts. Indeed, as early as June 18, 1967, King Hussein intimated that he was at last prepared to accept the State of Israel within the framework of a comprehensive peace settlement. Lacking the status of a popularly elected representative, however, the diminutive monarch was hardly in a position to negotiate authoritatively. Most of the Palestinians in his kingdom gave more attention to the "Voice of Cairo" than to the "Voice of Amman." Nasser had warned Hussein, too, that "the question of Jerusalem is not a purely Jordanian matter, but one for all Arabs and all Moslems." More ominously yet, Iraq maintained a division of troops along Jordan's northern border. It was not possible for Hussein to ignore the reaction of these hostile, left-wing governments.

Damascus, meanwhile, evinced less interest in a peace settlement than did any other of Israel's foes. Although the Golan Heights were in Israeli hands, the economic—as distinguished from the strategic—value of this plateau had never been very great. Moreover, the Ba'ath party, clinging to office by sufferance of a notoriously mercurial population, dared not make public acknowledgment either of Israel's victory or of Israel's right to exist. As a result, President Nurredin al-Atassi and his cabinet declined so much as to receive Dr. Jarring; the United Nations mediator simply bypassed Syria altogether. Two years later, in fact, the Hafez-Atassi regime in Damascus was overthrown by a group of officers under the leadership of General Hafez al-Assad, and based upon an even more uncertain power base of ultra-left-wing Alawite militants. Prospects for Syrian-Israeli peace thereafter became entirely unrealistic.

Among the various Arab leaders, Gamal Abd al-Nasser was the man for whom the June defeat had been the gravest humiliation. The loss of Sinai may not have inflicted a crippling economic blow, but the closure of Suez was far more painful; following their earlier precedent of 1956, the Egyptians had sunk ships in the Canal, effectively blocking it for traffic. The absence of maritime tolls subsequently was costing Egypt $30 million a month in lost revenues. The magnitude of this deprivation, together with the immolation of Egypt's armed forces, inevitably eroded Nasser's once unchallengeable personal prestige. For the while, he had been saved by his celebrated charisma, and by the centralist tradition in Egyptian society. Yet the president was by no means oblivious, following his battlefield humiliation in the Six-Day War, to the growing uncertainty of his tenure in office.

Nasser's initial priority, then, in the aftermath of disaster, was to reassert his authority over the revolutionary officers. He moved swiftly to that end, forcing Abd al-Hakim Amer and Shams Badran to resign. When other senior commanders angrily protested, Nasser ordered the latter's dismissal on June 11, and soon afterward purged hundreds of other officers. At this point, Amer himself decided to move to the counteroffensive. In August, he and his followers made plans to seize the headquarters of the armored corps, of the Eastern (Suez) Command, and of Camp Dahshar south of Cairo. Nasser and his aides would then be arrested. It was a close thing. The coup was nipped only hours before it was scheduled to be launched. Amer was seized, then "persuaded" to commit suicide. By October, Nasser was in full control once more.

Yet the principal anchor that sustained the Egyptian *rais* in the immediate aftermath of the 1967 debacle was the Soviet Union. Recognizing then that both Egypt and Syria were on the verge of collapse, Moscow dispatched President Nikolai Podgorny to Cairo on June 21, and to Damascus and Baghdad eight days later, with promises of immediate and decisive Soviet aid. Within two weeks, in fact, over 200 crated fighter planes were airlifted to these Arab countries, and throughout the summer three or four ships a week arrived in Alexandria and Latakia carrying other weaponry. By June of 1968, the Soviets had replaced fully $1.2 billion in military hardware lost by the Egyptians and Syrians. The vast replacement effort was supplemented, as well, by the arrival in Egypt of not less than 10,000 Soviet-bloc advisers and technicians. Their assignment was to participate in all phases of Egyptian military planning, training, and air defense.

Nasser reciprocated this largesse in January 1968 by granting the Soviet navy full support facilities at Port Saïd and Alexandria. Formalized three months later in a secret five-year pact, the naval agreement at long last provided the Russians with their coveted warm-water base in the Mediterranean. Moscow was interested in still other concessions, however. It pressed for a more emphatically "Socialist" orientation of the Egyptian economy. And once again Nasser obliged, agreeing to structure his heavy industry in an "authentically Socialist" manner. Thereafter, he dutifully parroted the Soviet line in international affairs, as well.

It was specifically the Egyptian president's success in quelling internal opposition, and in winning assurance of Soviet military and economic support, that allowed him subsequently to repudiate the "shame" of a negotiated peace. "We shall never surrender and shall not accept any peace that means surrender," he assured his shaken people on July 23, 1967. Earlier, on June 17, the foreign ministers of thirteen Arab countries had met in Kuwait to map a joint political strategy. Under heavy Egyptian pressure, the assembled delegates agreed to "restore Arab honor"—a key proviso that Israel and other nations seriously underestimated at the time. Later the kings and presidents of these nations gathered in Khartoum from August 29 to September 1 to pledge: no peace with Israel, no negotiations with Israel, no recognition of Israel, and "maintenance of the rights of the Palestinian people in their nation." To sustain their confrontation with the Zionist republic, moreover, the delegates established an inter-Arab fund to assist the war-ravaged economies of Egypt and Jordan. By then the Israelis, if not the Western members of the United Nations, sensed that their expectation of an imminent peace overture from the Arab world might be a fantasy.

There had been other, military, auguries of prolonged confrontation. Throughout late June and early July 1967, the Egyptians ignored the cease-fire and mounted several commando efforts to breach the Canal. These were easily foiled, but they provoked firefights, even artillery exchanges. Although Egypt and Israel subsequently allowed United Nations observers to be stationed on both sides of the waterway, the monitoring effort availed little. Fighting continued, and grew particularly intense by the autumn. One outburst of October 2 touched off a renewed exodus of Egyptian civilians from Suez City (60,000 of the town's 250,000 inhabitants already had fled). These eruptions reached a climax on October 21 with the sinking of the Israeli destroyer *Eilat* by Soviet-built Styx missiles fired by an Egyptian naval vessel off the Sinai coast, and Israel's retaliatory destruction of oil installations in Suez City.

The Jarring Mission to the Middle East in November and December 1967 similarly failed to advance the effort for peace. It is recalled that Damascus was unwilling even to receive the Swedish diplomat. The other Arab governments flatly declined to commit themselves to negotiations. Undaunted, Jarring proceeded afterward to set up headquarters in Cyprus, intending to bring Arab and Israeli representatives there. This, too, was wasted effort. A few months later, nevertheless, the mediator raised the possibility of encouraging bilateral Israeli-Arab talks in New York; then, toward the end of 1968, of a "next-door-rooms" formula, with Jarring shuttling between separate Israeli and Arab delegations. Nasser scotched these and other plans. A possible compromise solution of "nonbelligerency" (never peace) might eventually be possible, the Egyptian president hinted, but only after "full Israeli withdrawal" from occupied Arab territory. As Henry Kissinger wrote later, "[Nasser] never explained what incentive Israel had for withdrawal in the face of a peace settlement based solely on the unconditional withdrawal of the victor from the territory it had conquered." It was a nonstarter, and doubtless intended as such. For Nasser, the prospect even of offering recognition to Israel signified hardly less than a psychological trauma.

THE PLO UPSTAGES NASSER

Defiance was not yet a substitute for impotence, however. With Egypt and the other Arab states evidently incapable of blocking Israel's new army settlements on the West Bank, the Golan, and eastern Sinai, some Palestine Arabs devised their own response to this "creeping annexation." Before the war, it is recalled (p. 140), a growing campaign of border violence had been mounted by the al-Fatah organization. Now, after the June debacle, it was again this cabal of irregulars that revived its activities—and expanded them with shattering force and political influence throughout the Arab world. Leadership in the renewed guerrilla upsurge was provided by one Yasser Arafat, a balding, heavyset man in his late thirties, and a distant relative of the ex-Mufti of Jerusalem, Haj Muhammad Amin al-Husseini.

In September 1967, under Arafat's direction, the Fatah launched its postwar operations in several West Bank towns. Grenades were thrown at Israeli patrols.

To intimidate local Arabs commuting to Jewish work projects, bombs were detonated in village squares, in marketplaces and in bus terminals. From February 1968 on, as West Bank and Gaza Arabs continued to accept employment in integral Israel, episodes of Fatah sabotage similarly mounted in Jewish territory. Soon explosions were going off at the rate of thirty a month. Drastic as these measures were, however, Arafat and his followers were unsuccessful in their major purpose—of igniting a war of "national liberation" among the occupied Arab territories. Within months after their June victory, Israel's security forces were effectively countering every attempt to touch off a popular armed rising. Thus, by the end of 1968, some 1,400 Fatah members had been killed or captured in the West Bank alone, and Arafat himself was obliged to flee his secret headquarters in Nablus and to take refuge across the Jordan.

Thereafter, the guerrillas were thrown back to their pattern of the mid-1960s. They were limited to short forays across the river, to harassment of Jewish settlements in the Beit Sh'an and Jordan valleys. But, again, the Israelis refined their techniques of sealing off the Hashemite frontier, through patrols, ambushes, electrified fences, even retaliatory air strikes. In one such air retaliation of June 1968, the Jews destroyed the principal Fatah headquarters at es-Salt and killed more than seventy of Arafat's commandos. Ensconced deeply in Jordanian refugee camps, then, Fatah and other irregulars, now operating loosely under the umbrella of the "Palestine Liberation Organization," soon posed a far greater threat to King Hussein than to Israel. Indeed, the fedayeen managed to establish a virtual substate of their own on Hashemite territory, boasting immunity to Hashemite laws, claiming extraterritorial rights, organizing their own rival armies, and ultimately—by mob demonstrations and assassinations—even extracting from Hussein a veto over Jordanian government cabinet appointments.

THE WAR OF ATTRITION

Against this record of Palestinian guerrilla activism, Nasser's comparative impotence during most of 1967 and early 1968 appeared all the more glaring. Yet the Egyptian president would not allow himself to be overshadowed for long, either at home or in the Arab world at large. It hardly escaped him that, except for scattered Bedouin tribes, none of Egypt's citizens was under Israeli rule. When, therefore, at the Khartoum Conference of August–September 1967, he led the assembled Arab leaders in refusal to countenance negotiations with Israel, he understood shrewdly that he faced no imminent danger of Israeli reprisal against a hostage Egyptian population. By then, too, evidence of domestic unrest already was surfacing in the aftermath of defeat, led by a combination of students, Moslem fundamentalists, and crypto-Communists.

Under the circumstances, Nasser was convinced that he had more to gain politically now by salvaging his reputation on the battlefield.

As has been seen, the president's hand already was being strengthened by the Russians, who viewed Israel's pulverizing 1967 victory as an intolerable challenge to their own, no less than to Egypt's, hegemony in the Middle East. Fifteen months after the war, thanks to unprecedented infusions of Soviet weaponry and military advisers, Egypt's air and armored strength already surpassed its pre-1967 levels. Yet it seemed unlikely at first that the Egyptians were capable of launching a major counteroffensive against Israel. Nowhere did the Suez Canal appear to be suited to crossings in strength. The Sinai itself was formidable enough an obstacle, for that matter, once the Israelis began constructing defense installations in the peninsula.

As a result, the pattern of violence along the Canal developed erratically. In the early aftermath of war, it was characterized by sporadic outbursts. Each Egyptian probe from the west bank of the waterway evoked a tough counterblow from the Israelis. One particularly heavy artillery exchange in late summer of 1967, we recall, forced the evacuation of tens of thousands of civilians from Suez City and Ismailia. Then came the sinking of the Israeli destroyer *Eilat*, followed by Israeli shelling of Egyptian oil installations at Suez City. Egyptian infantry raids across the Canal in turn provoked Israeli helicopter-borne counterattacks against targets in the Egyptian interior.

Nevertheless, Israeli counterstrikes failed to deter the Egyptians from renewed artillery and commando attacks. The Canal was as effective a barrier for Egypt as it was for Israel, after all, and the slashing offensive war the Israelis had conducted in June 1967 plainly was out of the question afterward. By the autumn of 1968, a military standoff had developed. As it turned out, October 1968 witnessed a rising crescendo of Suez hostilities. In a single Saturday afternoon a massive Egyptian artillery barrage killed fifteen Israelis and demonstrated that Egypt had accumulated a vast superiority of men and equipment west of the Canal. Israel's response in November was to launch another heliborne raid deep inside Egypt, blowing the sluices of the Nag-Hamadi barrage and destroying power installations in the area. The Egyptians were not given pause. Rather, on March 8, 1969, they loosed a particularly concentrated shelling of Israeli fortifications on the east bank. Continuing for two days, the salvos inflicted dozens of Israeli casualties. The pattern of blow and counterblow continued during March and April.

By then the revived hostilities had developed into nothing less than an overt Egyptian "war of attrition." On April 23, 1969, Nasser announced that henceforth he would regard the June 1967 cease-fire agreement as null and void "due to Israel's refusal to implement the Security Council Resolution [242] of November 1967." His goal, quite simply, was to prevent the transformation of the Canal into a de facto border, and to accomplish this by wreaking such havoc on the understrength Israeli defense force that the Jews either would be forced back into Sinai, or their government compelled to accept a political solution on Cairo's terms. Nor were the Israelis sluggish in appreciating Nasser's logic. The devastating Egyptian bombardment of October 1968 clearly dictated a revision of tactics. "We must reply with a fighting refusal to any effort to push us off the cease-fire line," Dayan insisted. To ensure that posture, his troops began digging into hardened concrete and steel-reinforced bunkers. These were known subsequently as the Bar-Lev Line, after Israel's then chief of staff, General Chaim Bar-Lev. With the completion of the fortifications in March 1969, the Israeli general staff expected to withstand the developing war of attrition.

Yet the weight of prolonged Egyptian artillery bombardment, and of occasional Egyptian commando attacks in western Sinai, took its toll—of both sides. Israeli casualties rose to seventy a month by July 1969. Egypt's were not listed, but unquestionably were much higher. Dayan's response to enemy pressure was to intensify the countershelling of industrial and civilian targets across the Canal. Ismailia, Port Saïd, Port Fuad, and Port Tewfik were particularly hard hit, with numerous casualties and extensive damage. On July 20, Israeli air, land, and naval forces attacked positions in Gezira al-Qadra on the Gulf of Suez, shooting down five Egyptian MiGs in the process. Israeli fighter-bombers similarly began raiding Egyptian SAM-2 antiaircraft missile sites. At the end of the month, following two air encounters in which twelve additional MiGs were brought down, Nasser felt obliged to dismiss the commander of his air force. The change availed little. Soon afterward, on October 9, an Israeli amphibious force crossed the Gulf of Suez at Zafrarran. In a daring foray up the Nile, a commando unit of this expedition destroyed a network of military installations and killed over 100 Egyptian soldiers. It was a debacle for Egypt, and when Nasser finally learned of it, he replaced his chief of staff and his naval commander. The nation's air defense capability was virtually nonexistent by then, and the morale of the Egyptian army had all but collapsed. Only days afterward, Nasser himself suffered a serious heart attack and was put to bed for a month and a half. Israeli intelligence was apprised of this development. Tightening the screws, Dayan ordered air attacks launched on army bases deep inside Egypt. Thus, some twenty targets were bombed in January, February, and March of 1970. Israeli and American analysts estimated at this point that the Egyptians had suffered as many as 10,000 dead and wounded.

Nor were Israel's casualties negligible. By spring of 1970 they numbered approximately 2,000—approaching the losses incurred in the Six-Day War itself. Yet the nation drew some assurance not only from its continuing military supremacy but from the absence of the kind of international pressures it had experienced following the 1956 Sinai Campaign. Moscow was irredeemably hostile, of course. Except for France, however, now adopting an overtly pro-Arab stance, virtually all Western governments understood that Israel could not be bullied any longer into a unilateral evacuation of the occupied territories.

Washington was particularly supportive. After the 1967 war, the Johnson administration categorically endorsed Israel's insistence on direct negotiations with the Arabs, and its demand for a formal peace treaty assuring the Jewish state secure and defensible boundaries. In 1969 the newly elected Nixon administration reaffirmed this policy, agreeing to provide Israel with the latest model Phantom jets, far superior to the Soviet MiG interceptors then available to Egypt.

Notwithstanding this support, there were periods of tactical divergence between Jerusalem and Washington. As the winter of 1969 passed, with violence mounting ominously along the Canal, Washington and Moscow reached agreement on the format of a Big Four conference to deal with the Middle Eastern crisis. Ostensibly its purpose would be to "develop a substantive framework in which parties directly concerned can develop a dialogue." Yet the blueprint submitted by Secretary of State William Rogers on December 9, 1969, went well beyond a "format." Under the "Rogers Plan," Israel would evacuate all Arab lands in return for an Arab pledge of a binding peace treaty with Israel; Israel would be guaranteed freedom of passage through international waterways; the Palestine refugees would be allowed to choose between repatriation and compensation; Jordan and Israel would seek direct agreement on the future of Jerusalem; and the issues of Sharm es-Sheikh and Gaza would be reserved for future Egyptian-Israeli negotiations.

The scheme appalled the Israelis. Not since the Eisenhower-Dulles period had an American administration sought to define the scope of a projected Israeli withdrawal, and thereby to foreclose an Arab incentive for negotiations. Worse yet, from Jerusalem's viewpoint, was Rogers's contention that Israeli-Arab negotiations should follow the "Rhodes formula" of 1949. It was a "formula" that would have blurred the issue of whether Arabs and Israelis were talking face-to-face—for Israel the acid test of Arab sincerity and trustworthiness. In Eban's view (and in that of Henry Kissinger), the Rogers Plan was "undoubtedly one of the major errors of international diplomacy in the postwar era."

By this time, too, a new prime minister was sitting in Jerusalem. She was Mrs. Golda Meir, who had succeeded Eshkol upon the latter's death of a heart attack in March 1969. Reared in the United States, Golda Mabovich Meyerson had settled in Palestine in 1931. During the 1930s, her career in the labor federation and Labor party executives substantially paralleled those of Ben-Gurion and Eshkol. Afterward, as Israel's minister to Moscow, later as minister of labor, and then subsequently as foreign minister, Mrs. Meir consistently adopted a plainspoken, bluntly straightforward approach in her dealings with Israelis and non-Israelis alike. A seventy-one-year-old grandmother at the time she assumed the prime ministry, Mrs. Meir was incapable either by age or temperament of modifying her views of the Arabs as perennial enemies, with whom one dealt not in trust but out of strength. It was to her considerable relief, therefore, that Nasser himself rebuffed the Rogers scheme in December 1969, describing it as "one-sided and pro-Israeli." And the moment the Egyptians rejected the plan, the Soviets also felt obliged to renege. For the time being, the State Department dropped its exploratory notion of a Great Power solution.

THE SOVIET-ISRAELI CONFRONTATION

Until the autumn of 1969, Israel's military policy in the War of Attrition had remained one of controlled response. But the spectacular raid of October 9 across the Gulf of Suez was a terrifying humiliation for the Egyptians. Late in December, yet another Israeli amphibious raid captured the Red Sea island of Shadwan and transported off an entire marine radar station, killing 70 Egyptian troops in the process. Once Egypt was all but stripped of its radar protection, moreover, Israeli jets crossed the cease-fire line at will, bombing targets less than twelve miles from Cairo. Dayan coupled these raids with a warning, on January 7, 1970, that attacks into the interior would continue until Egypt's government respected the cease-fire along the Canal (from Washington, Yitzchak Rabin, the former chief of staff and currently Israel's ambassador to the United States, was pressing his government to launch bombing attacks on Cairo itself). Hereupon Nasser panicked. Departing on an urgent visit to Moscow, he explained his country's desperate plight to the Soviet leadership, and admitted that his own political tenure now was in doubt. Nasser then pleaded for Soviet bombers and pilots to be used for retaliatory attacks against Israeli cities.

The Russians demurred. They were unwilling to risk a confrontation with the United States. They did agree, however, to participate more actively in defending Egyptian military and civilian targets. Indeed, such a defense would fulfill an even more direct Soviet purpose. Russian pilots operating from Egyptian fields would be in a position to reconnoiter both the Mediterranean and the Red Sea—and Western naval forces in those regions. Accordingly, Soviet-manned planes began flying their reconnaissance missions from Egyptian bases. Others were on interception alert at fields around Cairo, even as Soviet personnel operated SAM-3 antiaircraft batteries around the Egyptian capital. For the first time in its history, then, Moscow had committed itself to direct participation in the defense of a non-Communist nation. Additionally, throughout the winter and spring of 1970, scores of freighters departed Black Sea ports with extensive new equipment for Egypt. Within six months, too, the Russians had increased to 14,000 the numbers of their instructors and advisers in Egypt, and had assembled an impressive naval flotilla of sixty vessels off the Egyptian coast—an armada nearly the equal of the United States Sixth Fleet.

Learning of these developments, the Israelis in April 1970 reluctantly suspended their deep penetration raids. On the other hand, as the Egyptians began moving new SAM missile and artillery batteries toward the Canal, Israeli air attacks on this equipment rapidly approached the scale and devastation of

American raids in Vietnam. The bombing and strafing failed to slow the Egyptian encroachment. Rather, with each Israeli raid, the Soviets expanded the perimeter of their defensive responsibilities, until at the end of June Russian pilots were flying combat patrols on the northern and southern outlets of the Canal, and only fifty miles from the Canal Zone itself. The Egyptian-Soviet defense system was further thickened with the introduction of SAM-4 and SAM-6 missiles, and in late June and early July these rockets shot down seven Israeli Phantoms. By then Jerusalem recognized that it was facing its gravest military crisis since the weeks preceding the 1967 war. The battle on the Canal had been transformed almost overnight into a Soviet-Israeli confrontation.

Thus, on July 25, a flight of Soviet MiGs jumped two Israeli light bombers attacking a position on the Canal's west bank. The Israelis escaped. Five days later, however, Israeli jets in turn ambushed a squadron of Soviet fighters over the Gulf of Suez, shooting down four of them. The shock of these encounters was at least as great for Moscow as for Jerusalem. The successful challenge of a Soviet-constructed air system, one superior even to that of the Warsaw Pact, might well have a grave impact on the European confrontation. Two days later, then, Soviet Air Marshal Pavel Kutakhov flew into Cairo. During Kutakhov's ensuing investigation, Soviet pilots avoided further contact with Israeli planes. The Meir government had warned clearly that it did not consider the Russians invincible, and that Israel was prepared to create a Vietnam for the Soviets, if the latter wanted it.

The Soviets did not. Still less did the Egyptians. As it happened, on June 19, 1970, Secretary of State Rogers had proposed a "breathing space" for the Middle East. The plan (the "second Rogers Plan") envisaged: the acceptance of a cease-fire on the Egyptian front for three months, subject to renewal; a public acceptance by Israel, Egypt, and Jordan of the Security Council's Resolution 242 and, specifically, the call for "withdrawal from territories occupied by war"; an undertaking for those three nations to negotiate under Dr. Jarring's auspices when the cease-fire began. An additional provision of the cease-fire would be a standstill, with neither Egypt nor Israel to bring missiles or artillery closer to the front than before.

Interestingly enough, the Rogers Plan had not won the full approbation of President Nixon's staff. Henry Kissinger, the national security adviser, had pleaded with Nixon to drop the scheme, to opt instead for a hard line with Nasser, to pour additional planes into Israel, and to warn the Egyptian leader that he must entertain no hope of regaining the Sinai through exclusive dependence on the USSR. Yet Nixon shared Rogers's concern that escalating warfare along the Canal might lead to an American-Soviet confrontation. If, as he anticipated, Nasser rejected the secretary of state's proposal, then an increase of American arms supplies to Israel would prove less of an incitement to the Third World.

Much to Kissinger's surprise, Nasser decided to give the plan favorable consideration. By refusing to provide additional deterrent weapons, the Soviets evidently had left him with little alternative. "Anwar, the Soviet Union is a hopeless case," Nasser admitted to Sadat. On June 29, therefore, the Egyptian president flew to Moscow for a second emergency conference. The War of Attrition had lasted seventeen months, he explained to Kosygin and to Leonid Brezhnev, and during that time Egypt had witnessed the destruction of its oil refineries. The Canal cities had become empty husks, denuded of their inhabitants. Military targets deep inside Egypt had been ravaged. Over 15,000 military and civilian casualties had been sustained. The morale of the armed forces and of the nation at large had virtually collapsed. Upon completing this litany, and outlining his country's near-helplessness, Nasser won Soviet endorsement for acceptance of the American proposal.

The Israeli government, on the other hand, was in a quandary about the Rogers Plan, for its acceptance would have produced major domestic consequences. To be sure, both the Eshkol and Meir cabinets had previously accepted Resolution 242 in general terms. But a specific promise now to withdraw from the full "Land of Israel" in the context of Jordanian negotiations was a very different proposition. Such a concession would virtually have ensured the departure of Menachem Begin and of other center-rightists from the "Government of National Unity." Mrs. Meir's first response, then, was negative—even shrill and hostile.

It was a reaction she was unable to sustain for long. In ensuing weeks, Nixon deepened his commitment to Israeli security, promising additional Phantom aircraft and full support of Israel's right to hold fast to the cease-fire lines until a peace agreement was negotiated and signed. In consequence, on August 6, the Israeli cabinet voted to accept the American cease-fire proposal. It did so only upon receiving Egyptian and Soviet assurances, through Rogers, of a missile "standstill" in the Canal area. The cease-fire thereupon went into effect the following day, August 7 (and Begin promptly left the cabinet).

Immediately afterward, however, new Soviet missiles were redeployed within the cease-fire area. The evidence of this violation was first detected by Israeli intelligence, and afterward—belatedly—by American spy satellites. By then, too, the influx of Soviet advisers, together with the astonishing growth of the Soviet naval armada in the Mediterranean, had convinced Washington that the Kremlin intended to use Egypt as a permanent base for the surveillance of the Sixth Fleet. This sense of joint betrayal and anxiety, in turn, laid the groundwork for a much closer American-Israeli understanding. At Kissinger's recommendation, the United States in ensuing months shipped Israel substantial quantities of jet planes and other sophisticated weapons. Additionally, Washington permitted Israeli scientists access to the latest in American weapons systems, to technology that seemed capable at the time of preventing indefinitely any Egyptian crossing of the Canal. To be sure, the Israelis had by no means emerged intact from the War of Attrition. The hemorrhage of young lives, the economic burden of protracted hostilities—in higher taxes and mounting inflation—were hardly less than nerve-racking to the Israeli people. Yet, despite their somber awareness that peace once again apparently was as much a chimera as in the pre-1967 era, none of them doubted that the nation's military posture remained essentially unshaken.

THE TRANSMUTATION OF PALESTINE ARAB VIOLENCE

On September 6, 1970, less than a month after the Israeli-Egyptian cease-fire, Jordan's King Hussein launched his army against the Palestine guerrilla strongholds in the refugee camps. During the ensuing ten-day campaign, nearly 2,000 fedayeen were killed. Soon the battle of "Black September," as it was later to be memorialized by the Palestinians, threatened to escalate into an international crisis. With Russian encouragement, Damascus sent an armored column across the Jordanian border. It was at this point, in turn, that Kissinger finally asserted himself as Nixon's chief Middle East adviser. The president conceded that Rogers's successive efforts thus far to placate the radical Arab states and their Soviet patron had been proven bankrupt—and had led to this newest crisis. At Kissinger's instigation, then, Nixon ordered the Sixth Fleet to move closer to the Lebanese coast. Simultaneously, he transmitted a discreet request to Jerusalem, asking the Israelis to make their military "presence" visible and substantial on the Golan Heights. The Meir government agreed.

Reassured by the tangible evidence of this emerging American-Israeli support, Hussein then proceeded to shock his enemies by counterattacking the Syrians. In the ensuing battle, his tanks and jets mauled the invading column, and the Syrians pulled back across the frontier. Thereafter, Hussein was free to consolidate his power against the remaining fedayeen. His army pressed its offensive during the winter months of 1970–71, bottling up the surviving guerrillas in the northeastern hill country. At last, in July 1971, the Hashemite army launched a decisive attack, moving on the fedayun encampments with tanks and infantry, rounding up some 2,000 prisoners and killing hundreds of them. Thoroughly demoralized, the guerrillas shifted their base of operations henceforth to Lebanon.

As matters worked out, Lebanese terrain was hardly less useful for guerrilla operations than was Jordan's. The southern border of this peaceful little trading nation was contiguous with Israel. As in Jordan, too, over 100,000 Palestinians were impacted into refugee camps nearby, and many of these refugees were potential recruits for Fatah and other PLO groups. Moreover, the government of Lebanon, traditionally polarized between Moslems and Christians, and intimidated in recent years by the neighboring Syrian army, was all but helpless to impose restrictions on fedayun movement and activity. As early as April 1970, Arab irregulars were sufficiently entrenched in Lebanese territory to begin rocket firings against Israeli border communities, and to lay ambushes for Israeli school buses and other vehicles.

The fedayeen developed additional techniques in their war against Israel. One of these, pioneered two years earlier, was a series of assaults on El Al, and subsequently on other airlines with service to Israel. The most spectacular of the attacks occurred in September 1970, when members of the "Popular Front for the Liberation of Palestine," one of the smaller guerrilla organizations under the PLO umbrella, hijacked four commercial airliners belonging to Swissair, Pan American, TWA, and BOAC. In a meticulously coordinated operation, 310 civilian hostages, including a number of Israelis and other Jews, were brought to a remote landing strip in the Jordanian desert. Eventually the passengers were released, but not until the British, West German, and Swiss governments agreed to release Palestinians convicted for earlier airport assaults on Israelis. It was this flagrant guerrilla violation of Hashemite territorial integrity, no less than of recognized standards of humane conduct, that provoked King Hussein's harsh counteroffensive of "Black September."

In terms of Israeli policy, the only real accomplishment of these abductions and killings, including a particularly horrifying massacre of eleven Israeli athletes in the 1972 Munich Olympic games, was to harden the Jewish state's opposition to rapprochement with the Palestinians. But their effect on the rest of the world was less certain. In Europe and the United States, the radical Left tended to equate fedayun violence with a legitimate Third World struggle for self-identity. At the least, in the aftermath of the War of Attrition, the Palestinians once again appeared to be relegating Egypt to the role of a passive partner.

EGYPTIAN TOTALITARIANISM AND MALAISE

It was hardly a consolation to Nasser that Egyptian dependence on the Soviet Union since 1967 apparently had become irreversible. We recall that, in the military sphere, this Communist support took the form of a powerful Soviet naval armada off the Egyptian coast; of thousands of instructors and technicians on the ground in Egypt; and of Soviet pilots flying reconnaissance missions from Egyptian bases. But, in the final analysis, it was the economic damage inflicted by the ongoing war with Israel that transformed Soviet trade and aid into an even more vital buttress of Egyptian survival. By 1970 the Soviet bloc absorbed fully 38 percent of Egypt's exports; even as Soviet-bloc products accounted for 92 percent of Egyptian non-agricultural imports in 1966. Most of these Soviet shipments were industrial, half of them equipment for entire factories and for other manufacturing enterprises. By the same token, the industrial sector of the Egyptian economy was shot through with Soviet-bloc technicians. Indeed, the Russians penetrated the everyday life of Cairo to a degree little realized in the West. One part of Zamalek, for example, a comparatively affluent residential section of Gezira Island, was known simply as the Russian Quarter; its best offices and homes were reserved for Soviet personnel. A large downtown movie house, the Odeon, specialized in Soviet films. The largest bookstore in town, the Darq al-Sharq, was given over entirely to Marxist literature and to Soviet technical works.

Yet this Russian presence, with its implications of ongoing economic and ideological penetration, simply exacerbated the malaise that had descended on the Egyptian people. Nowhere any longer did there appear evidence of Nasser's much-promised economic "takeoff." The filth and congestion of Cairo were profoundly aggravated by the influx of hundreds of thousands of refugees from the Canal cities. Shortages of the most elementary necessities were increasingly chronic. Lacking staples, bank clerks used pins to secure their office files. Taxi drivers turned off their motors at red lights. Offices kept candles handy in the likely event of electrical blackouts. No corner of the economy was spared the impact of the failed wars. By 1971 the loss of Suez Canal fees had totaled E£4 billion. The loss of the Sinai oil fields represented a potential production shortfall of over E£2 billion. The drop in tourism added another E£4 billion to the nation's losses. These deficits were only marginally offset by Soviet loans and grants, by annual subsidies paid to Egypt by Saudi Arabia, Kuwait, and Libya. Notwithstanding all the widely acclaimed technological and educational boot-raising since the revolution, Egypt remained, in plain fact, a desperately impoverished nation. Its people groaned under a raging inflation, a critical balance-of-payments gap, and a stupefying military budget of E£2.4 billion by 1973.

One of the most poignant aspects of the economic and psychological crisis was the fate of the nation's educated youth. Each year Egyptian universities were turning out 50,000 graduates. Less than a tenth of these young people could find meaningful employment in Egypt itself. The rest were guaranteed work of a sort, but mainly in an artificially swollen government bureaucracy, and at minimal salaries. Residing in congested quarters with their parents, lacking mortgage funds for new housing, few could marry. Not surprisingly, the frustration of these university graduates occasionally boiled over into demonstrations. The latent unrest was not lost on the government.

One traditional method of diverting it, of course, was to encourage retributive spasms against Egypt's vestigial Jewish community. Thus, of the less than 3,000 Jews remaining in the country, many were arrested and interned. Eventually most of these were allowed to depart for Europe; but of the few hundred who still remained, half were kept in prison, the others reduced to mendicancy and dependence for sheer survival on charitable remittances from Jewish organizations overseas. Meanwhile, the government resorted to other, somewhat less vicious, diversions. Among them were the construction of a huge soccer stadium (at a time when basic goods were in critically short supply); the exhibition of quasi-pornographic movies for the first time in Egyptian history; the virtual iconization of Um Kulthum, the renowned chanteuse, and the orchestration of her funeral into a mass orgy.

Nasser himself still commanded a certain veneration among the masses. Awe of authority and its concomitant political submissiveness remained enshrined in the traditions of the Egyptian people. Popular upheaval against the *rais* was out of the question, even in the doldrums of the post-1967 period; and Nasser had purged the government of active and potential enemies. Infusing the national mood of despondency, therefore, was an intensifying rictus of centralist totalitarianism. The intellectuals felt it most acutely. None ever knew who was an informer among even close friends in a purely cultural or social gathering. Telephones were tapped. Few Egyptian writers dared any longer express opposition to the regime, even obliquely. As a rule, they tended rather to glorify the "positive, fruitful work for the public's welfare under socialism." Thus, in an issue of the monthly *al-Kitab*, the distinguished essayist Ahmad Abbas Salih argued that "letting all flowers bloom . . . does not mean accepting a literature whose content is reactionary and opposed to Socialist solutions. . . . And it does not mean welcoming a literature that ignores the problems of modern Arab man to roam in total darkness after some abstract value." This faintheartedness hardly signified an affinity for the regime after 1967, and particularly after 1970. It was the consequence of simple despair. Indeed, the last five years of Nasser's rule were marked altogether by a dearth in creative writing.

If there was any hint of protest, it was less against the government itself than against its pan-Arabism. Criticism of this debilitating fixation had surfaced as far back as the collapse of the Egyptian-Syrian merger in 1961. But the defeat of 1967, and the subsequent emergence of the Palestinian issue as a factor in Arab politics, evoked further misgivings among the nation's intellectuals. It appeared to them that, despite Egypt's painful sacrifices on behalf of the Palestinians, the latter remained ungrateful and uncooperative. Thus, the entire doctrine of the "Arab Popular Liberation War," and its advocates, the Palestinian fedayeen, were increasingly challenged. Muhammad Husseinein Heykal, editor of *al-Ahram*, was the first to hint of an underlying disenchantment with the Palestinian "revolution," and to warn of a Great Power conflagration should the Palestine issue get out of hand. Heykal's views were echoed by Jalal es-Sayyid, a contributor to *al-Kitab*. The Palestinian groups were creating adventurism, danger, and suffering for Egypt, he warned. The implication was clear that the Egyptian people henceforth should go their own way.

To the extent that these and other criticisms were allowed, they may have reflected Nasser's personal disillusionment, his suspicion that popular support for military adventurism had begun to wane. He was not wrong. After the War of Attrition, the army's faith in the president never quite returned, nor with it the belief that Sinai—let alone Palestine—could be regained under his leadership. In the course of the author's interviews in Cairo some years later, officers, soldiers, students, and intellectuals alike made plain that, for a good half-decade by then, they had wanted an end to pan-Arabism, to the Palestinian "crusade," to the whole enervating business of war and deprivation.

No doubt a combination of these frustrations and punctured illusions exerted their effect on Nasser's physical resources. On September 28, 1970, the president was stricken by a massive coronary. He died within hours. Afterward, his funeral became the occasion for a typically Middle Eastern paroxysm of unbridled grief and lamentation. It was the *sayyid* who had fallen, after all, the leader who had made good on his promise to restore the nation's dignity. Yet, once the public orgy ended, it was possible more objectively to evaluate the impact of eighteen years of Nasserism on the Egyptian people. Assuredly the old colonial servitude to Great Britain and to Western financiers had been destroyed, and with it the corrupt, manipulable quasi-parliamentarism of the Farouk era. Unquestionably, too, the infrastructure of an industrial economy had been laid; at the least, Egypt was transformed into the preeminent industrial state of Africa and of the Arab Middle East. The class conflict similarly had been neutralized. National socialism and the benefits of a welfare state—mass medicine, mass education—all were now available.

But at what cost? Not less, surely, than the mutilation of Egypt's nascent democracy, the crisis of the intellectuals, and the collapse of educational standards. Worse yet, Nasser's putative "anti-imperialism" had been conducted in a decidedly imperial manner vis-à-vis Egypt's neighbors in Africa and the Middle East. And although the military cabal had established a technocratic, rational state, had erected an imposing pinnacle of military power, and had thrust Egypt to the forefront of the Afro-Asian world, it had done so at the price of a debased standard of living, of destroyed initiative, and of a nation virtually in pawn to the Soviet Union. Not least of all, the cost was to be measured in tens of thousands of lives extinguished in vainglorious pan-Arabist adventures against Israel. For a gentle, essentially peace-loving people, it was this latter payment, more even than the truncated Sinai, that appeared to be increasingly irretrievable.

XIV

THE NEW *RAIS* IN CAIRO

Vice-President Muhammad Anwar al-Sadat, nominated by the Arab Socialist Union and appointed by the People's Assembly as Nasser's successor, appeared in September 1970 to be little more than an interim choice. His background, to be sure, was virtually identical to that of others of the Young Officers who had assumed power in the 1952 revolution. The son of a small landowner in the Delta, one of thirteen children, he was married off to a village girl while still a teenager, and himself became the precocious father of three children (the marriage was later dissolved). In 1936, he joined Nasser, Amer, Salah Salem and the group of predominantly lower-middle-class youths who for the first time were granted admission to the nation's military academy.

Yet Sadat's resemblance to his classmate Nasser ended there. If the latter was cautious and brooding, Sadat was impulsive and physically reckless. He, too, participated in the anti-British plot during World War II. Actively abetting a pair of German spies, he was arrested in 1943 and dispatched to a prison camp in Upper Egypt. He escaped, was recaptured, escaped again, and managed to hide out in the teeming mosques of Cairo until the end of the war. An advocate of terrorism, he was barely dissuaded by Nasser from dynamiting the British embassy. Later, in 1945, he bungled an attempt on the life of the Wafdist leader, Mustafa Nahas, and finally was arrested several months afterward for his complicity in the assassination of Amin Osman, a former minister of finance. Eventually he was acquitted and released in 1948. Two years later, he retrieved his army commission.

By then Sadat was an active member of the Free Officers. A dutiful flunky of Nasser, he became a minister of education in the revolutionary regime; then, in 1957, served as secretary-general of the Islamic Congress. After a brief stint as editor of the newspaper *al-Goumhuriyya*, he was elected president of the People's Assembly in July 1960, a post he held for the next eight years. In December 1969 Nasser appointed him first vice-president. Throughout all these years, Sadat was regarded as a loyal follower of the revolution, reliable as an old soldier, but devoid of any apparent flair or imagination. Perhaps overlooked in this evaluation were his extensive travels under Nasser, both throughout Egypt and abroad. The experience unquestionably broadened him. Thus, he was impressed by the tradition of open debate he witnessed in the United States

180

Congress, a procedure he would reintroduce in Egypt's People's Assembly. After the debacle of 1967, moreover, and Amer's "suicide," Sadat became a trusted confidant of Nasser and was in a better position to study the latter's mistakes.

A dark-skinned half-Sudanese, fifty-one years old upon assuming the presidency, Sadat made a great show of warmth and traditionalism. He was much photographed with a prayer-spot on his forehead, often wearing the peasant's djellabiya. Solemnly, too, he professed his intention of maintaining the policies of the late, revered Nasser. "It was necessary," he insisted later, "to restore the Revolution to the original course planned by Gamal Abd al-Nasser which the entire people closely guarded." It seemed a reasonable approach at a time when political rivals were known to be lying in wait. Chief among these was Ali Sabri, vice-president and chairman of the Arab Socialist Union, and spokesman for the leftist intellectuals who advocated an even more militantly pro-Soviet political orientation. To augment his group, Sabri recruited cadres from the intelligence branch of the army, from the technocratic, industrial sector of the economy, and eventually from the high school graduates of the rural lower Delta. At the same time, Sabri and his followers attacked the central government, demanding an end to "half-measures," and the establishment of an authentically "Socialist" regime. It did not take this cabal long to test the new president's mettle.

The occasion was an agreement Sadat had signed on April 17, 1971, for a proposed Egyptian confederation with Libya and Syria. Forcing a confrontation in the executive of the ASU, Sabri and his associates outvoted Sadat on the confederation issue, five to three. Yet, apart from that step, which remained without practical effect, the Sabri group apparently planned no immediate further challenges to Sadat. When the president confounded them by fighting back, therefore, they were caught short. Indeed, displaying the bravado that had characterized his youthful career as a conspirator, Sadat struck hard. On May 2 he dismissed Ali Sabri from office. Two weeks later, he ordered the former vice-president and a number of the latter's followers arrested and put on trial for "crimes against the state." If the plotters counted on Soviet intercession on their behalf, they were soon disillusioned. On May 27, during a state visit to Cairo, Soviet President Nikolai Podgorny signed a fifteen-year Treaty of Friendship and Cooperation with Egypt. It was evident that Sadat's victory over his opponents was total. By the end of June, his reputation had soared. Ministers of government began hanging his picture beside Nasser's in their offices.

Thereafter, Sadat consolidated his position by exploiting a widely diffused, if inchoate, resentment against Nasser, following the latter's death. ". . . [T]he worst and ugliest feature of Nasser's legacy was what I have called a 'mountain of hatred,'" he wrote later, ". . . the spirit of hate which emanated in every direction and at every level, to the smallest family unit." Attributing to the former leader the destruction of Egypt's basic freedoms, Sadat himself promptly set about loosening the trappings of the police state—closing down detention centers, forbidding arrests without warrant (except, as in the case of Ali Sabri, for those suspected of "treason"), and permitting freedom of speech, if not yet of editorial opinion. Subsequently he kept his opposition fragmented through a "hullabaloo of elections": for new leaders of local athletic and social clubs, for union and professional organizations, for a constitutional assembly to guarantee new rights, and for the Arab Socialist Union. In this last case, however, Sadat shrewdly ensured that the ASU not only became more representative but also an instrument to fudge issues and to soften political confrontation.

What followed, together with the increase of personal freedoms, the demythologization of Nasser, and the gradual rise of Sadat's own popularity, was a subtle process of turning the country to the right. This the new president accomplished with calculated shrewdness. Since 1965, we recall, Egypt had faced a growing balance-of-payments crisis that disrupted and all but aborted Nasser's Second Five-Year Plan. The 1967 military disaster, with its vast emergency defense expenditures afterward, ultimately became so punishing that the nation found itself almost totally dependent on the Soviet Union and on the oil-producing Arab states. It was the hold of these latter—notably of Saudi Arabia and Kuwait—on Egypt's purse strings that unquestionably influenced Cairo's new trend toward economic orthodoxy. Sadat and his advisers recognized the urgent need to attract foreign capital, to open new opportunities for Western investment funds, and to attract petrodollars from the Persian Gulf States. He put the issue well later:

> We had, with crass stupidity, copied the Soviet pattern of socialism, although we lacked the necessary resources, technical capacities, and capital. . . . Any free enterprise system came to be regarded as odious capitalism and the private sector was synonymous with exploitation and robbery. Individual effort came to a standstill, and from this stemmed the terrible passivity of the people. . . . It was that withdrawal from . . . individual enterprise that marked the beginning of our abysmal economic collapse.

The government moved cautiously in its retreat from state socialism, never directly repudiating the previous policy. The omens were clear, however, particularly the appointment of the dynamic entrepreneur, Osman Ahmad Osman, as minister of housing and reconstruction. By 1975, too, all remaining leftists in the cabinet had been removed. Sadat's personal taste for luxury was also reflected in the new conservatism. After becoming president, he moved into a spacious house in Giza on the west bank of the Nile, and encouraged others to be relaxed in their economic habits, to drop their earlier inhibitions about displaying their money and possessions. The Egyptian people reacted well to this congenial approach.

THE ''YEAR OF DECISION''

Sadat's determination to alleviate his nation's economic plight seemed unaccompanied, at first, by any shift in the traditional posture of belligerency against Israel. Thus, in a speech before the People's Assembly on February 14, 1971, he vowed never to rest until every inch of Israeli-occupied land was restored. "We shall not be the generation that gave up the Palestinian people's rights," he assured his listeners. Yet Muhammad Husseinein Heykal, a close confidant of the new president's, floated a series of articles in *al-Ahram* that doubtless expressed official thinking. The existence of Israel was a political fact, Heykal observed, and accordingly all Egyptian efforts should be concentrated simply on undoing the territorial consequences of the 1967 defeat. The "eastern front" was nonexistent, after all, and the Palestinians were incapable of influencing anything. Heykal noted too that the United States in any case would never let Israel go under; and if it was more useful now to bargain for lost territory, then dialogue with the United States was the first, indispensable step in that process.

Heykal's articles provoked controversy in Egypt and contumely elsewhere in the Arab world, for no one doubted that they reflected Sadat's own views. In truth, as early as December 24, 1970, the president hinted of his desire for better relations with Washington by dispatching a special representative to attend the funeral of General Eisenhower. Shortly afterward, Sadat called in Donald Bergus, the American "attaché" at the Spanish embassy (but in fact the unofficial United States emissary to Cairo after the diplomatic rupture of 1967), and indicated his desire to "reduce tensions in the Middle East." Time was crucial, however. By February 1971 the first six-month period of the cease-fire was nearing an end, and the Nixon administration feared that if war resumed and the Soviet Union actively intervened, the United States would not be able to stand aside. Indeed, the American president was intensifying his pressure on Israel to resume the Jarring negotiations.

At almost the same time, in late January 1971, the Israelis ventured an unexpected initiative of their own. It is recalled that Dayan initially had expressed misgivings about advancing to the embankment of the Suez Canal. Now, four years later, the Israeli defense minister intimated to Washington the possibility of withdrawing his army as far as the Sinai passes, in this fashion defusing the confrontation along a vital international waterway. Keenly interested, the Americans promptly transmitted the message to Cairo. Thereupon, on February 4, Sadat coupled his announcement of a "thirty-day" extension of the cease-fire with his own proposal for reopening the Canal. His conditions were Israeli withdrawal from the eastern bank and agreement to implement Resolution 242. What Sadat had in mind, however, was by no means a replication of Dayan's overture. Instead, he envisaged a preliminary Israeli withdrawal not to the Gidi and Mitla passes but as far as al-Arish in eastern Sinai; and in return he demanded not an open-ended cease-fire and peace negotiations, but a continuation simply of the oblique Jarring negotiations. It was a less than forthcoming reply. Nevertheless, Israel responded cautiously, hinting that a permanent solution might be obtained on the basis of an Israeli "easement" at Sharm es-Sheikh. The issue of the West Bank and Gaza would be left for future negotiations.

Even before these views could be explored further, Gunnar Jarring, the United Nations mediator, publicly offered Israel and Egypt a blueprint of his own. It was for Egypt to recognize Israel and to accept an end to the war; and for Israel to undertake a full troop withdrawal to the original international boundary. The suggestion was an untimely one. By offering his full endorsement to Arab territorial claims, Jarring stripped Israel of its opportunity to negotiate even the smallest territorial adjustment. Yet, once again, as in December 1969, Secretary of State Rogers discerned a solution in the option of Israeli withdrawal, and on March 16, 1971, he entreated the Jerusalem government to accept the mediator's proposal. Three weeks later, in fact, Rogers traveled to Egypt and Israel to pursue this approach firsthand. By then it was plain that Sadat had extracted considerably more mileage from his own initiative than he had anticipated. At the least, he had signaled a reconciliation of views with Washington. Israel was thrown on the defensive, and its response now to Jarring's, and Rogers's, formula was so unimaginatively categorical and peremptory, so devoid of conciliatory counterproposals of its own, as in effect to hand Sadat an impressive diplomatic and propaganda victory. What the Egyptian president did not achieve, on the other hand, was an Israeli commitment to withdrawal. Other, less diplomatic, alternatives would have to be resorted to.

Until this point, Sadat was equally careful to maintain his posture of friendship with Moscow. Thus, in October 1970 he declared: "The United States wishes to sow dissension between us and the Soviet Union, but we shall not permit any shade of doubt on Soviet intentions." In January 1971 he repeated: "Our people must be warned against the deliberate plan aiming at sowing dissension between us and the Soviet Union." On May 27, 1971, we recall, shortly after purging Ali Sabri and the latter's followers, the president signed a new Soviet-Egyptian Treaty of Friendship and Cooperation. Dutifully, he pledged his government to follow a policy of "Socialist transformation," and to seek a further "coordination of positions" with the USSR in foreign affairs. For their part, the Soviets agreed to provide significant new quantities of economic and technological aid to Egypt, and to continue their training program for the Egyptian armed forces. It was plain that Moscow's gesture in offering this treaty was animated by self-interest, by an urgent hope, even at the last moment, of keeping Egypt from its threatened course of rapprochement with the United States and of disengagement with Israel. Alluding to the "coordination of positions," the Russians similarly expected to protect themselves against further Egyptian military surprises—the kind that took place in

1967 and 1970, with disastrous consequences. In short, they believed that they had acquired a veto over Egypt's resumption of warfare.

They did not achieve this goal, nor did they win assurance of alternative influence over Egyptian policy. Even during the period of heaviest economic dependence on the Soviet Union, for that matter, when Cairo's debt to the Communist-bloc nations reached E£3billion (by 1972), Egypt had remained considerably less than a Soviet satellite. Internally, the nation's proletariat had not grown to dramatic proportions, nor had the country's trade unions ever achieved the sense of class consciousness typical of their counterparts even in Western lands. Under Sadat now, too, the relaxation of "Socialist" restrictions could be interpreted as a warning to the Soviets. So could the announcement of a new cotton policy, in September 1971, abolishing barter deals with Moscow, and thus foreclosing the Soviets from their recent practice of marketing Egyptian cotton below the world price. In 1971 and 1972, trade between Egypt and the USSR actually declined—at a time when the new agreement called for a 50 percent increase in trade. Unnoticed also during this period was Sadat's rapprochement with King Feisal of Saudi Arabia, his policy of improving relations with all the conservative Persian Gulf regimes, and the modest and deferential manner with which he scrupulously disavowed any further Egyptian expansionist ambitions in the Arab world. Instead, in the summer of 1971, Sadat gave Feisal—and Moscow—a demonstration of Egypt's independence by helping restore General Gafar al-Nuwayri to power in the Sudan, following a brief Communist coup in that southern realm. And in September 1971, Sadat formally changed the name of the United Arab Republic to the Arab Republic of Egypt.

The man's ability to play both sides was impressive. Even as Soviet weapons and advisers continued pouring in throughout the summer and autumn of 1971, and the Israelis remained obdurate in their refusal to withdraw unilaterally from the Sinai, the Egyptian president insisted repeatedly that the moment of resolving the impasse with Israel was not far off. Whereupon, on November 1, he assumed personal command of the armed forces and ordered the newspapers to publish air raid instructions. Nor was Sadat necessarily bluffing. The evidence is substantial that he intended in the near future to resume some form of limited hostilities with Israel. In mid-November, however, perhaps mercifully for Egypt, India launched its invasion of East Pakistan. During the ensuing six weeks of fighting, the Soviets felt obliged to ensure the victory of their Indian ally by shipping the New Delhi regime important quantities of modern, sophisticated weaponry—much of it equipment originally intended for Egypt. Thereafter, on December 28, Sadat was obliged to inform the ASU that, "without additional Soviet help," Egypt could not go to war.

It was not an entirely convincing explanation. Too many blustering promises had been made in earlier months that 1971 would be the "Year of Decision" in the confrontation with Israel. The citizens of Cairo began making disparaging remarks. The saying became current that the "Year of Decision" had been extended several months by presidential decree. In January 1972 thousands of students took to the streets of Cairo, exhorting Sadat to "wage war or conclude peace." The standing army of over half a million men, the long periods of mobilization, and the bleak employment prospects for university graduates were becoming insupportable. "The Soviet agents inside Egypt made a laughing stock of the Year of Decision," Sadat complained later, "while I had to suppress my agony and conceal my wounds."

The new year developed unpromisingly. The Soviets had won a major proxy triumph as a result of India's victory over Pakistan. The American government, in turn, felt obliged to deny Moscow a similar propaganda breakthrough in the Middle East. To forestall that possibility, Washington announced the sale to Israel of additional Phantom jet aircraft. Yet the Nixon administration seriously miscalculated if it believed that its pro-Israel stance would inhibit Sadat's plans to renew the war. It succeeded only in outraging the Egyptian president. Sadat was increasingly alarmed at the cavalier treatment accorded his nation by both the Great Powers. In November 1971 the Soviets had hinted to Washington of a possible Soviet-American blueprint for a settlement in the Middle East. It would be a two-stage agreement: first, for opening the Canal; then only for an overall peace agreement based on the Jarring proposal. The idea was as horrifying to Sadat as it was to the Meir government in Jerusalem. He, at least, had made no commitment to permanent peace—no more than Israel had made a commitment to a nonnegotiated agreement based on full withdrawal.

THE DE-SOVIETIZATION OF EGYPT

At that point, Sadat decided to pay a visit to Moscow. He arrived on February 2, 1972, and remained three days. As Heykal revealed later, Sadat's purpose was to extract a firm Soviet commitment to provide Egypt with "the opportunity to be equal to Israel." He wanted assurances of a flood of arms, comparable to those received after 1967, when the time came for renewed warfare. The Russians were not forthcoming, however. Their Mediterranean strategy finally was bearing fruit. With their growing armada off the Egyptian coast, they had managed at last to reach naval parity with the United States Sixth Fleet. It was hardly the moment to transform parity into confrontation. Indeed, the opposite was the case. China by then had emerged as a serious threat in the Far East, and as a result Moscow preferred to explore all further possibilities of détente with Washington. A Middle Eastern war of broad dimensions might well have jeopardized those possibilities. Accordingly, the joint communiqué ending the Egyptian president's visit to Moscow did not include the usual reference this time to "full and cordial agreement."

Sadat was unwilling to give up. Determined not to allow the Middle East impasse to be relegated to the list of peripheral issues during Nixon's forthcoming summit visit to Moscow, he flew off once again to the Soviet capital on April 27. The impulsive gamble failed badly. In a deliberate snub, neither Brezhnev, Kosygin, nor Podgorny was on hand at the airport to greet the Egyptian leader, nor to see him off on April 29. No commitments of support were made. And afterward, as Sadat had feared, the Nixon visit to Moscow in late May produced a carefully orchestrated effort to paper over Great Power disagreement in the Middle East—as elsewhere. The effort actually represented little more than a façade. It bespoke tacit understanding of a serious gap between the Soviet and American positions. There had been three hours of tough talk on both sides, with the Russian leadership demanding full Israeli withdrawal to the 1967 lines, and Nixon categorically rejecting this approach. Confronted with immovable positions on each side, Brezhnev and Nixon agreed finally that the Middle East required further detailed discussions. Thus, upon Nixon's departure from Russia on May 29, a joint Soviet-American communiqué blandly declared that the two governments confirmed "their support for a peaceful settlement in the Middle East in accordance with Security Council Resolution 242," and reaffirmed "their desire to contribute" to the success of Dr. Jarring's mission (which by then had all but lapsed).

Refusing, nevertheless, to be placated by Soviet generalities, Sadat dispatched War Minister Muhammad Sadek to Moscow on June 8 with a detailed military shopping list. The war minister returned empty-handed. By then Sadat was in despair. He sensed the restiveness in his country. The Egyptian press was repeatedly criticizing the Soviets for the "low priority" they accorded the Middle East. Indeed, the Egyptian military, no less than the civilian public, was seething with anti-Russian frustration. There was reason for this sentiment. The Soviet military mission plainly was in Egypt for its own, not for Egyptian, purposes. In Heykal's words, the continued state of "no peace, no war" enabled the Russians to exploit Egypt as a strategic base without a reciprocal commitment to support decisive Egyptian action against Israel. Their huge desert air base at Garabalis, intended for reconnaissance missions over the Mediterranean, continued strictly off-limits to Egyptian personnel. So did half a dozen other Soviet air bases in Egypt. So, intermittently, did the best anchorage facilities at the port of Alexandria, and even major stretches of the Cairo-Alexandria highway. In their training sessions with Egyptian troops, moreover, the Soviet "advisers" evinced a contempt fully as palpable as that of their British predecessors. Worse yet, even as the Soviets tightened their grip on the Egyptian economy, they attempted simultaneously to penetrate the Egyptian security apparatus and the Arab Socialist Union. The flagrancy of this manipulation and infiltration was public knowledge by then in Egypt. Acutely aware of his nation's resentment and growing impatience, Sadat in turn began paying extensive "goodwill" visits to army and other military bases.

Thereafter, the president dispatched two letters to Brezhnev, requesting the

Soviet leader's assessment of the Moscow summit discussions with Nixon insofar as they related to the Middle East. The replies were studiously evasive—in fact, hardly more than a restatement of the Soviet-American communiqué of May 29. As Soviet Ambassador Vladimir Vinogradov read the second of Brezhnev's replies to Sadat on July 8, the Egyptian president listened carefully, then (as Heykal later related it), "twice asked if that was all, and the ambassador replied in the affirmative." Whereupon Sadat coldly informed Vinogradov that, effective July 17, the services of the Soviet military mission no longer would be required. Yet before putting this decision into effect, the president once again dispatched his war minister to Moscow on July 13 in a last-minute attempt to win assurances of military support. The visit was a total failure. Convinced that Sadat was bluffing, the Communist leadership remained adamant in denying Egypt offensive weaponry.

On July 18, Sadat publicly informed the ASU Central Committee that the Soviet military mission had been terminated. With these words the president electrified his country and the world. Not since Nasser nationalized the Suez Canal sixteen years earlier had an Egyptian leader so captured the imagination of his people. Crowds gathered to cheer Sadat outside his home. Cadis devoted their Friday sermons to the "punishment of the godless." Newspaper editorials, of course, were dithyrambic in their praise. "The expulsion of Soviet military personnel," Sadat wrote later, "was a signal reaffirmation of the end of classic imperialism as we have known it in recent centuries."

The Soviets accepted their eviction without protest. The departure of pilots, crews, advisers, and technicians went smoothly. Their families were gathered and flown out of Cairo or shipped out of Alexandria. Within a month, approximately 15,000 Soviet military personnel had been removed. Leaving with them were 150 combat aircraft and approximately 300 SAM missile units, equipment that had been operated by the Russians themselves. Initially, the evacuation could not fail to affect Moscow's strategic surveillance capability over the United States Sixth Fleet. Yet the Soviets quickly adjusted. Their own fleet still maintained its treaty access to Port Saïd and Alexandria; Sadat did not foreclose that. The Russians now simply kept more ships on station and depended more heavily on satellite reconnaissance.

As it happened, Sadat's decision was never intended to be irretrievable, or to seal off all possibilities of future cooperation. Its purpose, rather, was to allow Egypt greater freedom of military choice. ". . . Another important reason was that within the strategy I had laid down," he wrote later, "no war could be fought while Soviet experts worked in Egypt." This fact was entirely missed by the West, which attributed the expulsion solely to Moscow's failure to provide offensive weapons. In truth, few of those offensive weapons actually were critical to Sadat's purpose. The Soviets did not provide bombers, but these in any case would have been of limited value. Ground-to-ground missiles were notoriously inaccurate. The Egyptians possessed an ample supply of fighters, meanwhile, as well as vast quantities of artillery, armor, electronic equipment, and antiaircraft missiles. Far from being paralyzed in his ability to go to war, therefore, Sadat was now in a better position to move—liberated from Soviet restraint.

Nor would that restraint necessarily have been certain. On two occasions before October 1973, through his political initiatives in the United States and in the United Nations, Sadat had prudently assured himself of Soviet understanding and diplomatic support. Thus, a few months after the Russian exodus, he resumed correct, even mildly friendly, relations with Moscow. It was clear to both governments that he was casting about for a new strategy, one that would avoid the pathological dependence on the USSR of recent years, that would distract the West, and that in the end might even serve Moscow's advantage if the United States and Israel were lulled into complacency. As events developed, the Egyptian president succeeded in this nexus of ambitions, and to a more far-reaching extent than perhaps he had dared hope.

THE VIEW FROM JERUSALEM

Not surprisingly, the expulsion of the Soviet military mission aroused even greater satisfaction in Israel than in Egypt. Convinced that the greatest of their enemies would be weakened, Jerusalem subsequently allowed all political initiatives on the Middle East conflict to lapse. Henceforth, the Israeli government preoccupied itself with the Arab guerrilla campaign and with antiterrorist measures far more than with the basic questions of military balance. "The Munich massacre [of Israeli athletes at the 1972 summer Olympics]," recalled Eban, "the indecent support given to the assassins by Arab leaders, including President Sadat, the gloating that ran riot across the Arab world . . . all fortified Israelis in the feeling that peace with the Arab world was an Israeli dream. . . . At the same time, the Munich attack had reduced the international pressures upon us to make concessions to an adversary who seemed impervious to any human impulse. . . ."

In anticipation of the forthcoming Knesset elections, meanwhile, scheduled for October 31, 1973, bold-faced and self-congratulatory Labor placards greeted Israelis from kiosks and wall boards in every town and city:

> There is peace on the banks of the Canal, in the Sinai Desert, the Gaza Strip, the West Bank . . . and on the Golan. The lines are safe. The bridges are open. Jerusalem is united. . . . [Western diplomatic pressure on us] has relaxed, and our political position is stable. This is the result of a balanced, bold, and far-sighted policy. . . . You know that only the [Labor] Alignment could have accomplished this.

However politically motivated, the far-reaching claims expressed a quite genuine mood of national security. The War of Attrition had ended. For the most part, the borders were indeed quiet. The Arab guerrilla struggle continued, but no longer essentially on Israel's soil. If the military burden was heavy—indeed, very heavy—the nation thus far seemed prosperous enough to bear it.

Nor did the Labor Alignment permit itself to be outbid in its stance of intransigence on defense issues. Even Dayan no longer spoke, as he had occasionally in the past, of the need to "give up a lot of territory" for a peace settlement with Egypt and Jordan. Rather, in April 1973, he proclaimed the vision of "a new State of Israel with broad frontiers, strong and solid, with the authority of the Israeli Government extending from the Jordan to the Suez Canal." In these and other public statements, Israel's armed strength and its extended boundaries figured as the principal components of national security. This was not yet official policy. Publicly, Israel remained wedded to Security Council Resolution 242. It was the expansionist image, nevertheless, that Israel projected abroad.

All the more so, in August 1973, when the Labor Central Committee adopted a "compromise" program that allocated one and a quarter billion Israeli pounds for the development of the West Bank and Gaza, and for the integration of Arab agriculture and industry in those territories with Israel's own economy. More explicitly yet, the plan envisaged scores of Jewish settlements in the occupied areas, including a Golan Heights industrial center, a commercial-industrial center in the Jordan Valley, new industrial zones outside East Jerusalem, and a factory complex for the Jewish settlements that had been established in Yamit—essentially the Rafah area—in the northeastern Sinai. Under this format, Labor's platform for the territories differed little from that of Begin's right-wing Gachal bloc. Perhaps the one major point of departure was the Right's demand for outright annexation of the West Bank and the Golan, and of at least a part of the Sinai. Otherwise, the practical implications of Labor's blueprint were hardly less than imperialist.

The self-assurance of the scheme both reflected and influenced Israel's military posture. The nation regarded as decisive the defense in depth afforded by the captured territories. Even if the enemy were to strike first next time, war hardly was likely to threaten Israel's own population centers. Rather, hostilities would bring massive retaliation on the Egyptian Canal cities again, on Damascus and Amman. The obverse of this defensive posture admittedly was less comforting; Egyptian and Israeli forces were in direct proximity along the Canal, and Israel as a result had lost its crucial early-warning time. Thus, after 1967, the ministry of defense embarked upon the construction of an elaborate series of defensive positions in the Sinai, based on armor and artillery, and supported by a network of roads, maintenance depots, and air bases.

At the direction, moreover, of General Chaim Bar-Lev, the chief of staff, a line of forward bunkers was also established directly along the Sinai bank of the Canal itself. Its initial purpose was to serve mainly as a tripwire that would activate reinforcements waiting farther back in the Sinai. It is recalled, however, that during the War of Attrition the high command decided to strengthen these outposts against the mounting weight of Egyptian artillery salvos. Accordingly, at an expense of I£2 billion, some thirty major strongholds ultimately were built along the Canal. The new construction program did not go unchallenged. Several respected army commanders warned that the Bar-Lev fortifications would engender a "Maginot Line" psychology of fixed defenses, something alien to the nation's coveted traditions of mobility and retaliatory attack; and that the funds expended on the strongholds could be used more wisely to purchase another 1,500 tanks or 100 planes. The criticism was not stilled. Thus, when General David Elazar was appointed chief of staff in January 1973, he effected a "compromise" on the issue of the Bar-Lev Line simply by reducing the number of fortifications and troops along the Canal. Ten of the fortifications were closed outright, and troop strength in the remaining bunkers often was lowered to twenty men, or even less. As a result of this "compromise," then, the dividing line between the Bar-Lev outposts as a warning system and as an early-defense line was blurred. The subsequent lack of clarity on its purpose was to exact its toll in the first hours of combat on October 6, 1973.

The uncertainty of strategic posture was further reinforced by the configuration of the armed forces themselves. The Israeli general staff emerged from the Six-Day War certain of its ability to wage future battles with the identical weapons of a skilled, well-equipped air force and a powerful armored corps— the workhorses of Israel's spectacular 1967 victory. In later years, therefore, the military command placed unwonted emphasis upon armor and air, at the expense of infantry. Artillery, too, was neglected, as was infrared equipment, thus forfeiting Israel's much admired infantry traditions of night attack and surprise. Even mobilization techniques were allowed to ossify. At no time did the army's manpower staff devise a flexible, economically practicable method for limited call-ups along the various fronts.

The confusion of purposes reached directly to the top command. As minister of defense, Dayan gave over most of his time to the administration of the occupied territories. Little attention was paid to the actual status of the defense infrastructure. As a consequence of this neglect, the virus of politicization was allowed to infect the officer corps. Since the 1967 victory, generals had become Israel's new heroes, and many were sought out as natural vote-catchers for the nation's political parties. Soon entire units had commanders identified with various factions. In this manner, the barriers to political influence that Ben-Gurion had painstakingly erected in earlier years were allowed to collapse. So were the traditionally austere standards of military discipline. This was revealed most flagrantly during the alert called only hours before the outbreak of the 1973 war. Arriving at their units, reservists were met by a startling lack of organization. Often vehicular equipment had not been properly maintained and could not be started. Orders to reinforce battle positions frequently were not carried out. Soldiers went into action improperly dressed. Dayan had not bothered to concern himself with these matters.

Yet no irreparable harm was anticipated from a certain laxness. The Arabs surely would not be so precipitous as to risk full-scale war again. It was known, after all, that between 1967 and 1971 alone Israel's scientific output was double that of the entire Arab world. Nothing in any Arab country could match Israel's highly integrated and sophisticated defense industry. Dayan appeared not to be exaggerating, therefore, when he declared in April 1972 that Israel was not only the "most powerful force in the area," but also "the second most powerful state in the Mediterranean basin after France." The expulsion of Soviet advisors from Egypt hardly modified that view. On November 20 of the same year, the defense minister assured a visiting American Jewish mission that "Egypt's ability to renew war with Israel is now even more seriously reduced." General Ariel Sharon went further in June of 1973, asserting that "there is no target between Baghdad and Khartoum . . . that our army is unable to capture," and "with our present boundaries we have no security problem." The following month Yitzchak Rabin, the former chief of staff, declared in an article for the Israeli newspaper *Ma'ariv*: "There is no need to mobilize our forces whenever we hear Arab threats, nor when the enemy concentrates his forces along the cease-fire lines. . . . We are still living within a widening gap of military power in Israel's favor." Yigal Allon, a celebrated commander in Israel's war of independence and now a cabinet minister, stated flatly in June that "Egypt has no military option at all." In Israel at large, as in the Western world, this evaluation was accepted unquestioningly.

THE RECONSTRUCTION OF EGYPT'S ARMED FORCES

It was not accepted by Sadat. From the moment in July 1972 that he expelled the Soviet military mission, the Egyptian president resumed active preparations for war with Israel. The decision, as already noted, was hardly a sudden or impulsive one. "I used to tell Nasser," he wrote later, "that if we could recapture even four inches of Sinai territory . . . then the whole situation would change. . . . First to go would be the humiliation we had endured since the 1967 defeat; for, to cross into Sinai and hold on to any territory recaptured would restore our self-confidence." Upon coming to power, Sadat had ordered a thorough study of the cause of the 1967 humiliation, and had become convinced that Egypt's soldiers in fact had acquitted themselves bravely, that it was rather the senior officers of the general staff who had let them down. The new president was impressed, too, by the speed with which the armed services had mastered their new Soviet weapons and had organized new defense lines along the Suez Canal during the War of Attrition. Failing, then, to secure meaningful American pressure on Israel to elicit a favorable response to his offer of disengagement (pp. 183–84), Sadat turned decisively to the military option. In 1971 he allocated an additional E£127 million to the military budget.

The initial date Sadat had in mind for his limited offensive was November 1971. As recalled, the India-Pakistan War diverted the promised Soviet supplies. The offensive accordingly was rescheduled for November 15, 1972. This deadline also proved unworkable. Sadat found that he needed time to replace his defeatest war minister, General Muhammad Sadek, and to reinvigorate the morale of his armed forces. Sadek's replacement, General Ahmad Ismail Ali, was in fact a much stronger personality than his predecessor. Fifty-five years old, a veteran of World War II and of three subsequent wars against Israel, Ismail Ali had been appointed chief of operations following the death in action (during the War of Attrition) of General Abd al-Moneim Riad, and became Sadat's war minister two years later. Unlike his predecessor, Ismail Ali was a calm logician, a man who worked methodically and precisely, inspiring confidence among his subordinates as a no-nonsense type.

His deputy, Chief of Staff Sa'ad ed-Din Shazli, was temperamentally a very different man, an experienced combat fighter and something of a daredevil. Also a veteran of World War II, Shazli had led Egypt's paratroops in the 1956 war and later had distinguished himself in the 1967 conflict by leading the single Egyptian commando unit that had managed to penetrate briefly into Israeli lines. Immediately after the war, Shazli devoted his efforts to the improvement of army training. As chief of special forces, he vastly expanded the army's program of basic education for semiliterate recruits; even as he devised specialized courses for the 50,000 high school graduates who each year were inducted into the ranks. As chief of staff now, Shazli all but single-handedly transformed the army's former image as a press-gang of backward fellahin. It was under his aegis, for example, that the Israeli approach was adopted of closer officer-conscript relations. Emphasis henceforth was placed on the Israeli doctrine of requiring officers to lead their men personally into battle. Far greater attention, too, was given to the soldiers' individual welfare. Now, for the first time, conscripts received decent wages; their families were guaranteed support if they were killed or incapacitated in battle. All these factors produced a significant new *esprit de corps* among officers and men alike. So also did the rigors of training, particularly after the Soviet departure. Soldiers of all ranks appeared to be determined now to prove their mettle independently of Russian supervision.

Among the lessons learned from the Israelis, meanwhile, was the importance of initiative and surprise. The Egyptian command appreciated also that the Israeli army was built essentially for blitzkrieg, that it was unable to sustain the burden of total mobilization and heavy material expenditure for more than a few weeks at a time. Thus, initiative, surprise, and attrition were early cited by Ismail Ali and Shazli as the Egyptian doctrine for a future war. Indeed, both men had carefully studied their predecessors' errors in the Six-Day War— helped in no small degree by Israel's detailed and public accounts of its own battle tactics in that earlier struggle—and had begun taking important corrective measures. They understood with perfect clarity that their best hope was to concentrate on a limited objective. This envisaged a crossing of Suez and the deployment of infantry and armored forces on the east bank, without an immediate attempt to launch sweeping envelopments in the Sinai beyond Egyptian missile protection. Inasmuch as Israel had placed most of its emphasis on air superiority, Ismail Ali and Shazli correspondingly devoted their major efforts to powerful antiaircraft defenses. By October 1973 those defenses would comprise more than 800 missile launchers and a thousand antiaircraft guns of all types around the Canal alone. It was the densest system of its kind in the world. Moreover, when war came, the Israelis were amazed at the skill and courage with which Egyptian soldiers handled these weapons. It was the War of Attrition that had given the Egyptians two years of priceless battle training in their use.

In sum, Shazli's operational plan would exploit the best qualities of Egyptian troops, their stolid courage when executing modest, thoroughly rehearsed assignments and when fighting from established positions. To that end, in recent years, a simple but exhaustive training program had been carried out— first under Soviet guidance, then under Egyptian direction alone. Detailed models of Israeli fortifications were built. Under the supervision of the Egyptian army's chief engineer, General Gamal Ali, every stretch of Delta waterway that resembled the Canal was employed for bridging and crossing exercises. Research was carried out on methods best suited for destroying Israel's reinforced sand barriers on the eastern bank. When bulldozers and explosives were found to be ineffective, Gamal Ali came up with the idea of water cannon to break down the ramparts, in this fashion enabling bridge-carrying vehicles to establish beachheads on the Israeli-held shore. Thereafter, endless rehearsals were carried out in the erection of the bridges themselves, and within a tight deadline of six hours. No further time could be allowed for conveying tanks, ammunition, and guns to the infantry on the opposite bank; by then the anticipated Israeli counteroffensive would have developed. Months of practice went into these exercises, with each unit drilled relentlessly in a specified task, until every move became a reflex action.

SADAT'S DIPLOMATIC AND MILITARY PREPARATIONS

Sadat's determination to regain a foothold on the Sinai was hardly a secret— to Egyptian and Israeli alike. Yet few in Israel gave heed to his endless warnings of resumed hostilities, his proclamation of 1971, then of 1972, as the "Year of Decision." Those pronouncements appeared all the more empty following Sadat's expulsion of Soviet advisers in July 1972. By the same token, Israeli and Western observers managed to discount the fact that Egypt's armed forces had not been dismantled, after all—no more than had the vast quantities of Soviet weaponry accumulated since 1967. Neither did they appreciate the new freedom of action Cairo enjoyed once Soviet personnel departed Egyptian territory. In the meanwhile, goaded intolerably by Libya's militant young ruler, Colonel Muammar Qaddafi, Sadat launched a widely publicized "final diplomatic effort" to secure Israel's withdrawal from the Canal. In February 1973 he dispatched his national security adviser, Hafez Ismail, to Washington. Ismail's meeting with Nixon was cordial, but inconclusive; the American president made no commitment to exert pressure on the Israelis. Stung by this rebuff, Sadat then advised a *Newsweek* editor in March that the resumption of warfare was inevitable. "Everyone has fallen asleep over the Middle East," he observed bitterly, "but they will soon wake up."

The Egyptian leader still had a few alternatives at his disposal. He succeeded in raising the Middle East issue for debate in the UN Security Council on July 26, 1973. As anticipated, the United States used its veto to block a Security Council motion demanding Israeli withdrawal from the occupied territories. Sadat then had what he needed: a widely diffused impression that Egypt had exhausted all legitimate means to effect a political settlement. By then, too, he was well embarked on building a common strategy within the Arab camp. He was particularly successful with President Hafez al-Assad in Syria. The loss of the Golan Heights represented a permanent challenge to the Syrian Ba'athist junta. Ironically, it was the expulsion of Soviet advisers from Egypt that had strengthened Assad's bargaining position. In an effort to consolidate their position elsewhere in the Middle East, the Russians decided to ship unprecedented quantities of military equipment to Syria, including 300 new tanks, 300 jet fighters, and hundreds of late model SAM-6 missiles. In March 1973, therefore, when Sadat first proposed joint military action against Israel, Assad responded eagerly. Immediately afterward, in a series of meetings between the Egyptian and Syrian chiefs of staff, plans were laid for a two-pronged attack under Egyptian strategic command. A joint military headquarters was opened in the Cairo suburb of Medinat al-Nasr, under the direction of Egypt's General Ismail Ali. Although battlefield operations would be conducted separately by the Egyptian and Syrian general staffs, the joint command assumed responsibility for measures to ensure secrecy and to coordinate the timing of the offensive.

At the same time, Sadat set about wooing other allies, particularly King Feisal of Saudi Arabia, who had never disguised his hostility to the late Nasser's "Socialist" imperialism. Determined to enlist Feisal's support, Sadat visited Riyadh in August 1973. There he greeted the Saudi monarch with elaborate deference, reassured him that the pan-Arabist adventurism of Nasser no longer figured in Egyptian policy, and succeeded in winning a commitment of Saudi oil pressure against the West in the event renewed fighting against Israel went badly. Even earlier, in January, Saudi and other Persian Gulf money had been made available to Egypt for negotiating the purchase of up to $500 million in arms from Moscow. The sum was above and beyond the $250 million annual subsidy agreed upon at Khartoum in 1967.

Thereafter, Sadat proceeded to mend his fences with Hussein of Jordan. This was a somewhat more difficult task, for the Hashemite king's animus toward his Arab neighbors had been inflamed by the Syrian invasion attempt of three years earlier and by the recent murder in Cairo of Jordan's prime minister at the hands of Palestinian agents. Throughout June and July of 1973, nevertheless, Sadat conducted secret political discussions with representatives of the Hashemite government, and managed finally to dispell Hussein's misgivings. On September 10, Hussein and Assad arrived in Cairo in an effort to reach strategic agreement for the impending offensive. To clear the air, Assad for his part agreed to close down the PLO radio station that had been fanning opposition to Hussein's regime, and Hussein in turn announced amnesty to all Palestinian guerrillas held in Jordanian prisons. But Hussein also admitted his inability to conduct full-scale warfare. At best, he consented to pose a potential threat of attack across the Jordan River, tying down Israeli forces on the West Bank. Sadat and Assad accepted the commitment. On this basis the agreement was sealed.

It remained only to win assurance of Soviet military backing. That support plainly no longer could be taken for granted. Following their expulsion of the year before, the Russians were wary of major new commitments to Sadat. Nor was there certainty in Moscow that the Egyptians were a more potent military force now than in 1967. Sadat understood these Soviet reservations. On October 16, 1972, three months after the expulsion decree, he dispatched Prime Minister Aziz Sidqi to Moscow to see if a new understanding could be reached on arms supplies. The Russians were polite, but cautious. Sadat then decided to make an important conciliatory move. In December he extended the five-year agreement that granted the Soviets naval facilities in Egypt. The gesture succeeded. From Moscow's viewpoint, after all, Egypt remained a potentially vital fulcrum of Soviet strategy in the Middle East. It was a strategy of discouraging nonaligned Arab states from veering toward the West; and in that effort, Egypt, the largest of the Arab states, still carried unique prestige. So long as the weapons shipped to Egypt were "defensive," moreover, and Egyptian military intentions were limited, a renewed, carefully circumscribed offensive need not necessarily provoke a Soviet confrontation with the United States.

By then, too, yet another inducement for the shipment of weapons was Moscow's determination to "teach the Jews a lesson." The groundswell of Soviet Jewish demonstrations for emigration to Israel had become intolerable to the Kremlin leadership. It threatened to exacerbate similar demonstrations among other restive ethnic communities within the Soviet empire, and poisoned Soviet efforts to achieve most-favored-nation trading privileges with the United States. At the least, a renewed Arab-Israeli war might cripple the Zionist state economically, thus rendering more difficult Israel's task of absorbing large numbers of Soviet Jews. Weighing these various factors, the Soviet government agreed in February 1973 to meet Sadat's requests, and the following month full weapons deliveries once again were forthcoming. They included important quantities of the latest SAM missiles, including SAM-6s and SAM-7s, as well as limited numbers of SCUD and Frog ground-to-ground missiles as a threat to Israel's population centers.

By the summer of 1973, Sadat and Assad finally reached agreement on October 6 as the date for their offensive. The water table of the Canal would be low then, the moon high for night crossings. Politically and diplomatically, too, the timing would never be more opportune. Israel's position had weakened in Africa (p. 227). Europe was less than forthright in its own leadership. The Nixon administration was increasingly bedeviled by the Watergate scandal. The Israelis would be preoccupied with their own election campaign, they would be worshipping and fasting on their holy day of Yom Kippur, and in any case they would hardly expect an attack during the Moslem religious observance of Ramadan.

Between them, the Egyptians and Syrians would have at their disposal approximately 750,000 men under arms—three times the number of troops the Israelis could mobilize. Their commanders knew that the Jews still were relying on air power to neutralize this quantitative advantage. The Egyptians possessed a substantial air fleet of 550 combat planes, and the Syrians 310, against Israel's 480. Yet even if Jordanian and Iraqi planes also were available for combat, this ratio probably would not have been adequate against Israel's superb pilots. Hence Cairo and Damascus agreed to rely on missiles to blunt Israeli air power. SAM rockets already had proved their value during the last days of the War of Attrition. Their use now could be decisive. Once Israeli planes were driven from the combat zone, ground battle alone would tell the story. And here, in addition to their vast numerical superiority in manpower, the Egyptians possessed 2,000 tanks of the latest Soviet model; the Syrians, 1,200. The Israeli armored force consisted of 1,700 tanks, a number of them obsolescent. Moreover, the Egyptians and Syrians had accumulated 3,300 guns of all varieties, four times the quantity of Israeli artillery, as well as several thousand new "Sagger" antitank rockets. With this agglomeration of manpower and equipment, and with their forces operating from short interior lines, the Arab leadership regarded the prognosis for a solid advance on both fronts as better than even.

Everything depended upon simultaneous initiative and surprise, however. The Israelis had enjoyed those advantages in 1967. Sadat and Assad were determined that the situation should be reversed now. In the late summer of 1973 only the two Arab leaders, their war ministers and chiefs of staff, knew the exact date set for the offensive; and it was not until October 2 that General Ismail Ali flew to Damascus to inform Assad that zero hour would be 2:00 P.M. on the sixth. Otherwise, all officers and men were told that their intensive training maneuvers were simply routine exercises. Those "exercises" were conducted daily up to October 6, with Egyptian regiments coming down to the waterline of the Canal each day in full view of the Israelis, then apparently returning each night. In fact, selected regimental units remained on after darkness, hidden behind ramparts on the western embankment. As early as October 3, meanwhile, commando patrols were dispatched behind Israeli lines, pinpointing communication centers and key signal installations. Among other tidbits of information, the commandos learned that Israeli forces—in theory 14 battalions in Sinai and along the Canal—were down to mere skeletal size. Even the troops in the Bar-Lev bunkers had been reduced to a pitiable 2,000, barely half their listed strength in peacetime.

The Israelis were not oblivious to the scope of Egyptian maneuvers, or to the fact that large quantities of men and equipment were being accumulated along the waterway. Neither did it escape them that, in the north, the Syrians were augmenting their tank and artillery forces in triple lines extending from the northeastern Golan plain to the very outskirts of Damascus. Yet the Israeli military intelligence branch persuaded itself that these maneuvers and reinforcements were essentially defensive: that, in the south, they represented merely another gambit in Sadat's annual war of nerves; and, in the north, that they signified little more than Assad's response to an air battle of September 13, when Israeli jets had shot down thirteen Syrian MiGs near the port of Latakia.

Sadat and his advisers fostered this illusion. In the last months before October, the Egyptian president allowed reports to be circulated of growing "tensions" between Cairo and Moscow, of Soviet unwillingness to provide Egypt with new weaponry following the July 1972 expulsion. Abd al-Satar al-Tawil, military correspondent of *Rus al-Yusuf*, later described Sadat's strategy:

> The brilliant plan of political camouflage was based on large-scale diplomatic activity. From time to time several emissaries would fly, as Sadat's representatives, all over the world: to Washington, London, Moscow, New Delhi, Peking and Africa. The Arabic press would print large headlines referring to . . . diplomatic, or political, activities. Reports would appear on the travels of the former foreign minister, Dr. Murad Ghaleb, and [the current foreign minister] Dr. Muhammad Hassan al-Zayat, of the former special adviser for national security, Hafez Ismail, and of other political personalities such as Hassan Sabri al-Khouli, Ashraf Mawaran, and others.

In this campaign of subterfuge, Arab foreign ministers attending the UN General Assembly session in New York gathered on September 25 with Henry Kissinger, the recently appointed American secretary of state. Possessing no information themselves on the impending offensive, the ministers were instructed to schedule a follow-up meeting with Kissinger for several months later (the secretary had not yet so much as examined the department's Middle

Eastern file). Its purpose would be to discuss a "course of procedures" leading to substantive negotiations on the Middle East. This ostensible reliance on diplomacy was reaffirmed as late as October 5 in a cordial private meeting between Kissinger and Egyptian Foreign Minister Zayat.

Finally, in these last days before the offensive, information was leaked to *al-Ahram* that Egyptian officers were about to make a Ramadan pilgrimage to Mecca, and that the Rumanian defense minister was scheduled to visit Cairo on October 8. On October 3, too, the Egyptian cabinet held its weekly meeting, the discussions largely revolving around the moribund issue of an Egyptian-Libyan union. No martial atmosphere prevailed in Damascus or Cairo. Lights remained on. Civilian routine continued as normal. Thirty minutes before the scheduled attack Egyptian troops strolled along the Canal bank, without weapons or helmets. The tail end of seven fat years, they would be the last thirty minutes of unqualified self-assurance the Israeli people would remember—perhaps for a generation or more to come.

XV

OCTOBER 1973: THE FIFTH ARAB-ISRAELI WAR

A FAILURE OF ISRAELI PERCEPTION

Israel had not failed to respond with vigor to earlier threatened crises, particularly in September 1970 and in May 1973. On the latter occasion, civil war in Lebanon had appeared likely to provoke a Syrian move into Lebanese territory. The government reacted by ordering an immediate and substantial mobilization. Troop reinforcements were deployed along the Golan and, preemptively, along the Canal. The threatened Syrian move turned out to be a false alarm, however, and one that cost Israel's economy I£11 million. Indeed, the economic factor would weigh heavily in Jerusalem's reluctance to mobilize again in the autumn of 1973. Not that Israeli military leaders took the danger lightly. Fearing additional developments with Syria ever since the air battle of September 13, Dayan warned of more serious fighting to come. But the minister of defense was less concerned about Egypt. ". . . [If] we were forced to retire to the second line in the south," he observed, "it would not prove catastrophic, for this withdrawal would involve no more than lines of defense in a desert area."

Thus, even as the Egyptian and Syrian armies steadily reinforced their front lines throughout the fall, conducting large-scale exercises and trundling heavy equipment forward, the Israeli general staff refrained from issuing a public warning. The nation was in the midst of its election campaign, after all, and the government's proudest boast was of tranquillity along its borders. Instead, every effort was taken to avoid outward signs of crisis, lest these provoke Arab retaliatory measures. Press references to Arab military movements were censored. The occupied Golan was left open to tourists. If Israel was preoccupied with security issues, these related mainly to outbursts of Arab terrorism against its citizens and against other Jews abroad. Terrorism in fact was the principal item on the agenda of a cabinet meeting on October 3. In the wake of an Arab hijacking of a trainload of Soviet Jews in Vienna, Mrs. Meir had flown to Austria in a vain effort to dissuade Chancellor Bruno Kreisky from closing Jewish Agency transit facilities in the Austrian capital. Returning now to Israel, Mrs. Meir was obliged to report on the failure of her visit. In advance of the cabinet meeting, the prime minister, Dayan, and several other ministers briefly discussed Egyptian and Syrian troop concentrations, but the group agreed unanimously that war was not imminent.

The truth was that Dayan and his staff already possessed important information on Arab preparations. To monitor Egyptian military activities, the defense intelligence branch had planted its own highly sophisticated listening devices in the Sinai. Their data in turn were supplemented by United States SAMOS satellites and by high-flying reconnaissance airplanes. The latter's photographs ordinarily were shared with Israel. Thus, on October 4, a secret American electronic surveillance station in Iran detected a suspiciously large volume of signals traffic over the Canal Zone communications system. Reports also were coming in of a major Syrian army deployment in front of Damascus. The CIA passed this information on to Israel.

Other warning signs had been accumulating throughout September and early October. These included reports that Sadat had notified Yasser Arafat of impending hostilities, that Syria had alerted its SAM defenses following the air battle of September 13, and that Egypt had hardened roads leading to the Canal. In late September, contingents of Syrian troops that normally were stationed on the Jordanian border were shifted to the Golan cease-fire line. On October 2, the Israelis similarly learned that Cairo had ordered a "full alert" in the northern and central zones of the Canal, ostensibly for defensive purposes. That same day Damascus put its army on "extreme alert," called up reservists and retired officers, and made extensive hospital preparations in southern Syria. On October 5, monitored Egyptian communications traffic revealed that a new code was in effect. On October 4, 5, and 6, reports arrived in Israel that Moscow was carrying out an emergency airlift to evacuate families and dependents of Soviet advisers in Syria and Egypt, and that Soviet naval ships were leaving Alexandria and Port Saïd.

In short, the portents of war were everywhere, and Israel did not read them correctly. The intelligence chiefs, the army commanders, and the political leadership alike had made up their minds that Sadat and Assad would surely understand, as Israel understood, that a far-reaching offensive operation was unthinkable without dominant air power; and the Egyptians and Syrians were unlikely to possess effective bomber forces for several years. This was the "Misconception"—as Israeli journalists termed it in their later commentary— that inhibited a broader and more imaginative understanding of Arab frustration and revanchism.

As a result, reaction to the Arab concentration of forces came belatedly, indeed, not until October 5, the eve of the Jewish Day of Atonement, Yom Kippur. It was then only, faced with overwhelming evidence of large-scale enemy preparations, that the general staff agreed to declare a "C" alert. Yet even this configuration fell short of mobilization, and represented essentially a warning to the standing army. Then, just before dawn of the next day, General

Eliahu Zeira, director of Israeli military intelligence, received word from a highly-placed informer in the Arab camp. It was a warning to be taken seriously: an Egyptian and Syrian offensive would begin at sunset that very October 6. Immediately Dayan and General David Elazar, the chief of staff, were notified. So was Prime Minister Meir, who in turn called an emergency meeting of her most trusted cabinet advisers for 8:00 A.M.

Once reaching Mrs. Meir's Tel Aviv office, Elazar requested a preemptive air strike. He was decisively overruled. Both Dayan and Mrs. Meir agreed that Israel could not risk a diplomatic quarantine. This time the armed forces' one alternative was to absorb the first blow and to rely upon defense in depth. The debate on mobilization was lengthier and more acrimonious. Elazar pressed for a total call-up. Dayan demurred. Such a move was both unnecessary and overly costly, he argued. The defense minister suggested instead a partial mobilization of some 100,000 to 120,000 armored corps reservists who would be ordered to their units without delay. Mrs. Meir endorsed this compromise. As the meeting adjourned, the decision was reached to warn Egypt and Syria through Washington. If the enemy leaders realized that their planned attack was known in Israel, possibly they would cancel it. Word thereupon was dispatched to Kissinger. Deeply concerned, the secretary of state promptly issued an appeal for restraint to the Arab governments. Until the very outbreak of fighting, nevertheless, Kissinger was more fearful of an Israeli preemptive strike than of an Egyptian-Syrian offensive. Had he received confirmed advance evidence of the impending Arab assault, his warnings to Cairo and Damascus would have been much tougher—and possibly effective.

In Israel, meanwhile, the mobilization of armored corps personnel had begun. Although it was possible on Yom Kippur to contact the largest number of reservists at their homes or in synagogues, over twenty-four hours would pass before all men reached their units. The skeletal force of troops at the Bar-Lev fortifications (most of the men were at home on leave for the holy day) refused to take seriously the likelihood of more than isolated Egyptian commando crossings. On the Golan front, too, troops anticipated at most a few hours or even a day of battle, the kind they had withstood earlier. And in the unlikely event that Syrian or Egyptian assaults should come in greater strength, the availability of powerful Israeli armored units in the rear, together with air support, seemed adequate to hold the line until additional reservists arrived. All these plans, however, were based on the assumption that the Arab offensive would not begin before sunset, and that substantial reinforcements would be mobilized and transported to their positions by the time hostilities began. Matters did not work out that way. At 2:00 P.M. on October 6, as the Israeli cabinet gathered in emergency session, a military aide suddenly entered the conference room and whispered urgently to Mrs. Meir. The enemy onslaught had begun.

A TIDAL WAVE ACROSS SUEZ

It had begun with a vengeance, with thousands of shells and bombs exploding across the eastern bank of the Suez Canal and along the cease-fire line of the Golan Heights. Enemy planes roared overhead, strafing deep behind Israel's forward positions. After a lengthy artillery barrage on the Golan, two Syrian armored divisions and three mechanized infantry divisions began rumbling across the cease-fire line, pouring through gaps in the Golan defenses and cracking the Israeli front in two sectors. In the northern sector, 200 tanks burst through the lightly manned Israeli picket line, and the thin network of Nachal (farmer-soldier) settlements, to invest al-Quneitra, "capital" of the Golan. In the central-southern sector, one Syrian column penetrated toward Nafach, the base camp that served as Israeli headquarters on the plateau; another pushed down toward the Jordan River bridges, leading to integral Israel. At the foot of the Golan, in Israel's Chula and Jordan valleys, kibbutz settlements began hastily evacuating their children, preparing to resist the enemy with light arms. It was danger of a magnitude that had not faced Israel's northern communities since the first Syrian invasion in 1948.

Approximately 230 miles to the southwest, meanwhile, during these same hours of October 6–7, the Israelis were testing the power of one of the largest standing armies in the world. Positioned along the Canal were five Egyptian infantry divisions, three mixed infantry-and-tank divisions, and twenty-two independent infantry, commando, and paratroop brigades. Facing these 600,000 men in the Sinai along the 110 miles of Canal were precisely 436 Israeli soldiers in eleven isolated bunkers, together with three tanks and seven artillery batteries. General Avraham Mendler, Israel's southern armored force commander, had 177 operational tanks at his disposal some five miles behind the line. An additional twenty miles to the rear, guarding the Mitla and Gidi passes, was a full Israeli armored division. It was the intention of General Shmuel Gonen, the southern front commander, to move this reserve armor forward the moment enemy forces reached the trip wire of the Canal fortifications. In the scope and brilliance of their operation, however, the Egyptians disrupted this tidy plan.

At 2:00 P.M. of October 6, as Sadat's planes attacked air bases and radar stations behind the Israeli lines, the full weight of Egyptian artillery opened up along the entire front. When the barrage reached its crescendo, the first wave of 8,000 Egyptian infantry moved across the waterway in fiberglass boats. In response, Israel's jets were loosed indiscriminately against the amphibious forces—only to be shot down in large numbers by SAM-6 missile salvos, and by other antiaircraft weapons. From then on there was little that the Israeli air force, or, still less, the shell-shocked Israeli reservists in the fortifications, could do to halt the crossings. By nightfall, 30,000 Egyptian infantrymen had attained a beachhead throughout the eastern length of the Canal, and several units had pushed on between and behind the Bar-Lev positions to a depth of three miles into Sinai.

It was still a vulnerable foothold, however. Without armor support, the amphibious force remained exposed to Israeli tank counterattack. Indeed, within the first ninety minutes of combat, General Mendler's Centurions were rushed forward to strike at the Egyptian infantry while the latter still remained near the water's edge. But the Israeli armored crews encountered a shocking surprise. Lying in ambush, courageously holding their ground against the formidable spectacle of Israeli tanks bearing down on them, the Egyptians fired hundreds of portable rockets. The weapons proved devastatingly effective, scouring Israeli armor, wiping out entire tank crews with each blast. By morning of October 7, only thirty of the Israeli Centurions remained operable. It was a vivid example of the transformation that had been wrought in Egyptian *esprit de corps*.

At the same time, under the resourceful leadership of Brigadier General Hassan Abu Saada, a division commander in the Egyptian Second Army's northern sector, other troops with powerful Soviet-made water pumps blew gaps in the sand embankments along the eastern bank. In this fashion an opening was cleared for bridgeheads. Thus, within less than six hours (and well ahead of training schedule), eleven bridges spanned the Canal. By early afternoon of October 7, 300 tanks and five mixed infantry-and-armored divisions had crossed the waterway. Linking up three miles east of the Canal, these forces entirely outflanked the Bar-Lev Line. It was a remarkable achievement. General Shazli, the chief of staff, had expected his army to suffer as many as 10,000 casualties in the opening phase of the offensive. Instead, Egyptian dead totaled 180 men. Yet, once having put two armies, the Second and the Third, on the Canal's eastern bank, Shazli was uninterested at first in advancing much deeper into the Sinai. His orders, rather, were for the troops to "lock elbows" north and south, to make their bridgehead a continuous front. And a day later, when the Egyptians renewed their drive eastward, it was a slow, methodical affair, more concerned with securing their own flanks against the expected Israeli counterattack than with seizing large areas of desert. This was the logical fulfillment of Shazli's and Ismail Ali's doctrine: to stay under the missile umbrella, under no circumstances to risk exposure to Israel's air force.

During those first thirty-six hours of combat, Moshe Dayan sensed the magnitude of the Egyptian crossing. He was convinced then that the Israelis must retire quickly to a second line, fighting within a belt of some twelve miles from the Canal until their strength was replenished. In the meanwhile, priority should be given to the northern front, where the Syrians were threatening a major breakthrough into Israel itself. The cabinet ministers reacted badly to Dayan's suggestion. They agreed with Chief of Staff Elazar that the situation remained "under control," and that the army should strike immediately to push the Egyptians back across the Canal. It was wishful thinking. The mobilization effort was lagging on both fronts. Days would pass before the reserve armored units could reach the distant Sinai. With insufficient transport vehicles available, many of Israel's tanks were obliged to cover up to 150 miles of desert on their own engines and treads. Worse yet, the southern command even then was throwing groups of reservists into immediate delaying actions on a piecemeal basis. Understrength and loosely coordinated, these units often were knocked out by Egyptian Sagger rockets.

Until his manpower could be fully organized, therefore, Gonen, the southern front commander, tried simultaneously to buy time without losing territory. Throughout October 7 he ordered his single armored division west of the Mitla and Gidi passes to fight a holding action. Yet, as the situation worsened, and as the plight of the surviving troops in the fortifications became desperate, Gonen was obliged to abandon this approach and to order his major reserve of 250 tanks directly forward to the Canal. There the armored brigade was expected to liberate the besieged strong points; then, afterward, to seize one of the Egyptian bridges and to cross over to the west bank. It was an ill-conceived gamble, designed essentially for conflicting objectives—one of rescue, the other of counteroffensive. Nevertheless, the Israeli armored brigade dutifully moved out of its staging base on the morning of October 8. Almost immediately it encountered the full fury of Egyptian Saggers and artillery. Slowly, as the day passed, the Israeli tank crews were ravaged. By evening, only 90 of their Centurions remained out of the original 250. At midday of October 9, Gonen ordered the remaining armor pulled back.

That same night of October 9, after a grim cabinet session, Dayan flew down to the Sinai for a meeting with Elazar and with senior officers of the southern command. The defense minister was in a trembling rage. Gonen's armor had not been deployed in time for the Egyptian attack. Neither were the Bar-Lev bunkers evacuated when there still had been time to do so. The counterattack, hobbled by its confusion of purposes, had failed lamentably. As Dayan wrote later: "When we finally concentrated a suitable force [in Sinai], which had battled a whole day, that, too, had been wasted, frittered away, all for nothing."

At the defense minister's uncompromising orders, Israeli forces in the Sinai were arrayed henceforth in an exclusively defensive posture. Full priority was to be given to the Syrian front. And even as the Israelis subsequently withdrew, the Egyptians for their part appeared content with their initial gains. In ensuing days they continued to wage a low-keyed war of attrition, still advancing their infantry in small leaps at night and mopping up occasional pockets of Israeli resistance. These latter included the remnants of the Bar-Lev fortifications, whose defenders now received permission to surrender. General Gonen meanwhile regrouped his lines fourteen miles east of Suez.

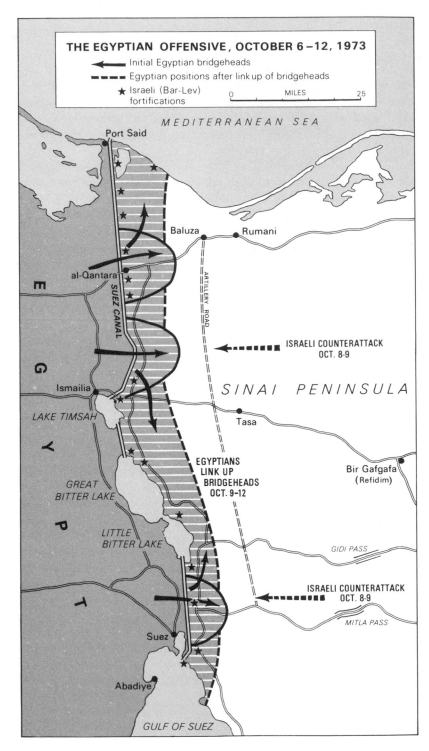

THE EGYPTIAN OFFENSIVE, OCTOBER 6–12, 1973

Initial Egyptian bridgeheads

Egyptian positions after link up of bridgeheads

★ Israeli (Bar-Lev) fortifications

0   MILES   25

MEDITERRANEAN SEA

Port Said

Baluza   Rumani

al-Qantara

SUEZ CANAL

ARTILLERY ROAD

ISRAELI COUNTERATTACK
OCT. 8-9

E
G
Y
P
T

Ismailia

SINAI PENINSULA

LAKE TIMSAH

Tasa

Bir Gafgafa
(Refidim)

EGYPTIANS
LINK UP
BRIDGEHEADS
OCT. 9-12

GREAT
BITTER LAKE

LITTLE
BITTER LAKE

GIDI PASS

ISRAELI COUNTERATTACK
OCT. 8-9

MITLA PASS

Suez

Abadiye

GULF OF SUEZ

During October 9 and 10 the Egyptians continued to pour massive reserves of armor and other heavy equipment into the Sinai. But in fact the Israelis, too, were strengthening their lines with reservists. While giving strategic priority to the northern front, they felt it necessary to keep the Egyptians off-balance by venturing a limited counteroffensive. This was launched in the afternoon of the tenth, and continued until the following morning. It was indecisive. By the same token, the Israeli air force persevered in its raids on missile bases and on other targets along the Canal. It lost twenty-three more planes. Nothing stopped the mounting Egyptian concentration of manpower. A *Newsweek* editor, Arnaud de Borchgrave, visited the Canal on the tenth. He wrote:

> There was none of the usual chaos I had come to expect of troop movements. . . . We found ourselves bumper to bumper with hundreds of other military vehicles, all waiting to cross the canal via pontoon bridges. But there was no confusion, no disorder. One by one, the army trucks eased their way down the small hill. . . . As we climbed the opposite embankment and surged into the Sinai, there were vehicles as far as I could see. Many were moving out in long convoys that stretched to the horizon. Covered with camouflaged netting, they drove briskly off, each carefully maintaining a 50-yard distance from the one ahead.

It was a painful moment of appraisal for Israel's leaders. Dayan expressed the universal reaction: "As for the fighting standard of the [Egyptian] soldiers, I can sum it up in one sentence: They did not run away."

A COMPETITION OF PATRONS

At the outset, then, the most important of Egypt's victories was less over the Bar-Lev Line than over fear, an inhibition that Israel had fostered systematically through years of tough retaliatory raids and occasional major campaigns. Since the 1967 blitzkrieg, few in Israel would have predicted this revival of enemy nerve. Yet the Egyptians made no secret that the quest for avenged honor was a vital ingredient of their renewed offensive of October 6. Thus, on October 8, at the height of Egyptian success, Chief of Staff Shazli could declare in an order of the day to his troops: "The war has retrieved Arab honor. Even if we shall be defeated now, no one can say that the Egyptian soldier is not a superior fighter." In contrast to 1967, moreover, there were few initial boasts of epic victories. Rather, the Egyptian people were warned that they faced a hard and protracted war (as has been seen, an extended campaign of attrition in fact was crucial to Egypt's strategy). The mood both in Egypt and in Syria was subdued.

Israel, conversely, entered the war in a miasma of confusion and deception. The government's first reaction, that of concealment, was intended to disguise its own blunders. On the afternoon of October 6, the defense ministry released only the cryptic announcement that hostilities had begun. In the early evening, Mrs. Meir declared on radio and television that the "Israel Defense Forces are fighting back and repulsing the attack. . . . We have no doubt about our victory, but we consider the resumption of the Egyptian-Syrian aggression as tantamount to an act of madness." Dayan spoke shortly afterward, radiating confidence, promising victory "in the coming few days." As late as October 8, Elazar informed a press conference that the turning point was just ahead, and "[o]ur aim is to teach [the Arabs] a lesson and to win a decisive and significant victory. . . ."

The Arabs meanwhile had their own news sources, and in the beginning these were more accurate than Israel's. In fact, it was from live pictures on Jordanian television that Israelis first learned that the Egyptians had overrun the Bar-Lev Line. It was from Syrian photographs released in Western newspapers that Israelis discovered that the Mount Hermon position in the north had been captured on the first day of the war. Not until October 9 did the Meir government belatedly admit that a hard struggle lay ahead and that "no soaring visions should be nurtured of elegant and rapid conquest." It was an understatement. By then the manpower strength alone of the combined Arab armies was three times that of the Six-Day War: 1,000,000 troops as against their earlier 300,000. With a discipline born of long practice, the Israeli population turned stolidly to its wartime routine of blackouts, volunteer service, and blood donating. Nevertheless, the government's confidence in its military leadership was sufficiently shaken to prompt the recall of six retired generals to service, among them Bar-Lev, Hod, Yariv, and Sharon.

By noon of October 9, as noted, after nearly three days of fighting, Dayan and the general staff had decided to shift the bulk of the reserves originally allocated for Sinai to the Golan front. This was a reversal of the strategy adopted in previous wars (except for 1948), but it was dictated by the prospect of an imminent breakthrough of Syrian armor into integral Israel. Moreover, the failure by then of Israel's counterattack on the Egyptian front suggested that victory in the south in any event would take much longer. Almost immediately, the air force began a systematic offensive against the Syrian economy. The major Syrian power stations, fuel reservoirs, and electric grids all were destroyed or crippled. The losses in Israeli planes and pilots were heavy, but the raids gradually levered the Syrian missile system back from the front, and this withdrawal in turn opened up new possibilities for tactical air cover over the Golan.

For two and a half days, since the outbreak of the war, Israel's two outnumbered brigades on the plateau had been waging a frenzied rearguard battle against a Syrian offensive that threatened to inundate the entirety of northeastern Israel. By dawn of the ninth, however, additional tank reinforcements began to reach the Golan, and an Israeli counterattack began, moving along the El Al-Rafid axis. It was slow, grinding work against heavy Syrian defenses both of armor and artillery, but by early afternoon of the tenth, the Syrians had been driven back to the original "Purple Line," the 1967 cease-fire line. President Assad's commanders had thrown the fullest element of their strength into the offensive, with every advantage of numbers, surprise, and equipment—and now their crack offensive divisions lay smoking and ruined along the Golan.

The Egyptian campaign far transcended the Suez battlefield. Actually, it extended more than a thousand miles from Suez, to the Bab al-Mandeb Strait, lying between the eastern bulge of Africa and the southwestern corner of the Arabian peninsula. In this narrow estuary, the route of passage between the Red Sea and the Indian Ocean, the Egyptians had leased the island of Perim from the People's Democratic Republic of Yemen, and were using it as Nasser had used Sharm es-Sheikh in 1967, to blockade the traffic of oil tankers to Israel's Negev port of Eilat. In fact, the October War in all its battlefronts and maritime zones projected international implications critical enough to require decisive Great Power action. Within two hours of the Arab attack, therefore, the United States was calling for a cease-fire and a return to the original pre-October lines. The effort was altogether wasted. Riding the crest of their initial victories, the Egyptians and Syrians hardly were constrained to accept a cease-fire linked to withdrawal. Nevertheless, when the UN Security Council met on October 8, the American representative solemnly repeated the proposal: a cease-fire based on an immediate return of Egyptian and Syrian forces to the pre-October lines. The Soviet delegation neatly blocked the appeal by insisting on a full Israeli withdrawal to the pre-1967 frontiers; while the French and British called only for a cease-fire in place. Immobilized by the Soviet-American impasse, the Security Council dispersed. And, for the while, the Arabs and Russians were not dissatisfied with this inaction. Time was working against Israel, they believed.

It was a view shared by Henry Kissinger. Accordingly, on October 10, the secretary of state changed his tack and sought to persuade Israel to accept a cease-fire in place. At first he was rebuffed. Two days later, however, the Israelis began issuing anguished pleas for weapons and ammunition, and a dispirited Mrs. Meir went out of her way to signal Israel's willingness to talk, should the Arabs offer any kind of cease-fire. Ironically, the Soviets began to entertain doubts of Syria's ability to hang on, and of Egypt's capacity to push much farther into the Sinai. They hinted to Kissinger, therefore, that Sadat might now be responsive at least to a call for a cease-fire in place. In fact, the Egyptian president was not responsive. Convinced that his army would sustain its initial momentum, he rejected the notion of a cease-fire in any shape or form—and thus unwittingly threw away the diplomatic opportunities of an impressive military victory. Whatever the course of diplomacy, meanwhile, Moscow was determined that the Arabs should not have to forfeit their early gains on the battlefield. Relays of Soviet vessels were unloading thousands of tons of weapons at Alexandria and Latakia harbors. As early as October 9, too, the Soviets launched an unprecedented airlift to the Arabs. From Hungarian bases, a succession of giant Antonov transports carried guns, tanks, SAM missiles, and dismantled fighter planes to military airfields in Syria and Egypt. Between October 9 and October 22, these Soviet flights averaged thirty a day.

Both the flagrancy and magnitude of the Soviet intercession were a grave shock to Secretary of State Kissinger. He understood well that if Moscow's credibility and prestige were now at stake, so too were Washington's. In earlier years, serving as the President's national security adviser, Kissinger had deliberately adopted a low profile on Middle Eastern affairs. Conscious of his vulnerability as a Jew, he had preferred whenever possible to leave the Arab-Israel issue to the State Department. Neither, on the other hand, had he ever disguised his belief that the United States bore a "historic commitment" to Israel, and that the preservation of Israel ultimately was in the national interest. Now, on October 9, Kissinger reached a major decision, and won Nixon's full support for it.

The Soviets had to be blocked, the secretary insisted, and not simply for Israel's sake. Two years earlier the Russians had consolidated their influence in northeast Asia by supporting India's victory over Pakistan. An identical Communist breakthrough could not now be permitted in the Middle East. A substantial infusion of American weapons would help Israel turn the tide, would restore the military balance in the East Mediterranean, and thus provide Washington with diplomatic leverage to shape the postwar negotiations. In sum, it was vital for the Arabs to be convinced that they could never win a victory under Soviet patronage alone. Kissinger's position on this issue was entirely forthright; his determination to provide Israel with an immediate airlift of weapons was unqualified. Eban wrote afterward:

> As late as Monday night [October 8], Israel was telling the United States that we were on the verge of victory. . . . The need for massive reinforcement only became evident on Tuesday. The President ruled favorably the same night. . . . By Saturday [October 13], the operation was in full swing. I had the impression that the driving force in surmounting the obstacles [in the Pentagon] was Kissinger, who knew that there could not be a cease-fire, let alone a negotiation, unless the military situation gave an incentive to stop the fighting. For those who know the bureaucratic ways in Washington, the astonishing fact is that the airlift was in massive motion about three days after it was first conceived.

By October 13, then, Phantom jets began flying to Israel via the Azores. Among the weapons the United States was delivering to Israel were 36 A-4 Skyhawks and 32 Phantoms, most of them from air force stocks, but a few supplied directly from the production line at the McDonald-Douglas factory in St. Louis. From military airfields in New Jersey and Delaware, giant C-130 and C-5 cargo planes, loaded with tanks, shells, helicopters, spare transmissions, electronic jamming equipment, antiradar missiles and "smart bombs," began a round-the-clock airlift. As the first American planes taxied to a stop at Israel's Lydda airport on October 14, their cargoes of ordnance were unloaded and rushed immediately to the fronts. In this manner, between October 14 and November 14, the United States transported 22,000 tons of equipment in 566 flights. Much also came later by sea. The weapons lift by then had saved Israel's war effort. "I hate to think what our situation would have been if the United States had withheld its aid," wrote Dayan later, "or what we would do if Washington were to turn its back on Israel one of these days."

THE COUNTER-CROSSING

By October 10, meanwhile, Israeli forces had driven the Syrians back beyond the initial 1967 cease-fire line. That same evening, Dayan and the general staff agreed that it was necessary to penetrate at least twelve miles farther. Only then could the Syrians be neutralized as a factor in the war. Consequently, Israeli armor and infantry brigades proceeded during the next two days to advance over stiff resistance, ultimately wresting control of the main Damascus road network. In the process, they also liquidated two Iraqi armored brigades, and severely mauled a Hashemite brigade that had arrived on the Syrian front as an oblique gesture of Jordanian support. By October 18, the Israelis were ensconced only twenty-two miles from Damascus and had indeed neutralized Syria as a factor in the war.

By then, also, the Jews could take satisfaction from other accomplishments. Despite heavy losses against Egyptian and Syrian antiaircraft fire, their air force kept Israel—even most of Sinai and the Golan—sealed tightly against enemy air forays. Not less than 450 Arab planes were shot down in dogfights, another 48 by antiaircraft fire (in one of these, Sadat's youngest brother, a pilot, lost his life). Israel's losses to aerial combat were 20 planes. There were days near the end of the war when the Syrians and Egyptians hurled virtually all their remaining air power into battle, losing the equivalent of entire squadrons. Most of the Arab planes were destroyed with their pilots and navigators (unlike 1967), and the loss of these trained crews would be felt for years to come. The Israeli navy also acquitted itself particularly well during the October fighting. While the Egyptians blockaded the Bab al-Mandeb Strait, the Israelis promptly launched their own counterblockade of the Gulf of Suez, interdicting the shipment of Egypt-bound oil. By war's end, Israel's fast, compact missile vessels had succeeded not only in keeping the northern shipping lanes open, but also had sunk 19 Arab ships, including 10 missile boats, without a loss.

In the interval, on October 11, the day after Israel's armored brigades cracked the Syrian defenses, Elazar and the general staff agreed that the principal military effort could safely be transferred henceforth to the Sinai theater. By then, 70,000 Egyptian troops had crossed the Suez waterway and had established an unbroken front six miles in depth. Within the guidelines of the "Soviet doctrine," they could be expected at any moment to launch a major second-stage breakthrough. It was in fact an accurate appraisal of Egyptian intentions. The question for Cairo was simply one of timing. Chief of Staff Shazli favored an immediate transfer of armor from the west bank and a two-column thrust into Sinai and down the Gulf of Suez. War Minister Ismail Ali was inclined to caution, however. Preferring still to broaden his front, he ordered Shazli for the time being to reinforce his armor and artillery; later there would be opportunity to consider an offensive.

At the same time, in a mirror image of Egyptian strategy, Israel's southern front commander, General Gonen, had been instructed after his disastrous setback of October 8–9 to fight a war of containment in the Sinai, to block any serious enemy advance toward the key passes. The next few days were not wasted. Accelerating their mobilization, the Israelis reprovisioned their troops in Sinai and repaired their damaged equipment. Between October 9 and October 13, General Avraham Adan's armored division, which had carried the heaviest brunt of the ill-fated counterattack, was entirely reinforced. Long columns of tanks and personnel carriers began arriving now from the Golan and from Israel. The wall of armor before the Mitla and Gidi passes was solidly buttressed.

Yet it was not the general staff's purpose to become enmeshed in a static war of attrition. All military plans since 1968 had anticipated a swift counterattack across the Canal that would take the battle into the Egyptian heartland. During that earlier period, General Ariel Sharon was the southern front commander, and it was he who had initiated these preparations. A staging location had been chosen at the juncture of the Canal and the northern tip of the Great Bitter Lake, and leveled there for an extensive parking-lot compound. Little could be done to activate the crossover plan in the first critical days of the war. On October 6, Sharon was called back from retirement to assume command of a hastily mobilized reserve division, and on October 8–9 he shared with Adan the abortive counterattack against the Egyptian beachhead. It was during this otherwise costly and unsuccessful effort that one of Sharon's battalions reached a crossroads near the Canal-Great Bitter Lake juncture and discovered something of great importance. Entirely by coincidence, a "seam" had opened between the Egyptian Second Army to the north and the Egyptian Third Army to the south—directly at the spot where the compound had been prepared several years before.

Reporting his discovery to southern front headquarters, Sharon asked permission to organize his division for an immediate crossing. Gonen turned him down. If Sharon's force were decimated (as was Adan's that same day), nothing would remain to block a further Egyptian advance in the Sinai. It was also known that the Egyptians were holding two divisions in reserve on the west bank of the Canal, and that a good part of this force would have to be destroyed before an attempted Israeli crossing. Gonen was equally emphatic that the Egyptian reserves should not be attacked west of the Suez, but rather induced across the Canal, beyond their artillery and missile protection. There they could be counterattacked in a direct slugging match.

For Cairo, as it happened, the collapse of Syrian forces on the Golan dramatically altered the strategic picture. To alleviate pressure on the northern front, Damascus by then was issuing frantic appeals for a renewed Egyptian offensive in the Sinai. Ismail Ali was not unmoved by these entreaties. Yet he recognized that a major offensive from his beachhead would require an advance beyond his missile cover. He was prepared to run this risk, but he would not do so without additional tanks. Accordingly, on the morning of October 11, the defense minister ordered the transfer of his Twenty-First Armored Division, comprising 500 tanks, from the west bank to the Sinai, and for the next two days he continued moving armor and troops eastward across the pontoon bridges in preparation for a decisive thrust against the Gidi and Mitla passes. The Israelis meanwhile hurriedly deployed 430 of their own tanks west of the passes. Soon nearly 1,500 tanks were crowded into the western Sinai, more armor than had participated in the battle of al-Alamein thirty-one years before. Finally, at dawn on October 14, the Egyptians launched their full strength eastward, with the principal attack developing toward the Gidi Pass. The battle lasted half a day, and it was a slaughter. Over 250 Egyptian tanks and hundreds of personnel carriers were destroyed. By the time the firing died down at midafternoon, Israel had established total control of the field.

Now at last the Israeli command turned its full attention to Sharon's plan for a crossing. It sensed that the mauling of the Egyptian Twenty-First Armored would force additional quantities of the enemy's tank reserves across the Canal, in this fashion leaving the west bank even more vulnerable to a surprise crossing. By then too, the American airlift was moving into full gear, and new equipment was being integrated. On the night of October 14, therefore, Dayan and Elazar discussed the scheme with the cabinet and the latter gave its approval for the offensive. Whereupon a gratified Sharon immediately began working out the operational details. By his plan, Adan's forces would gain the staging area of the waterway by attacking to the north of the compound. This would also serve the purpose of mounting a diversion. Sharon's own battalions would then cross first, to be followed later by the bulk of Adan's armor.

The operation began at 5:00 P.M. of the fifteenth, as one of Adan's tank columns launched its assigned diversionary attack northward toward Ismailia. Simultaneously, Sharon's infantry and engineering troops pushed southward through sand dunes toward the Great Bitter Lake. There the Israelis moved for the "seam" between the Egyptian Second and Third armies. And there, suddenly, a few thousand yards to the north of the Great Bitter Lake, this task force was struck by heavy Egyptian fire. An enemy unit had belatedly discovered the Israeli advance. A furious tank battle then erupted. It would continue for the next two days. Only one of Sharon's columns managed to break through to the compound at the water's edge. Unwilling to wait for the portable bridges and the rest of his fording units, however, the burly paratroop commander decided to begin the crossing immediately. He would use the handful of rubber rafts and small pontoons then available. Thus, toward evening, 200 infantrymen silently paddled over to the west bank. They went undetected.

The worst difficulties in fact were encountered not on the west bank, but on the east, at the operation's staging zone. Fully 6,000 Egyptians were emplaced throughout the area. With substantial armor and artillery, they launched a hell of fire precisely at the moment that Sharon's engineers were struggling to assemble vital bridging equipment. Eventually the Israeli vanguard was compelled to lash tanks onto barges and send them chugging slowly across the water. By 9:00 A.M. of the sixteenth, a mere 30 tanks and 2,000 men had reached the west bank. By any conventional military standard, Sharon's attempt to establish a foothold on the west bank had failed. Yet, incredibly, the Egyptians were laggard in discerning Israel's amphibious operation at the compound. They assumed that the Jews simply were counterattacking their— Egyptian—bridgehead in Sinai. This failure of intelligence was all the more astonishing inasmuch as Cairo had not been unaware of the potential threat of a crossing. Apparently the Egyptian army, long inured to positional warfare, with its six years of defensive attritional doctrine, had become office-bound in its staff procedures. Intelligence assessments were made at fixed-time committee meetings rather than on a round-the-clock basis—as fast-moving warfare demanded. Reaction to the Israeli offensive, as a consequence, was slow and piecemeal.

Typically, Sharon wasted little time in exploiting Cairo's inertia. He decided at this point to bring over additional men and supplies, on rafts, on dinghies, on anything that would float, without pausing to enlarge the staging zone on the east bank or to get bridges across. By the next day, October 16, the murderous struggle for the compound on the east shore began shifting in Israel's favor. At heavy cost, battling for every yard, Adan's armor gradually forced the Egyptians back from the roads north of the Great Bitter Lake. Early that morning, his tanks had fought their way through to the water's edge, towing the bridge's first pontoon. In the next hours more pontoons arrived. Despite heavy Egyptian shelling, Israeli engineers managed to complete the bridge. By early afternoon of the seventeenth, the first of Adan's armored columns began crossing over.

Until then, the Egyptians had assumed that the Israelis at most were launching a small, commando-like raid, and news of Sharon's initial makeshift crossing was not transmitted by GHQ to Sadat himself. When the president addressed his People's Assembly at noon on the sixteenth, he was still unaware of the new development. For that matter, when officers of Egypt's Second Army, responsible for the security of that sector, were informed by Palestinian units of the Israeli crossover in their area, their first response was: "You must be dreaming." Only later, following Mrs. Meir's announcement of the crossover in a speech before the Knesset (two hours after Sadat's address to the People's Assembly), did it become known that an Israeli task force had crossed Suez in the Bitter Lake region—and in more than patrol strength. Whereupon General Shazli visited Second Army headquarters and ordered the derelict officers shot.

By the evening of the seventeenth, as Cairo finally awakened to the danger implicit in the Israeli crossover, Egyptian forces on the west bank were limited to a single mechanized division and a single paratroop brigade near the capital, and to a single Kuwaiti brigade and a Palestinian brigade closest to the point of Israeli penetration. Now, therefore, Shazli asked Sadat's immediate permission to withdraw 200 tanks from Sinai and rush them back across the Canal. The president vacillated. Before agreeing to this humiliation, he allowed thirty-six hours to pass. In the meanwhile, Shazli had ordered the Egyptian Second and Third armies to converge on the Israeli east bank staging area. It was too late. The enemy's reinforcements were strengthening and widening that corridor, and by nightfall of the eighteenth General Adan already had 150 tanks across on the west bank. There his armor began systematically destroying SAM missile batteries, tearing great holes in Egyptian air defenses. With the newly provided American electronic guidance systems, Israeli fighter-bombers soon were devastating Egyptian antiaircraft units.

Assured of air cover, moreover, Israeli engineers completed a second bridge by late morning of October 18, near the town of Deversoir. Larger supply columns began rolling over, including two full armored divisions of 300 tanks and 15,000 troops. Thereafter the invasion force fanned out on the west bank to destroy additional SAM batteries along a fifteen-mile stretch of the Canal. With Egyptian air defenses all but obliterated by then, the Israeli tankers encountered little difficulty in battering through makeshift enemy ground resistance and pushing south along the rich agricultural terrain of the Canal's west bank. By then, in fact, the pattern of the war was decisively broken. "Our objective is to punish the Arabs until they are unable to make war again," declared the Israeli military spokesman. "We intend to crush their armies and kill a hell of a lot of young soldiers. The essential thing is to plant in the minds of young noncommissioned Arab officers—those who survive this war and who will be the leaders of the next generation—that war will simply be no solution."

SADAT IN PANIC. SOVIET-AMERICAN CONFRONTATION

Watching these Middle Eastern developments with growing concern, the Soviets as early as October 12 began issuing their first warnings—and provoking American naval countermaneuvers. Finally, on October 15, Prime Minister Alexei Kosygin flew into Cairo personally for urgent discussions with Sadat. In five extended meetings during the next three days, Kosygin outlined for the Egyptian leader a plan to end hostilities. Its terms included a cease-fire in place; an Israeli withdrawal to the pre-1967 boundaries, with only minor changes; an international peace conference to negotiate a final settlement, which then would be "guaranteed" by the Soviet Union and the United States. Yet Sadat was recalcitrant. The gravity of his army's position still had not dawned on him. In his address to the People's Assembly on October 16, he made no mention of the Israeli crossing. Rather, after an hour of self-congratulation, he proceeded to demand full Israeli withdrawal to the pre-1967 lines, then a "total solution" of the Palestine question. To that end, he intimated, he was prepared to take part in an international peace conference.

In Jerusalem, meanwhile, the cabinet sensed that the crossing of the Canal offered Israel its first authentic diplomatic leverage since the outbreak of war, and the ministers now were in no hurry for a cease-fire. "In this situation," Eban wrote later, "we had no reason to accelerate international discussions." The Israeli divisions had moved sixteen miles into Egypt, and it was then only that Sadat began to awaken to the full implications of Israel's counteroffensive. Thereupon he raised a vital question with Kosygin: What would happen if Cairo agreed to a cease-fire and Jerusalem did not? Kosygin in turn assured his Egyptian host that Moscow stood ready to enforce a cease-fire—alone, if necessary. But, in turn, Egypt would have to accept the concept of direct Egyptian-Israeli negotiations within an international peace conference. At that point, with distinct lack of enthusiasm, Sadat endorsed the Russian proposal. Later he rationalized his acceptance:

> The United States was taking part in the war to save Israel. . . . For the previous ten days I had been fighting—entirely alone—against the Americans with their modern equipment . . . while the Soviet Union stood . . . ready to stab me in the back if I lost 85 or 90 percent of my arms, just as in 1967. It was obvious that the United States could destroy my entire air defense system with the TV-camera bombs, and thus give the Israelis the "open skies" of Egypt they had enjoyed in 1967.

Two hours after the decision was reached, Kosygin departed Cairo. His government's next move was to secure American cooperation.

That same night of the eighteenth, Soviet Ambassador Anatoly Dobrynin in

Washington presented Kissinger with a Soviet cease-fire proposal based on total Israeli withdrawal from "all" occupied lands, including Jerusalem. It was an obvious nonstarter, and the secretary of state rejected it. The next morning, however, Dobrynin transmitted Brezhnev's personal message to Kissinger, requesting the latter to fly immediately to Moscow for "urgent consultations." The veiled threat of unilateral Soviet action in the Middle East was too palpable to ignore. It was in fact "murderously dangerous," Kissinger admitted to the president. With Nixon's approval, the secretary emplaned for Moscow before sunrise on October 20, bringing with him the "power of attorney" to sign any agreement in the president's name. His jet landed in the Soviet capital at 7:30 that evening. Allowing him no time to rest, the Russian leadership hustled him into immediate discussions. There was reason for their haste. The implications of Israel's counter-crossing were all too clear by then, and with it the potential for yet another Egyptian debacle. By the time substantive conversations were under way in the Kremlin, the Israelis had managed to put three bridges across the Canal, and three armored divisions were grinding ahead at full tilt through Egypt's west bank supply lines. It was manifestly Israel's intention to seize control of the entire western length of the waterway, in this fashion outflanking and annihilating Egyptian forces in the Sinai.

Thus, in Moscow, with both Russians and Americans fully apprised of the battlefield situation, Kissinger laid down his conditions for a cease-fire in place. An end to the fighting, he insisted, would have to be linked subsequently to direct peace negotiations between Arabs and Israelis. Kosygin and Brezhnev met these terms—and swiftly ensured that Sadat would also acquiesce. The results of their agreement were immediately conveyed, via Washington, in a personal communication from Nixon to Mrs. Meir. The dispatch reached the Israeli prime minister at midnight of October 21, during an emergency cabinet session. In his message, the president cordially but firmly requested the Israeli government to accept the terms of the Kissinger-Soviet understanding. He noted that the agreement would endorse a Security Council request for a cease-fire in place, and therefore could be accepted by Israel from a position of strength. The battlefield situation had been substantially rectified in Israel's favor, after all, and American weapons shipments to Israel would continue even after a cease-fire. The president observed finally that the Soviets at least had endorsed the principle of direct negotiations between the two sides, as had Sadat. The deal was a good one for Israel, Nixon emphasized.

The cabinet discussed the proposal through the night. Although indignant that the American government had presented them with a virtual ultimatum, the ministers agreed that Israel was in a vastly improved military position; and that politically, too, the country would have achieved its long-cherished desideratum of face-to-face peace discussions with the Arabs. Even the original Security Council Resolution 242, calling for the establishment of a just and lasting peace, had not explicitly committed Egypt or other Arab governments to a "negotiating" process, but rather had appointed a mediator. The cabinet appreciated, as well, that if Israeli forces continued their offensive west of the Canal, they might crush Egyptian resistance; but they would also risk Soviet intervention and American ire. At the least, additional fighting would cost additional Israeli lives. The decision was unanimous, then. Mrs. Meir sent word to Kissinger of her government's acceptance.

Kissinger in turn promptly radioed his staff in Washington, instructing them to call for an emergency meeting of the Security Council. This was done, and the Soviets co-sponsored the request. The United Nations body met early on October 22. With only China abstaining, it approved the Soviet-American appeal for a cease-fire in place, to go into effect within twelve hours. The resolution—Security Council Resolution 338—called for the parties "to start immediately after the cease-fire the implementation of Security Council Resolution 242 [of 1967] in all of its parts." It further stipulated that, "immediately and concurrently" with the cease-fire, negotiations should commence between Egypt and Israel under "appropriate auspices" with the aim of establishing a "just and durable" peace in the Middle East. Privately, too, both Washington and Moscow made known that they favored an exchange of prisoners of war, a matter of intense importance to Israel.

Stopping off in Israel en route home from Moscow, Kissinger then informed the Israeli cabinet for the first time of the American-Soviet plan for a Geneva peace conference. The format envisaged Israel and the Arab states conferring under joint American-Soviet chairmanship, thus allowing the United States a determining role at the conclave. It was vital, Kissinger emphasized, that the conference take place before the end of the year; otherwise Egypt, under pressure from more radical governments, would withdraw its consent, and the opportunity for committing the Arabs to the negotiating principle might then have been wasted. Even an opening session alone would be worthwhile, the secretary added; the conference might then adjourn without going into substantive discussions, leaving the door open for private bargaining elsewhere. The Israelis agreed. It had not escaped them that the United Nations resolution had neglected to establish machinery to supervise the cease-fire. This omission by itself would provide Israel's army further leeway to consolidate its gains.

The Meir government consequently joined Egypt and Jordan in accepting the cease-fire that same day, October 22. Syria's grudging acceptance came two days later. For the Israeli general staff, time now became vital in their effort to spring the trap on the Canal's west bank before the cease-fire came into effect at 6:50 P.M. To the north, Israeli tank columns were encountering increasingly heavy resistance as they moved up the Ismailia-Suez road. In the south, however, their armor had better luck, driving forward in a pincers movement toward the confluence of the Little Bitter Lake and the Canal, then thrusting toward Suez City. Although Israel's tankers did not quite reach the Gulf of

Suez, the cease-fire deadline found the Egyptian Third Army with its main supply lines cut, large numbers of its troops in flight, 8,000 of them already prisoners in Israel's hands, and its main force of 20,000 men on the east bank in mortal danger.

At this point, in a last frenzied effort to crack the Israeli vise, and to open a corridor to the Third Army, Egyptian infantry on the east bank's southern sector ignored the cease-fire, and throughout the night of October 22–23 struck repeatedly at Israeli tank emplacements. Immediately, then, General Gonen ordered his troops to continue their drive southward, and to tighten their grip. The orders were followed with alacrity. By early afternoon of the twenty-third, Adan's division had gained control of the access road to Suez City and had captured the port of Adabiye, the southernmost outlet of the Canal. As a consequence, Israeli forces by then were solidly emplaced on the Gulf of Suez, all roads and approaches linking Suez to Cairo were severed, and the plight of the Egyptian Third Army on the east bank was all but terminal.

During the morning of October 23, meanwhile, Sadat loosed a volley of panic-stricken appeals for Soviet intercession. Moscow complied the same day. In a tough ultimatum to the United States government, it warned that the Israelis must withdraw immediately to the October 22 cease-fire line; otherwise, the Soviet Union would inflict "the most serious consequences" upon them. Back in Washington, Kissinger immediately contacted Israeli Ambassador Simcha Dinitz and emphasized that he expected Israel to observe the terms of the cease-fire "scrupulously." The secretary of state appreciated that more than a truce was at issue. If the beleaguered Egyptians were denied a supply corridor, and their army allowed to disintegrate, the kind of military stalemate that would ensure productive negotiations afterward would collapse with it. So would Kissinger's credibility between the warring Middle Eastern factions.

At dusk on October 23 Kissinger and Soviet Ambassador Dobrynin together formulated the text for a new cease-fire resolution. Winning Security Council approval late that evening, the resolution—number 339—exhorted Egypt and Israel to end hostilities forthwith, and to return to positions occupied at the October 22 deadline. This time, too, the Council authorized the immediate dispatch of United Nations observers to monitor the truce. Yet the problem of identifying the original cease-fire line was not a simple one. As both sides maneuvered for advantage, fighting continued. On the morning of October 24, a Red Cross convoy en route to the Egyptian Third Army was turned back by Israeli troops as it reached Suez City. By then Sadat was thoroughly unnerved. Cabling emergency appeals to Moscow and Washington, he implored both governments to organize a joint force to police a Suez cease-fire. Thus it was, for the third time in less than two decades, that the Arab-Israeli imbroglio— and, specifically, warfare between Egypt and Israel—brought the United States and the Soviet Union to the threshold of confrontation.

Moscow endorsed Sadat's appeal. Determined to keep Soviet troops out of the

Middle East, Kissinger flatly rejected it. Accordingly, on the evening of October 24, Brezhnev dispatched a harsh personal message to Nixon, demanding that Soviet and American contingents be flown immediately to Egypt. "I will say it straight," the Soviet leader warned, "that if you find it impossible to act together with us in this matter, we would be faced with the necessity urgently to consider the question of taking appropriate steps unilaterally." Implicit in the threat was the likelihood of a full-scale Soviet rescue effort of the Egyptian Third Army.

Meeting this challenge vigorously, Kissinger and the National Security Council recommended an immediate military alert. Nixon concurred. At 11:30 P.M. on October 24, all United States military commands throughout the world were placed on "Defcom B," just before acute alert. An additional aircraft carrier was dispatched toward the Mediterranean. As Kissinger intended, Soviet monitoring stations picked up these movements immediately—and at that point the crisis was promptly resolved. A full-scale military confrontation with the United States was unthinkable to the Kremlin leadership. Early in the afternoon of October 25, Brezhnev instructed his ambassador at the United Nations to drop the appeal for a Soviet-American peacekeeping expedition. Subsequently, the Russians accepted the American formulation of a UN force that would exclude troops of the Great Powers. So did the Security Council on the afternoon of the twenty-fifth.

Wasting little time, UN Secretary-General Kurt Waldheim announced the next day that the first contingents of a 7,000-man UNEF force (taken from Austrian, Finnish, and Swedish units among the United Nations peacekeeping forces operating in Cyprus) already had reached Egypt. They had been assigned to patrol the anomalous, jigsawed series of battle zones along the Suez front. When the fighting stopped, then, Israeli divisions had penetrated from the Canal twenty-five miles into Egypt, dominating the west bank between Ismailia and the Gulf of Suez. On the east bank, Egyptian forces were deployed along the Bar-Lev Line to a depth of three to five miles, apart from an extensive Israeli corridor northeast of the Great Bitter Lake.

The Egyptians chose to put their own interpretation on the altered posture of their armies. It was summarized in a government communiqué of October 25:

> When the order to cease fire was issued at 1842, 22 October 1973, our forces east of the Canal were holding firmly to the land they had recaptured in Sinai. The enemy did not succeed by its repeated attacks against bridgeheads east of the Canal in gaining any part of them, excluding the Deversoir area, where some enemy forces succeeded in infiltrating and spread out in areas west of the Canal. . . . The position of our forces this morning can be summarized as follows:
> . . . The area [of Sinai] controlled by our forces east of the Canal is 3,000 square kilometers. . . . [T]here are some subsidiary enemy units scattered and intermingled among our forces in certain sectors west of

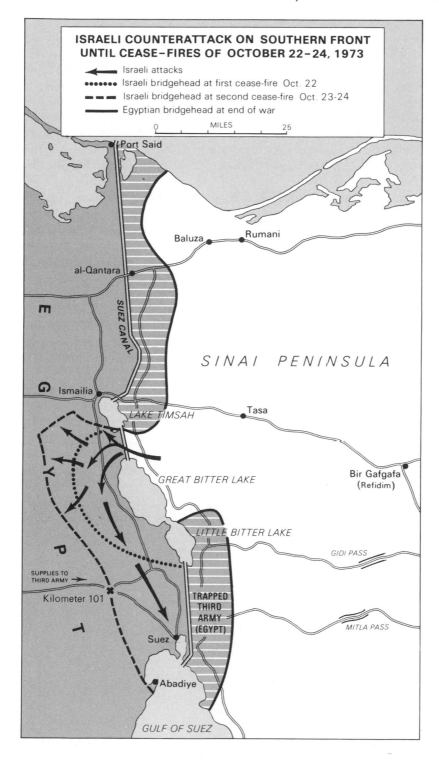

**ISRAELI COUNTERATTACK ON SOUTHERN FRONT
UNTIL CEASE−FIRES OF OCTOBER 22−24, 1973**

Israeli attacks
•••••• Israeli bridgehead at first cease-fire Oct. 22
▬ ▬ ▬ Israeli bridgehead at second cease-fire Oct. 23-24
▬▬▬ Egyptian bridgehead at end of war

0　　　　MILES　　　25

Port Said

Baluza　　Rumani

al-Qantara

SUEZ CANAL

E

G

SINAI　PENINSULA

Ismailia

LAKE TIMSAH　　Tasa

Y

GREAT BITTER LAKE

Bir Gafgafa
(Refidim)

LITTLE BITTER LAKE

P

GIDI PASS

SUPPLIES TO
THIRD ARMY

Kilometer 101

TRAPPED
THIRD
ARMY
(EGYPT)

MITLA PASS

T

Suez

Abadiye

GULF OF SUEZ

> the Canal behind the southern axis as far as Adabiya port . . . [but]
> . . . there are no enemy forces at all in any of the main towns of the
> Canal—Suez, Ismailia, or Port Said. . . . Supplies continue to reach
> all our forces regularly. They have not stopped for one moment and
> our forces continue to hold our positions firmly in Sinai.

It was the version that Sadat sold to his people, not only in the final stage of the
1973 war, but in ensuing years, as well. Accepted unquestioningly, even
gratefully, by the credulous majority of his nation, it offered him the political
latitude for all his subsequent diplomatic initiatives in the Egyptian-Israeli
confrontation.

Nixon, meanwhile, had asked Congress on October 19 for a $2.2 billion
appropriation in military aid to Israel. Yet the reason he adduced, "to maintain
a balance of forces and thus achieve stability," was a warning to the Israelis. The
president clearly was intent on achieving the kind of military standoff that would
lead to diplomatic compromise in the Middle East. Thus, in ensuing days,
Nixon and Kissinger left no doubt that the initial accommodation they expected
from Israel was a supply route to Egypt's Third Army, which since October 21
had been cut off from food and medical provisions. For his part, Sadat
understood that the fate of these 20,000 troops was essentially in American
hands now, and indeed Kissinger had given a commitment that they would not
be allowed to perish. Beyond American support on this issue, moreover, Sadat
possessed an additional bargaining weapon against the Israelis. It was some 200
Israeli prisoners in Egyptian hands, men whose welfare was hardly less than an
obsession to the little Jewish nation. Cairo now refused so much as to discuss a
prisoner exchange or even a release of prisoners' names unless a convoy were
allowed through to the Third Army.

On October 26, that army made a final despairing effort to improve its
position. Under heavy artillery cover, its tanks mounted an attack on Israeli
pontoon bridges south of the Little Bitter Lake. The ensuing battle was savage,
but the Egyptians were thrown back with severe loss of life. By then, with both
sides chastened and prepared for compromise, Kissinger was able to negotiate
with Israeli and Egyptian representatives directly. After four hours of triangular
discussions, a formula was devised by which a single Red Cross convoy of
medical and food supplies would be allowed through Israeli lines. To work out
the details, senior officers from both sides met under United Nations auspices
early on October 26 at a clearing on the Suez-Cairo highway, sixty-three miles
from the Egyptian capital. This was Kilometer 101, inside Israeli-occupied
territory west of the Canal, and the discussions there signified the first official,
direct contacts between Egyptians and Israelis since the collapse of the Mixed
Armistice Commission seventeen years before. The conversations were crisp,
businesslike, and successful. On October 28, a 100-truck convoy, operated by

United Nations personnel, was inspected by Israeli troops and allowed to pass through to Egyptian lines. In return, Cairo supplied the United Nations with a list of wounded Israeli prisoners of war, and the Red Cross was allowed to visit these men. It was clear by then that hostilities would not be resumed. The most brutal of the five conflicts between Egypt and Israel had come to an end.

XVI

THE RAMIFICATIONS

OF OCTOBER

THE MILITARY LESSONS OF THE WAR

Within months after the end of hostilities, a tentative balance sheet could be drawn on the military lessons of the war. On Israel's side, blunders plainly had contributed to sacrifices in manpower and matériel. The most far-reaching miscalculation had been the assumption that territorial depth would take the place of early warning. As has been seen, this error led directly to critical lapses of intelligence evaluation, for Israel's preparations had been oriented almost exclusively to a preemptive attack or to a swift, devastating counterpunch. No one had foreseen prolonged blocking battles. It was an irony, then, that in earlier wars Israel had achieved military victories from borders it had considered unsafe; while during the 1973 conflict it was initially defeated from lines it regarded as very secure. By the same token, the October conflict had also taught Israel the risks of disproportionate reliance upon a superior air force and armor. The Egyptians and Syrians had succeeded, at least partially, in neutralizing Israel's planes and tanks with missiles and antitank rockets. For the underpopulated Zionist republic, with its numerically small army, the demographic implications of a possible future shift to large-scale infantry warfare were unsettling.

But the Arabs, too, had committed serious mistakes. Obsessed in the earliest phase of the offensive by the importance of missile protection, the Egyptian general staff had failed to exploit Israel's critical shortage of reinforcements by moving boldly and imaginatively to capture the Sinai passes. Had they done so, they would have deprived Israel of time to mobilize adequate reserves at a moment when the Jews were locked in a desperate, rearguard struggle on the Golan, far closer to home. No doubt some of the blame was Sadat's. With refreshing candor, the Egyptian president admitted later that he had been almost entirely fixated by the limited political and psychological purpose he envisaged for his offensive. Wherever responsibility accrued, this equivocation ultimately permitted the Israelis once again to fight on a single front at a time; first concentrating their resources against the more immediate Syrian danger; then turning their full attention to the Canal front. It was a strategic gift to Israel that, in a sense, was also made possible by the absence of a joint Arab headquarters and a supreme commander with power to issue operational orders on both fronts. As in past wars with the Jews, there was no substitute for an integrated command.

Yet the balance sheet did not consist of blunders or miscalculations alone— either for Jews or Arabs. In the case of Israel, once fighting began, valor and resourcefulness more than compensated for errors in intelligence and preparation. Indeed, in the last analysis, Israel's armed forces had won the most notable victory in their history. The combined Arab forces had launched their offensive with a quantity of troops and weapons exceeding those available to NATO in Europe, and had done so against a small country with a population unready and an army not yet mobilized. Despite the unprecedented scope and mechanized fury of the war, the surprise attack on two fronts, the incomparable advantages in Arab manpower and—at the outset—in army matériel, the Israelis had held on, their forces had battled with a heroism approaching the superhuman, and eventually they had penetrated well beyond the 1967 Golan cease-fire line in the north, even as their bridgehead on the west bank of the Canal had more than neutralized Egypt's capture of the Bar-Lev Line.

If there was a clear perception of victory in Israel, however, the Egyptians could derive equal satisfaction from their own performance. During extensive interviews carried out with Egyptian veterans of the 1973 war, the author was particularly struck by the recurrent motif of pride—a mirror image of the euphoria he had encountered in Israel following the 1967 conflict. The reaction of Mustafa Abd al-Nabi Mustafa was typical. An infantry sergeant in the war, assigned to the Seventh Division of the Third Army, Mustafa participated in the armored attack on the Gidi Pass. Throughout the inferno of that battle, the young noncom ministered ceaselessly to the wounded, carrying them back to the field hospital under heavy fire and air strafing (he was subsequently decorated). Mustafa recalled the army doctors, no less exhausted than he, devotedly treating an interminable procession of burned and mutilated soldiers. Later, once the Israelis broke through to the west bank to encircle the Third Army, Mustafa and his companions were cut off for many days from food, medicine, fuel, and ammunition. Their commander, General Ahmad Badawi, put the troops on tight rations, and made each day's allocation of food and water suffice for three days. Unlike the 1967 war, there was no panic, no thought of surrender. If morale remained high, it was sustained by the shared exultation of the initial Canal-crossing, and by the inspirational courage of the officers. In short, it was this courage under adversity that Mustafa remembered as the supreme achievement of the October War.

The Israelis, for their part, needed no pictures drawn of the grim cost of their belated victory. The nation had sustained 2,552 dead and over 5,000 wounded in the eighteen days of fighting, with a high proportion of officers among the casualties. Some Israeli families lost more than one son. This was painful attrition for a tiny nation, and the number of dead and wounded would continue to rise in ensuing months, until the final Syrian-Israeli disengagement. It was scant consolation that the enemy had endured far higher casualties. The Arabs could afford them. The economic costs, too, were hardly less painful than the physical and psychological wounds. Egypt's wartime expenditures may have come to $8 billion, but Israel's reached at least half that in equipment and damaged property alone. As a consequence of manpower mobilization, the decline in Israeli production and exports raised the total economic cost to $7 billion—the equivalent of the nation's GNP for an entire year. Additionally, the fighting disclosed that Israel's efficient lines of internal communication no longer offered as great an advantage as before; that quick, cheap victories were a thing of the past; that staying power, not the blitzkrieg, would be a key in the future; and that possibly only the wealthiest of superpowers could sustain this kind of warfare in the years to come. From 1973 on, as a result, a defensive approach appeared to fixate the Israelis, and the nation's future strategy was increasingly to be based on powerful, but static, fortifications—until recently the Arab military doctrine.

Thus, at the moment that a euphoria of pride and renewed self-confidence swept through Egypt, painful questions were being asked in Israel, often in shaken whispers. Five debilitating wars had taken place within the state's short history—indeed, within the memory of a single generation. What, then, did peace look like? How much longer could this endless hemorrhage in lives and material resources be sustained? Could even temporary victory be achieved again, for that matter, now that the Soviets had made clear that they no longer would permit the Arabs to suffer a decisive defeat on the battlefield? Even as the firing died down in the last week of October, and negotiations were begun for opening a supply route to Egyptian forces in southern Sinai, the Israeli people well understood that a threshold somehow had been crossed between two eras.

ISRAEL IN ISOLATION.
UNITED STATES MEDIATION AND INITIAL DISENGAGEMENT

The familiar ritual was to begin once more: the protracted diplomatic stalemate, the quest by Egypt for assurance of a reprovisioned army and of regained land; and, by Israel, for at least an intermediate security in the wake of a dearly achieved military triumph. Under American pressure, the Israelis had reluctantly allowed a Red Cross supply convoy to pass through their lines to the beleaguered Egyptian Third Army. But afterward the Meir government was unprepared to offer further concessions until the Egyptians made available a full list of Israeli prisoners of war. Nor could there be any question of a return to Israel's October 22 positions on the west bank of the Canal, as the Egyptians demanded. Concessions had to be mutual, Mrs. Meir insisted. As it turned out, the prime minister's difficulties were to be less with Cairo than with Washington.

Impressed by Sadat's seeming moderation, his professed wish for resumed ties with the United States, and his avowed interest in peace, Secretary of State Kissinger had assured Cairo of his intention not merely to negotiate a permanent supply corridor to the Third Army, but to persuade Israel gradually to evacuate the Sinai altogether—in return for a stable peace treaty. At this point, on October 31, Mrs. Meir flew to Washington to meet personally with Kissinger and Nixon, and to express her government's resentment. By what moral obligation, she asked, was Israel to pay a higher price than Egypt for accommodation? It was Egypt, after all, that had launched the war, and that had failed subsequently to win it. Kissinger appreciated the prime minister's logic. But he reminded her that the cost to Israel in blood and treasure had been exceptionally high. Surely Israel would be willing now to risk an exchange of territory in return for permanent peace?

Moreover, Kissinger did not need to remind Mrs. Meir that Israel currently found itself in a state of diplomatic near-isolation. Support for the Egyptian-Arab cause had been expressed not only by Communist and Moslem nations but by nearly the entire Third World. Even in Africa, the site of Israel's most impressive diplomatic achievements in the 1960s, the special relationship the Jewish nation had built through years of patient effort now appeared to have been dissipated. Since its victory in the 1967 war, and its occupation of the Sinai, the Zionist republic reemerged in African eyes as something of an imperialist power. That impression was confirmed in the October War. By crossing the Suez Canal into African Egypt, Israel forfeited its last tenuous foothold on African affections. In all, the thirty-two African nations that had maintained close relations with the Jewish state over the years now severed their ties. The diplomatic defeat was shattering.

Yet it was the erosion of European support that proved even more traumatic for the Israelis—and for the Americans. Solicitous of Arab goodwill, London now imposed an embargo on the spare tank parts it had contracted to sell to Israel. The West German government scrupulously refrained from expressing partisanship in the Arab-Israeli conflict. France publicly maintained the diplomatic support for the Arab cause it had adopted since the Six-Day War. Determined, moreover, to achieve a relaxation of tensions with the Soviets, America's NATO allies collapsed like paper bags during the rival Soviet and United States airlifts to the Middle East. Ankara permitted Soviet planes en route to Syria to violate Turkish air space. British Prime Minister Edward Heath rejected a personal appeal from Nixon for American landing rights in Cyprus. Greece barred American planes altogether. Bonn initially allowed the United States use of Bremerhaven harbor for the shipment to Israel of American ordnance stored in West Germany; but later, at Arab insistence, it withdrew this permission.

Even more basic in the foundering of the Atlantic alliance, however, was the impact of the Arabs' single most potent weapon, the oil embargo. As a consequence of Sadat's shrewd advance diplomacy, the petroleum ministers of the Arab oil-producing nations gathered in Kuwait on October 17, 1973. There, within hours, they decided to cut oil production by 5 percent, and in succeeding months further to reduce their output, "depending on the Middle Eastern situation." Eventually the ministers established various categories among the Western nations, upgrading or reducing the latter's oil quotas in direct relation to their support of the Arab cause against Israel. Afterward, once the American airlift began, the Arab oil-producers, even such traditional friends as Saudi Arabia, declared a total ban on oil shipments to the United States. It was similarly under the façade of the war crisis that the Arabs exploited the opportunity to launch a drastic escalation of oil prices. Within days the depleted oil shipments and price rises forced the British, French, Italian, and Benelux governments to introduce tight controls on oil use. Britain was obliged to reduce its factory work schedule to four days a week. Italy's ocean liners were kept in port for lack of fuel. Frantic to placate the Arabs, the Common Market ministers now released a statement urging Israel to return all occupied Arab lands and to take into account "the rights of the Palestinians." The Arabs were not placated. Their oil reductions continued, the agony in Western Europe—and soon in the United States—mounted, and with it Israel's sense of diplomatic isolation.

These were the circumstances under which Kissinger sought, and achieved, a more flexible bargaining position from Mrs. Meir. The secretary was determined to widen his search for accommodation, moreover, by protecting his flanks in the Arab world. To that end, he embarked on a five-nation swing through the Middle East between November 5 and 9. The visits went well. He was received by the Arab leaders as a "messenger of peace," the only man, after all, who could persuade the Israelis to disgorge occupied territory. In a cordial meeting with Sadat on November 7, Kissinger persuaded the Egyptian leader to modify his demand for an immediate Israeli withdrawal to the October 22 cease-fire line, and instead to put this narrow issue in the broader context of a general disengagement of Israeli and Egyptian troops. Both sides, in any event, recognized that the current truce lines were too precariously entwined to survive. Kissinger meanwhile assured Sadat that, at a peace conference later, the United States would exert its influence on the Israelis to carry out a more generous withdrawal in the Sinai.

To achieve this long-cherished peace conference, however, Israel would have to make concessions even now, principally on the issue of a supply corridor. Thus, after many hours of negotiations between the Israeli government and Kissinger's staff, a compromise was reached, and later endorsed by the Egyptians. It provided that both Israel and Egypt would immediately begin talks under United Nations auspices "on the disengagement and separation of forces"; that a permanent supply corridor would be opened to the Egyptian Third Army on the east bank; and that a full exchange of prisoners would take place. On November 15, as the first scheduled United Nations convoys began rolling into Suez City and across the waterway to the Third Army, Egypt released 238 Israeli prisoners of war, and Israel returned some 8,000 Egyptians.

At the same time, during the interval before the impending peace conference, Israeli and Egyptian military representatives continued to meet at Kilometer 101 on the Suez-Cairo highway. Their hope was to negotiate Kissinger's proposal for an additional military disengagement of the two armies, each ensconced precariously behind the lines of the other. The discussions were brittle, occasionally harsh. The Egyptians demanded an extensive Israeli withdrawal deep into Sinai. The Israelis pressed for at least a partial Egyptian retreat to the west bank. By early December, with no agreement in sight, the Kilometer 101 talks were suspended. At this point, then, Kissinger departed for yet another Middle East swing. He was determined at all costs to sustain the diplomatic momentum, to nudge the belligerents into a Geneva peace conference later in the month. With the exception of Syria, whose government would not so much as furnish a list of Israeli POWs, the secretary's efforts were fruitful. During visits to Cairo, Amman, and Jerusalem, he won a tripartite commitment to a peace conference, the first such ever to take place between Israel and the Arabs since the Lausanne discussions in 1949.

On December 22, the foreign ministers of Egypt, Jordan, Israel, the United States, and the Soviet Union gathered at Geneva's Palais des Nations. The atmosphere was cold. The Arab and Israeli delegations did indeed sit in the same room, but they entered by separate doors, and only after a forty-five-minute delay to ensure that neither party actually was seated next to the other. When the proceedings began, Egypt's Foreign Minister, Ismail Fahmi, launched into an uncompromising attack upon the Israelis, their presence on Arab territory, and their obligation to clear out promptly. Eban answered in the same terse spirit for Israel. The following day, by prearrangement, the conference "temporarily" adjourned, with the understanding that Egypt and Israel would continue talks at the military level for a disengagement of forces as the next stage toward peace. It had been a short "conference," but there appeared every likelihood that discussions would resume later at Geneva. Kissinger's accomplishment was unquestionably a major one.

By then Israel was in the midst of its renewed election campaigning. The Labor party fully recognized that its maximalist pre-October stance on the occupied territories was out of date. The realities of the costly war, Israel's losses in life and treasure, and its diplomatic isolation precluded any chance of too hard a line. Thus, Labor's new electoral platform, while insisting on "defensible borders that will ensure Israel's ability to protect itself effectively," offered hope as well for a peace based on "territorial compromise." By the same token, Sadat was determined that the radical Arab nations would not dictate his policy. He was his own man now; his political leverage had dramatically widened following the capture of the Bar-Lev Line. By evincing flexibility, moreover, he enjoyed a unique opportunity to achieve through Kissinger's intercession what his generals had failed to win on the battlefield. As Foreign Minister Fahmi put it: "What other country [but the United States] can force Israel to withdraw?" On that basis, Egypt had resumed diplomatic relations with Washington.

Despite the subsequent failure, then, of Israeli and Egyptian military negotiating teams at Kilometer 101 to reach a disengagement agreement on their own, neither Jerusalem nor Cairo despaired that all opportunity for compromise had been exhausted. Rather, at the suggestion of both governments, Kissinger departed Washington on January 10, 1974, for yet a third effort at shuttle diplomacy. He brought with him this time a proposal that had been submitted to him earlier in Washington by Moshe Dayan. It was a hint that Israel might countenance a retreat from the eastern bank of the Canal to the Sinai passes, on condition that Egypt agreed to open the waterway immediately, then to rehabilitate the Canal cities, and to lift the Bab al-Mandeb blockade. The idea was not new; Dayan had floated it unsuccessfully in 1971 (p. 183). This time, however, Sadat decided to accept the idea in principle. Hereupon Kissinger flew directly to Israel for a working dinner with Israeli leaders in Jerusalem.

It was during this evening meeting of January 12 that the context of Middle Eastern negotiations suddenly shifted. Kissinger informed his hosts that Sadat had offered an immediate disengagement agreement, a pact to be mediated by the secretary himself, as an alternative to continuing either the Geneva or the Kilometer 101 talks. It was a breathtaking departure. The Israelis were confronted now with a crucial choice. On the one hand, the opportunity for face-to-face negotiations had been a major inducement for the Meir government originally to accept a cease-fire, and subsequently to open a corridor to the Egyptian Third Army. Yet perhaps even more attractive was the possibility now, through Kissinger's good offices, to defuse the threat of a new explosion between the entwined armies. In truth, during the ten and a half weeks since the cease-fire of October 24, there had been no end to combat. Some 500 incidents had been initiated by the Egyptians, and the Israelis had suffered fifteen killed and sixty-five wounded. The danger of yet another major eruption was a nagging fear in every Israeli mind, for it appeared unlikely that Sadat would long be able to conceal from his nation the precarious status of the Third Army, or the proximity of Israeli forces to his major cities. In any event, little progress had been made through direct negotiations, either at Kilometer 101 or at Geneva. Even less could be expected at a renewed peace conference attended by hostile Soviet and Arab foreign ministers. On the spot, therefore, the Israelis made the choice for indirect negotiations; they preferred not to risk additional loss of life.

The decision soon produced tangible results. Shuttling in his presidential jet transport between Aswan and Tel Aviv, occasionally formulating compromise suggestions of his own, Kissinger swiftly narrowed the difference between the two sides. On January 17 he cabled Nixon that agreement on troop disengagement had been reached; the following day Israeli General David Elazar and Egyptian General Muhammad al-Gamassi would sign the document at Kilometer 101. The Geneva Conference, which had opened to fanfare only four weeks earlier, played no part in the disengagement agreement.

The key feature of the accord manifestly reflected American and world pressure on Israel. It was for the Israelis to withdraw both from the west bank of the Canal and from their advanced positions on the east bank to a distance of some twelve miles into Sinai. Although the pullback represented no essential weakening of Israel's defensive position—the Gidi and Mitla passes would not be abandoned—it did signify a unilateral Israeli move. The withdrawal was qualified, however, by Sadat's agreement to limit the Egyptian military presence on the east bank to a mere 7,000 troops in a limited geographical zone. A middle—buffer—zone would be occupied by United Nations troops, while a third zone would be held by the Israelis under the same constraints imposed on the Egyptians due east of the Canal.

In addition to the official bilateral agreement, eight of a series of eleven "private" letters from Nixon to Sadat and to Mrs. Meir were countersigned by both Middle Eastern leaders, thus representing Egypt's and Israel's commitment not to each other but to a third party, the United States. The most important of the "private" communications included Sadat's assurances that his government would set about clearing the waterway and rebuilding the Canal cities, in effect making the Suez area a hostage to peace; and that nonmilitary cargoes to or from Israel would be allowed passage through the Canal, although not in Israeli vessels. Nixon's letter to Mrs. Meir, in turn, confirmed that the United States would supply aerial reconnaissance of the disengagement area, and would be "fully responsive on a continuing and long-term basis to Israel's military equipment requirements." The final codicil of the bilateral agreement proclaimed the document to be a "first step toward a final, just, and durable peace according to the provisions of Security Council Resolution 338 and within the framework of the Geneva Conference."

Throughout the next week and a half, the mutual extrication of forces was accomplished with little difficulty. Both sides honored their agreements. Indeed, by then Kissinger was known both in Egypt and in Israel as a "miracle man." It was precisely his success in mediating the disengagement, and his promise to undertake a similar effort between Israel and Syria, that persuaded the Arab oil-producing nations on March 18 to end their embargo against the West. Factories in Europe and in the United States gradually resumed full production. Traffic began to move freely again. The atmosphere seemingly was conducive for a parallel Syrian-Israeli disengagement. Manifestly, the task of negotiating an accord would not be easy. Syrian hostility toward Israel remained more deeply embedded than in any other Arab nation. Nevertheless, the Assad

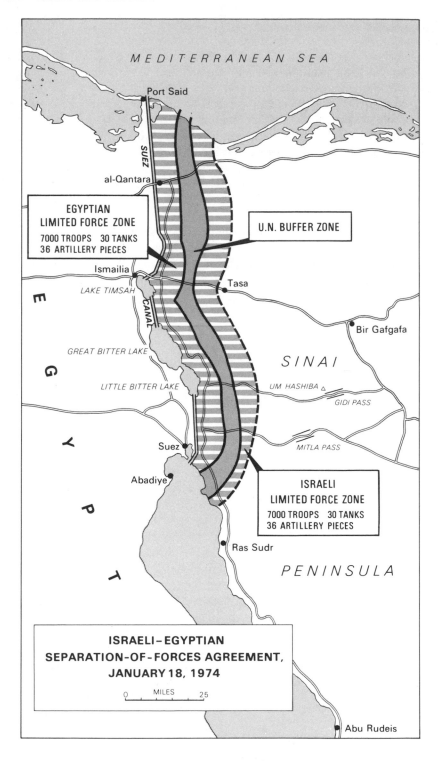

MEDITERRANEAN SEA

Port Said

SUEZ

al-Qantara

EGYPTIAN
LIMITED FORCE ZONE
7000 TROOPS   30 TANKS
36 ARTILLERY PIECES

U.N. BUFFER ZONE

Ismailia

LAKE TIMSAH

CANAL

Tasa

• Bir Gafgafa

GREAT BITTER LAKE

SINAI

LITTLE BITTER LAKE

UM HASHIBA △

GIDI PASS

Suez

MITLA PASS

Abadiye

ISRAELI
LIMITED FORCE ZONE
7000 TROOPS   30 TANKS
36 ARTILLERY PIECES

E
G
Y
P
T

• Ras Sudr

PENINSULA

ISRAELI–EGYPTIAN
SEPARATION-OF-FORCES AGREEMENT,
JANUARY 18, 1974

0   MILES   25

Abu Rudeis

government recognized that the Russians could offer Syria only weapons and more fighting, without assurance of returned territory. The United States conceivably could do better. In late April 1974, therefore, Kissinger departed again for the Middle East. Continuing without interruption for the next thirty-two days, this last shuttle between Damascus and Tel Aviv was the longest and most arduous of his experience. But at last, on May 31, an agreement was signed in Geneva.

The accord established a new and binding cease-fire. Israeli forces were obliged to withdraw to positions slightly west of the pre-October cease-fire line. Syrian forces would advance to a line east of that earlier frontier. As along the Suez Canal, the retreat effected no serious weakening of Israel's defensive posture. A demilitarized buffer zone was established between the two armies, with equal and parallel "areas of limitation in armament and forces" on each side. The buffer itself was to be patrolled by 1,250 United Nations "observers." Unlike the 1949 Israeli-Syrian armistice agreement, Damascus this time refused to guarantee that "paramilitary forces" would be forbidden to commit "warlike or hostile" acts against Israel; Assad was politically too weak to disown activities by the various Palestine guerrilla organizations. On the other hand, the United States reassured Israel, again by "private" letter, that legitimate acts of self-defense against guerrilla raids would be permissible. Whereupon the Israeli Knesset voted to approve the agreement. Almost immediately afterward, prisoners of war were exchanged. In the next three weeks the troop disengagement was carried out on schedule. As in Sinai, the likelihood of renewed hostilities in the north faded.

THE FALL OF GOLDA MEIR

Meanwhile, elections for Israel's Eighth Knesset, postponed for two months due to the war and afterward rescheduled for December 31, were held under the shadow of the nation's heavy manpower losses and the threat of renewed fighting. The fall of the Bar-Lev Line and the pulverizing Syrian offensive had thrown the nation into shock. Yet, whatever the mood of disillusionment with the Labor government, few citizens believed that Menachem Begin and his right-wing Gachal colleagues could be trusted to explore all opportunities for peace. As a result, the December elections left the political configuration essentially unchanged. Gachal gained eight seats, but remained a minority bloc. Accounting for 51 out of 120 members, Labor managed to survive as the dominant force in the Knesset. It could still put together a coalition.

As matters developed, the new government experienced the shortest life span in Israel's history, collapsing only three weeks after presenting its cabinet to the Knesset. What torpedoed the coalition was an "official report" on the recent war. In the immediate aftermath of the cease-fire, the press and members of all political parties had angrily demanded an explanation for the army's grievous initial defeats. Responding to this furor, the government on November 18 appointed a commission of respected, nonpolitical figures to investigate the intelligence breakdown preceding the enemy attack, and the military's lack of preparedness for the Egyptian-Syrian offensives. By early April, the commission had held extensive hearings and had taken much evidence in writing. It decided then to issue an "interim" report without waiting for the investigation to be completed. The deliberations already had consumed many months, after all, and in the meanwhile public debate over the October War was developing into an unmanageable clamor.

The interim report concluded that the defense forces had received more than sufficient warning of an impending attack. Their belated response to this information could only have been attributed to the obdurate "Conception" that, without clear superiority in air power, neither Egypt nor Syria would dare resort to full-scale war. The commission then recommended the dismissal of General Zeira, the intelligence chief, and of his three deputies (this recommendation was duly accepted and carried out). The report also observed that no defensive plan had been prepared for the eventuality of a surprise attack, and that a partial mobilization should have been requested at least a week before the war. Holding Chief of Staff Elazar accountable for these errors, the commission sorrowfully recommended his dismissal, as well. It did not, on the other hand, presume to judge the "parliamentary responsibility" of Prime Minister Meir or of Defense Minister Dayan for the initial failures, observing that the issue fell "outside the scope of this inquiry."

On April 2, the day the report was submitted to the government, Elazar offered his resignation. Yet the chief of staff insisted, resentfully, that Dayan at least shared responsibility for events leading to the war. It was a criticism ventilated far more emphatically by the press and by the nation at large. Demobilized soldiers, academicians, writers, and others began organizing public meetings calling for Dayan's resignation, and similar appeals were heard within the Labor party. Begin's Gachal faction meanwhile requested an extraordinary session of the Knesset to debate a motion of nonconfidence in the government. In anticipation of that debate, which was fixed for April 11, tensions within the Labor party rose to a degree unequaled since the Lavon Affair of the early 1960s. It was by no means certain this time that the party's members would close ranks to support the government. Whereupon, exasperated and exhausted, Mrs. Meir decided not to risk the vote of confidence. Instead, she submitted her resignation, thereby causing the fall of her cabinet.

Labor's most urgent task at this point was to find a successor to the redoubtable old woman. The major contest ultimately devolved between Ben-Gurion's former protégé, the able and highly respected Shimon Peres, currently serving as minister of information, and Yitzchak Rabin, chief of staff during the Six-Day War, later ambassador to Washington, and most recently minister of labor. Unlike Peres, Rabin was a newcomer to politics. This was to his advantage now. So were his credentials as a military hero, as a man untainted by the setbacks of the recent war, and as one with presumably well-developed contacts in the United States government. Eventually, on April 22, Rabin was chosen by Labor's central committee in a tight election. At fifty-one, he was the first native-born prime minister in Israel's history. His choice for foreign minister, Yigal Allon, whose deputy he had been in Israel's war of independence, was also native-born.

HENRY KISSINGER AND SECOND-STAGE DISENGAGEMENT

By April 22, Washington was intensively reviewing its Middle Eastern alternatives. Oil was the State Department's obsession, a consuming anxiety lest a fresh outburst of Arab-Israeli hostilities revive the Arab petroleum embargo. To avoid that disaster at any cost, Kissinger began sounding out Cairo and Jerusalem in the spring of 1—74 on the possibility of renewed—indirect— negotiations for additional disengagement. The response was affirmative. Sadat by then was less than eager to return to Geneva. Under Soviet pressure, a reconvened conference would have ensured a common Arab stance of intransigence; any possibility of further Israeli withdrawal would have been doomed. Kissinger's mediation seemed a better choice.

The Rabin government agreed. The new prime minister presided over a shaky coalition. He had won his mandate from the Knesset by assuring the centrists and religionists that negotiations on the West Bank ("the historic Land of Israel") would not take place without new national elections. To forestall discussions with Hussein on the Palestine issue, therefore, Rabin was prepared to seek an immediate accommodation with Egypt. In fact, this may have been a blunder. Even if an agreement with Hussein had not been attainable, a good-faith effort to negotiate might at least have created the appearance of movement on the eastern front, in this fashion undercutting radical Arab opposition to Hussein. Before Rabin could reconsider, however, on October 26, 1974 an Arab summit conference in Rabat, Morocco, stripped Hussein of his right to negotiate for the Palestine Arabs at all, and instead appointed Yasser Arafat as exclusive spokesman on this issue. The Israeli prime minister unquestionably had succeeded in avoiding the much-feared general election; but, inadvertently, he had paved the road for Arafat to the speaker's rostrum at the UN General Assembly and at other international forums.

At best, Rabin's decision to avoid Geneva, to bypass Hussein, and to rely on Kissinger's mediation with Egypt, was a gamble. The initial goal he and his foreign minister, Allon, had in mind was something less than a peace treaty with the Egyptians, but an understanding at least credible enough to establish an atmosphere of mutual trust in which peaceful conditions might gradually emerge over the years. The extent of a Sinai withdrawal would be determined by the range of meaningful Egyptian political concessions: in short, "a piece of territory for a piece of peace." The territory at stake here, first and foremost, was the Mitla and Gidi passes. Less than forty miles from the Canal, the two defiles represented the only practicable access routes to eastern Sinai. They also guarded Israel's huge military air base at Refidim (Bir Gafgafa) and dominated passage to the Israeli-operated Abu Rudeis oil fields. These latter had been developed at the cost of hundreds of millions of dollars by Israel-licensed companies since the 1967 war, and by 1973 provided Israel with nearly half its energy supplies. In possession of Gidi and Mitla, Israel could defend itself, and an important part of its economic future, with relatively small forces. For this reason, shortly after the 1967 victory, Israeli military engineers had elaborately fortified the passes with a network of trenches, miniforts, caves, and tank redoubts. Since the October War, moreover, Israel had spent an additional $150 million on roads, mine fields, communications, and outposts to reinforce the Mitla-Gidi line.

For the appropriate political concessions, Rabin and his cabinet were prepared to abandon this vast military infrastructure. Indeed, Rabin, Allon, and Peres (who had joined the cabinet as defense minister) were equally prepared to withdraw from the Abu Rudeis oil field and from the smaller oil facilities at Ras Sudr. They asked in return simply a meaningful Egyptian commitment to nonbelligerency. Such a declaration not only would preclude resort to force; it would render illegal any further blockades of international waterways, including the Suez Canal, and would provide the framework for liquidating economic and even propaganda warfare against Israel. This was the message from the Israelis that Kissinger took with him as he departed for Egypt on a renewed effort of shuttle diplomacy. The secretary arrived in Aswan on March 8, 1975, and proceeded immediately to discussions with Sadat and Foreign Minister Ismail Fahmi.

Sadat's demands, on the other hand, were essentially territorial. He and his advisers sought the restoration of much more than simply the desert passes. They had in mind approximately 40 percent of the Sinai, extending two-thirds of the way to al-Arish. Plainly, this was a far larger concession than Israel had anticipated at the outset. Even so, once Gidi and Mitla were abandoned, a few extra miles would not prove crucial, and there would still be room for negotiation. Among other problems to be worked out were those of demilitarization and nonbelligerency. The Egyptians opposed a total demilitarization of the area to be evacuated by Israel, including the passes; they demanded instead the right to move their army forward as the Israelis withdrew. Yet because Kissinger sympathized with Israel's position here, a narrowing of viewpoints on this issue was also conceivable. Where the Egyptians remained adamant was on the question of nonbelligerency. Such a commitment, Sadat insisted, was feasible only after Israel had withdrawn from all occupied territories on each of the three fronts: Egyptian, Syrian, and Jordanian. On this point, conversely, Kissinger's sympathy was with the Egyptians, and he finally persuaded Rabin to forgo a public renunciation of belligerency by Egypt in return for assurance at least of the "practical elements" of nonbelligerency.

The Israelis were quite specific on those elements, however. They wanted a guarantee not merely of free navigation for their cargoes through the Canal (Sadat had made this concession a year earlier), but the passage of mixed Israeli and other crews on non-Israeli ships through the Canal, and direct third-party tourism between Egypt and Israel, with direct (foreign) airline travel between the two countries. Not least of all, the Israelis wanted time, an assurance that a UNEF force in the buffer zone would not be challenged in six months or so, or its mandate overturned by Great Power veto. Finally, Rabin demanded mixed Israeli-Egyptian patrols for the buffer zone. If only on the military level, these joint units would establish the human contacts that Israel had forfeited by agreeing not to resume the Geneva Peace Conference.

On none of these provisions was Sadat forthcoming. Neither did the Israelis win support from Kissinger, who repeatedly entreated them to display greater flexibility. Under this pressure, Rabin consented finally to abandon his demands for mixed crews through the Canal, even for joint army patrols. But he would not compromise elsewhere. At Kissinger's behest, then, President Gerald Ford, who the previous August had replaced Nixon at the White House, cabled a warning to Rabin that the United States would be obliged to "reappraise" its Middle Eastern policy if the Israelis were not more accommodating. On the other hand, the president was prepared to offer the kind of open-ended military aid that would compensate the Israelis for any territory they abandoned in the Sinai. The inducement proved unavailing. Rabin and his colleagues would not abandon their last natural barriers in Sinai for the "chimera" of American support. Accordingly, in the final week of March 1975, Kissinger dropped his shuttle negotiations and returned to Washington. At his recommendation, President Ford in turn withheld assurance of future American arms shipments. Yet even then Rabin would not be shaken. Together with his ministerial colleagues, he was convinced that Egypt needed peace as badly as did Israel.

The prime minister was not mistaken. Despite vast infusions of Arab oil money, the war had cost Egypt heavily. In 1974 the nation's annual inflation rate had climbed to 40 percent. Its population groaned under the weight of a military budget that approached a fifth of Egypt's GNP. In 1975, too, the government was spending $900 million in food subsidies alone. The state was crippled by underproduction and its public services were malfunctioning to the brink of collapse. Angered, meanwhile, by Cairo's new warmth toward the United States, Moscow had turned down Sadat's appeal to reschedule Egypt's debt payments (estimated at nearly $7 billion). If, then, American help was needed for diplomatic pressure on Israel, that aid was hardly less indispensable for rescuing and revamping Egypt's chaotic economy.

Indeed, it was to launch that revival that Sadat had authorized minesweeping and debris removal from the Canal in the aftermath of the disengagement agreement of January 1974. With extensive American and West European participation, the task was completed by the spring of 1975 (pp. 246–47). Thus it was, only three days after the failure of Kissinger's March shuttle negotiations, that Sadat decided to gamble on a propaganda victory and on economic recovery. He announced that he would open the Canal on June 4, and would proceed forthwith to rebuild the Canal cities. Actually, the Egyptian president had little choice. His people no longer possessed either the strength or the willpower for renewed warfare. Sadat himself all but admitted this helplessness during a meeting with President Ford in Salzburg, on June 1, when he suggested that there was perhaps after all a certain limited room for "maneuver" with Israel.

As a gesture of their own goodwill, meanwhile, the Israelis announced on June 3 that they would match Egypt's decision to open the Canal by pulling back half their authorized tanks and troops some eighteen to twenty-five miles from the waterway. The evacuation similarly had the effect of reducing tensions between Jerusalem and Washington. Shortly afterward, in the second week of June, Rabin flew to the American capital to engage in his own effort at fence-mending. The ensuing talks with Ford and Kissinger were tough, and at first were less than productive. But a later meeting between Rabin and Kissinger in Germany, on July 13, offered a hint of a breakthrough. With renewed assurance of political support at home, the Israeli leader indicated that he, too, was willing now to make additional concessions, particularly in territorial withdrawals; and that, like Sadat, he favored picking up the thread of indirect diplomacy.

THE BREAKTHROUGH TO INTERIM WITHDRAWAL

Triangular discussions were quietly resumed. This time they took the form of negotiations in Washington between Kissinger and the Israeli and Egyptian ambassadors, the latter two passing on to the secretary their governments' proposals and counterproposals. Slowly the gulf between the opposing positions began to narrow. And when finally only a minimum of details remained to be clarified, Kissinger departed once again for the Middle East on August 20, 1975. An additional week and a half of travel were needed between Tel Aviv and Alexandria to secure "clarifications," but on September 1 the second-stage, interim, disengagement was initialed at last by Sadat and Rabin.

The territorial and military features of the agreement were incorporated into a public accord and annex. Under the text of these documents, Rabin acquiesced in Sadat's demand to withdraw Israel's forces some eighteen to twenty miles east of their current positions. The key sites of the evacuated areas this time included the length of the Mitla and Gidi passes, and the portion of southwestern Sinai encompassing the Abu Rudeis and Ras Sudr oil fields. Yet the nature of this military evacuation was highly qualified, and Israel's defensive posture was affected only minimally. Egyptian forces would take over only a small part—between two and four miles—of the territory abandoned by Israel east of the Canal. The rest, including the passes, would be occupied by United Nations troops in a new and much wider buffer zone, except for a shrunken corridor extending along the coast to the oil installations, and even these would be demilitarized. Moreover, Israeli forces were allowed to position themselves on hills dominating the eastern entrances to the defiles. The Egyptians enjoyed no such rights at the western edges of the passes. For that matter, even the restricted zone of Egyptian advance was confined exclusively to limited forces. Nor would Israel be obliged to redeploy its forces east of Mitla and Gidi until five months after the signing; there would be time during the interval to remove all fortified installations and equipment.

Under the provisions of the new accord, to be sure, Israel failed to win a public Egyptian declaration of nonbelligerency, or assurance of compensation for the oil fields it had explored, developed, and was now abandoning. Even so, the commitments extracted from Egypt were hardly negligible. Each side agreed to avoid "resort to the threat or use of force or military blockade against the other." The Egyptians reaffirmed the right of nonmilitary cargoes destined for, or coming from, Israel, to use the Canal. In a private communication to Washington, Sadat further pledged to relax Egypt's boycott of selected foreign companies doing business with Israel, and to ease his government's pressure on African and other nations wishing to resume diplomatic ties with Israel. And, too, the accord was noncancelable for a minimum of three years.

By far the most significant feature of the agreement, however, was the active role assumed by the United States to ensure both the cease-fire and the balance of power in the Middle East. Although Egyptian and Israeli electronic warning stations were permitted at either end of the Mitla and Gidi passes, neither side would allow the other to man additional stations within the defiles themselves. Nor would either entrust this monitoring responsibility to the traditionally unreliable United Nations. Thus, during his meeting with Ford at Salzburg, the Egyptian president volunteered the intriguing notion of using American technicians to operate a group of auxiliary stations in both the Mitla and Gidi passes. The proposal was instantly accepted by the Israelis. In their view, no other gesture would lend such credence to Washington's vested interest in Middle Eastern stability. Kissinger agreed. So did Ford; and so, eventually, did key members of the United States Senate. The compact was thereupon refined. In its final version, it took the form of three additional watch stations to be established by the United States and operated by some 200 American civilian personnel within the UNEF buffer zone in the two Sinai passes.

Other American assurances proved hardly less vital to Israel. Since the collapse of the original March 1975 shuttle effort, the Rabin government had warned Kissinger that Israel would require meaningful compensation in exchange for abandonment of the passes and of the Abu Rudeis oil fields. With Egypt refusing that compensation, it was Washington that would have to make Israel whole. In the ensuing negotiations of spring and summer, therefore, Kissinger was engaged as much in negotiating an American-Israeli understanding as in completing agreement between Jerusalem and Cairo. Except for the issue of technicians, the American-Israeli "entente" was not incorporated into the public accord, but took the form rather of a series of "private" letters from Ford to the Israeli government. These letters included assurance of an uninterrupted flow of modern weapons systems to Israel, and a promise to request Congress for grants and loans totaling between $2 billion and $3 billion annually for the next five years to help underwrite Israel's backbreaking military and civilian expenditures. Not the least of those expenditures was the cost of oil supplies to be acquired elsewhere, once Abu Rudeis and Ras Sudr went back to the Egyptians. In the event, too, of an oil embargo against Israel by Iranian or other suppliers during the next five years, the United States would guarantee the Israelis adequate quantities of fuel, if necessary from American stocks.

Perhaps the most meaningful of Washington's assurances to the Rabin government was the American undertaking to refrain from pressing Israel for additional unilateral withdrawals from the Golan or from the West Bank; to withhold recognition of the PLO as long as the latter declined to accept UN Resolution 242; and to "consult closely" with Israel in the event of a future threat to Middle Eastern peace either by Egypt or by an "outside power." The implication of American military support was far-reaching. In truth, these various American economic, diplomatic, and military commitments left no doubt that the United States was doing what great and wealthy nations had always done. In effect, it was buying an interregnum of quietude for its own strategic purposes.

Yet if the Americans were forthcoming, their contributions to the Sinai disengagement merely accentuated the grudging nature of Egypt's concessions. Sadat offered no statement of nonbelligerency, or any provision for the sale of Sinai oil to Israel, or for neutral party tourism between the two countries. The right of Israeli cargoes to pass through the Canal had been acknowledged in the earlier January 1974 disengagement agreement. It was a right, then, for which Israel in effect had paid twice. Sadat emphasized the purely military nature of the latest accord, moreover, by the representatives he dispatched to the signing ceremony in Geneva on September 4, 1975. They were army officers, and low-ranking ones at that. Cairo's agreement to moderate its boycott on foreign companies doing business with Israel, to reduce the scale of its diplomatic and propaganda warfare, appeared not in the public accord, but rather in the exchange of letters with the United States. Indeed, Sadat emphasized repeatedly that his negotiations at no time had been with the Israelis, but rather with the Americans. A final political understanding with the Zionist enemy apparently still remained unthinkable.

Sadat's suspicion was a mirror image of Israel's. The shortcomings of the agreement were not lost on its Israeli critics, on Begin, Dayan, and on others of the Center-Right. The Rabin government, they warned, was abandoning vital strategic defenses in exchange for purely American guarantees. Could full value be placed on those assurances? Would the United States be prepared to risk the ire of the entire Arab world by heeding its "private" military and diplomatic commitments to Israel? Recalling the fate of Eisenhower's 1957 guarantees in the blockade crisis of ten years later, these critics were skeptical. To ventilate their apprehensions, Begin and his Gachal followers organized large-scale demonstrations against the accord on September 2. At one point some 25,000 marchers paraded angrily near the Knesset and the prime minister's office. Even so, the virulence of public protest evidently did not reflect a national consensus. On September 3, the Knesset signified its willingness to venture a "risk for peace." It endorsed the interim agreement by the unexpectedly large majority of 70 to 43.

MALAISE IN ISRAEL. REVIVED CONFIDENCE IN EGYPT

The passage of nearly two years since the October War had not eased the shock of that conflict for the Israelis. In 1973 the threat of Soviet intervention had obliged the government to call a military halt just short of final victory or of any logical strategic goal. Pressure from Washington in 1974–75 had compelled an Israeli retreat from the Canal without even a definitive Egyptian commitment to nonbelligerency. The implications for the future were grave. So were the economic costs of less than final peace. Before 1973, the prevailing wisdom had assumed that Israel, with its resilient economy and skilled work force, somehow could hold its own in any Middle Eastern arms race. But in the first year and a half since the October War, nearly $3 billion in Soviet and French weaponry had flowed into Egypt and Syria, most of it underwritten by the Persian Gulf oil nations. By a ratio of at least one to three, Israel had to match these acquisitions. It was also obliged to pull tens of thousands of men and women out of the economy for extended terms of military service. As a result of these pressures, in 1974 the little nation's defense budget rose to $3.6 billion— or a staggering 33 percent of its GNP. And in March of that year Israel's foreign currency reserves declined to $1 billion, the "red line" danger mark. By then foreign loans had to be exploited for all they were worth. Inasmuch as the country already was supporting a debt load of $5.5 billion, the sheer cost of servicing this debt, of drawing upon shrinking hard currency reserves to pay for imports (their prices often doubled or even tripled by the escalation of oil prices), fueled Israel's soaring inflation. The price level jumped 56 percent in 1974 alone.

It was the nation's diplomatic isolation, no less than the economic burdens

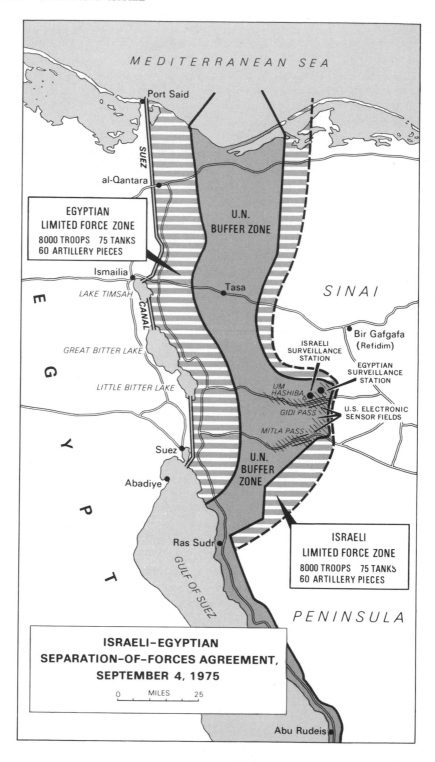

MEDITERRANEAN SEA

Port Said

SUEZ

al-Qantara

**EGYPTIAN
LIMITED FORCE ZONE**
8000 TROOPS   75 TANKS
60 ARTILLERY PIECES

U.N.
BUFFER ZONE

Ismailia

LAKE TIMSAH

CANAL

Tasa

SINAI

E

GREAT BITTER LAKE

Bir Gafgafa
(Refidim)

ISRAELI
SURVEILLANCE
STATION

G

LITTLE BITTER LAKE

EGYPTIAN
SURVEILLANCE
STATION

UM
HASHIBA

GIDI PASS

U.S. ELECTRONIC
SENSOR FIELDS

MITLA PASS

Suez

Y

U.N.
BUFFER
ZONE

Abadiye

**ISRAELI
LIMITED FORCE ZONE**
8000 TROOPS   75 TANKS
60 ARTILLERY PIECES

Ras Sudr

P

GULF OF SUEZ

PENINSULA

T

**ISRAELI–EGYPTIAN
SEPARATION–OF–FORCES AGREEMENT,
SEPTEMBER 4, 1975**

0   MILES   25

Abu Rudeis

and the physical losses of the war, that added its impact to the cumulative malaise of the mid- and latter-1970s. There was virtually no forum in which Israel could escape this pressure. In early July 1975, for example, the UN International Women's Year Conference in Mexico City called for the elimination of Zionism as one of the world's "great evils, along with colonialism, neocolonialism, imperialism, foreign domination and occupation, apartheid and racial discrimination. . . ." In November 1975, the UN General Assembly endorsed a resolution describing Israel as "the racist regime in occupied Palestine," and stigmatizing Zionism as a "form of racialism and racial discrimination." Just prior to adopting this measure, the General Assembly passed two other resolutions, one calling for the participation of the PLO in future sessions of the Geneva Conference, the other establishing a committee to promote "the exercise of the inalienable rights of the Palestinian people." A month later, on December 5, the General Assembly ordered the Jewish state to return all occupied Arab land "without qualification [that is, without the qualification of peace treaties]," and to restore the "legitimate rights of the Palestinians." Additional diplomatic reverses could be anticipated in the future.

Egypt, too, did not escape the war without heavy cost. In terms of absolute manpower losses, it paid even more cruelly: 7,700 dead and at least three times that many wounded. For a warm, family-oriented people, it was little consolation that the nation's demographic base was far larger than Israel's. Sadat recalled: "I lost my younger brother, who was like a son to me, five minutes after the start of the October War. I have seen the victims of that war—young people destined to spend the rest of their lives in wheelchairs." By the same token, Egypt's economic losses were at least twice those of Israel. Psychologically, nevertheless, the Egyptian army's impressive early performance more than compensated for the wounds of conflict. Once the electrifying news was released that the Bar-Lev Line had been captured, Yusuf Idris, an eminent poet-politician and former critic of Sadat, wrote a panegyric entitled "Deliverance":

> I had never before believed in the role of the individual in history.
> I did not know that one person alone, in setting his own will, set that of
>   a Nation, and the history of a people, and the strength of a
>   civilization.
> But the hero, Anwar al-Sadat, is beyond my ken.
> He crushed the defeat lying deep within us all when he resolved upon
>   the crossing.
> And by his decision not only the army crossed the Canal
> but the people crossed with it and transcended their submissiveness and
>   misery, left behind their humiliation and shame. . . .
> The crossing is deliverance.
> (Translation by John Waterbury)

It was a sentiment echoed in every newspaper, in every radio and television program, in every school pageant, in every music hall. There was no need for governmental orchestration. The mood of euphoria was altogether spontaneous. Typical were the comments of Egyptians participating in a specially convened "International Symposium on the 1973 War." "As a result of the war, Egypt and the Arab nations restored their honor and dignity" (Dr. Sufi Hassan Abu Thaleb, dean of Cairo University and later speaker of the People's Assembly); or "We, here in Egypt, regained confidence in ourselves and in the possibility of establishing a just peace" (Vice-President Hosni Mubarek).

The author recalls with particular vividness the account of Major General Hassan Abu Saada, a division commander in the Second Army during the 1973 war. Having successfully crossed the Canal, Abu Saada's troops on the morning of October 7 were attacked by three Israeli armored battalions of General Avraham Adan's division. The Egyptian commander allowed the Israeli Centurions to penetrate, then ambushed them with Sagger rockets. Seventy-three Israeli tanks were destroyed in the inferno. One of the officers captured was an Israeli battalion commander, Colonel Assaf Yaguri. When Yaguri was brought to Abu Saada personally the next morning, the Egyptian offered his prisoner a cigarette and tea, reassured him that he and his men would be well treated, that the Egyptians were civilized people. Abu Saada was as good as his word. "When you are victorious," he commented later, "you can afford to be generous and noble." And, in fact, this forbearance proved to be a critical factor in everything that followed, not least of all in Anwar al-Sadat's subsequent diplomatic initiatives. The Egyptian people had been restored to dignity.

XVII

SADAT OPENS THE DOOR

POLITICAL LIBERALIZATION

It is recalled that, shortly after consolidating his power in May 1971, Sadat embarked upon a program of desocialization and de-Sovietization. Two and a half years later, with his popularity immeasurably enhanced following the October War, the Egyptian leader felt secure enough to launch an intensified "liberalization in all fields." The phrase envisaged a far-reaching political as well as economic overhaul of Egyptian society. Nothing else and nothing less would reverse the stagnation of the late 1960s and early 1970s. Within two months after the first disengagement agreement with Israel, therefore, Egypt's concentration camps were almost entirely vacated. Even earlier, in an attempt to recruit to his cause many former opponents of Nasser, Sadat had begun granting amnesties to journalists, to cashiered army officers and government ministers. It was the president's hope to establish a new consensus among his nation's more conservative religious and social subgroups.

Encouraged in turn by this new relaxation, some of Egypt's most distinguished artists, writers, and professional figures began making invidious comparisons between the "agony of Nasser's totalitarian years" and the revived humanism at last ventilating almost every corner of national life. Public gratification increased in 1974 when Sadat restored the judiciary's independence, opened the doors once again to expatriate Egyptians, and canceled numerous extralegal measures that had been adopted during eighteen years of Nasserism. Yet the contrast most frequently drawn now was between Nasser's palpable failure in the war of 1967 and Sadat's widely heralded success in 1973. Thus, at the international conference sponsored by Cairo University on the second anniversary of the October War (p. 244), Egypt's participants adverted repeatedly to the "glorious triumph of 1973" and stressed that in 1967 "the political leadership," not the armed forces, had been responsible for defeat. Accordingly, with the denigration of Nasser emerged the cult of Sadat.

Throughout the mid- and latter-1970s, as acclaim for the new "openness," the new "democratization," generated a psychological momentum, Sadat decided that Egypt might well be ripe for a gradual transition to a multiparty system. In 1977, therefore, he approved the transformation of the Arab Socialist Union's three "trends" into formal political parties. The moderate-center Misr bloc—Sadat's own preference—was overwhelmingly the largest. Of the "independent" outer wings, that of the Right followed the old Wafdist line; that of the Left included several radical Socialist delegates who harked back to the Ali Sabri tradition. Sadat indulged them all. But, firmly, he warned the People's Assembly that no party would be allowed to organize exclusively on the basis of class or religion, or to advocate a violent alteration of the republican system of government. In sum, neither Communists, Fascists, nor Ikhwan-style religious extremists would be tolerated. Like his friend, the shah of Iran, Sadat plainly regarded the existence of an authentic opposition as something of a luxury. With the cooperation of Dr. Sufi Abu Thaleb, speaker of the People's Assembly, he preferred to temper the new democratization with a cautious blend of gradualism.

ECONOMIC DECENTRALIZATION

It was critical, too, that political liberalization be accompanied by wider economic opportunity, for the immediate impact of the 1973 war had been to exacerbate the nation's economic plight. To be sure, material privations could still be borne by the Egyptian people in the exaltation following the capture of the Bar-Lev Line. The government enjoyed a certain margin to formulate new alternatives. Nevertheless, the priority objective now was to devise an even more impressive and far-reaching economic "New Look." To that end, Sadat and his advisers were intent upon linking Western capital and technology with Egyptian manpower and markets. It was a process of rejuvenation, in turn, that depended with near-mathematical certitude upon the restoration of tranquillity and functional peace in the area. The disengagements of 1974–75 represented the first step in that process. The opening of the Suez Canal and reconstruction of the Canal cities were to be the next step.

Sadat's dramatic announcement that the Canal would reopen in June 1975, we recall, was interpreted initially as a silent olive branch to Israel. But its principal significance was economic. The throttled waterway had cost Egypt $13 billion in inflated shipping costs and lost tolls. Worse yet, seven years of intermittent bombardment had driven three-quarters of a million people away from the once-prosperous western bank, had left the Canal cities ghostly ruins, and had transformed Cairo into a fulminating malignancy. As early as the spring of 1974, therefore, the technical work of clearance was launched. The task was a prodigious one. It was necessary to remove from the waterway dozens of sunken vessels, hundreds of thousands of mines and other unexploded ordnance. Additional hundreds of thousands of mines had to be disinterred from the banks of the Canal. Although the United States was granted the commission to undertake the task of clearing and rebuilding, British, French, and Russian technicians all subsequently collaborated, with the Egyptians supplying the largest part of the manpower. The work was dangerous as well as complex and arduous. More than one hundred Egyptians died in the operation.

Hardly less monumental was the financial expense of clearance. It would in fact be an ongoing cost, for the government intended systematically to broaden the Canal until the waterway accommodated 200,000-ton tankers. Thus, as early as June 1975, the month Suez was reopened for traffic, $1.2 billion already had been spent to dredge hundreds of millions of cubic meters of earth, to build decantation basins, to remove old revetments and construct new ones, and to establish a network of electronic controls for safer and more rapid ship transit. Much of the funding for these projects was supplied by loans from the World Bank ($100 million) and from various Arab Persian Gulf sources ($140 million). Yet the Egyptian government itself agreed each year to contribute 10 percent of the Canal Authority's income, an annual commitment of at least $40 million. Altogether, the undertaking was destined to be the largest of its kind in modern Egyptian history, exceeding even the Aswan High Dam. If the investment was vast, however, so were the expected returns. It was anticipated that, by 1985, following the enlargements and other improvements, tonnage passing through the Canal might well approach two billion annually, while annual income from transit fees could reach $1.1 billion. Once the waterway was opened, too, the Western financial community doubtless would be prepared to consider additional funds for irrigation, for fishing and tourist facilities, and for other investments likely to nurture Egypt's economic growth.

In Sadat's list of priorities, the next goal, after opening the waterway itself, was to rebuild the three major Canal cities of Port Saïd, Ismailia, and Suez, and to make them habitable again for the hundreds of thousands of residents who had fled the area since 1967. To employ these people, the president and his advisers similarly planned the establishment of an international free zone at Port Saïd, and of major industries—cement, petrochemicals, fertilizers, refineries, among others—in the Canal Zone. The trans-Canal hinterland would also be expanded. A system of concrete culverts would be fabricated and laid beneath the Canal to transfer water from the Nile to the Sinai, in this fashion irrigating and reclaiming at least 350,000 acres of wilderness as a local source of food for the Canal cities. Indeed, so wedded was Sadat to this vision of a revived national economy, that through the week of November 20, 1974 he conducted a national referendum on his "October Working Paper," a broad-sweeping charter outlining the country's goals for the ensuing twenty-five years.

To ensure fulfillment of his grandiose economic scheme, moreover, Sadat's "Open Door" policy was aimed at encouraging the private sector to join the government in developing new employment opportunities and new technology. Thus, in 1974 and again in 1977, a series of investment laws lifted export and import regulations, established yet additional free zones, and granted Egyptian businessmen permission to make deals in foreign currencies. The number of joint projects and public ventures in turn increased to 381 by October 1977, with total investments valued at E£3.25 billion. As an inducement for encouraging savings investment, the government similarly exempted interest on deposits from taxation, and allowed shares and bonds registered in hard currency to circulate on the stock exchange.

It was significant, too, that voices from the past were heard again for the first time in nearly two decades. Almost all were persons who had fallen out with Nasser, such men as Saba Habashi, a former minister of finance and bitter critic of Nasser's socialism; and Ahmad Abu al-Fath, a "retired" editor of *al-Misri* (a nationalist paper, since defunct), and once a forthright advocate of parliamentary democracy and free enterprise. Conversely, Prime Minister Abd al-Aziz Higazi, who had launched the "Open Door" policy even before the October War, was relieved of his post in April 1975. It appeared that he was moving too slowly for Sadat's taste. By then the president was all but consumed with impatience to achieve Egypt's new era of growth and development.

CULTIVATION OF THE WEST. REJECTION OF SOVIET PATRONAGE

It was plain, nevertheless, that an "Open Door" for Egyptian initiative would not by itself have accomplished this goal. Additional funds were urgently needed from abroad. Some of the capital might be available from the Persian Gulf oil-producing states—in the event their leaders regarded the investment as a safe one. One of those who did was Reza Shah Pahlavi. In 1974, the Iranian ruler committed $700 million in aid and investment to Egypt. The Saudi government also extended an important loan of $200 million. Yet for Sadat, it was the West, and particularly the United States, that represented the limitless source of funds and technology that alone could revive his nation's future. To ensure access to this perceived cornucopia, the Egyptian president resumed diplomatic relations with the United States almost immediately after the 1973 war. And, as he hoped, American businessmen began to test the quality of Egypt's moderate new economic climate. David Rockefeller and other influential corporation executives arrived for firsthand investigation and consultation. These visitors were intent upon learning what, specifically, in addition to moderation, Egypt had to offer foreign investors.

One inducement, in fact, was the country's geographic location as a crossroads astride the heavily traveled trade routes between Europe and the Far East. It was a strategic importance that would grow with the opening of the Canal and the improvement of port facilities at Alexandria, Port Saïd, and Mersa Matruh on the Mediterranean, and at Suez City and Safaga on the Red Sea. Internally, too, Egypt enjoyed a relatively sophisticated infrastructure of roads, railroads, river transport, and power supply. This communications network in turn made available to investors Egypt's not inconsiderable domestic market of some 42 million people—by far the largest population in the Middle East. Still an additional advantage was Egypt's reservoir of skilled and semiskilled cheap labor and its unusually large supply of managerial personnel. Thus far, many of the latter had been obliged to find employment abroad, especially in the Persian Gulf. But now foreign investors could tap these reserves. Presumably they would be gratified to know that the right to strike did not exist in Egypt. Workers were docile and loyal, as a rule. The government itself defused potential unrest by subsidizing food.

Admittedly, the buying power of Egypt's impoverished population was not yet a compelling incentive. Neither was Egypt's "sophisticated" communications infrastructure; it was already overburdened and malfunctioning, particularly its telephone and telex facilities. And one of the least satisfactory features for overseas investors was the sclerosis of Egypt's awesome bureaucracy. The legacy of more than a decade of Nasserist socialism, administrative chaos both in government and industry remained truly Kafkaesque. By Nasser's design, too, laws and regulations to attract foreign investment in that earlier period were either restrictive or totally absent. European and American capital in turn had kept its distance from Egypt.

Then, in 1971, to help channel Western funds into the country, Sadat launched a more liberal foreign investment code and established the Egyptian International Bank for Trade and Development under the direction of Dr. Abd al-Moneim al-Qaysuni, a respected economist of orthodox views. At the time, these measures had little impact, for the confrontation with Israel still went on. But with the disengagements that followed the October War, the moment seemed appropriate to introduce new legislation to attract foreign capital. The most important of the new directives was Law 43, enacted by the People's Assembly in June 1974. Priority areas were defined, allowing the government to offer important tax benefits, including a guarantee that investments from overseas no longer would be subject to nationalization or confiscation "except through lawful process." Additionally, foreign investment projects would be exempted from all government regulation affecting wages, worker participation on management boards, or profit-sharing. During a five- to eight-year grace period, foreign companies would even be spared exposure to commercial or industrial profits taxes. In specially designated free zones, too, Western firms might freely import and export building materials, capital goods, or their own manufactures, again without paying customs or export duties. Capital transfers were allowed without restriction between the free zones and all foreign countries.

As they assessed the nation's future, Sadat's economists similarly anticipated that a calmer atmosphere in the region would enable tourism to become a steady source of hard currency. In 1977 some 680,000 tourists visited Egypt, not less than 80 percent of them from neighboring Arab states, and their receipts amounted to an impressive E£70 million. The goal for 1980 was E£250 million, much of this to come from hundreds of thousands of free-spending—Western—tourists. Yet another potential bonanza was the oil reservoir of the Sinai, both at Abu Rudeis and Ras Sudr and at other fields under exploration. The chances were regarded as favorable that these wells could transform Egypt into an oil exporter, bringing in as much as $1 billion by the early 1980s. To be sure, many other problems demanded solution before any of these possibilities could be realized. Central among them were the huge foreign debt that had to be serviced and the reorganization of Egypt's surrealistic bureaucracy. And beyond all others, as shall be seen, was the need to terminate the state of war with Israel.

During the mid- and latter 1970s, meanwhile, the Soviets were increasingly alarmed by the sudden Egyptian reorientation toward the West, and especially toward the United States. The offhand adjournment of the Geneva Conference in December 1973, the visible evidence afterward of Sadat's preference for the Kissinger track toward disengagement, represented a bitter disappointment for Moscow. In ensuing months, therefore, the Russians pressed Sadat to resume the Geneva Conference. For his part, the Egyptian president was careful not to reject these appeals out of hand. He simply refused to be pinned down to a specific date. There was logic in this procrastination. The presence of the Soviets and of the hard-line confrontation states at Geneva would have been a virtual guarantee of failure. Exasperated by Sadat's evasiveness, then, Leonid Brezhnev in January 1974 suddenly canceled his planned visit to Cairo. Afterward, Soviet commentators embarked on a furious editorial campaign against Egypt's undisguised rapprochement with the United States, its drift away from "scientific socialism," its growing "dependence" on Western private capital.

Sadat in turn was unwilling to accept this criticism supinely. During his May Day speech at Helwan in 1974, he rebuked Moscow for denying Egypt the diplomatic flexibility the Soviets claimed for themselves. "For the American Chase Manhattan Bank to open a branch in Moscow is acceptable," Sadat scoffed, "but for the same bank to open a branch in Egypt is considered a threat. American, German, and Japanese investment to build factories in Russia and exploit the gas fields of Siberia is acceptable, but the use of such funds to reconstruct the Canal towns and to reclaim the Western Desert is unacceptable. This is political adolescence."

Then, in March 1976, the Egyptian president officially and irretrievably transformed his government's relationship with the USSR. On the fourteenth of that month he called for the termination of the 1971 Soviet-Egyptian Treaty of Friendship and Cooperation. The "request" was approved by the People's Assembly within twenty-four hours. In his speech to the Assembly that same day, Sadat explained his decision. The Soviets had consistently opposed the "trend toward peace which has taken shape" since the October War, he pointed out. They had also opposed Egypt's "Open Door" policy, its "sovereign right" to carry out its own social and political changes. With growing indignation, Sadat observed that Moscow had declined to reschedule Egypt's debt repayment or to meet Egypt's military needs. On the contrary, the Soviets had gone so far as to demand interest payments on its current outstanding military loans. In an additional, gratuitous twist of the blade, moreover, the Russians had refused to overhaul Egypt's planes or to provide spare parts; even had forbidden India, which manufactured MiG-21 engines on license from the USSR, to offer this service. As far as Sadat was concerned, the vindictive infringement of Egypt's capacity for self-defense was the ultimate affront. For a brief while longer, he refrained from denying the Soviet fleet access to Egyptian ports. But on April 4, responding to the "public will," he canceled these naval privileges altogether. It was accordingly at this point that the Soviet adventure in Egypt, launched with a spectacular weapons deal twenty-one years earlier, and sustained thereafter with an apparently limitless effulgence of economic, diplomatic, and military patronage, expired in a mutual farrago of acrimony.

THE NEED FOR PEACE

In giving Moscow the back of his hand, opening new lines to Washington, and decentralizing and liberalizing his regime, Sadat was acting with a keen awareness of the tangible benefits his people expected as a result of the 1973 war. They had anticipated an instant boom in the aftermath of the first disengagement agreement with Israel. What they had gotten instead, thus far, was an inflationary spiral of near-uncontrollable proportions and a growing uncertainty of meaningful economic improvements. The Egyptian president appreciated that he would have to move far more quickly to satisfy the nation's insistence on a better life. For that matter, even the most spectacular economic success was likely to be dwarfed by an inexorable demographic reality: within a quarter-century Egypt's population almost certainly would have grown to at least 60 million inhabitants. Long before the end of his own tenure in office, therefore, Sadat would have to find a way of liberating his people from their centuries-old dependence on a narrow green belt along the 500-mile stretch of Nile Valley. Alternative sources of food and settlement were desperately needed.

The president was convinced that these sources were available. In addition to his far-reaching plans for the Sinai (p. 247), and the cultivation of some 800,000 acres of land below the Aswan Dam, Sadat nurtured an even more audacious vision. It was the reclamation of nearly two million acres in the Western Desert, between the green belt and Egypt's western borders. Underneath that arid wilderness, running from the Sudanese border through the Qattara Depression to al-Alamein in the north, were a series of underground reservoirs connecting the major oases. Egyptians referred to this subterranean treasure as the "Second Nile." It was Sadat's bold ambition to use the electricity generated by Aswan to pump that water into an irrigation network for the desert; to launch a surge of expansion in the west comparable to the nineteenth-century opening of the American frontier. In fact, this view may have been too roseate. By the best geological estimates, not more than 100,000 acres of the Western Desert were within reach of irrigation. East of the Nile, moreover, new lands and new Canal cities were capable of absorbing only a small fraction of the nation's anticipated population explosion.

Whatever the nation's prospects for the future, there were in any case acute current needs to be met. The shortage of food was among them. In 1975 alone, Egypt was obliged to import some four million tons of grain, flour, edible oils, beans, meat, and sugar. The housing shortage may have been even more critical. As early as 1965, some 100,000 migrants a year were arriving in Cairo. Three years later, the city's population density had reached 23,000 per square kilometer—and this well before the heaviest influx of Canal refugees touched off by the War of Attrition. After 1968, the government was spending $90 million annually in hardship allowances for hundreds of thousands of evacuees from Suez, Port Saïd, Ismailia, and the smaller Canal towns. Although the refugees initially were dispersed in villages outside Cairo, rather than in the heart of the capital, their circumstances were grim. Vegetating on the dole, crowded like animals into wretched one-room dwellings, they were becoming an increasingly restive and volatile group. Together with the eight million other inhabitants of Cairo, impacted into a city with public facilities for perhaps one million, they all but shattered the capital's motor abilities. In any Western nation, congestion of this magnitude would long since have erupted into serious violence.

In truth, the social structure of the nation as a whole faced disintegration. Although most of the benefits of the Nasser period remained—free schools and universities, subsidized food and rents, virtually guaranteed job-tenure—Egypt remained a welfare state grafted onto an altogether nonsupportive economy. The university graduates continued to pose an especially critical problem. Scrabbling for a pitiably attenuated number of meaningful jobs, most of these young men and women eventually found their niche in the government's swollen bureaucracy. Their disillusionment was soul-shattering, and the initial reaction to it was a frantic search for escape abroad. Only the best of the nation's young people managed to escape to the Persian Gulf or elsewhere, however. The weak and second-class were left to survive at home. It was the frustration of these latter that now boiled over into occasional public demonstrations. Indeed, there were major outbreaks of students, and then of workers, in Cairo on

January 1, 1975, and in the textile center of Mehalla al-Qubra in early April of
that year. The refrain against Sadat went:

Ya basha, ya bey, mish 'arafin na'akal wal-gazm'hamsa giney—
O Pasha, O Bey, we don't eat and shoes go for five pounds.
Ya batl al-Uktubir, fayn al-futur?—O Hero of October, where is our
breakfast?

Compounding the problem of economic development since 1967, moreover,
was the burden of remaining on a perpetual war footing. For Egypt, the issue
quite literally had become one of guns or butter. In 1971, Hedrick Smith, an
American observer, wrote of his latest visit: "Probably the most profound, yet
subtle, change that I sensed in Egypt was what seemed to be a genuine
willingness to make peace with Israel. Before the 1967 war, even thoughtful and
moderate Egyptians wanted to shut Israel out of their minds. The Arabs could
not destroy it; they would acknowledge that much. But it was not to be
accepted. This attitude has . . . softened. . . ." After 1973, in fact, and the
restoration of Egyptian honor, that attitude was altogether reversed. During his
interviews with Egyptian veterans after the October War, the author encountered the new pacifism in full force. Typical was the reaction of one Atef
Mitlawi Ahmad, a corporal who had been wounded in the battle for the Gidi
Pass. Ahmad no longer was impressed by the Israelis as supermen; he had
discovered to his satisfaction that they were mere mortals. Neither, by the same
token, did he regard them any longer as perennial ogres. Favoring a settlement
with them, he was willing, even eager, to receive them as guests in his home.
"We have fought so long for the Palestinians," he explained. "Now it is time for
us to think of ourselves, of our own future, and of a more realistic approach to
all our neighbors—including the Israelis." This viewpoint was repeated without
variation. Sadat himself phrased it succinctly in his autobiographical *In Search
of Identity:*

In conclusion, I must put on record that the Egyptian people differ
from many other peoples, even within the Arab world. We have
recovered our pride and self-confidence after the October 1973 battle,
just as our armed forces did. We are no longer motivated by
"complexes"—whether defeatist "inferiority" ones or those born out of
suspicion and hate. And this is why the opposing sides met soon after
the battle dust had settled to talk matters over. . . . With the fighting
over, we harbored nothing but respect for one another.

And, he might have added, a mutually anguished passion for peace.

XVIII

THE QUEST FOR PEACE

The sea change in Egypt's political and economic direction throughout the latter 1970s was paralleled by a fascinating, and not entirely dissimilar, upheaval in Israel. It was anticipated by widely publicized episodes of bribery and corruption at the highest level of government: in the exploitation of the Sinai oil wells and of the National Water Board for the profit of public officials; in the embezzlement of tens of millions of pounds from the Israel Corporation, a national venture to encourage the country's economic development; in the revelation of earlier misconduct by the man nominated as governor of the Bank of Israel; and ultimately in the resignation of Prime Minister Yitzchak Rabin from his party chairmanship as a result of his wife's conviction for possessing an illegal bank account abroad.

In consequence of these and other failures of public trust, the parliamentary election of May 17, 1977, evicted Labor from office for the first time in Israel's history and brought Menachem Begin to the prime ministry as chairman of a rightist political coalition. In truth, the electorate had by no means registered its approbation of this veteran fire-eater as its national spokesman; for his own bloc, Likud (a recent coalition of Gachal and other right-wing elements), had picked up a mere four seats over its equivalent showing in 1973. Rather, the vote signified essentially a repudiation of Labor's flaccidity and venality, its failure to check the rampant political nepotism and industrial unrest that had all but paralyzed Israel's economic growth.

Nevertheless, the mathematical exigencies of the nation's party coalition system enabled Begin on June 20 to patch together a narrow alliance of religious and other conservative factions, and his prime ministry became a fact of life with which the somewhat disconcerted citizens of Israel dutifully prepared to cope. Begin himself, now sixty-four years old, a slight, balding, bespectacled man of uncertain health, left no doubt of his intention to chart an avowedly revisionist course, both in domestic and in foreign policy. Upon assuming the reins of government, he, like Sadat, began dispensing with many of the statist regulations and subsidies that, in his view, had cribbed national productivity. At the same time, he publicly reaffirmed his support for broadened Israeli settlement on the West Bank. Since 1967, in fact, in common with many others of all political loyalties, Begin had contemptuously rejected a description of the occupied territories as either "occupied" or "West Bank," and had insisted, rather, that they be known by their biblical appellation of Judea and Samaria. This was no mere gesture of ingratiation toward the religious parties— those whose vital support provided the margin of safety in his coalition cabinet. It bespoke as well Begin's tenacious and lifelong commitment, as commander of the pre-state dissident underground Etzel no less than as Israel's first minister, to a wholly redeemed "Land of Israel."

Polish-born, Menachem Begin had studied law at Warsaw University, taking his degree in 1935. It was in that year, too, that he first met and was overwhelmed by Vladimir Jabotinsky, the brilliant poet-orator who had founded the Revisionist wing of the Zionist movement. Jabotinsky's teachings were simply stated: every Jew had a right to enter Palestine; only active retaliation would deter the Arabs; Jewish armed force alone, not collaboration with the British, would ensure a Jewish state for the historic "Land of Israel"—that is, Palestine (including Transjordan) in its entirety. Enthralled by Jabotinsky's maximalism, Begin soon assumed the leadership of the Revisionist youth movement in Poland. It was a leadership that nearly proved his undoing. When the Soviet army occupied eastern Poland in September 1939, following the Nazi invasion from the west, Begin was promptly arrested by the Russians for his Zionist "reactionary" activities. Unflinching, the young prisoner stubbornly defended his Zionist ideals before his judges and, later, before his guards and fellow prisoners in a Siberian labor camp. His subsequent eighteen-month ordeal in the "white nights" of Soviet imprisonment may well have toughened Begin's soul irretrievably. So did the discovery later of his parents' death in a Nazi concentration camp.

In 1942, as part of a three-way deal between Moscow, the Western Allies, and the expatriate Polish government in London, several thousand Polish prisoners in the Soviet Union were allowed to enlist in the "Polish Army in Exile" commanded by General Wladyslaw Anders. Begin was one of these. For him, even membership in an army of blatantly anti-Semitic Poles was a welcome avenue of escape from the Soviet nightmare. It soon proved better than that. Eight months after his enlistment in the Anders army, the emigré force was dispatched to Palestine for advanced training under the British. And there at last, in his beloved Land of Israel, Begin promptly deserted his Polish unit and disappeared into the companionship of the Etzel—the Revisionist paramilitary organization. Almost immediately, his earlier reputation in Poland won him a leadership role in this group. Thereafter he infused the Etzel with his own grim militancy of purpose, his uncompromising determination to hound the British out of Palestine, to open the gates of Jewish immigration, and eventually to proclaim a sovereign Jewish state.

Under Begin's direction, the underground movement intensified its assaults on British military installations. More than occasionally, it killed or wounded British personnel, extorted funds from Jewish businessmen, even "executed"

Jewish collaborators and informers. On July 22, 1946, a group of Etzel members dynamited the wing of Jerusalem's King David Hotel that had been occupied by the British Criminal Investigation Department. Over 90 Englishmen, Arabs, and Jews were killed in the explosion. Subsequently the Etzel members found themselves pariahs among Jews no less than among the British. Execrated by the Jewish Agency, under threat of hanging or of long prison terms at the hands of the British, they adopted false names and moved from one hiding place to another. Begin himself masqueraded as a bearded rabbi. Nothing deterred him or his followers. Rather, they widened the scope of their attacks, ultimately paralyzing British military communications in large areas of Jewish Palestine. As it developed, many factors—diplomatic, political, economic—played a role in forcing Britain to abandon its Palestine mandate, but the dissident underground guerrilla campaign unquestionably was significant among them.

Yet the departure of the British was hardly enough to satisfy Begin. His reaction to the United Nations Partition Resolution of November 29, 1947, was typical. "The partition of the homeland is illegal," he warned on November 30. "It will never be recognized. . . . It will not bind the Jewish people. Jerusalem was and will forever be our capital. The Land of Israel will be restored to the people of Israel. All of it. And forever." When the independence of Israel was declared on May 14, 1948, Begin was on the Etzel radio that same night, broadcasting his rejection of the partition boundaries in language the late Jabotinsky would have approved. "The homeland is historically and geographically an entity," he insisted. "Whoever fails to recognize our right to the entire homeland does not recognize our right to any of its territories. We shall never yield our natural and eternal right. We shall bear the vision of a full liberation." It is worth noting that the Etzel's uncompromising claim to dominion over the entirety of Palestine was also prefigured in the ferocity of its independent military operations against the Arabs. Thus, on April 9, 1948, the Etzel's massacre of 200 Arab men, women, and children in the village of Deir Yassin was a warning that parallel Arab atrocities against Jews elsewhere would be matched blow for blow.

To be sure, once the Palestine war ended and the Republic of Israel was secured, the Revisionist-Etzel group agreed to be reincarnated and legalized as the Cherut party. As a minority faction in the Israeli Knesset, however, Begin and his followers remained as militantly right-wing as ever. By the 1960s, supported increasingly by the urban underprivileged, and particularly by the Oriental Jews, who were closed out of the European Jewish establishment, Cherut eventually became the single most important reservoir of opposition to the Labor-controlled government. The personal hatred between Begin and Ben-Gurion surely did little to mitigate this opposition; the two men could hardly bring themselves to address each other directly. The latter as a result was prepared to strike a coalition agreement with virtually any of Israel's parties—

but never with the Communists or with Cherut. Nor were tensions between Labor and Cherut eased, in the aftermath of the 1956 Sinai War, when Ben-Gurion agreed finally to withdraw Israel's troops from Sinai and Gaza. Accusing the prime minister of "cowardice" in bending under American pressure, Begin once again crossed the threshold of party doctrine into rampant demagoguery.

It was all the more remarkable, therefore, in the May–June crisis of 1967, that Begin acted with courage, even greatness, in suggesting that Ben-Gurion be invited back to replace the indecisive Levi Eshkol as prime minister. Nevertheless, once hostilities erupted and then were victoriously concluded, the right-wing leader's vision characteristically shifted again from national survival to territorial annexation. Continuing on after the war as minister without portfolio in the Government of National Unity, Begin regarded it as his mission henceforth to protect the "liberated" areas of Palestine, to ensure the "inalienable right of the Jewish people to Judea and Samaria." Then came the prolonged agony of the War of Attrition. Once the cabinet decided in August 1970 to accept the "Rogers Plan," which envisaged not merely a cease-fire but compliance with UN Resolution 242 (alluding to "withdrawal . . . from territories occupied in the recent conflict"), Begin promptly withdrew from the government coalition. For him, there would be no compromise on the issue of the "Land of Israel."

Before the parliamentary elections in the spring of 1977, therefore, Begin and his group—now further expanded to include additional rightist and centrist factions, and known henceforth as Likud—formulated an uncompromising platform. Its key foreign policy provision declared:

> The right of the Jewish people to the Land of Israel is eternal and inalienable and is an integral part of its right to security and peace. Judea and Samaria shall therefore not be relinquished for foreign rule; between the sea and the Jordan, there will be Jewish sovereignty alone.

Nor was the program ambiguous in its claim to eastern Sinai, and its demand that the rest of the peninsula be demilitarized in perpetuity. Indeed, Begin himself let it be known that he intended to purchase a retirement home in Yamit (the Rafah cluster of settlements). It was with this less than conciliatory approach after the May elections that Likud suddenly found itself the dominant political bloc in a new rightist government.

Moreover, Begin further astonished supporters and opponents alike by the person he nominated for foreign minister in his new cabinet. It was Moshe Dayan. Seemingly discredited by the reverses of the 1973 war and by the subsequent fall of the Meir government, Dayan until then had been considered politically a closed case. Yet Begin sensed that this former Ben-Gurion protégé, an arch-pragmatist, was less than doctrinaire on such non-Palestinian issues as the Sinai. It was Dayan, after all, who had repeatedly opposed the notion of holding fast to the Suez Canal line. As he saw it, the blockage of an international waterway was a standing provocation both to Egypt and to the international maritime community. The risks of that provocation outweighed any military advantages of defense in depth. Much of the western Sinai, for that matter, was possibly superfluous in the burden it represented of extended supply lines and costly fortifications. We recall that, even before the War of Attrition, Dayan had hinted of significant Israeli withdrawals in return for practical Egyptian nonbelligerency. After the October War, too, the augmented role of the United States in negotiating disengagement provided a new dimension to Dayan's initial scheme. By removing the threat of war, Kissinger's shuttle diplomacy had created a built-in momentum toward a compromise agreement. Israel had become attuned to the prospect of gradual withdrawal from at least part of Sinai.

Thereafter, during secret talks between Rabin and Kissinger in 1976, the then Israeli prime minister had intimated his willingness to pull back farther to the al-Arish-Ras Muhammad line in exchange for an end to the state of belligerency—a trade-off of two-thirds of Sinai for an agreement that would be less than formal peace. Upon assuming the prime ministry himself, Begin shared this interest in a trade-off. What he had in mind, however, was less an exchange of Sinai territory for nonbelligerency than a trade-off for the West Bank—for the "Greater Land of Israel," the ideological obsession of his adult lifetime. In first conceiving, and subsequently endorsing, the notion of evacuating Sinai, Dayan, with his considerable record as a "hawk," would be indispensable now to Begin in selling the idea of such a trade-off—first to Egypt, and then to the Knesset. For his part, Dayan sought an assurance of his own before accepting membership in the new cabinet. This was Begin's willingness to forgo his traditional insistence upon formally annexing the West Bank. Such a claim, Dayan believed, would prejudice Israel's credibility in a revived Geneva peace conference. Begin concurred.

Accordingly, from the earliest weeks of his incumbency, with the advice and encouragement of Dayan, the prime minister began dispatching signals to Cairo of his desire to strike a deal. One signal took the form of a trip to Bucharest on August 26, a five-day ceremonial visit that included two lengthy personal conversations on Middle Eastern issues between Begin and Rumanian President Nicolae Ceausescu. Over the years, Ceausescu had managed to preserve a working relationship with both the Eastern and Western camps. In June 1967, his was the only Communist government to have refrained from severing diplomatic ties with Israel. On several occasions since then, he had offered his intermediary services to Egypt and Israel. Begin was determined to exploit that offer now. Emphasizing to the Rumanian leader his willingness to give Sadat "extensive satisfaction" on the Sinai, the Israeli premier expressed a desire to consider seriously joint Egyptian-Israeli intelligence and even joint defense measures against Libyan terrorism and against Soviet penetration in the Middle

East and the Horn of Africa; and, finally, to negotiate some form of autonomous Arab administration for Gaza and the West Bank. Whatever Begin's ulterior motive of de facto Israeli rule over Palestine, these were important, even breathtaking, concessions, and Ceausescu promptly ensured that both their letter and spirit were duly transmitted to Cairo.

Yet a second Israeli signal took the form of Dayan's instructions to Meir Rosenne, the legal adviser of the foreign ministry, to devise a working draft of a possible Egyptian-Israeli peace treaty. Thorough and punctilious to the last degree, Rosenne consulted scores of treaty models, then came up with a 46-point document that elaborated upon the basic principles outlined by Begin in Rumania. The draft was promptly sent off to Washington for examination. Carefully scrutinized by State Department officials, the treaty impressed Secretary of State Cyrus Vance sufficiently for the latter to request President Jimmy Carter's personal intercession with the Egyptians. On September 10, therefore, the document was followed to Cairo by a personal letter from Carter to Sadat. It was an appeal to the Egyptian president to test Begin's good intentions by acceding to an early revival of the Geneva Conference.

THE DECISION TO ''BREACH THE BARRIER OF SUSPICION''

Sadat's reaction to these Israeli feelers at first was somewhat equivocal. Earlier, it will be recalled, his response to Israeli overtures had been considerably less than enthusiastic (p. 183–84). The Egyptian leader had emphasized repeatedly that the issues of Sinai and of the Golan were intimately linked to the burning question of occupied Palestinian territory. "Now, in my first peace strategy," he wrote later, ". . . I do not deny the State of Israel's right to be recognized by all the countries of the region, provided that . . . a peace agreement should . . . [establish] a Palestinian state on the West Bank of the Jordan and in the Gaza Strip, and Israel should withdraw from the territories occupied in 1967. . . ." It was an approach less than likely to set Begin to dancing in the streets. Indeed, there appeared no room whatever for dialogue in these irreconcilable positions.

In July 1977, however, even in advance of Begin's visit to Rumania and the dispatch of Rosenne's draft treaty, the possibilities for discourse had suddenly improved—as a consequence of a fascinating twist of history. For some years, Colonel Muamar al-Qaddafi's revolutionary Libyan government had been exhorting Sadat to reactivate the Syrian-Egyptian-Libyan Confederation, to detach Egypt from the American connection, and to resume a decisive confrontation with the Jewish state. The Egyptian leader remained unmoved by these appeals. Thereafter, as Sadat negotiated two disengagement agreements with Israel and made plain his fullest intention of orbiting even closer to the

United States, Qaddafi in turn became increasingly splenetic in his diatribes against his "Arab brother." Ugly territorial issues suddenly were raised along the Egyptian-Libyan frontier in the Western Desert, and Qaddafi authorized a dangerous massing of troops along this border area.

In the summer of 1977, Israel's director of military intelligence drew Begin's attention to a scheme organized by Qaddafi to assassinate Sadat. The conspiracy had been discovered by accident. Qaddafi's "hit" team consisted mainly of Palestinians, men always closely followed by Israeli agents. In the past, whenever these plots had not been aimed specifically at Jews, they had been directed against such Arab conservatives as Hussein of Jordan or Feisal of Saudi Arabia. Israeli intelligence as a rule had turned over its information to the American CIA, which then had warned the intended victims under its own by-line. This time, however, Begin suggested that the information be given "directly" to the Egyptians. For that purpose, Morocco was a useful channel.

Morocco's King Hassan II was a proven moderate. Like his forebears of the Alawi dynasty, he had always accorded his nation's Jewish minority the fullest measure of tolerance and equality, and had periodically called for a fusion of "Jewish genius and Arab might" in building the Maghreb Third World. In turn, from 1975 on, Israel had secretly offered Hassan its aid in fighting the Algerian-supported Polisaro guerrillas in the western Sahara. The king was not ungrateful, and in ensuing years he had sought to bring Israel and Egypt together. Now, with Hassan's cooperation as intermediary, Israel's intelligence chief promptly flew to Casablanca and met there with his Egyptian counterpart, Lieutenant General Kamal Hassan Ali (later to become Egypt's minister of war). Hassan Ali was stunned by the evidence the Israeli brought with him. It included extensive details, even names and addresses of the would-be assassins in Cairo. The information was promptly transmitted to the Egyptian secret police, who moved in and seized the conspirators with all incriminating documents and weapons. Five days later, Sadat launched a trip-hammer border war against Libya. His planes blasted Qaddafi's radar installations, and his troops mauled the Libyan ground forces in a series of bloody clashes. Simultaneously, Begin announced in the Knesset that Israel would do nothing to disturb the Egyptians in the Sinai while they were engaged with Libya.

Sadat was not unappreciative of this Israeli role. Initially, like other Arab leaders, he had been appalled by Begin's victory and by the hardliners the new prime minister had brought with him into the Israeli cabinet. In addition to Dayan, the latter included General Ezer Weizman, the former air force commander, who currently assumed the post of minister of defense; and General Ariel Sharon, the hero of the 1973 Canal countercrossing, who accepted the agriculture ministry. But now all Sadat's earlier premonitions had to be reassessed. Begin's conversation with Ceausescu and the Rosenne draft treaty evidently were to be taken seriously. The secret, personal letter from President Carter, urging a resumption of the Geneva Conference, was intended as yet another inducement to give the Israelis a chance to prove their good intentions. In fact, the idea of a revived Geneva Conference was distinctly unappealing to Sadat. With its envisaged Soviet, Palestinian, and Syrian participation, such a conclave appeared all but certain to end in a stalemate. On the other hand, if a private Egyptian-Israeli understanding could be reached in advance of Geneva, the Egyptian president no longer was categorically opposed to exploring that possibility. At this point, he dispatched a message to the Israelis, again via Morocco. Jerusalem responded.

On September 4, Foreign Minister Dayan flew off secretly to Fez, arriving (by way of Paris) in a private jet supplied by King Hassan. There the Moroccan ruler confirmed Sadat's interest in achieving bilateral Egyptian-Israeli agreement. Would the Israelis be prepared to negotiate in a spirit of flexibility? Dayan's response was emphatically affirmative. Hassan then promised to convey this message to Egypt. The reaction in Cairo apparently was equally favorable. Less than two weeks later, on September 16, Dayan once again emplaned for Morocco. This time his destination was Rabat. Awaiting him in the capital city was Egyptian Deputy Prime Minister Hassan al-Tohami. Fifty-five years old, a right-winger, Tohami had never been trusted by the late Nasser, who had "exiled" him to Vienna as Egypt's ambassador and as the official delegate to the International Atomic Energy Commission. In Austria, Tohami had met Prime Minister Bruno Kreisky, and had become friendly with Kreisky's Jewish millionaire friend, Dr. Karl Kahana. Kahana in turn was sought out by the Israelis when Sadat inherited the Egyptian presidency. The following year, when Tohami became a close confidant of Sadat—who appointed him deputy prime minister and coordinator of intelligence services—the Israelis sent word through Kahana that they regarded Tohami as a potential intermediary. He was an intermediary, in turn, whom Sadat was quite willing to use.

It was thus from Tohami that Dayan learned of Sadat's willingness in principle to anticipate a revived Geneva Conference by negotiating an Egyptian-Israeli nonbelligerency agreement—and perhaps even more. But the price was stiff. It was a commitment by Israel to return the entire Sinai to Egyptian sovereignty, to withdraw "every last soldier" from Egyptian soil, and to countenance some sort of "Palestinian arrangement" linking the West Bank and Gaza with Jordan. Tohami added that Sadat was willing to offer Israel every possible security guarantee, including United Nations forces stationed on both sides of the Sinai border. In a revelation of the changed circumstances that made these negotiations possible, Tohami also informed Dayan straight out that Egypt did indeed expect Israel's active help in its conflict with Libya, and in confronting the emergent threat of Soviet penetration in Africa.

Dayan's response was equally forthright. Israel was prepared to restore full Egyptian sovereignty over the Sinai, he explained, although not to abandon its enclave of settlements in the northeastern corner of the peninsula or its key air bases near the Gulf of Aqaba. Neither would Israel contemplate withdrawing its troops and settlements from the West Bank and Gaza. Even on these issues, however, there was room for negotiation and conceivably for some tactical compromise. The conversation was frank and cordial, lasting seven hours, with King Hassan himself popping in and out occasionally to ensure that discussions went smoothly. When the meeting ended, both Tohami and Dayan agreed to present the other's proposals to their heads of government; and, if approval were forthcoming, they would return to Morocco within two weeks carrying more detailed outlines for a final peace.

Begin was acutely interested in the Egyptian reaction. He fully shared Sadat's concern about American pressure for a restructured Geneva Conference. By then, in fact, the Carter administration had developed a distinct blueprint of its own for the Middle East. The plan was modeled largely on a 1975 Brookings Institution report, one of whose signatories was Professor Zbigniew Brzezinski of Columbia University, the man who now served as the president's national security adviser. The report had concluded that the Kissinger step-by-step approach had gone as far as it could; that the moment was ripe at last for a comprehensive settlement; but that this was not possible without the establishment of an internationally recognized Palestinian "entity" on the West Bank. Two months after his inauguration, Carter had stated publicly that there "has to be a homeland provided for the Palestinian refugees." Begin was shaken. No American president had ever made this statement publicly, and Carter repeated it several times in ensuing weeks.

Then, on September 19, meeting with Dayan in Washington to discuss a resuscitated Geneva Conference, President Carter issued a virtual ultimatum: the Palestinians would be represented at Geneva, and Israel eventually would have to accept a Palestinian "entity" or "homeland" on the West Bank and Gaza; Israel's settlements on the West Bank and Gaza were "illegal" and should be withdrawn. Whatever the president's expectations, he was unprepared for Dayan's flinty response. The government of Israel would never accept an independent Palestinian state or the evacuation of its settlements from the West Bank, declared the foreign minister, and it rejected categorically the very notion of discussions of any kind with a representative of the PLO. Furthermore, Israel had severe misgivings about the idea of Soviet participation in a peace conference. Inasmuch as Kissinger had deftly managed to exclude the USSR from Middle Eastern negotiations after Geneva, the clock should not be turned back.

Dayan's adamant stance was influenced, of course, by his earlier meeting in Rabat. Tohami had made it plain that Sadat wanted the Sinai returned, that leeway for negotiation on other issues still existed. In fact, the Egyptian president, who by then had reappraised his nation's desperate situation, its vicious circle of war and poverty (pp. 252–53), had concluded that the root cause of Israel's obduracy was the psychological barrier of distrust. This obstacle had to be breached, Sadat was convinced, to enable the Israelis to overcome their "legalistic preoccupation with technicalities." He wrote later: "It was then that I drew, almost unconsciously, on the inner strength I had developed in Cell 54 of Cairo Central Prison—a strength, call it a talent or capacity, for change." In short, he was determined to launch a totally fresh approach to elicit Israeli trust.

At this point, on October 30, Sadat departed for Bucharest to conduct extended talks of his own with Ceausescu. The Rumanian president this time communicated Begin's message in fullest detail. "I asked Ceausescu about his impressions," Sadat wrote afterward. "He said: 'Begin wants a solution.'" This was heartening. All the more so inasmuch as Begin, some months earlier, had visited the Yamit cluster of eighteen Israeli settlements in Sinai and had insisted that the Jewish farmers and their wives and children there would stay put. Now it seemed clear that the impression conveyed by Tohami of the meeting with Dayan was accurate. Begin was softening his stand. Moreover, as leader of a right-wing bloc, he would actually be in a better position than the Laborites to sell the Knesset a deal on Sinai.

On October 31 Sadat continued on from Rumania to Iran and Saudi Arabia for conferences with the restrained and temperate leaders of those Persian Gulf states. In Teheran, the shah offered the Egyptian president further encouragement to pursue the line of negotiations with Begin. The Iranian ruler's arguments were not based exclusively on his own innate moderation on the Arab-Israel issue. Three months earlier, during the first week of August, Dayan also had visited Teheran, and in an audience with the shah had requested the latter's good offices. Israel's inducements for Egypt were essentially those repeated later in Bucharest and in the Rosenne draft treaty. Once again, then, Sadat was exposed to the full force of conciliatory intercession.

It was at this point that the Egyptian leader made a historic, and possibly impulsive, decision. It was not uninfluenced by the man's deeply rooted flair for the dramatic. Here it is worth noting that, upon finishing secondary school and before his acceptance by the military academy in 1936, Sadat had given serious thought to pursuing a career as an actor. He had once requested a job in a local Cairo theater. Even afterward, following his graduation from the military academy, nearly all his subsequent actions—his spying, his assassination attempts—continued to reveal his instinct for the dramatic gesture. So did his unexpected move, later, in expelling the Russians from Egypt; and so, for that matter, did his unilateral decision to open the Suez Canal in June 1975. What Sadat had in mind now, however, was an authentic *coup de théâtre*. At first he envisaged an invitation to leaders of the Arab confrontation states to a meeting in Jerusalem, at the Knesset, *"to make it absolutely clear to Premier Begin that we were determined to prepare seriously for Geneva. . . ."* Presumably the hard issues then would be resolved before the Soviets and the PLO could sabotage an agreement. But later, in Teheran and Riyadh, Sadat tempered this grandiose scheme. There was little likelihood, after all, of other Arab rulers joining him.

This sober appraisal was reaffirmed on November 5, shortly after his return to Cairo, when he was visited by Jordan's King Hussein. The Hashemite ruler was eager to learn the results of Sadat's meeting with Ceausescu. Earlier, on August 22, in a secret meeting with Dayan in London, Hussein had rejected any notion of a private "deal" with the Israelis on the West Bank. His principal concern now was to ensure that no such commitment was tendered on Jordan's behalf by Egypt. Sadat offered that assurance, but pressed the king to reconsider. Hussein demurred; the idea was premature, he insisted. The Egyptian president in turn was neither surprised nor discountenanced. By then the principal element in his new initiative was clearly fixed in his mind: he would go to Jerusalem—on his own. Again, with his instinct for the grand gesture, he chose a ceremonial occasion to reveal his decision. It was the formal opening of the People's Assembly on November 9, 1977. Addressing the legislators, speaking emotionally of the need for peace in the Middle East, Sadat accused Israel of raising artificial stumbling blocks. "There is no power on earth that can stop me from demanding total Israeli withdrawal from occupied lands and the recovery of Palestinian rights, including their right to set up an independent state." Thus far the refrain was a familiar one. Immediately afterward, however, the president unveiled his secret plan. "I am ready to go to the Israeli parliament itself," he declared, "and discuss it with them."

A VISIT TO JERUSALEM

The announcement stunned the Egyptian government and people alike. Disconcerted (although less by his president's intention to secure peace than by his failure to countenance exploratory, low-level negotiations), Foreign Minister Ismail Fahmi promptly resigned. Editorial reaction, too, at first remained noncommittal. In Washington, Carter and the State Department, anticipating at most a resumption of the Geneva Conference, greeted Sadat's statement with a silence less eloquent than confused. Only several days later did the United States government register its belated, and somewhat constipated, approbation. Ironically, in Jerusalem, Begin was hardly less astounded. Earlier that month unusually large numbers of Egyptian troops had been concentrated on the western side of the Canal, a buildup that confused the Israelis and threw their military into a frenzy of reconnaissance flights. At the time, Begin had even wondered if the Tohami-Dayan talks in Morocco had merely been a ruse. But now those fears were allayed.

The only remaining question was the proper response to Sadat's extraordinary overture. On November 10, Begin made a direct broadcast to the Egyptian people on Israel's Arabic-language frequency. After reviewing the "tragic, completely unnecessary conflict between our two nations," the prime minister went on to assure his listeners that, should the Egyptian president agree to visit Israel, he would be accorded "all the hospitality which both the Egyptian and Israeli peoples have inherited from our common father, Abraham. . . ." When in response Sadat noted that he had not received a "formal" invitation, Begin on November 15 handed an official letter to United States Ambassador Samuel Lewis, ceremonially inviting Sadat to address the Knesset. The invitation, for November 20, was promptly accepted.

The day after receiving Begin's letter, Sadat flew off to Damascus in an effort to win the approval, or at least the understanding, of President Assad. The four-hour meeting was acrimonious. Assad had not disguised his bitterness at Sadat following the Egyptian-Israeli disengagement agreements of 1974–75. It was his feeling that Egypt had abandoned Syria at a time when Israeli troops were still emplaced on the Golan plateau. Afterward, Sadat for his part had criticized Assad's intervention in the Lebanese civil war. It was plain that the old rift between the Nile Valley and the Fertile Crescent had opened again. The meeting of November 16 did nothing to heal it. Thus, by the time Sadat returned to Cairo and made final preparations to depart for Israel, Syria's Ba'ath regime proclaimed a day of national mourning and broadcast "funeral" eulogies in memory of Sadat. Newspapers in Baghdad similarly anathematized the Egyptian president as a traitor to the Arab people.

Sadat would not be deterred. On the morning of November 18, thirty-six hours before his planned departure for Israel, an Egyptian airliner flew into Lydda, the first Arab plane ever to land officially at an Israeli airport. Its passengers were Egyptian protocol and security personnel dispatched to help work out preparations for the impending trip. In cooperation with the Israeli secret service, the visitors organized a security ring of a magnitude never equaled in Israel. Other Israeli officials, meanwhile, were embarking on urgent, last-minute preparations of their own. Egyptian flags had to be sewn. The military orchestra required copies of the Egyptian national anthem. Hospitals had to be supplied with quantities of reserve blood matching the types of Sadat and his associates. Operating theaters were placed on an emergency footing. Twenty-four hours before Sadat's arrival, the Israeli police arrested and detained known Arab "unreliables" on the West Bank. At last, on Saturday evening of November 19, at the close of the Jewish Sabbath, Sadat fulfilled his promise. He emplaned for Israel.

The flight of the presidential jet to Ben-Gurion airport in Lydda consumed a mere hour and a half, but within that time span a gulf of thirty years of bloodshed and agonized intransigence seemingly was breached. Throughout the world, tens of millions of television viewers watched in breathless fascination as Sadat and his entourage disembarked to a twenty-one-gun Israeli salute, then made their way cordially down a waiting line of dignitaries that included President Ephraim Katzir, Begin, Dayan, the former prime ministers, Meir and Rabin, and other distinguished figures. Viewing these proceedings on their sets at home, many Egyptians wept at the honor accorded their president. Afterward, Sadat and his party were driven in a tightly guarded motorcade to Jerusalem, and to their suites at the King David Hotel.

The wonder and excitement grew the following morning, the twentieth, as Sadat went directly for prayer services to the al-Aqsa Mosque in East Jerusalem. There he was greeted enthusiastically by some 6,000 waiting Arabs. From the mosque, the president was conducted by Begin on a personal tour of Yad vaShem, Israel's Holocaust Memorial shrine, and thereafter to luncheon with other Israeli officials. Finally, in the afternoon, he was ceremoniously ushered into the Knesset building, to the sound of trumpets and an unprecedented burst of applause from the assembled parliament members. And here at last Sadat delivered his promised address. It consumed forty minutes, and proved to be significantly less than an endorsement of Israel's diplomatic stance. Speaking in Arabic, his words simultaneously broadcast to Egypt and to the rest of the world, the visiting president emphasized that

> the first fact is that no one can build his happiness at the expense of the misery of others. . . . I have not come here for a separate agreement between Egypt and Israel. An interim peace between Egypt and Israel . . . will not bring permanent peace based on justice in the entire region. . . . Second, I have not come to you to seek partial peace . . . [a] third disengagement agreement in Sinai or in Golan or the West Bank. For this would mean . . . merely delaying the lighting of the fuse.

Having genuflected to the other Arab nations, then, Sadat went on to reassure his Israeli listeners, to give them what they had been waiting thirty years to hear, openly and formally, and through face-to-face dialogue:

> In all sincerity I tell you that we welcome you among us with full security and safety. . . . We used to reject you. . . . We had our reasons and our fears, yes. . . . [But] I declare it to the whole world that we accept to live with you in permanent peace based on justice. . . . Today, through my visit to you I ask you, why do we not stretch out our hands with faith and sincerity so that together we might destroy this barrier [of distrust]? Why should we not meet with faith and sincerity so that together we might remove all suspicion of fear, betrayal, and bad intentions? . . .

In response to this extraordinary overture, Begin, who had not been permitted to read Sadat's speech in advance, was obliged to extemporize. He began graciously enough, praising Sadat, sharing the Egyptian leader's commitment to peace. But the prime minister made it emphatically clear that Jerusalem would never be divided again, or the West Bank transformed into a PLO state. It was a stern warning. "I invite King Hussein to visit us," Begin concluded, "and to discuss with us all problems that require discussions between him and us. And also the legitimate spokesman of the Arabs of the Land of Israel [a less than tactful allusion to the West Bank and the Gaza Strip]. I invite them to come and meet with us for discussions. . . ."

Several hours later, Sadat and Begin sat on the stage of the Jerusalem Theater, facing two thousand representatives of the media, equably fielding questions, maintaining the public façade of cordiality. It may only have been a façade, for Sadat by then had learned of Begin's unconciliatory meeting earlier that day with a group of Egyptian editors, his unbudging opposition to any notion of Arab self-determination on the West Bank, and his insistence on Jewish possession of the entire unified city of Jerusalem. At the banquet that night in Sadat's honor, therefore, the mood was subdued. The tough speeches in the Knesset, and Begin's session with the editors, had dispelled some of the earlier optimism on both sides. Sadat remained silent, pecking listlessly at his food. The two leaders nevertheless went on to private conversation afterward. During an eighty-minute discussion, they managed to reach agreement on three principles. These were: the rejection of war between Egypt and Israel; the formal restoration of Egyptian sovereignty over the Sinai Peninsula; and the demilitarization of the largest part of the Sinai, with limited Egyptian forces to be stationed exclusively in the area adjoining the Suez Canal, including the Mitla and Gidi passes. It was similarly agreed that talks would continue in the future. To that end, a framework for these additional contacts was prepared, envisaging future meetings between ministers, exchanges of notes, even direct-line telephone conversations between Sadat and Begin. The next afternoon, November 21, Sadat flew back to Cairo and to a tumultuous reception by the Egyptian people. However stage-managed, the welcoming crowds left no doubt that their enthusiasm for the president's mission of peace was deeply, even passionately, felt.

THE AFTERMATH OF EUPHORIA

Soon afterward, the changes in Egypt's official propaganda line became dramatically visible. In their allusions to Israel, radio announcers dropped the term "enemy." On Radio Cairo's military wavelength, the program "The Sounds of the Battlefront" gave way to a new format, "The Flags of Peace." Nor did broadcasts or newspaper articles describe the PLO any longer as the exclusive representative of the Palestinian people. Peace was the new motif, and it was evident that nothing should be permitted to occlude its chances. Returning to his office, Sadat encountered a flood of congratulatory telegrams from his fellow citizens, and particularly from writers and other intellectuals. As far back as 1973, in the aftermath of the October War, many of these latter had called on the president to seek a compromise accommodation with Israel, rather than to allow "university degrees to be thrown away on the sands of the battlefield." Now, to their gratification, it appeared that Sadat had been listening.

Elsewhere, however, in the Libyan capital of Tripoli, a harried inter-Arab conference opened on December 2, and became the occasion for a frantic, if disorganized, effort to intimidate Sadat in his peace initiative. The Tripoli meetings did not go smoothly. Torn by disputes between the PLO, the Syrians, and the Iraqis, the conference produced little more than a majority declaration, on December 5, calling upon its members to "freeze" diplomatic and commercial relations with Egypt, to include Egypt henceforth in the anti-Israel boycott, even to transfer the Arab League headquarters from Cairo to Tunis. In the end, nothing emerged from these proposals. The Saudi government was not prepared yet to condemn Sadat's initiative. Hussein, too, refused to commit himself at Tripoli.

As it happened, Sadat had met again with the Jordanian ruler within a week after his, Sadat's, return from Jerusalem, and had exerted all his eloquence and charm in conjuring up a vision of the West Bank restored to Hashemite rule. But Hussein preferred to temporize, neither accepting nor rejecting Sadat's appeal to share in the peace process. It was his hope, rather, that sufficient American pressure might be exerted on Israel to persuade the Zionist state at least to issue a "declaration of principles," giving some sign of movement on Palestine, and thereby offering Jordan an inducement for joining the peace talks. Otherwise, he feared that Sadat's initiative would fail, that he, Hussein, would be exposed again to Arab radicalism. In truth, the Hashemite king had conducted numerous meetings of his own with Israeli leaders in recent years, and had made it a point scrupulously to inform Sadat about them. Those contacts had been secret, however, and when Sadat now called for him to enter the limelight of public negotiations, Hussein demurred.

Meanwhile, Begin too was exposed to intense pressure from both Cairo and Washington to match the spirit of Sadat's gesture. This appeal was reiterated by Hassan al-Tohami in a second meeting with Dayan in Marrakesh on December 3. The Israeli foreign minister once again emphasized his government's willingness to restore the Sinai to Egyptian sovereignty, for Israel to withdraw to the old international border. That withdrawal would take place in two stages, however. In the first, it would extend just beyond the al-Arish-Ras Muhammad axis, leaving Israel in control of Sharm es-Sheikh, of the Rafah salient—the "Via Maris," the historic route of Egyptian invasion in northeastern Sinai—and of a cluster of Israeli military airfields; all Sinai east of the Gidi and Mitla passes would be demilitarized. The second stage, that of final withdrawal, would not be completed until the year 2000, and even then the last evacuated areas would remain under United Nations supervision. A more detailed outline of the Israeli position was formulated by the prime minister's legal adviser, Professor Aharon Barak, who elaborated upon the envisaged peace with Egypt and "autonomy" for the Arab residents of the occupied territories. It was this plan that Begin himself carried off to Washington, and that he submitted to President Carter and to Secretary of State Vance on December 16.

It was a curious document. If Begin's—and Dayan's—proposal for the Sinai was tightly qualified, the scheme for the West Bank and Gaza was only superficially more attractive. Indeed, it was evident that the prime minister still was thinking in terms of a unified Land of Israel. With twenty-four Jewish settlements already functioning on the occupied territories, Begin had brought with him a carefully developed right-wing blueprint for the Arabs living under Israeli rule. It was to accord them a degree of self-government that would be limited essentially to cultural and economic autonomy. To be sure, the formula envisaged termination of the military government in Judea, Samaria, and the Gaza district. In its stead, the elective administrative council Begin favored would deal with educational and religious affairs, with health and social welfare, with finance and industry, commerce and tourism, and with justice and local police forces. On the other hand, security and public order would remain the exclusive responsibility of the Israeli authorities. Although Arab inhabitants in these districts would be granted free choice either of Israeli or Jordanian citizenship, they would not be entitled to opt for citizenship in their own autonomous community. Not least of all, residents of Israel would be entitled to acquire land and to settle in the occupied territories. This was a fundamental point for Israeli right-wingers and religionists. At their insistence, Begin's document emphasized that "Israel stands by its right and its claim of sovereignty" to these areas. In a gesture of "moderation," however, "in the knowledge that other claims exist," Israel was prepared for the time being to leave the issue of sovereignty in abeyance.

It was a far cry from the sort of Palestinian entity that Sadat originally had in mind. For that matter, it fell well short of the minimal concessions that Carter and his aides regarded as basic to a peace agreement. Nevertheless, the Americans cautiously observed that the formula was "encouraging," that it offered a "fair basis for negotiations." In that seemingly qualified manner, Washington in turn transmitted the plan to Cairo. Yet once Begin returned to Israel, and revealed the document publicly to the Knesset, he discovered that it aroused serious opposition among his own supporters and Laborites alike. The formula appeared to open the door to the evolution of a Palestinian state, they argued. In truth, this contingency was furthest from the prime minister's intention. Taken aback by the outburst of criticism, however, Begin was obliged to modify the plan sharply before the cabinet finally ratified it on December 23. The amendments ensured that Israel would assume responsibility not only for public law and order in the autonomous areas, but also for the "permanent security" of its borders; that refugees would be allowed to return to the areas only in "reasonable" numbers and according to the "unanimous" decision of a joint Israeli-Jordanian-Palestinian committee; that the extent of an administrative council's legislative authority would have to be "unanimously" agreed upon by the committee; that only Israeli citizens or Arabs who had assumed Israeli citizenship would be entitled to purchase land in the territories. Furthermore, the entire plan was conditional upon the establishment of final peace between Egypt and Israel.

Even as he read the original document that had been sent on to him by Washington, Sadat became increasingly chagrined. He had bypassed Geneva and Washington for direct talks with Begin, and now he was suddenly being presented with a formula that Begin was advertising as an Israeli-American plan. He regarded it as a bad plan—and well before the Israeli cabinet qualified it even more stringently. Nevertheless, still optimistic that the spirit of his initiative would be reciprocated, Sadat allowed Israeli-Egyptian talks to proceed along the lines first outlined in Jerusalem. Those talks actually had begun in Cairo on December 16, the day of Begin's visit to Washington. Israel's delegation was led by Eliahu Ben-Elissar, the director-general of Begin's office, and its purpose was to lay the groundwork for more far-reaching political discussions to commence several days later. Although Ben-Elissar and his colleagues, Meir Rosenne and General Avraham Tamir, were received correctly, it soon became clear that they had not been authorized to engage in substantive negotiations. The Cairo discussions began in some confusion, therefore, and both sides soon became entrapped in wrangling over procedural issues.

The principal achievement of the Cairo conference was psychological; it afforded opportunity for extended direct contacts between Israelis and Egyptians. Those encounters included an elaborate tour of Cairo, even of the Khan al-Kalili bazaar, where the Israelis were warmly greeted by Egyptian merchants and passersby alike. Neither were the visitors unmoved by their brief, ceremonial visit to the Sharei Shamayim Synagogue on Adli Basha Street. The few aged Jews who were on hand to shout tearful huzzahs for Sadat and Begin were essentially derelicts, the impoverished relics of a once proud community. For them, at least, the arrival of their Israeli brethren signified a distinct revival of status. In ensuing weeks, they began entering the synagogue through the front door again rather than furtively, through a side entrance, as had been their custom in recent decades.

The visits gained momentum. On December 19, Defense Minister Ezer Weizman, whose warm and engaging personality had appealed to Sadat when the two men first met in Jerusalem, flew to Egypt to confer with his opposite number, General Muhammad Abd al-Ghani al-Gamassi, then to meet briefly again with Sadat. It was in this second conference that the Egyptian president courteously but firmly made clear to Weizman that Israel's proposal for retaining settlements and airfields in eastern Sinai was unacceptable. Finally, on December 25, Begin himself was welcomed by Sadat in a coldly formal reception at Ismailia, beside the Suez Canal. There the Israeli prime minister began the discussions with a statement of apparently sweeping magnanimity, offering to deliver the whole of the Sinai back to Egypt, with the Egyptians to resume full sovereignty up to the recognized international border. He added only a single qualification, the one Dayan had presented in the second meeting with Tohami, and that Begin had submitted in the Washington formula. Israel of course would retain its Sinai air bases, as well as its network of settlements in the Rafah salient, until the end of the century; and would expect "special arrangements" along the Strait of Tiran.

Sadat's response was identical to the one he had given Weizman, but far more brittle. In Rabat as well as in Bucharest, Egypt had been promised sovereignty over the entire Sinai. What kind of sovereignty was this? the president asked. It was an affront the Egyptian people would not condone even for an instant. And when he listened afterward to Begin's detailed recitation of Israel's autonomy proposal for the West Bank, he restrained himself only with difficulty. The plan would have to be "studied in detail," he observed tightly. Yet if tension was mounting between the two sides, Sadat did not wish to foreclose negotiations barely a month after his gambled visit to Jerusalem. As a result, the one-day conference ended only with the announcement that talks would resume in January on a double track, with meetings of a joint Egyptian-Israeli political committee in Jerusalem, and of a joint committee of military representatives in Cairo. To Begin, this represented genuine progress. In a state of near-exultation once again, the prime minister returned home "a happy man" (as he stated to the press). His experts, on the other hand, had been considerably more sensitive to Sadat's reaction. They did not share their prime minister's widely professed optimism.

THE ROAD TO CAMP DAVID

There was cause for these misgivings. Even then the Egyptian leader was dispatching messages to Carter in Washington, to Prime Minister Callahan in London, to President Giscard d'Estaing in Paris, complaining of Israel's tough stand. "Israel is no less a 'rejectionist state' than is Syria," he declared in an interview granted the Egyptian magazine, *Uktubir*. "She has sown the wind and will therefore reap the whirlwind." In truth, so deeply perturbed was Sadat by Begin's convoluted reaction to his initiative that he invited Weizman—whom he had come increasingly to like and trust—to return for yet another visit, this one to Aswan on January 11, 1978. During their conversation, the president opened out to his guest. The Palestinians were not his central preoccupation in life, he admitted. It was true that, at the Rabat summit conference in 1974, Egypt had joined with other Arab states in designating the PLO as the "sole legal representative of the Palestinians." But he, Sadat, had had his doubts even then, and in ensuing years he had been urging the PLO's executive council to moderate its stand in order that it might share in the political process. Specifically, he had asked the PLO to recognize UN Resolution 242, and with it Israel's right to exist in peace and security.

Arafat had flatly rejected the demand. Instead, more recently, the PLO appeared to be returning to terrorism. (A month later, on February 2, 1978, two Palestinians murdered Sadat's close friend, Yusuf al-Sabai, editor in chief of *al-Ahram*, then seized Egyptian hostages at Nicosia airport. An Egyptian commando force dispatched to rescue the hostages failed, costing many lives.) Sadat made it clear to Weizman, then, that he had written off the PLO. Neither was he a fanatic on the issue of total self-determination for the occupied territories. He would settle for any sort of arrangement that would not shame him before the Arab world. But for the moment, Sadat went on, the question of Palestine would be left aside. There was the more immediate problem of Sinai to be addressed. He wanted it all back, and, except for certain agreed-upon demilitarized zones, he wanted it back unconditionally; on this point there was no change in the Egyptian position. The Israeli defense minister, in turn, now saw little possibility of accommodation.

Upon receiving an account of Sadat's counterproposal from Weizman afterward, Begin was in a dilemma. Admittedly, Sinai possessed no historic importance for the prime minister. Yet, for security reasons, he was loath to abandon both the air bases and the Israeli settlements in the Rafah salient. Even earlier, he had turned over the Sinai issue to a special committee led by Dayan and Sharon (the latter the most unregenerate "hawk" in the Israeli cabinet). The two men had studied the question, and now, unknown to Weizman, had come up with a "compromise" solution. It was to present the Egyptians with a *fait accompli* by establishing a new cluster of "dummy settlements" in Sinai. These presumably could be used as a trade-off later for Rafah and the air bases. The scheme was less than inspired. Sadat exploded upon hearing it. So did Weizman, who warned Begin by telephone from Egypt that the settlements were poisoning the atmosphere of negotiations. When Carter in Washington added his own protest to the *"fait accompli,"* Begin finally relented. The Israeli bulldozers were withdrawn.

Almost immediately, then, according to agreement reached earlier between Sadat and Begin in Ismailia, talks between Egyptians and Israelis resumed on the military level in Cairo. Gamassi and Weizman led their respective delegations. The Israelis once again began with their maximal demand, insisting on their prerogative to retain the Rafah settlements and their main airfields in Sinai. There were ten of these air bases, and they provided Israel with extensive defense in depth against air attack not only from Egypt but—in the case of the Etzion air base near Eilat—from Saudi Arabia as well. Moreover, the Sinai alone offered Israel terrain broad enough for dispersing combat planes safely. It was no secret, after all, that Israel's air force had tripled since the 1967 war. If the Sinai bases were abandoned, hundreds of new Israeli jets now would have to be concentrated again within the narrow, and vulnerable, wedge of integral Israel. This was a situation as dangerous for Egypt as for Israel, Weizman insisted, for it virtually ensured the likelihood of a preemptive Israeli attack against Egypt at the first sign of tension. Yet the argument did not register on Gamassi or on the latter's colleagues. The Egyptian military men were unwilling to make the slightest concession either on airfields or on Israeli settlements. All would have to go. There was no bridging the gap between the two sides. Finally, on January 13, both delegations agreed to suspend further talks until the political committee opened its discussions in Jerusalem.

Those meetings began four days later, on January 17, in the presence of Secretary of State Vance, who had arrived as Jimmy Carter's personal representative. Nominally, Foreign Minister Ibrahim Kamil led the Egyptian delegation. In fact, Kamil and his staff were "guided" every step of the way by a special committee established by Sadat in Cairo, and, as a result, there was little room for flexible discussions in the Israeli capital. More probably the talks would have collapsed in any case. In advance, both sides had agreed to a moratorium on accusations and recriminations. Yet, upon arrival at Ben-Gurion airport, Kamil issued an uncompromising statement of Egypt's maximalist position. "The lower the rank of the participants," Dayan observed sourly later, "the greater was their rigidity." Whereupon, at the banquet convened the evening of January 17 in honor of the Egyptian visitors, Begin offered a "toast." Typically (for Begin), the "toast" became a hectoring polemic, extolling the virtues of a united Jerusalem, of Judea and Samaria linked permanently to Israel, and warning of the dangers of Arab self-determination in the administered territories. Shocked by this obtuseness, Kamil in turn promptly telephoned Sadat, insisting that the Israeli premier had all but foreclosed meaningful negotiations. Sadat agreed. Despite Cyrus Vance's harried intermediary efforts, the Egyptian delegation was recalled only forty-eight hours after its arrival in Jerusalem.

For his part, Dayan was tempted to retaliate by calling off the military talks in Cairo. Yet, by telephone from the Egyptian capital, Weizman dissuaded him, explaining that he, Weizman, had developed a valuable personal rapport with his counterpart, War Minister Gamassi. Returning to discussions, then, Weizman intimated to the Egyptians that he and his colleagues were authorized to evince a certain "flexibility" on the airfields. Perhaps not all of them were indispensable to Israel. Perhaps, too, he suggested, there was room for compromise even on the issue of Israeli settlements in eastern Sinai. Might they not be placed under United Nations jurisdiction? Seemingly interested, Gamassi countered with a "compromise" proposal of his own. Should Israel withdraw its settlements from Sinai, this would not necessarily be regarded as a precedent for other areas. The implications for the West Bank and Gaza were clear. In some excitement, Weizman flew back to Israel hoping to elicit a counteroffer from the government. He was turned down. Precedent or no precedent, the settlements must remain in Sinai for the foreseeable future, Begin and the cabinet insisted, and they must remain exclusively under Israeli jurisdiction.

No doubt strategic considerations influenced the ministers' response. Yet, as Weizman himself later admitted, a deeper psychological factor may have played a role.

> Many of us had grown accustomed to regarding the Sinai as an integral part of the state of Israel. We had toured the length and breadth of the peninsula; the bathing beaches in the Sharm el-Sheik area were regularly inundated by hordes of vacationing Israelis. Radio and television reported the weather forecast for southern Sinai and the Gulf of Aqaba in the same routine fashion as they quoted temperatures for the Galilee and the coastal plain. Furthermore, there was a new generation that could hardly remember Israel within the pre-June 1967 borders. For these young Israelis, the desert peninsula was part of their native landscape.
>
> Suddenly, the Egyptians were confronting us with the demand that we give up the peninsula, whose size is much bigger than the entire country before 1967—in exchange for something abstract and intangible. This demand provided fertile ground for the seeds of mistrust that had lain dormant in the collective unconscious during the weeks when the peace euphoria was at its height. Many Israelis suddenly recalled that they really didn't have a great deal of trust in the Arabs.

Whatever the Israelis' motivations, Sadat could be concerned only with their formal response. With none forthcoming, he flew off despairingly to Washington on February 2, where he appealed directly to Carter. The American president was altogether sympathetic. He stated his views pungently to Weizman, moreover, who arrived in Washington three weeks later to discuss an American military aid package. Taken aback, the Israeli defense minister warned Begin by telephone that the issue of settlements—both in Sinai and on the West Bank—were hopelessly freezing the atmosphere in the United States. Indeed, the prime minister experienced this chill personally on his third visit to the White House on March 22. Only days earlier, his cabinet had authorized the establishment of new settlements in Judea and Samaria. Carter and his staff now reacted vigorously and emphatically. Their opposition to Israel's "expansionism" beyond any of its frontiers was implacable. Begin told his aides later that his meeting with the president this time was "one of the worst moments of my life." And on his return to Jerusalem he faced a new challenge to his leadership, a rising "Peace Now" movement among hundreds of thousands of exasperated Israeli moderates. Depressed, and troubled as well by a heart ailment, Begin was hospitalized and for several weeks afterward was unable to exert active leadership. When he returned at last to cabinet meetings, his behavior remained curiously listless and unfocused.

In the interval, Weizman was called back for two additional meetings with Sadat. The first took place in Cairo on March 30, and was secret. Once it became clear that the impasse on Sinai continued between the two men, Sadat shifted his attention to the West Bank. "The test for both of us is the Palestinian problem," he insisted. "I must tell my people that I have induced the Israelis to withdraw from the West Bank. I have excluded the PLO from my lexicon. By their own behavior, they have excluded themselves from the negotiations. . . . I don't care whether Hussein comes in or not. The West Bank should be demilitarized. Any solution must guarantee your security. We shall try to find a suitable formula." As it happened, the president's "suitable formula" could not yet rule out the possibility of Palestinian "self-determination," a concept anathema to all Israelis, Weizman included. The discussions ended in a mood of pessimism.

Then, four months later, in July, proceeding to Vienna for a conference, Sadat once again invited Weizman to meet with him en route in Salzburg. The Israeli defense minister reached the Austrian city on the thirteenth of the month, and the ensuing discussion between the two men was, as always, cordial. It was also very frank. "Ezer, if I can make no further progress toward peace by October," the Egyptian leader warned, "I shall resign." Once again, Sadat insisted upon a full, if phased, withdrawal of Israeli settlements from Sinai. On the issue of Palestine, he repeated to Weizman his earlier intimation of willingness to accept a rather more modest plan for Arab quasi-autonomy on the West Bank. But in the interim, Sadat added, his only hope of salvaging his position in the Arab world was to extract some dramatic, unilateral gesture of good faith by Israel—possibly an Israeli turnover of al-Arish or of Mount Sinai. Weizman listened attentively to this confession, and not without sympathy. The next day he flew back to Israel to report to the cabinet. Sadat was asking for little more than a "fig leaf," he insisted. Surely Israel owed the man a more forthcoming posture on the West Bank. At the least, the requested "gesture of goodwill" ought not to be too difficult to manage in Sinai.

Five days later, however, on July 19, before Begin and his associates could formulate a response to Sadat's appeal, Foreign Minister Dayan met in Leeds

Castle, England, with his Egyptian counterpart, Ibrahim Kamil, and with Secretary of State Vance. And here, rather to Dayan's surprise, the Egyptian diplomat evinced no willingness at all to settle for a "fig leaf." Instead, he adhered strictly to the original, maximalist, line. The inhabitants of the West Bank must be allowed full and authentic self-determination, Kamil insisted; and all Israeli settlements in Sinai, no less than all Israeli air bases there, must be abandoned without qualification and restored to unalloyed Egyptian sovereignty. Neither would there be a separate Egyptian-Israeli peace; a Middle Eastern accord must be all-inclusive.

At this point the Israeli government was in a quandary. What was Egypt's true policy? Weizman believed Sadat. Dayan believed Kamil—although, by the same token, the Israeli foreign minister now accepted the sincerity of the Egyptian desire for peace. For Begin, in any case, there could be only one response. Sadat would be offered no "fig leaf." "Nothing for nothing," the prime minister informed a press conference. Both the inelegance and the intransigence of the reply enraged Sadat. Accordingly, on July 27, he ordered Israel's military delegation in Cairo to depart. As the Egyptian president saw it, there was no further point in direct negotiations with the Begin government; henceforth all communications would go through Washington. By then, in fact, it appeared that Sadat's widely heralded peace initiative was all but moribund. The Egyptian leader had gambled his nation's prestige in the Arab world, and his personal reputation among the Egyptian people, on his dramatic trip to Jerusalem. It had been his assumption that Israel, in return for an authentic peace agreement with its largest Moslem neighbor, would be prepared to relinquish its enclave in Sinai and agree in principle to withdraw from the West Bank.

Now Sadat understood that the Israelis, deeply suspicious after years of confrontation and isolation, were not to be won over that easily. Even the Americans were unsuccessful in bridging the gap between the two sides. By the summer of 1978, and in the six months that had passed since the collapse of the political committee in Jerusalem, the Americans had presented numerous draft proposals of their own, laying particular emphasis on timetables of Israeli withdrawal both in Sinai and on the West Bank. Most of these suggestions got short shrift from Jerusalem. Secretary of State Vance's shuttle diplomacy was not more successful. First spending August 5 and 6 in Jerusalem conferring with the Israelis, then meeting afterward with Egyptian officials in Alexandria, Vance was obliged to return home without any imminent prospect of breakthrough.

And yet it was this very lack of success that now evoked a critical procedural agreement between the Israelis and Egyptians, and virtually at the last moment. Revealed in Washington on August 8, the announcement was a shocker. Sadat and Begin had consented to meet jointly with Carter at the latter's presidential retreat of Camp David on September 5. It would be the first direct encounter between the Israeli and Egyptian leaders since their abortive discussions in Ismailia on December 25, 1977, and it would take place at the urgent request of Jimmy Carter himself. Apprised that the two nations were reaching a critical, perhaps irreconcilable, standoff in their historic quest for an accommodation, the American president had determined that the lost momentum for Middle Eastern peace would now have to be restored by any diplomatic artifice, and if necessary by exercising the fullest political influence of the most powerful country in the free world.

XIX

A FRAGILE ACCORD

At a news conference on August 17, 1978, President Jimmy Carter explained his purpose in convening a tripartite summit between himself, Sadat, and Begin. It was his intention to dampen "the vituperation that has been sweeping back and forth between government leaders," and to encourage both Sadat and Begin to display "flexibility." The president's sense of urgency was justified. Not only had the millennialist hopes aroused by Sadat's visit to Jerusalem long since been dissipated, but recriminations between the two Middle Eastern statesmen were being loosed against a blizzard of press accusations and counteraccusations. Once, in a terse press interview of May 14, Sadat had even hinted that the October War might not after all be the last conflict between his nation and Israel. The mood of despair and rising bitterness plainly had to be reversed.

In fact, the notion of a summit had been initiated by Sadat himself early in August, during a conversation with United States Ambassador Herman Eilts. There was ample precedent for detailed American involvement in the peace process. Kissinger had initiated this activist role. More recently, in the aftermath of Sadat's visit to Jerusalem, the function exercised by the United States fell somewhere between Israel's preference for an American mediator and Egypt's preference for an American arbitrator. President Carter, Vice-President Walter Mondale, Secretary of State Vance, Assistant Secretary of State Harold Saunders, National Security Council Adviser William Quandt, Ambassadors Samuel Lewis and Herman Eilts, and Ambassador-at-Large Alfred Atherton, Jr., all carried letters, messages, proposals, invitations, and other communications between the parties. In addition to serving as "messenger" for the talks, the United States offered its advice and counsel, formulated proposals of its own, commented on the proposals of others, consulted on the progress of the talks, and used its persuasive powers to seek out compromises.

Transmitted to Israel via Washington, Sadat's proposal for a summit conference was warmly received by the Begin government. This time, it was noted, the Egyptian president demanded no prior Israeli commitment to full evacuation from the territories. In any case, both Dayan and Defense Minister Ezer Weizman had long suspected that Egypt's professional diplomats were endemically hostile to Israel, and that only Sadat himself could be trusted to move imaginatively and incisively to a compromise solution. For their part, the

Americans discerned a useful model for this tripartite "pressure cooker" approach to final negotiation. It could be found in President Theodore Roosevelt's mediation in the 1905 Russo-Japanese Peace Conference in Portsmouth, New Hampshire. There, in a wing of a United States naval base, the three parties had been kept in near-monastic seclusion until an agreement finally was hammered out. The pattern would be no less useful for Jimmy Carter and his advisers now.

In anticipation of the forthcoming Camp David conference, meanwhile, General Avraham Tamir, Weizman's deputy at the recently suspended military talks in Cairo, chaired a committee that included Meir Rosenne and Eliahu Ben-Elissar, the latter director-general of the prime minister's office, to draw up a new working document of Israel's position. Reflecting Weizman's view, the committee's eighty-page "Blue Paper" argued that Israel's principal objective under all circumstances must remain a separate peace with Egypt. To achieve that goal, the government now had to envisage special arrangements for the Sinai bases and settlements that would assure Egypt meaningful sovereignty; Sadat would accept nothing less. As for the West Bank and Gaza, the report went on, the key must be verbal flexibility, both to fulfill American expectations and to satisfy the Egyptian president's need for a "fig leaf."

Even on the Palestine issue, however, it was the committee's view that Israel was obliged to insist on three provisions: its right to maintain both its troops and its settlements on the West Bank; its right ultimately to assert its own claim to sovereignty over the area; and its flat rejection of a Palestinian state. Dayan read this "Blue Paper" for the first time en route to Washington and Camp David (except for authorizing a committee report, Israel's senior ministers had engaged in little advance preparation) and was not impressed. He was certain the Egyptians would never accept a formula that offered the Palestinians so little; even as he and Begin were unprepared to withdraw all Israeli settlements and air bases from Sinai.

And, at the outset, the foreign minister's reservations appeared justified. On September 5, a warm, late-summer afternoon, Sadat and Begin arrived separately with their entourages at the presidential retreat in Maryland's Cacoctin Mountains. Despite the carefully orchestrated atmosphere of informality—all participants were encouraged to wear sport clothes—it soon became evident that negotiations would be difficult and protracted. That same evening, the Egyptians made the final corrections on their own position paper. Sadat read the document aloud to Carter and Begin the next afternoon, in the presidential cabin. "It included every tough demand the Arabs ever made on us," reported one Israeli participant later, "from return of the 1948 refugees and reparations for all previous Arab-Israeli wars to complete withdrawal to the 1967 lines and a renewed division of Jerusalem." Whereupon, incensed, Begin threatened to walk out of the conference. Eventually he was persuaded to remain by Dayan; but after two additional harsh meetings between the Middle

Eastern leaders that same day, Israel's senior legal adviser, Professor Aharon Barak, cautioned Zbigniew Brzezinski not to bring Sadat and Begin together again for working sessions. In any case, the ensuing four days of prolonged discussions between staff members of the three sides generated little substantive progress.

Finally, early on September 10, Begin accepted Dayan's suggestion to come up with an "affirmative" statement of policy, one that at least would project an atmosphere of flexibility. Yet the prime minister's hastily devised statement evinced only one small change in Israel's approach. It agreed to a phased reduction of Israel's military presence on the West Bank. Otherwise, there would be no abandonment of Israel's key airfields in Sinai, no evacuation of Israeli settlements in the Rafah salient, no agreement to withdraw Israeli settlements from the West Bank, and no restrictions on the prerogative of Israeli citizens to buy land and build homes in Judea, Samaria, and Gaza. The Egyptian response, not surprisingly, was frigid.

Even as tensions between the two delegations mounted, Carter, Vance, and Brzezinski continued to negotiate quietly from cabin to cabin. The American president's command of the issues at all times was masterful, his presentation of his own views increasingly forceful. With his legal advisers, he submitted version after version of "compromise" drafts. By the end of the conference, twenty-three such drafts would have been formulated. All possible areas of potential agreement were reviewed and refined, in turn, by Professor Aharon Barak and by Dr. Osama al-Baz, the brilliant, Harvard-trained deputy minister of state for foreign affairs (and Sadat's closest adviser). At last, on the seventh day of discussions, September 12, Dayan returned from a conversation with Sadat, having discerned a faint possibility of agreement. "Concentrate on the Sinai issues," he told his colleagues. "I'm sure this is what Sadat really wants." Indeed, this had been Weizman's instinct all along, following earlier discussions with Sadat in Egypt and Austria, and it was reflected in the "Blue Paper" formulated by his deputy.

By then Dayan also sensed that the Tamir document might offer a viable approach, after all, that a deal might be reached on a "fig leaf" for the West Bank—provided Israel demonstrated flexibility on the Sinai. In short, Sadat's adamant stand on Palestine conceivably had been adopted for bargaining purposes. The Americans soon learned of this shift in Israeli emphasis. Although Brzezinski still feared leaving the Palestine issue in limbo, Carter overruled him. "Let's get agreement on first things first," the president insisted. Thereafter, the Sinai and West Bank issues were separated, with only ambiguous terminology agreed upon as linkage. There would be two distinct agreements, in Carter's plan, one dealing with peace between Israel and Egypt, the second dealing with a wider-ranging settlement of the Middle Eastern conflict.

For his part, Begin still intended to remain firm on the question of Sinai airfields and settlements. Yet by then Dayan had been substantially won over to Sadat's position: full evacuation of the Sinai was crucial if there was to be peace. On the morning of the fourteenth, too, Carter summoned Dayan to his cabin and added his own warning. It was a grim one. Peace was out of the question unless Israel agreed to remove its Sinai settlements, the president observed. Moreover, in the event war broke out on the issue of the Rafah salient, Israel would not be able to count on American support. Dayan was sobered by the ultimatum. Soon afterward, he was given further pause by his meeting with Sadat in the latter's cabin. Nerve-frazzled and exasperated, the Egyptian leader announced his intention to depart Camp David; he had sent word for a helicopter to be made ready. Point-blank, he asked Dayan now: would Begin yield on the Sinai or not? The Israeli foreign minister was uncertain. "Begin is a strong man," he replied, "but he hasn't got a mandate [from the cabinet] to do anything further."

"Kindly convey this from me to Begin," exclaimed Sadat. "Settlements, never! Why are you coming to me with such ideas you know I'll never agree to? Why should we torture President Carter with us?"

Unexpectedly, then, Sadat added a sweetener. He hinted at the possibility of full diplomatic relations only nine months after signing a peace treaty, if Israel agreed to withdraw its settlements from Sinai. No mention whatever was made of Palestine. Sensing the possibility of compromise, Dayan returned immediately to his prime minister and added his own appeal for moderation. Begin listened carefully. Although he did not yet commit himself, he reflected painstakingly on the issue of Sinai throughout the night of the fourteenth. The following evening, too, Carter met personally with Begin, and in a tough, four-hour conversation tightened the screw. In the event agreement were not reached the next day, he, the president, would terminate the conference and present a full report to Congress. The intimation was clear that the report would blame Israel for the failure of negotiations. Carter tempered the warning with an inducement, however, by reaffirming an offer first tendered by Vance and by Defense Secretary Harold Brown in response to a query by Weizman. If Begin agreed to abandon his nation's Sinai air bases, the United States, at its own expense, would build Israel two military air bases of "important scope and with extensive facilities." Moreover, these bases would be completed in the Negev before Israel's last phased evacuation from Sinai.

That same evening, contemplating the president's offer, the Israeli prime minister received an unexpected telephone call from Jerusalem. It was from Ariel Sharon. Unknown to Begin, Tamir and Weizman had conceived the scheme of telephoning Sharon in advance, and of requesting the latter's intercession with the prime minister. Sharon had agreed. At this point, then, much to Begin's surprise, the hawkish former general declared that he, Sharon, anticipated no unmanageable security risks in evacuating the Sinai settlements, provided Israel held firm on the West Bank. Hereupon Begin decided to give in. He did so grudgingly, still fearing the political consequences at home. But he knew, too, that Sadat had his own serious problems by then; that his foreign minister, Ibrahim Kamil, had submitted his resignation upon learning of the proposed "fig leaf" for the West Bank. Indeed, Begin acceded not only to the Egyptian demand for evacuating the Sinai bases and settlements, but also to the precondition that the West Bank and Gaza agreements be signed in advance of the understanding on Sinai, thereby avoiding at least the appearance of a separate Egyptian-Israeli accommodation. These were not unimportant concessions.

THE FRAMEWORKS OF AGREEMENT

The two components of agreement would be entitled, respectively, a "Framework for Peace in the Middle East" and a "Framework for the Conclusion of a Peace Treaty between Egypt and Israel." Under this rubric, it was the second framework that related exclusively to Egyptian-Israeli issues, and that provided for: the full exercise of Egyptian sovereignty up to the old international Sinai-Palestine border; the withdrawal of all Israeli armed forces and settlements from the Sinai; the use by Egypt of abandoned Israeli airfields for civilian purposes only; the right of free passage by Israeli ships through the Gulf of Suez, the Suez Canal, the Strait of Tiran, and the Gulf of Aqaba; and (provided the Hashemite government agreed) the construction of a highway between Sinai and Jordan near Eilat with guaranteed free and peaceful passage by Egypt and Jordan.

More detailed provisions were worked out for a phased withdrawal of Israeli troops, to be completed between two and three years after a final peace treaty was ratified; for limited Egyptian forces in certain key areas; for United Nations forces in specified areas of the Sinai, troops that could be removed only with the formal approval of the Security Council; and, following ratification of the treaty and completion by Israel of the first phase of its withdrawal from Sinai (after nine months), the establishment of diplomatic and other normal commercial and cultural relations between Egypt and Israel. As in the 1975 disengagement, American commitments to Israel—in this case the promises to build air bases in the Negev and to supply extensive military hardware—were not incorporated into the text of the formal agreement, but were outlined rather in separate understandings between the Israeli prime minister and the American president.

It was a good arrangement for both sides. The Egyptians were guaranteed the return of all their land, and the evacuation from it of every last Israeli soldier and settler. Israel won assurance that, for a maximum of three years following treaty ratification, its forces could remain along a line extending from just east of al-Arish down to Ras Muhammad at the southern tip of the Sinai Peninsula—thereby leaving 40 percent of the Sinai in Israeli hands. Even more important was the fact that for at least two years of this period, full, normalized relations would be maintained between the two countries, including the exchange of ambassadors, the opening of borders, and cultural and commercial interchange. As Yitzchak Rabin admitted with approval later: "I cannot overemphasize the importance of testing Egypt's intentions not merely by virtue of what the Egyptians say, but by what they do for more than two years while Israel continues to hold on to such a large proportion of the Sinai."

Preceding the Egyptian-Israeli understanding, however, was a far more complex "framework" dealing with the West Bank and Gaza. It envisaged the participation of Egypt, Israel, Jordan, and "the representatives of the Palestinian people" in negotiations on the resolution of "the Palestinian problem in all its aspects." The negotiations anticipated three stages. In the first, Egypt, Jordan, and Israel would deal with the "modalities" for establishing an elected self-governing authority in the West Bank and Gaza, and would define that authority's powers and responsibilities. Egypt and Jordan might include West Bank and Gaza Palestinians in their respective delegations. Secondly, after the self-governing authority itself was established and inaugurated, a transitional period of five years would begin, and Israel would dismantle its military government and withdraw its troops to specified security locations.

In the third stage, and not later than the third year after the onset of the transitional period, negotiations would be undertaken between Israel, Egypt, Jordan, and—this time—elected representatives of the Palestinians (again, those currently living in the West Bank and Gaza itself) to determine the final status of the administered areas. A separate committee of Israelis, Jordanians, and elected West Bank and Gaza Arabs would negotiate a final peace treaty between Israel and Jordan. These discussions not only would "take into account" the agreement reached on the final status of the West Bank and Gaza, but would ensure recognition of "the legitimate rights of the Palestinian people."

In the aftermath of Camp David, to be sure, Sadat ventured to interpret the agreement on the West Bank and Gaza as a major commitment by Israel to the Palestinians. After all, it included promises of "full autonomy" and respect for the "legitimate rights of the Palestinian people"—phrases Israel had always resisted—and assurance of early troop withdrawal. The "framework" declared, too, that peace treaties should similarly be negotiated between Israel and Jordan, Syria, and Lebanon. Yet, in perspective, it seemed unlikely that Sadat had achieved (or, as Weizman had insisted all along, had expected to achieve) more than a "fig leaf" on the Palestine issue. He had entered the conference asserting that he would insist on a forthright commitment from Begin to withdraw entirely from the West Bank at some future date. Instead, he had agreed eventually to a convoluted, amorphous formula—essentially Israel's—that postponed the entire question of final Israeli withdrawal for future negotiations.

By its anticipatory inclusion of Jordan in the discussions, moreover, the formula apparently precluded the Arabs' widely proclaimed desideratum of a Palestinian state. Indeed, the agreement endorsed Israel's right to take "all necessary measures" to assure "the security of Israel . . . during the transitional period and beyond." Beyond? Possibly "beyond" the five-year transitional period? Finally, the sensitive issue of Jerusalem was not so much as touched upon in the accord, but instead was relegated to separate letters from Sadat and Begin to Carter, each presenting conflicting views on the city's future. In effect, then, Sadat had given his approval to what amounted to a separate Egyptian-Israeli peace agreement, and to a scheme for the West Bank that differed little in spirit from the plan first submitted by Begin—via the United States—in December 1977. Yet even if, as both sides doubtless hoped, agreement eventually were reached on the intractable issues of the West Bank, Gaza, and Jerusalem, at least in the interval the protracted negotiations would not interfere with the building of peace between Egypt and Israel. The agreement was a good one for Begin.

Neither was it without its important advantages for Sadat. The Egyptian president received other assurances that (as Weizman had suspected from the beginning) evidently meant more to him than an ideal resolution of the Palestine question. As a result of the Camp David agreement, Egypt would be able not merely to regain the Sinai, but to shift its troops from the Israeli front to the Libyan border. Indeed, this strategic redeployment was one of several verbal understandings reached between Sadat, Begin, and Carter. Expanded cooperation between the Egyptian and Israeli intelligence services was another. Additionally, the Egyptian army now would be able to reduce its standing forces by half, to about 200,000 men. It would be restructured and streamlined with modern American equipment. These deliveries of ordnance, in turn, would be linked to Egyptian progress in carrying out the Camp David accords, up to and including the establishment of full diplomatic relations with Israel; even as the United States would organize a Western economic consortium to help replace Arab funds cut off from Egypt in retaliation for Camp David. Israel, too, of course, was promised a significant infusion of American economic and military aid, of advanced jet aircraft and access to American weapons technology.

Thereupon, after twelve days of touch-and-go negotiations, a bone-weary Carter summoned the two Middle Eastern leaders to his lodge for a festive toast. That night, September 17, a televised ceremony of signing took place at the White House, in the presence of selected members of Congress and other dignitaries. The president himself outlined the substance of agreement, observed that a formal peace treaty between Egypt and Israel was to be negotiated and completed within the next three months, and emphasized the

American commitment to "participate fully in all subsequent negotiations relating to the future" of the West Bank and Gaza. Sadat and Begin then personally saluted each other and Carter in separate addresses. On the following evening the three leaders appeared again before a special joint session of the full Congress, this time with Carter the principal speaker, congratulating his two Middle Eastern guests, and basking in the triumph of his diplomatic tour de force. Under the TV lights, onlookers were treated to the spectacle of Begin and Sadat embracing before an audience of cheering legislators. Manifestly, the road to peace seemed shorter.

In fact, Begin appeared to move forthrightly on that road by honoring a promise he had made in one of the Camp David "side letters," namely, to place before the Knesset the issue of removing the Sinai settlements. On the other hand, the prime minister was unwilling to make the vote a matter of party discipline, and there was reason for concern that some of his closest political supporters would oppose withdrawal. None had to be reminded of the strategic role fulfilled by these border villages. It was a function so palpable that the Laborites, ironically, had earlier taken a firmer stand on the settlements than had the right-wing Likud bloc. For them, the Rafah salient provided a security guarantee that was far more legitimate to Israel's self-interest than the Right's historical-biblical obsession with Judea and Samaria. In mid-September, meanwhile, the settlers themselves vented their outrage by mounting demonstrations and a protest "drive-in" through the heart of Jerusalem. Begin's worries were soon dispelled, however. Labor's central committee agreed that the settlements issue could not be allowed to block the prospects for peace, even as the Gachal bloc similarly declined to embarrass its leader. The question of the West Bank and Jerusalem, after all, had conveniently been postponed for long and intricate future negotiations, and under terms not necessarily unfavorable to Israel. Thus it was, on September 27, that the Knesset cast its vote of 84 to 19 to approve the Camp David framework and to remove the 3,000 Israeli settlers from Sinai.

In the aftermath of the historic conference, Sadat, like Begin, was not without grave concerns of his own. Plainly, these were evoked by the anticipated hostile reaction of the Arab world. To defuse that expected outburst, the Egyptian president flew directly from the United States to Morocco. There he hoped to ensure himself of the support at least of King Hassan. But this time the Moroccan sovereign was cautious and noncommittal. So was Hussein of Jordan, who declined even to meet with Sadat, much less to consider a proposal to join the upcoming Palestinian negotiations. In Saudi Arabia, King Khaled remained ominously silent. As a result, Sadat was obliged to conduct his Rabat press conference in isolation. Afterward, he flew on to Cairo. There, at least, he entertained no concern whatever about the public response.

Nor was Sadat wrong. Greeted rapturously, he was escorted to his home in a triumphant—if carefully orchestrated—reception of nearly a million people.

With their president, the citizens of Egypt were convinced that peace was in sight, that the lost Sinai would be restored in short order, that the standing army would now be reduced, that Western investment capital would soon be forthcoming, and that, with all these bounties, a quantum leap was imminent in the nation's standard of living. These hopes appeared further vindicated in late November when the Nobel Peace Prize was awarded jointly to Sadat and Begin.

THE DEDIABOLIZATION OF ISRAEL AND JEWRY

One of the Egyptian leader's principal tasks, in the wake of his initial visit to Jerusalem, and most particularly after the Camp David breakthrough, was to dissipate the animus against Israel, Zionism, and the Jews that had been systematically fostered in his country throughout nearly four decades. The residue of hostility was formidable. It was during the apogee of the Nasser epoch, for example, in the 1960s, that the Catholic Church decided to "exonerate" the Jews of responsibility for the Crucifixion. Almost immediately, the theologians of al-Azhar University chose to impute this "exoneration" to the machinations of world Zionism. During the 1960s, too, Egyptian literature borrowed heavily in its description of Jews from the notorious *Protocols of the Elders of Zion*. The government itself printed several editions of the *Protocols* in Arabic, English, and French, and sold copies to the PLO for distribution. Not infrequently, Nasser, and even Sadat, cited the *Protocols* in their speeches.

More insidiously yet, school textbooks brimmed over with references to the Jews as spies, usurers, embezzlers, as committed enemies of Islam since the time of Muhammad. Various early Moslem works had accused the Jews of attempting to kill the Prophet. In the 1960s and early 1970s, Egyptian publicists and propagandists magnified these claims dramatically, and embellished them in pictures, songs, and televison programs. As recently as the summer of 1977, the weekly magazine *Uktubir*, edited by Anis Mansour, a self-styled philosopher-poet and close journalistic confidant of Sadat, published a serialized Arabic version of an old French book called *The Evil Found in the Talmud*. Mansour's rendition was lavishly endowed with accounts of Jewish blood rituals and caricatures of hook-nosed sadists wielding long daggers.

Now, however, in the wake of his peace initiative, Sadat felt obliged to turn off these spigots of enmity and to redefine the image of the ugly Israeli—and the ugly Jew. Fortunately, the typical Egyptian possessed a shallow capacity for sustained hatred. For him, life was too short to be mired in bile (an attitude often mistaken for cowardice). By subjecting the Israelis to initial defeat, the recent war curiously had brought them down to life-size, even had humanized them for the first time, and as a consequence had made it possible for Egyptians to engage in peace negotiations with them.

For professional soldiers, moreover, for officers like Major General Ahmad Badawi, Egypt's chief of staff in 1978, there was practical advantage to be gained in the dediabolization of Israel. Concerned increasingly by the unpredictable aberrations of a psychotic Libyan neighbor, and by the widening Soviet penetration of the Horn of Africa and the Persian Gulf, Badawi admitted that the possibility of Egyptian-Israeli military cooperation was no longer altogether remote. Turks and Greeks had managed intermittently to cooperate within the framework of NATO, after all. By the same token, the quasi-official Institute for Palestine and Zionist Studies, founded to "know the enemy," was directed now to utilize the talents of its fifteen staffers and twenty part-time researchers, and the resources of its vast library of Israeli books and journals, for the "reeducation" of public opinion in anticipation of peace. To that end, the institute's numerous published monographs on Israel were carefully stripped of all polemics. A major new research program was devoted instead to the likely consequences of normalized relations between Egypt and Israel. Earlier, the consensus had been that Israel would dominate the relationship economically. More recently, however, it was the institute's conclusion that Egypt's economy was potentially competitive with Israel's. If Israeli technology was adapted in large measure from the United States, Egypt was capable of exploiting the same source.

Perhaps more telling evidence yet of the government's sincerity was its campaign to dediabolize the Jews and Israel in the eyes of Egyptian school-children. Here, interestingly enough, men like Dr. Abd al-Fatah Arafa and his colleagues had been preparing for a new era since the October War. In their obscure offices at the ministry of education, Arafa and other curriculum supervisors already were well embarked on the revision of textbooks and social science courses for the peace treaty they were sure was coming. Denunciations of Israel, attacks on Zionism, and appeals for armed struggle were eliminated and replaced by "just the facts." Arafa, who held the position of chancellor of history, geography, and civics for Egypt's public schools, noted proudly in June 1979 that "no books that are presently in the schools will have to be removed to convey the new reality of peace. It has been at least five years since anti-Israel diatribes appeared in our curriculum."

Of equal significance in the new reconciliation was the muting of the desire for *jihad*—holy war—by Egypt's religious leadership. Dr. Abd al-Moneim al-Nimr, vice-rector of al-Azhar University, exemplified this change. An elderly theologian, robed and turbaned, Nimr assured the author that he personally no longer would entertain objections to peaceful coexistence with Israel. But what of *jihad*? the vice-rector was asked. Smiling tolerantly, Nimr replied that *jihad* was mandatory only if an enemy attacked Egypt. The entire purpose of *jihad* was defensive. If Israel lived in peace with Egypt, then *jihad* did not apply. The old mufti's assurances were rationalization, of course, an adaptation of religious doctrine to fit political exigencies. But this was hardly an innovation of Islam's.

Yet the most telling insight into the change of national mood, conceivably, was the welcome accorded visiting Israelis. Among these were journalists, university professors, archaeologists, scientists, doctors, and other professionals who were selectively granted admission to Egypt in the aftermath of Camp David. The newcomers were greeted cordially by their Egyptian counterparts, and with visible emotion by the Egyptian man in the street. Elated by the long-postponed opportunity of meeting Israeli intellectuals, the nation's most distinguished literary critic, Dr. Lewis Awad, a contributing editor of *al-Ahram* and formerly a professor of literature at Cairo University, expressed his own eagerness in turn to visit Israel, even to accept a guest professorship there—should it be offered. Awad's sentiments were heartily echoed by the venerated novelist, Naguib Mahfuz. Indeed, for Mahfuz, who had been deeply touched by the recent visit of Professor Mattiyahu Peled of Tel Aviv University (the translator into Hebrew of several of Mahfuz's best-known works), peace signified an opportunity to lift the intolerable economic burden on Egypt, to allow cultured Egyptians to secure the best of Western writing again, and to facilitate a broad cultural exchange between Egypt, Israel, and the West.

In Israel, meanwhile, the vista of peace created a tense ambivalence between hallucination and disbelief. Only half-jestingly, travel agents spoke of possible two-way excursions between the former enemies, even as they ventured to raise the prospects of Middle East package tours that no longer would be circum-scribed by complex, indirect dog-leg stopovers in Greece or Cyprus. For the average Israeli, of course, the radiant vision of escape from more than thirty years of claustrophobia, from the brooding peril of war and endless human and economic sacrifice, was overwhelming. Nevertheless, well accustomed by then to disappointments in the aftermath of earlier confrontations with their Arab neighbors—and most notably in the aftermath of the Six-Day and October wars—Israelis were cautious about articulating that vision in detail. They waited, their hopes and dreams still barely at the threshold of consciousness. Fate dare not be tempted.

SADAT ALTERS HIS PRECONDITIONS

Under the terms of the Camp David framework, Egypt and Israel were to reach agreement "on the modalities and the timetable for the implementation of their obligations under the [impending peace] treaty." To that purpose, on October 12, 1978, an Egyptian team headed by Defense Minister Kamal Hassan Ali and Acting Foreign Minister Butros Butros-Ghali, and an Israeli team led by Dayan and Weizman, gathered at Washington's Blair House to negotiate the details of a pact. At first, in the presence of Secretary Vance (as always, an active participant), the discussions began in a cordial atmosphere.

Despite reservations within the Israeli cabinet that the timetable of phased withdrawal from Sinai was too abrupt, Dayan and Weizman intended to honor the September understanding punctiliously. The negotiators on both sides were hopeful, therefore, that the final ceremonial signing of an Egyptian-Israeli treaty would take place not on December 17—the deadline set at Camp David—but as early as November 19, the first anniversary of Sadat's visit to Jerusalem.

Yet the days went by and draft treaty after draft treaty failed to win mutual acceptance. It soon became clear that one of the difficulties postponing final agreement was the issue of future Israeli settlements on the West Bank. At Camp David no language on the question had appeared in the Framework of Agreement. Nevertheless, it was the understanding both of the Americans and of the Egyptians that Israel would call a halt to new settlements until the Palestinians elected their self-governing council. After that, the question of new settlements presumably would be negotiated between Israel, on the one hand, and Egypt, Jordan, and the West Bank Arabs, on the other. Within days after Camp David, however, Begin let it be known that the settlement "freeze" applied only for the three months (or less) that were required to complete and sign the Egyptian-Israeli peace treaty. Chivied by the religionists in his coalition to remain "honest," the Israeli prime minister now flatly refused to budge from this stance. The moratorium on new Jewish settlements would be short-lived, he warned. It was a shocking provocation to the Egyptians—even as Carter's pained silence afterward was a meaningful insight to the Arab rejectionists of American (and Egyptian) ineffectuality on a crucial test issue.

Far from adopting a conciliatory posture, Begin also asserted Israel's right not merely to establish new settlements in the foreseeable future, but to claim its sovereignty over the West Bank altogether. "It is our land," he insisted vehemently at a banquet in New York, only two days after the Camp David agreement (Sadat had not yet departed the United States). Nor was the prime minister's intransigence on this issue mitigated by a visit to the Middle East in late October by Assistant Secretary of State Harold Saunders. In an effort to win Jordanian and Palestinian cooperation for the autonomy plan, Saunders assured his Arab hosts that autonomy at best represented an interim program, that Israel eventually would dismantle its settlements in the occupied territories altogether. Infuriated by this palpable misreading of Begin's intention, the Israeli cabinet thereupon announced plans to "thicken" Jewish settlements in Judea and Samaria from the moment the three-month Egyptian-Israeli treaty deadline ended. The pronouncement left Sadat in an acutely uncomfortable position, and the Carter administration hardly less so.

Immediately following the Camp David signings, Carter had instructed Secretary Vance to embark on a tour of Middle Eastern capitals in an attempt to secure wider Arab understanding of the "Framework of Agreement." Thus, upon reaching the Hashemite capital of Amman, Vance focused mainly on the question of Jordanian participation in a final agreement on Palestine. The effort did not go well. King Hussein and his cabinet intensively cross-examined their visitor, then explained the risks the monarch courted if he defied the Arab hard-liners—that is, endorsed a document that did not call for total Israeli withdrawal from the West Bank, the Golan Heights, and Jerusalem. In Riyadh, the secretary encountered an equally brittle response from the Saudi cabinet. And, under the influence of the PLO, virtually all West Bank mayors denounced the Camp David accord, declaring their intention to boycott any planned elections for an administrative council.

If the Americans were given pause by this tepid reception, Sadat could only have been more gravely concerned. Notwithstanding his triumphant welcome in Cairo, the Egyptian president understood by then that a large part of the Arab world was anathematizing him for his "sellout" of the Palestinians. Worse yet, restiveness exsited within the Egyptian diplomatic corps itself, and, as we recall, lately the foreign minister, Ibrahim Kamil—himself a successor to Ismail Fahmi—had resigned in protest. Before the People's Assembly on November 2, therefore, Sadat painstakingly repeated the elaborate preamble to the "frame-works," emphasizing the primacy of a West Bank solution over an exclusively Egyptian-Israeli pact. The agreements did not relate to Egypt alone, he insisted, but to Jordan and Syria, as well, and to the Palestinians and the Lebanese, "and that is the [only] accessible road to the liberation of the Arab land after 1967. . . ." The president added that members of the PLO were not specifically debarred from negotiating on Palestinian autonomy, provided that they lived on the West Bank; but if they chose not to take part, he, Sadat, would speak for them. "I cannot think that they shall object to alleviating the hardship suffered by the Palestinian people in the occupied land. . . . I do not think they would object to real participation in the paving of the road to an overall solution." Negotiation under the Camp David format was the Palestinians' last best chance now, he argued.

Sadat's appeal evoked no favor elsewhere in the Arab world. Even as he addressed the People's Assembly on November 2, emissaries from the Arab states were meeting again in Baghdad to discuss further measures against Egypt and against an emergent Egyptian-Israeli treaty. Initiative for the conference this time had come from Iraq itself, whose Ba'athist regime intended to end that nation's long years of isolation and to project Iraq as a new leader of the Arab world. Yet, much to Sadat's dismay, the Saudis also participated in the Baghdad conclave. Crown Prince Fahd shared the bitterness of the radicals at Egypt's "sellout" of the Palestinians. For him, the volatile Palestinian guerrilla movements were fully as dangerous to Middle Eastern stability as were the left-wing Ba'athist governments of Iraq and Syria. In the crown prince's view, the various PLO factions could be assuaged now only by the establishment of a fully autonomous entity on the West Bank, a regime assured of its future right to self-determination. Accordingly, with Saudi endorsement, the conference ended by detailing the sanctions to be imposed on Egypt if the latter signed the pact with Israel. The punitive measures would include a termination of all Persian Gulf financial aid to the Cairo government, a formal and final severance of diplomatic relations, and a tight embargo on Egyptian companies known to be trading with Israel. This time, too, a fund was established to provide additional financial aid to Syria, Jordan, and the PLO; as well as an offer of up to $15 billion in loans and grants over the ensuing five years to Egypt itself—provided Sadat repudiated the impending treaty.

The Baghdad Conference was a serious blow to the Egyptian president. Those closest to him admitted later that he was gravely shaken. Until the last moment, it had been his expectation that the Saudis under no circumstances would join the radical Arab governments in common cause against Egypt. Now, well after the fact, Sadat appreciated that evidently he had let Israel off too easily. At the outset, he had been willing to leave unspecified the connection between the timing of the peace treaty and the first moves toward West Bank autonomy. Admittedly, the implication of a political—or at least a moral—linkage was well understood and quietly accepted by both sides. In the immediate aftermath of Camp David, nevertheless, Egypt had agreed, and Israel had emphasized, that the two frameworks were each designed to stand alone. After all, no one could guarantee that Jordan and the West Bank Palestinians would ever consent to participate in negotiations; and an Egyptian-Israeli peace treaty should not remain hostage to Arab indecision elsewhere. But now Sadat felt constrained to alter that understanding. On November 3, even as peace talks were continuing at Washington's Blair House, Egypt's Acting Foreign Minister Butros-Ghali suddenly announced a shift in his government's position. It was an alteration simultaneously confirmed in a private letter from Sadat to Begin. Under the new format, Egypt would have to insist on a definite timetable for Palestinian autonomy before committing itself to a formal treaty.

Begin and his colleagues expressed their shock. Meeting urgently four days later, the Israeli cabinet rejected the Egyptian proposal out of hand. Indeed, the linkage between a peace treaty and negotiations on Palestine already were "too close" for several of the ministers' taste. When yet additional requested changes for the draft treaty were floated by Cairo, they were given even shorter shrift. One new demand called for a review after five years of the security arrangements, including all demilitarized and limited force zones, that had been negotiated earlier for Sinai. Another alteration related to Israel's interim withdrawal to the al-Arish-Ras Muhammad line. To save face among his own political constituents, Sadat now asked Jerusalem to make the "gesture" of withdrawal within six months, rather than nine months, following signature of the treaty. The Begin government's response was an indignant refusal. Nor did the Israelis react favorably to an additional Egyptian proposal, this one suggesting an Egyptian "presence" in Gaza during elections there for the administrative council. Such a "presence" would intimidate local Arab voters, Jerusalem explained.

In a countermove that suggested their revived distrust of the Egyptians, Begin and his associates now submitted two desiderata of their own. One raised the issue of priority of treaties. It had been understood at Camp David that the Egyptian-Israeli accord would be enacted without regard to Egypt's obligations to other Arab nations—that is, obligations for mutual defense in the event of war with Israel. Under pressure from the Arab world, however, and particularly from Syria, the Egyptians were now arguing that their current treaty engagements to other Arab countries must take priority. But again the Israelis were adamant, and insisted this time that, without a specific provision—Article VI in the draft treaty—clarifying the primacy of Egyptian-Israeli peace, the document would be meaningless. The second Israeli amendment defined their claim to Sinai oil. As a consequence of growing unrest in Iran, a nation that supplied 40 percent of Israel's petroleum, Jerusalem wanted ironclad assurance of its right at least to purchase Sinai oil from Egypt; and to guarantee that right, the Neptune Oil Company, a private firm then under Israeli contract in the Sinai, should remain the principal conduit of Sinai oil. The Egyptians coldly rejected these demands. By the end of 1978, then, the likelihood of peace once again had suddenly been clouded.

Notwithstanding these difficulties, the Egyptian president still appeared committed to a treaty with Israel. Lashing out repeatedly at Arab critics of his initiative, on November 4 he turned down the Baghdad offer of $15 billion, even snubbed a delegation sent to Cairo by the rejectionist states. "All the billions in the world cannot buy the will of Egypt," Sadat later declared to a cheering People's Assembly. A week and a half afterward, he agreed to extend the mandate of the United Nations peacekeeping force in the Sinai for an additional nine months, to July 24, 1979. Yet the depth of Arab outrage unquestionably had to be taken seriously. In a cautionary gesture, therefore, Sadat refused in December to participate personally in the Nobel Peace Prize ceremony (although Begin flew to Oslo to accept his share of the award).

Meanwhile, the three-month deadline for completing the Egyptian-Israeli treaty was approaching. From December 11 on, as a result, Cyrus Vance spent a week shuttling between Cairo and Jerusalem in an urgent final effort to broker an agreement by December 17. On the issue of linkage, it developed that Sadat was prepared to compromise on something less than a definite timetable for Palestinian autonomy. A "target date" for the installation of the locally elected West Bank council would be acceptable. So would a merely symbolic Egyptian "presence" in Gaza in a preliminary election there. In return for these concessions, Sadat had persuaded Vance to accept the principle of yet another letter to be annexed to the envisaged treaty. This one would delay the exchange of Egyptian and Israeli ambassadors until one month after control of the West

Bank and Gaza had passed to an autonomous authority. It was a revision, Sadat and Vance agreed, that would give Israel meaningful incentive to fulfill its pledges on the occupied territories. But here again the effort was wasted. Begin and his advisers made clear that they had gone as far as they dared at Camp David. In rejecting Sadat's (and Vance's) amendment, the Israeli prime minister emphasized once more that extraneous forces—that is, local Palestinian resistance—easily could doom the establishment of meaningful autonomy, or even elections to an administrative council. It was a warning that was fully supported by the Labor opposition.

In Begin's case, however, the argument was at least partly a rationalization. His own conception of autonomy was less than forthright. At no time had he envisaged more than a limited town- or village-level jurisdiction for a Palestinian council. He was still the man who, six years earlier, in an updated preface to his 1948 autobiography, had written: "It is our duty, fathers and sons, to see to it that the artificial [1949 Rhodes Armistice] line which disappeared [in the 1967 war] never returns. We must not yield our natural and eternal right." Nor would he abandon his lifelong fixation with an undivided Land of Israel even now, in the afterglow of Camp David. As a result, then, of Egypt's altered stance and Israeli opposition, the deadline for signing was not reached. Returning to Washington on December 16, Vance gave his president a harshly anti-Israel accounting, and Carter thereupon publicly condemned Israel for inflexibility.

The mood in Cairo was equally despondent. In an interview that same December 16, Acting Foreign Minister Butros-Ghali underlined the importance his government attached to Arab public opinion elsewhere, and specifically in the Persian Gulf nations. Tens of thousands of Egyptians were employed in those kingdoms and emirates, Butros-Ghali explained, and their remittances to kinsmen in Egypt were worth hundreds of millions of dollars annually. "We cannot cut ourselves off from that," he insisted. Already some of these Egyptian technicians were being replaced with Koreans and Pakistanis. "In twenty years, too, the Gulf nations will equal Egypt in educational and political influence, as they already far surpass us in wealth; and as a consequence Egyptian diplomatic leverage will have to be shared with them. It may be that by then our leadership for moderation will also be gone." But was Israel not justified in fearing that "too much autonomy too soon" in the West Bank would convert that territory into a PLO state, Butros-Ghali was asked; into an Arafat regime tempted to sign defense agreements with Cubans and Russians? The acting foreign minister dismissed this possibility. His government was prepared to limit the power of such an entity, he argued, by incorporating into its very constitution an Austrian-style neutrality. Indeed, he and his staff had spent months analyzing historical precedents to reassure the Israelis on this issue. After a period of autonomy or statehood—"we do not say it has to be statehood"—a Palestinian entity would be obliged for reasons of its own economic survival to federate with Jordan, "or even with Israel—we would not care."

But without such an entity, the acting foreign minister warned, the Palestinians would remain an embittered and explosive element, as dangerous for Egypt as for Israel. Butros-Ghali was careful to add, at this point, that the seething presence of millions of refugees was no less fraught with risk for the conservative Saudi government. (Soon afterward, in March 1979, Riyadh canceled Prince Fahd's scheduled visit to Washington. It was plain that the Saudis were concerned by the upheaval of radical elements in the Arab world and feared too intimate a connection with the United States, and with the latter's role in negotiating the Camp David agreement.) Inasmuch as the Saudis could not long tolerate that refugee danger, Butros-Ghali continued, the Egyptians for their part were obliged to insist on some sort of linkage between an Egyptian-Israeli treaty and a guaranteed autonomous status for the Palestinians. The acting foreign minister's tone was one of frustration and exhaustion, possibly not unaffected by awareness of his own responsibility for having shifted the ground rules after Camp David. "We shall keep striving," he promised, "but passing the three-month deadline was a terrible blow." By implication, the blow was a grave one to Sadat's prestige. "A grave blow to peace," lamented Butros-Ghali. And to Sadat's chances for a decisive turnabout in Egypt's economy.

Following Vance's departure on December 16, 1978, the task of shuttle diplomacy was left to a specially appointed State Department mediator, Alfred Atherton, Jr. But after two weeks of strenuous negotiations in Jerusalem and Cairo, during which he and his staff came up with ten draft versions of a treaty, Atherton returned to Washington as empty-handed as had the secretary. All the basic stumbling blocks remained: linkage of the Israeli-Egyptian accord to implementation of civil autonomy on the West Bank and in Gaza; priority of Egypt's mutual defense pacts over an Egyptian-Israeli treaty; a review of Sinai security arrangements after five years; an Egyptian "presence" in Gaza; timing of the exchange of ambassadors between the two countries; and availability of Sinai oil to Israel. None of these issues appeared to be close to resolution. In a brief meeting between Dayan and Egyptian Prime Minister Mustafa Khalil in Brussels on December 22, the one concession Israel appeared ready to make was to "consider" advancing the date of its withdrawal from al-Arish. Otherwise, the deadlock between the two sides remained. Nor was it resolved in a second— foreign ministers'—meeting at Camp David, from February 20 to February 24. Conferring with both delegations, President Carter was barely able to contain his frustration. "The occasional smile with which he tempered his words was thin and fleeting," Dayan recalled afterward, "never extending beyond lips and teeth. His expression was grave, his look harsh."

For that matter, newspaper editorials both in Egypt and Israel began to express a fatigued, muted sense of déjà vu. Was the high hope aroused by

Sadat's historic visit to Jerusalem in 1977 to be regarded now as little more than a meteoric, but evanescent, episode in the long succession of failures: the Rhodes Armistice of 1949, the PCC negotiations at Lausanne during 1949–50, the intermittent MAC contacts of the 1950s, United Nations Resolution 242, the disengagement agreements of 1974–75? Was Camp David, too, to be nothing more than another fading landmark on an endless and chimerical quest for peace?

THE PRECARIOUS EMBRACE

CARTER'S GAMBLE ON A BREAKTHROUGH

The last week of February 1979 began in an atmosphere of deep pessimism. Sadat had rejected an invitation from Carter to attend a second summit, and Begin was unwilling to meet with Sadat's subordinate, Prime Minister Mustafa Khalil. At best, the Israeli leader agreed to visit Washington for discussions with Carter. It was during that visit of March 1, however, and in the ensuing three-and-a-half days of exceptionally tough conversations with Begin at the White House, that the president finally won his guest's approval for several imaginative new proposals. A telephone call to Sadat in Cairo followed. Immediately afterward, Carter announced his plans for a new initiative, one potentially even more spectacular than Camp David. In a calculated decision to expose the dignity of his person and his office to the high-risk buzz saw of Middle Eastern negotiations, he would travel personally to Egypt and Israel in an effort to secure a final breakthrough on the peace agreement.

The president in fact had come up with ideas on two seemingly intractable issues. Addressing the question of "linkage" between an Israeli-Egyptian treaty and Palestinian autonomy, he now proposed a "side letter" to the treaty in which Israel would agree to complete "negotiations" for West Bank-Gaza elections within one year of a treaty signing. The suggestion did not require that elections actually take place within a year, and thereby would leave Israel blameless in the event Jordanian or Palestinian noncooperation delayed elections. On the possible conflict between the treaty and Egypt's obligations to other Arab nations, Carter proposed simply that the Egyptian-Israeli pact be regarded as binding, without specifying that it necessarily took precedence over Egypt's other treaties. Both Sadat and Begin discerned possibilities in these formulas. Indeed, Begin cabled Jerusalem afterward, declaring that he had achieved a "great victory."

On March 7, Carter, Vance, Brzezinski, Secretary of Defense Harold Brown, and their respective aides, departed for the Middle East, arriving in Cairo the next day. Thirty-six hours of intensive discussions with Sadat and his associates followed, interspersed with an elaborate state banquet for the American president, and a moving address by Carter to the People's Assembly on March 10. Several hours later, Carter traveled on to Israel in high spirits, having won

Sadat's agreement to a vaguely worded timetable for future negotiations on West Bank and Gaza elections. In Israel, the president was cordially received; but the next day, in the course of a tense, seven-hour bargaining session with Begin and Dayan, Carter and his staff learned that difficult issues still remained. These did not relate to the unspecified timetable for Palestinian elections, or to the compromise American wording of Article VI (referring to the issue of Egypt's prior treaty commitments). The Israelis accepted these changes. But they asked for clarifications on their other demands. These included: a guaranteed right to purchase 2.5 million tons of Sinai oil from Egypt annually as compensation for wells Israel had developed in the Sinai; the timing of an exchange of ambassadors, with the Israelis still maintaining that this exchange should proceed as originally agreed, midway through their army's withdrawal from the Sinai; and Egypt's claims to a "presence" during elections in Gaza. Begin and his colleagues were flatly unyielding on these issues.

The atmosphere was not encouraging. Nor did it improve on the afternoon of March 12, when Carter addressed the Knesset and obliquely lectured Begin on the need for flexibility. In turn, the American president was obliged afterward to sit in pained embarrassment as Begin's speech of response was interrupted by the tasteless hectoring of several right-wing members. It was a bleak moment for Carter. He had gambled more than his diplomatic credibility in this unprecedented initiative to Egypt and Israel. His very political future in the United States, after three years of less than scintillating executive accomplishment or public approval, now appeared seriously in jeopardy. Yet, unknown to him, the prospects for a breakthrough were not yet altogether frozen. Dayan and Vance were quietly, but urgently, experimenting with compromise solutions. Defense Secretary Brown, meanwhile, dangled a tantalizing list of ordnance the United States could provide Israel, as well as meaningful promises of American military and diplomatic support in the event of a threat to Israeli security. Finally, on the morning of March 13, a breakfast meeting between Carter and Begin confirmed that a tentative understanding had been achieved between Dayan and Vance—literally at the final moment. Astounded, then jubilant, at what he envisaged as a definitive series of Israeli concessions, the president immediately departed on his jet transport for an unscheduled stopover in Cairo.

Once in the Egyptian capital, Carter met with Sadat in the airport VIP lounge and reviewed the issues that had been worked out in Jerusalem. Several of the Egyptian officials continued to demur, but Sadat decided that enough progress had been made. Typically, he ended the haggling with a magisterial wave of his hand, endorsing the agreement on the spot. Carter's eyes visibly misted. In Sadat's presence, the American president excitedly telephoned Begin in Jerusalem. The Israeli prime minister was gratified by Carter's report. Soon afterward, in a gesture of conciliation to Egypt, he released sixty-six jailed Palestinian guerrillas.

THE SUBSTANCE OF COMPROMISE

What had been agreed upon in the hectic five days of meeting were two revised accords, understandings that eventually would be incorporated into a formal treaty, three annexes, an appendix, agreed minutes, and six letters. As at Camp David, one of the accords was an outline of a comprehensive peace for Palestine; although in this case, at the Israelis' insistence, the plan was defined in "side letters" from Sadat and Begin to Carter. The second accord was the actual peace treaty itself, to be signed directly between Egypt and Israel. In the former, the two parties agreed to begin negotiations on Palestinian self-rule one month after ratification of the Egyptian-Israeli treaty, to invite Jordan to participate in those negotiations, and to authorize the participation of West Bank and Gaza Arabs in the Egyptian and Jordanian delegations. Should Jordan decline to join the negotiations, Egypt and Israel would carry on alone. In any case, both parties agreed to make a "good faith" effort to reach agreement on Palestinian autonomy within one year. While the participants would seek to organize elections for a self-governing entity in the West Bank and Gaza, and to define the role and responsibility of that entity, there would be no guarantee that elections actually would take place.

In the event elections were carried out, however, then one month after the establishment of the autonomous entity, Israel would end its military administration in the occupied areas and withdraw its troops to specified strong points. And, as agreed at Camp David, a five-year transition period would then begin. Although no details were cited in the brief communications to the American president, it was assumed that negotiations on the subsequent fate of the West Bank and Gaza would adhere to the Camp David format. Still to be decided were the eventual disposition of Israeli settlements on the West Bank and Israel's right to maintain specified military outposts on these territories. This time, the question of Jerusalem was not so much as mentioned; it had been foreclosed by Sadat's and Begin's "side letters" to Carter as part of the Camp David accords.

Yet because Israel had agreed to a "good faith" effort in its anticipated negotiations on the West Bank, and Egypt in turn had forgone its demand for a timetabled "linkage" between Palestinian elections and ratification of a peace treaty, the way was open for other compromises, specifically on the Egyptian-Israeli pact. The latter was a very formal and legalistic document. Under its Article VI, the new wording read: "This treaty does not affect . . . the rights and obligations of the parties under the Charter of the United Nations." It was a formulation that enabled Sadat to assure other Arab nations that, under Article 51 of the United Nations Charter, Egypt reserved the right to come to their aid should they be directly attacked by Israel. Israel, conversely, received its own assurance in subsection 5 of this provision: "Subject to Article 103 of the United Nations Charter, in the event of a conflict between the obligations of the parties under the present treaty and any of their obligations, the obligations of this treaty will be binding and implemented." The minutes appended to the document went on to state that "there is no assertion that this Treaty prevails over other Treaties or agreements, or that other Treaties or agreements prevail over this Treaty." In short, Egypt and Israel simply would not argue in public about treaty procedures.

Otherwise, Camp David's three-year schedule of phased Israeli withdrawal from the Sinai ostensibly remained in effect. In a carefully delimited chronological sequence of evacuation, to be protected each step of the way by the temporary interposition of UNEF troops, Israeli forces would pull back initially to the al-Arish-Ras Muhammad line nine months following ratification of the peace treaty. During sharp bargaining in Jerusalem, however, the Israelis actually had consented to make the necessary "gesture" of withdrawal within six months. The advanced timetable would not be stipulated in writing. In fact, two weeks later, Begin felt confident enough in Israel's position to embellish his gesture. He assured Sadat that Israeli troops would withdraw to the interim line only two months later—and fully seven months ahead of schedule. Responding "as a man of honor" to this Israeli commitment, Sadat for his part confirmed in Annex III and, more specifically, in a personal letter to Carter, that both nations would exchange ambassadors and establish normal diplomatic relations one month after Israeli forces had moved to the new line. In this fashion, Israel shared in the advantages of the foreshortened schedule. Additionally, Sadat relinquished his demand for early and separate Gaza elections, with Egyptian representatives to be present during the voting; the issue would be left to the forthcoming autonomy talks. Neither would Sadat insist any longer on a review of Sinai security arrangements "after five years." Instead, those arrangements would be evaluated on a nonspecified basis, and only with the mutual agreement of both parties.

The oil question between the two countries, like Begin's last-minute gesture of accelerated troop withdrawal, was resolved only through haggling the night before the signature ceremony, and defined in "minutes" attached to Annex III of the treaty. Referring to the anticipated development of Egyptian-Israeli economic relations as envisaged in the text of the treaty itself, the minutes provided that "such relations will include normal commercial sales of oil by Egypt to Israel, and that Israel shall be fully entitled to make bids for Egypt-origin oil not needed for Egyptian domestic consumption, and Egypt and its oil concessionaires will entertain bids made by Israel, on the same basis and terms as apply to other bidders for such oil." This Egyptian commitment was quietly reinforced a few hours after the treaty-signing ceremony by an American "Memorandum of Agreement" to Israel to maintain the latter's oil supplies, in the event of a boycott, for not less than fifteen years—that is, for ten years beyond the earlier Ford commitment to Rabin.

A few last points of contention remained after Carter's triumphant return to Washington. Egyptian Prime Minister Khalil took umbrage at an even more wide-ranging provision in the American "Memorandum of Agreement" to Israel. Worked out between Dayan and Vance, it now formalized Defense Secretary Brown's initial offer in Jerusalem. The document confirmed Washington's understanding (subject to congressional approval)

> to provide support it deems appropriate for proper actions taken by Israel in response to such demonstrated violations of the Treaty of Peace. In particular, if a violation of the Treaty of Peace is deemed to threaten the security of Israel, including, inter alia, a blockade of Israel's use of international waterways, a violation of the provisions of the Treaty of Peace concerning limitation of forces or an armed attack against Israel, the United States will be prepared to consider, on an urgent basis, such measures as the strengthening of the United States presence in the area, the providing of emergency supplies to Israel, and the exercise of maritime rights in order to put an end to the violation.

The memorandum further articulated Washington's commitment to block any action in the United Nations that could adversely affect the peace treaty; to "be responsive to the military and economic assistance requirements of Israel," and to impose restrictions on "weapons supplied any country which might transfer them without authorization to a third party for use in an armed attack against Israel." (Saudi Arabia and Jordan clearly were implied here). It was a major American commitment, all but a unilateral treaty of defense for Israel, and plainly a critical factor in winning Begin's final acceptance of the peace document. For this reason, Prime Minister Khalil argued, it was prejudicial to Egypt; the memorandum was based on the manifest assumption that Egypt alone was liable to violate the impending treaty. But the State Department reminded Khalil that it had offered a similar commitment to Egypt, and that the latter had refused it.

In truth, the Egyptians had little reason for complaint. Under a separate understanding, the Americans had agreed to provide them with some $2 billion in airplanes, tanks, and antiaircraft weapons. Israel, to be sure, would receive $3 billion in military and financial help. These aid pledges supplemented the "normal" assistance the United States earlier had provided the two Middle Eastern countries, a package that in 1979 totaled $750 million to Egypt and $1.8 billion to Israel—the bulk of this latter to be applied to the construction of two air bases in the Negev Desert. There were inducements aplenty for both sides, in any case, and they paved the way for lower-level Egyptian and Israeli negotiators to resolve the few remaining details. The treaty was scheduled for signing in Washington on March 26, 1979.

THE FORMALIZATION OF COMPROMISE

In the period between Carter's dramatic breakthrough and the ceremony of signing, other spokesmen for the Arab world were predictably apoplectic. By then not a shred of doubt remained that Sadat had abandoned their cause irretrievably. Between March 28 and 30, representatives of nineteen Arab nations met again in Baghdad and voted unanimously to sever all remaining political and economic ties with Egypt. This time, too, Saudi Arabia and Kuwait formally canceled the large-scale aid they had promised to underwrite Egypt's intended purchase of American jet fighters. No reference was made to the scores of thousands of Egyptians working in these Persian Gulf nations, but their employment future manifestly remained uncertain. Nevertheless, these announced punitive measures did not appear to faze Sadat. The Egyptian president had committed himself too extensively by then to forfeit the blessings of peace he anticipated for his nation; his gamble would have to be pursued to the end. Begin's reasoning followed the same line. So, notwithstanding a few die-hard extremists from the "Land of Israel" movement, did the Israeli Knesset's. On March 22 the parliament voted to ratify the peace pact, and by the all but unprecedented vote of 95 to 18. Accordingly, four days later, in a White House ceremony attended by the Israeli and Egyptian delegations, by UN Secretary-General Waldheim, and by high officials of the American government and other dignitaries, Sadat and Begin affixed their signatures to a formal treaty of peace between their two countries.

The preamble dutifully invoked the "framework" signed at Camp David, the United Nations Resolutions 242 and 338, and emphasized again the intention of both nations to conclude peace not only between themselves "but also between Israel and each of [Israel's] other Arab neighbors. . . ." The document went on to terminate the state of war between Egypt and Israel. Israel committed itself to withdraw all its armed forces "and civilians" from the Sinai. Egypt pledged itself to use Israel's evacuated airfields in the peninsula exclusively for civilian purposes. Each party agreed to respect the other's sovereignty, territorial integrity, and political independence, as well as the other's right to live in peace within "secure and recognized boundaries" (another Israeli victory, implying boundaries to be negotiated in the east). Pledging also to refrain from the use or threat of force, directly or indirectly, both sides undertook to conduct normal diplomatic, economic, and cultural relations with each other, and to remove all discriminatory barriers to the free movement of people and goods.

The treaty proceeded to outline four permanent limited-force zones in the Sinai and within a narrow strip of Negev territory adjacent to the Sinai (an important concession by Israel), and the stationing of United Nations troops and observers in the last—eastern—two of these zones. None of the United Nations personnel would be drawn from the Great Powers, but would come, rather, from other nations upon whose participation both Egypt and Israel agreed. Nor were the United Nations forces to be evacuated from their assigned zones unless specifically authorized to do so by the Security Council, acting on a unanimous vote of its five permanent members. Israeli ships and cargoes in any event were to be assured free access through the Strait of Tiran, as well as through the Suez Canal. Although, as has been seen, the treaty finessed the question of Egypt's prior defense pacts, the mutual determination to avoid potentially troubling incidents was apparent even in the smallest details. Thus, an Egyptian liaison office in al-Arish and an Israeli liaison office in Beersheba would be connected by a direct telephone "hot" line. Israeli war memorials would be erected in the Sinai and Egyptian war memorials in Israel, each side agreeing to respect and maintain in good condition these tributes to the other's fallen soldiers.

In a broader spirit of accord, meanwhile, the appendix to Annex I provided that, as soon as possible, and not later than six months after the completion of Israel's interim withdrawal, Egypt and Israel would enter into negotiations aimed at reaching agreement on trade and commerce, the free two-way movement of nationals into each other's territories, the termination of all hostile propaganda against each other, the establishment of normal postal, telephone, cable, radio, and other communications between the two countries, and the construction of a highway between Egypt, Israel, and—with Amman's consent—Jordan, near Eilat for mutual use. Finally, in accompanying letters attached to the peace treaty, Begin and Sadat confirmed to Carter their understanding on the issue of the West Bank and Gaza, a meeting of the minds that ensured the signature of the peace treaty itself.

As in the Camp David agreement, those accompanying letters also stated Egyptian and Israeli understanding that the United States would participate fully in all stages of Palestinian autonomy negotiations, as well as in all phases of enforcing the Egyptian-Israeli treaty. In his letters of reply to the two Middle Eastern leaders, Carter affirmed that, in the event of a treaty violation, the United States (subject to congressional approval) would confer with the parties and "take such other action as it may deem appropriate to achieve compliance with the treaty." Carter similarly acquiesced in the request for the United States to conduct aerial monitoring over Sinai, during the three-year period of Israeli withdrawal; and also, should the Security Council refuse to authorize the permanent stationing of United Nations personnel in the designated zones of withdrawal, "to take those steps necessary to ensure" the establishment and maintenance of "an acceptable alternative multinational force." These commitments, in addition to other American assurances of military aid to Egypt and to Israel, and the promise to become involved in the negotiations on the West Bank and Gaza, made plain again how fundamental both Jerusalem and Cairo envisaged the American role to be, and how categorically both rejected any Soviet participation in their affairs.

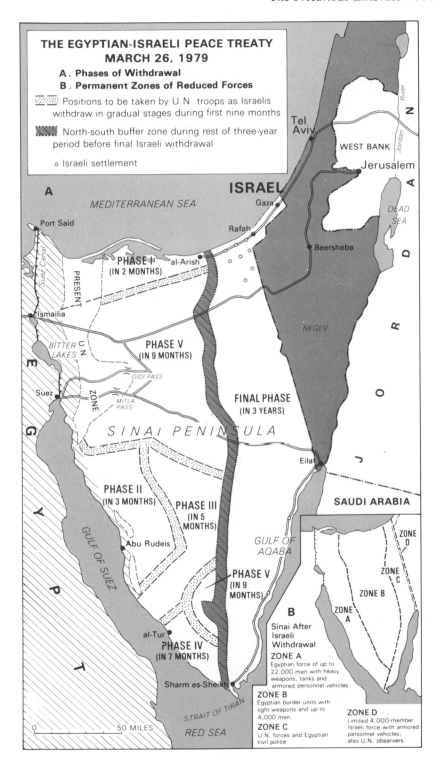

**THE EGYPTIAN-ISRAELI PEACE TREATY
MARCH 26, 1979**
A. Phases of Withdrawal
B. Permanent Zones of Reduced Forces

Positions to be taken by U.N. troops as Israelis withdraw in gradual stages during first nine months

North-south buffer zone during rest of three-year period before final Israeli withdrawal

o Israeli settlement

A

MEDITERRANEAN SEA

Port Said

ISRAEL

Gaza

Rafah

Tel Aviv

WEST BANK

Jerusalem

DEAD SEA

Beersheba

Jordan River

J O R D A N

PHASE I
(IN 2 MONTHS)
al-Arish

PRESENT

Ismailia

BITTER LAKES

U N   Z O N E

GIDI PASS

Suez

MITLA PASS

PHASE V
(IN 9 MONTHS)

NEGEV

S I N A I   P E N I N S U L A

FINAL PHASE
(IN 3 YEARS)

Eilat

E G Y P T

GULF OF SUEZ

PHASE II
(IN 3 MONTHS)

PHASE III
(IN 5 MONTHS)

Abu Rudeis

SAUDI ARABIA

GULF OF AQABA

PHASE V
(IN 9 MONTHS)

B

Sinai After Israeli Withdrawal

ZONE A
Egyptian force of up to 22,000 men with heavy weapons, tanks and armored personnel vehicles.

ZONE B
Egyptian border units with light weapons and up to 4,000 men.

ZONE C
U.N. forces and Egyptian civil police.

ZONE D
Limited 4,000-member Israeli force with armored personnel vehicles; also U.N. observers.

ZONE D

ZONE C

ZONE B

ZONE A

al-Tur

PHASE IV
(IN 7 MONTHS)

Sharm es-Sheikh

STRAIT OF TIRAN

RED SEA

0 _____ 50 MILES

THE CHALLENGES OF THE FUTURE

In the aftermath of the peace-signing ceremony, no one in Cairo, Jerusalem, or Washington tended to underestimate the problems that yet remained. Those difficulties related not only to the formidable negotiations that lay ahead on the implementation of the scheduled peace between Egypt and Israel themselves, but to the infinitely more entangled problems of the West Bank and Gaza. It was permissible, nevertheless, for Henry Kissinger (a guest at the White House ceremony) to take satisfaction in the proven validity of the step-by-step approach he had pioneered between 1973 and 1975. Vindicated with the former secretary of state were those moderates both in Egypt and Israel who had not despaired of their leadership's capacity to achieve a pragmatic modus vivendi.

It is worth recalling that the Western press had not initially shared that faith. Upon assuming office in October 1970, Sadat was proclaimed by the *New York Times* to be an "intense, impulsive, and deeply religious man who is a bitter foe of Israel and one of the most outspoken critics of the United States." A year later, the *Economist* asserted that "Sadat is not the man. . . . Egypt may have to accept that neither war nor a full, signed peace is possible with Israel. . . . It needs a new leader to face that prospect." Begin evoked the identical misgivings. In April 1977, American newspapers lamented the election of a former "terrorist" as Israel's prime minister. The *Wall Street Journal* argued that Begin's election "skews peace hopes." "Tough, decisive, and unyielding" was the evaluation of the *Christian Science Monitor*. The European pundit Eric Rouleau assured readers of *Le Monde* that "Begin is known for his ideological intransigence." In *Time*, Begin's name could not appear without pejoratives clinging to it like a ligature: "inflexible," "hard-line," "unyielding," "arrogant," "extreme"—even "the major obstacle to peace."

None of these appellations was necessarily off the mark, given the context of the time and the backgrounds of the two leaders. Yet all missed the sense of priority that animated Sadat and Begin, the passionate desire of each to break the lockstep of war and endless human tragedy. In the case of the former, that determination was informed by the critical need to rescue his paralyzed economy. For the latter, it was precisely the doctrinaire obsession with the West Bank—with Judea and Samaria—that opened out opportunities for flexibility on the Sinai. Nor was there any way to minimize the sacrifices each leader knowingly had incurred by accepting compromise. In the case of Sadat, forfeiture of a guaranteed linkage between the peace treaty and a detailed schedule of uncompromised autonomy for the West Bank and Gaza ensured the imprecations of the Arab world, the termination of political relations with nineteen Arab states, and the withdrawal of Saudi and Kuwaiti financial support. It is recalled that the Baghdad summit conference of March 1979 had reached agreement even to shift the site of Arab League headquarters from Cairo to Tunis. The blow was a harsh one for the Egyptian president.

Conceivably his nation would survive the loss of Persian Gulf assistance. Even so, the sanctions voted in Baghdad represented specifically the psychological and political challenge to Egyptian leadership that Butros-Ghali had feared, and it was a measure of Sadat's vision and courage that he had steeled himself to withstand it.

Begin paid no less heavy a price for his decision to withdraw from the totality of the Sinai. During its thirteen years of occupation, Israel had invested in that critical buffer peninsula $10 billion in military installations and $2 billion in roads and settlements. Now, within a period of three years, the Israelis were obliged to remove this vast infrastructure—to remove much of it, in fact, within a period of nine months. From the logistical viewpoint alone, the statistics of transfer were awesome. Initial calculations suggested that not less than 62,000 transport-days were needed to evacuate some 75,000 tons of equipment. In addition to ten air bases, two of them comparable to the largest military fields available to NATO, the Israelis would have to dismantle and relocate 70 other military camps and installations ecompassing 2,700 buildings.

Worse yet, the transplantation of this mass of arms and equipment required the construction of approximately 50 new camps in the Negev Desert, and 450 miles of new road. The Israelis would have to lay waterlines and electric cables, as well, to build sewage treatment plants and thousands of family housing units. To compensate for the loss of its electronic warning stations on the Sinai ranges, moreover, Israel would become dependent subsequently on an expensive airborne system, coupled with a ground sensor concept and advanced radar technologies. In the view of analysts at the Rand Corporation, the new strategic reality in the Middle East would place heavy demands on Israel's intelligence-gathering capability, and these in turn would impose onerous new burdens on the Israeli defense budget.

At Camp David, to be sure, the United States had undertaken to construct two major air bases in the Negev, and this represented a not insignificant contribution to Israel's total cost of relocation—about 25 percent of the projected $4 billion total. The problem for the Israelis would be to find the remainder. Perhaps, notwithstanding the crippled circumstances of the nation's economy (by 1980 the annual inflation rate had climbed to 130 percent), and the fact that imported labor would build the new airfields—thus siphoning off funds that otherwise would have remained in Israel—the needed balance somehow could be generated over a period of twenty years. But most certainly this could not be done within the three years of phased evacuation required by the peace treaty. It was surprising, as a result, that funding provisions for the withdrawal were not settled at Camp David. Yet, even during the period of Begin's hardest bargaining with Carter in Jerusalem, no additional American commitment was extracted beyond open-ended promises of access to American weapons systems, and of military and diplomatic support in the event of treaty violation. Even more ominously, Israel would carry the back-breaking burden of withdrawal just at the moment when it was preparing to abandon its Sinai oil supplies. During the past decade, those supplies had met half the nation's energy requirements. During its period of occupation, moreover, Israel had invested $5 billion to develop Sinai's wells—and now was giving all that up, too. There could be little doubt, then, that Begin, like Sadat, was taking a prodigious gamble for peace.

Were the economic prospects of peace sufficient to compensate both nations for that gamble? For the risk of an Arab quarantine, in the case of Egypt; and the abandonment of defense in depth, of energy reserves, and of vastly expensive installations and settlements, in the case of Israel? For the longer term, elimination of the threat of war between the two Middle Eastern nations unquestionably was worth almost any immediate economic sacrifice. To Sadat and his advisers, the opportunity for reducing the size of Egypt's standing army, for assuring uninterrupted traffic in a revived and renovated Suez Canal, for gaining access to a reopened Sinai and to Western capital invested in a nation at peace—all were decisive inducements. It was not unlikely, in fact, that the Sinai alone would prove a vital reservoir of natural resources: of coal, manganese, phosphates, and, above all, of oil. Between 1977 and 1979, Egypt had earned some $500 million from the oil fields returned by Israel, from wells that were producing a million barrels a day by the end of the decade. In the short run, however, without major Western investment, neither the reduction of military expenditures nor the availability of oil income alone was certain to compensate Egypt for the loss of Persian Gulf subsidies, nor dramatically to improve its standard of living.

For Israel, the question was pertinent whether much was to be gained in accumulated revenues by trade with Egypt (during the 1930s, after all, Egypt had served as Palestine's main trading partner). In fact, the prospects of renewed two-way commerce remained unimpressive for the near future. By the early 1970s, the Egyptian and Israeli economies were no longer complementary. If Israel was less than entirely self-sufficient in foodstuffs, neither did it offer a substantial market for Egyptian agricultural products. Conversely, Israeli technology would have to compete on the—still limited—Egyptian market against the products of the United States, Europe, and Japan. Without doubt, the availability of purchased Egyptian oil could be of importance to Israel; it would obviate the transportation costs of shipments from Mexico. Yet Israel's access to Syria and Lebanon was certain to remain closed, even as Egypt was likely to remain under punitive Arab quarantine. As a result, the kind of wider regional economic development that alone could assure the new treaty partners meaningful prosperity was far distant. So were plans even for large-scale, two-way tourism between Egypt and Israel. Tourism was a luxury that itself depended on mutually strengthened economic infrastructures, and that strength could not be generated exclusively from within. For both countries, therefore, the underlying economic advantages of peace were to be found less in trade, or even in reduced military expenditures, than in opportunities to attract Western development capital—to the funds that alone offered the key to the prosperity coveted by both sides. American and European companies, it was believed, would surely be less hesitant to invest in Israeli or Egyptian projects once the threat of hostilities was lifted.

Perhaps in the longer run, too, as a consequence of Egyptian-Israeli peace, there existed a serious chance of a new shift in the center of Middle Eastern gravity. This was a matter of decisive importance to the United States and Western Europe as they evaluated the possibilities of regional defense in the area. Iran, formerly a bulwark of Western strength in the Persian Gulf, had lapsed into paralysis following the overthrow of the shah, then had been mauled by an invading Iraqi army in the Shatt al-Arab. The Saudi monarchy, exposed to dangerous new economic and social crosscurrents, appeared to be an increasingly uncertain pillar of Middle Eastern stability. Turkey, yet another erstwhile bastion against Soviet imperialism, one of the earliest members of NATO, was drifting into political chaos and its economy had all but ceased to function. In the southern Mediterranean, meanwhile, the singular Colonel Qaddafi had transformed Libya into the principal staging base of radical terrorism throughout the Third World.

With a sentient appraisal of these critical new developments, and of the unique opportunities they presented to Soviet infiltration, the military staffs of both Egypt and Israel were quietly raising the level of their intelligence cooperation in the Maghreb and in the Horn of Africa. It was a tacit alliance soon to be joined by a third, rather more weighty, partner. By 1980, the United States already had authorized joint air force "training" exercises from Egyptian bases. Indeed, it had launched its military transports from Egyptian fields in an abortive effort to rescue American hostages in Iran. By the same token, Washington was considering seriously Israel's invitation for the Sixth Fleet to use the naval facilities of Haifa and Ashdod. If, as a result, a new bulwark of Western strength had to be forged in the Middle East, Egypt and Israel seemed more likely candidates for that role than at any time since the early 1950s.

Yet much preliminary work had to be accomplished before the two former enemies could negotiate a partnership within the non-Communist world less inimical, for example, than that of Greece and Turkey. Under the circumstances, an important factor in defining the new relationship was the progress that could be made in nurturing a Palestinian entity to self-government in the West Bank and Gaza. Sadat's reputation in the Arab world largely depended on his ability to deliver this autonomy. The timetable of a year for organizing West Bank elections was not hard and fast. Indeed, it would not be reached, for the Israeli prime minister and his cabinet adopted a hard line, insisting on the narrowest degree of administrative jurisdiction for the Palestine Arabs, gratuitously proclaiming united Jerusalem to be the capital of Israel, ordering the preemptive bombardment of Iraq's nuclear reactor; and, as a result, discussions between Israeli and Egyptian negotiating teams periodically broke down, or were suspended, amidst mutual recriminations.

Nevertheless, a partnership could still be forged, and progress on other levels of the emerging relationship might yet be achieved, in the attitude each nation adopted toward the culture of the other. In the case of Egypt, admittedly, few enough Jews remained to become the objects of a revived governmental toleration and benevolence. Yet, in its approach to the Jewish people at large, no less than to the Republic of Israel, Sadat's program of dediabolization somehow would have to be transformed into one of forthright appreciation. In this effort, little could be accomplished without additional courses on the university level in Jewish history and in the Hebrew language; or, on the secondary school level, without a further "objectification" of Zionist history.

In the case of Israel, the process of normalization depended upon a fundamental reintroduction to Arab civilization in its larger contours. It was Cairo's hope, in fact, that the emergence of Israel's Oriental Jews as the nation's majority would encourage this trend. Although Israel's universities were notably strong in their departments of Arabic and Arab history and politics, a wide-ranging program of studies devoted to the surrounding majority culture still required extensive integration into the nation's school system. In the aftermath of the Six-Day War, the ministry of education had begun encouraging secondary-school pupils to study Arabic as their second foreign language. It appeared likelier now that this discipline would be required. Even more attention, too, was all but certain to be given to courses in Arab history and to Islamic religious ideology. At the least, this emerging shift in curriculum would go far to ameliorate relations between Israel's Jewish and Arab citizens, to help dissipate the latter's sense of anomie in a Zionist state.

There could be little doubt that, left to their own instincts, spared the incitement of chauvinist governments, the Egyptian people were fully capable of accepting the Israelis as neighbors, even as friends. War remained as abhorrent to the typical Nile farmer or Delta city dweller in the late twentieth century as in the Twentieth Dynasty of antiquity. Now, as then, the Egyptians preserved a *Weltanschauung* so enamored of life that escape from death remained their overriding obsession. Throughout history, much of their leisure energy, their national wealth, their intellectual endeavors were dedicated to a conspiracy for eluding death. The Pyramids, the Colossi of Memnon, the Temple of Karnak, the innumerable mummies and frescoes of paradise still visible to the contemporary tourist—these were but artistic refinements of a passion for eternal life that had unceasingly animated Egyptian civilization. In *The Book of the Dead*, a hieroglyphic of the First Millennium before the Common Era, that passion was limned in a characteristic exhortation:

> I shall not decay, I shall not rot, I shall not putrefy, I shall not become worms, I shall not see corruption before the eye of Shu. I shall exist! I

shall live! I shall flourish! I shall flourish! I shall wake up in contentment; I shall not putrefy; my intestines shall not perish; I shall not suffer injury. My eye shall not decay; the form of my face shall not disappear; my ear shall not become deaf. My head shall not be separated from my neck. My tongue shall not be removed, my nose shall not be cut off . . . and no evil defect shall befall me. My body shall be enduring; it shall not perish. It shall not be destroyed, nor shall it be turned back whence it entered into this Land of Eternity!

It was Sadat who invoked this tradition as he turned to the cause of peace. "Our cultural depths are there," he insisted, "our cultural roots are alive, as vigorous as ever after more than 7,000 years. Those who are surprised by what we do simply cannot understand this fact. They cannot grasp the real nature of a people who are working for a modern civilization comparable to the one they erected thousands of years ago in freedom and peace." It was a civilization that virtually all Egyptians wished to see revived and enriched—from the humblest fellah, the first to be exposed to shrapnel and destruction in wartime; to the typical university student, desperate for a creative vocation and assurance of economic advancement; to the nation's artists, writers, and scientists, grateful at last for the opportunity of uninhibited self-expression, but longing with equal intensity for a literate and affluent audience. The chances were at least even that this passion for peace—for life itself—would survive the protracted negotiations that lay ahead with Israel on the issue of Palestinian autonomy, and the vindictive *cordon sanitaire* imposed on Egypt by the surrounding Arab world.

THE PRECARIOUS EMBRACE

A week after the treaty-signing, Menachem Begin departed on his first official visit to the capital of the former enemy. He was met at the Cairo airport by Vice-President Hosni Mubarak. The welcoming ceremony lasted a bare ten minutes. The crowds Begin encountered as he drove through Cairo's thoroughfares were far smaller than those that had greeted Sadat in Israel seventeen months before. The prime minister appeared unperturbed. After spending most of April 2 on a guided tour of the principal tourist sights, then visiting the Sharei Shamayim Synagogue, Begin attended a state dinner hosted by Sadat. Again he was correctly, if less than enthusiastically, received by the several hundred assembled dignitaries. This time—in a foreign land—the Israeli leader struck a conciliatory note. He praised Sadat, the Egyptian people, the courage and honor of Egypt's fighting men. The remarks evoked applause. For his part, Sadat replied in a vein more cordial than any he had employed toward Israel (and Begin) since his trip to Jerusalem. "We fought and will go on fighting," he declared, "but this time we fight for understanding and love, not for grudge, so that there may be no more wars, for the prosperity of our countries, for the peace of our peoples and the peace of the whole world."

During the twenty-eight-hour visit, the two leaders issued a joint communiqué announcing that Israel, as a token of goodwill, would relinquish its control over al-Arish on May 26, seven months ahead of schedule. Representing the next logical phase—after the disengagement agreements of 1974 and 1975—of Israel's contractual three-year process of withdrawal from the entire Sinai Peninsula, here was the dramatic unilateral gesture that Begin once had scorned ("nothing for nothing"), but which at last had been quietly tendered, first through Carter in Jerusalem, then afterward in more personal detail ("my word of honor") from Begin to Sadat in Washington on March 25, as an inducement for the Egyptian leader to accept the peace treaty. On May 27, the communiqué went on, Sadat and Begin would meet in al-Arish, and from there the two men would travel on to Beersheba, Israel. During their visits in both towns, Sadat and Begin would ceremonially declare the Egyptian-Israeli border open, then would formally inaugurate an air corridor between Cairo and Tel Aviv. As matters turned out, Egyptian visas for these new travel opportunities would be issued to Israelis on a tightly selected basis. Nor was Cairo prepared yet to allow direct service by the national airline of either land. Substantially more progress on the issue of Palestinian autonomy was needed before Sadat was willing to acknowledge that the spirit, as well as the letter, of the peace treaty had been fulfilled. Even so, in al-Arish the faint penumbra of that spirit appeared to flare up spontaneously.

It happened that both leaders had agreed to make of the al-Arish ceremony an occasion for a display of *sulh*, a peace far deeper than the perfunctory Arab *salaam*, and denoting a more authentic reconciliation. To that end, Defense Ministers Weizman and Hassan Ali worked out the arrangements for a humanizing feature, a symbolic meeting of wounded veterans from both sides. Accordingly, a selected group of fifty Egyptian war casualties and an equal number of their Israeli counterparts were brought to the Sinai coastal town. Their meeting was a good deal more than symbolic. It was cordial, even emotional. In the cinema hall of al-Arish, the one-legged Egyptian lieutenant colonel appraised the Israeli sitting beside him. He was a young man, possibly not yet thirty, and it was evident that one of his eyes was glass.

"Ahmad al-Ghani," said the colonel, extending his hand.

"Ilan Halpern," replied the Israeli. He returned the Egyptian's grip with his left hand. Only then did Ghani notice the steel hook protruding from Halpern's right sleeve.

The colonel nodded gravely. "Was it in Sinai?"

"In Jerusalem," said the Israeli. "During the Six-Day War." He explained then that a Jordanian grenade had inflicted the damage. "The next thing I remember was waking up in the Hadassah Hospital, and the eye and hand were gone."

"Mine was in seventy-three," smiled the colonel. He recounted the story of the crossing, the shrapnel that had parted him from his leg. The two men exchanged cigarettes.

Soon afterward they were joined by other Israeli and Egyptian veterans. One of the latter was a man of Ghani's age, Niazi al-Saïd, a surgeon in the Cairo Military Hospital. His account was of service as a battalion doctor in the Second Army. During the heavy armored battles of October 7, as Saïd ministered to the procession of wounded, a shell had dropped nearby, mangling his right leg. Refusing evacuation, he had continued treating other casualties until he fainted from loss of blood. Proudly now, he displayed his commendation medal: Hero of Egypt.

Several feet away, an Israeli pilot, Captain Ilan Lev, shared reminiscences with an Egyptian flier, Major Ibrahim Disai. Both men had suffered wounds in the 1973 fighting. Other veterans gathered in small clusters, chatting warmly with their former enemies. Cigarettes and mementos were exchanged, then addresses. At a corner of the auditorium a demobilized Israeli armored corps sergeant, Motti Ashkenazi, engaged in a long, intense conversation with an Egyptian colonel, Muhammad al-Saïd. Like his namesake, Niazi al-Saïd, the Egyptian was a military doctor, a plastic surgeon; and, by chance, Ashkenazi had been seriously burned while climbing out of his flaming tank on the second day of the October War. "I'd like to examine you, Motti," said the Egyptian doctor. "It would be best if you could visit me at my clinic. It's a special rehabilitation center that was established under the patronage of Mrs. Sadat. We have excellent facilities there, and I've developed an effective treatment for wounds of your kind."

"We have excellent facilities, too," said Ashkenazi, "but I certainly would be privileged to have you examine me."

"Then perhaps I can do it in Israel," smiled the colonel. "Just get me permission and I'll come."

Nearby sat a young Israeli, wearing a skullcap. Avi Chaim was one of the troops who had defended a stronghold in the Bar-Lev Line. Taken prisoner by the Egyptians, he had been photographed departing his bunker with a Torah in his arms. Sitting next to him, by pure coincidence, was Major Muhammad al-Had, commanding officer of the very platoon that had overrun Avi Chaim's bunker. The two men were studying photographs of each other's families, clucking in admiration. An older Israeli officer, one of his arms missing, suddenly rapped a table for attention. Introducing himself as the chairman of his nation's disabled veterans organization, he expressed a wish to present "our Egyptian friends" with a little souvenir of the ocasion. Decorated plates then were distributed, bearing the words "shalom" and "salaam." At this point, Ahmad Muhsein, a man in his mid-thirties, pulled himself upright on crutches: "It's good to share our war experiences at such a meeting," he declared emotionally, "but we must now talk about the future, in order to avoid more wars. What unites all of us, the war-crippled of Egypt and Israel, is our knowledge of the ugliness of war, its lack of reason." Muhsein's remarks were greeted with prolonged applause.

Before conversations could be resumed, an honor guard of Egyptian and Israeli paratroopers at the cinema entrance snapped to attention. It was 1:15 P.M. Precisely on schedule, President Sadat, Prime Minister Begin, and Secretary of State Vance entered the auditorium. For the next few minutes the three statesmen circulated informally among the wounded, chatting, shaking hands, posing for pictures with their arms around individual veterans. Once the excitement subsided, the Egyptian president addressed the audience: "Premier Begin and I have decided to give maximum impetus to the movement for peace," he declared, "and to continue together the common effort to end the suffering of the countries in this area. . . . Your sacrifices will not be in vain; the road is open to peace. Together we shall light the candle of life, consolation, and redemption."

Begin echoed these sentiments, pledging his nation to peace, then intoning the Hebrew prayer: "Shehechiyanu. . . . Let us pray to God and bless Him for allowing us to live and to reach this moment." After a few additional words of congratulations from Secretary Vance, Begin addressed the group once more. "During a conversation that lasted barely a quarter of an hour," he said, "President Sadat and I have decided officially to confirm here, at al-Arish, the opening of the borders between Israel and Egypt. Citizens of Egypt can visit Israel, and citizens of Israel can visit Egypt."

The room erupted again in prolonged applause. In the exhilaration of the moment, Israelis and Egyptians hugged each other. Secretary Vance, normally a low-keyed Yankee, turned his head away, but not before a reporter had caught the glint of tears in his eyes.

Was this indeed a new beginning, a watershed betokening an era of reconciliation, of understanding and mutual cooperation? It was much to expect for perhaps the most notoriously strife-torn region in the world. Grave obstacles remained: among them the organization of a multinational peace-keeping force in the Sinai; the awesomely complex process of negotiating Palestinian autonomy; the even more emotionally charged problem of Jerusalem; and, over the longer span, the reestablishment of Egypt's historic and cultural ties with the Arab hinterland. Each of these issues, and others, conceivably might yet serve as a provocation for terminating the brief experiment of peace. There had been other formal treaties, after all, between other countries, even among the Arab nations themselves, and none had offered a celestial guarantee of indefinite quietude or accommodation. Rather, what had been established at Camp David, at Washington, and at al-Arish was a precedent. In their future relations with each other, diplomats and international lawyers on both sides at least would find it possible to hark back not alone to a tradition of unrelieved enmity, but to an impressive model for communication, for personalized, firsthand discourse. In a Middle East saturated with archaeological tels, with monuments and brooding folkloristic memories, it seemed not unlikely that the touchstone of a peace treaty also should evoke a certain venerated historical resonance.

BIBLIOGRAPHY

This compendium is presented topically. Some works are listed, as appropriate, under more than one heading.

Egypt's Struggle for Freedom until British Evacuation

Awad, Mohammed. "Egypt, Great Britain and the Sudan: The Egyptian View," *Middle East Journal*, July 1947.

Collins, R. O., and R. L. Tignor. *Egypt and the Sudan*. Englewood Cliffs, N.J., 1967.

Colombe, Marcel. *L'évolution de l'Égypte: 1923–1950*. Paris, 1951.

Eden, Anthony (Earl of Avon). *Full Circle*. London, 1960.

Eppler, Johann. *Rommel ruft Kairo: Aus dem Tagebuch eines Spiones*. Bielefeld, 1959.

Fitzsimons, M. A. *The Foreign Policy of the British Labour Government, 1945–1951*. South Bend, Ind., 1953.

Francis-Williams, Edward. *Ernest Bevin*. London, 1952.

——, ed. *A Prime Minister Remembers: The War and Post-War Memoirs of the Right Honorable Earl Attlee*. London, 1962.

Harris, Christina. *Nationalism and Revolution in Egypt*. The Hague, 1964.

Hirszkowicz, Lukasz. *The Third Reich and the Arab East*. London, 1966.

Hourani, Albert. "The Anglo-Egyptian Agreement: Some Causes and Implications," *Middle East Journal*, Summer 1955.

Hussein, Ahmad. *The Story of Egypt and Anglo-Egyptian Relations*. New York, 1947.

Issawi, Charles. *Egypt: An Economic and Social Analysis*. New York, 1947.

Khalid, Wasim. *Al-Kifah al-Sirri Didda al-Ingiliz* [The Underground Struggle against the British]. Cairo, 1963.

Lacouture, Jean and Simone. *Egypt in Transition*. New York, 1958.

Lugol, Jean. *Egypt and World War II*. Cairo, 1945.

Marlowe, John. *Anglo-Egyptian Relations, 1800–1956*. London, 1964.

Marsot, Afaf Lufti al-Sayyid. *Egypt's Liberal Experiment: 1922–1936*. Berkeley, 1977.

Monroe, Elizabeth. "British Interests in the Middle East," *Middle East Journal*, Spring, 1948.

——. "Mr. Bevin's Arab Policy," in *St. Antony's Papers*, No. 11, London, 1961.

Naguib, Mohammed. *Egypt's Destiny.* New York, 1955.

Nation Associates. *The Record of Collaboration of King Farouk of Egypt with the Nazis, and their Ally, the Mufti.* New York, 1948.

Richmond, John C. B. *Egypt, 1798–1952: Her Advance Toward a Modern Identity.* New York, 1977.

Royal Institute of International Affairs. *Great Britain and Egypt, 1914–1951.* London, 1951.

Sachar, Howard M. *Europe Leaves the Middle East, 1936–1954.* New York, 1972.

Sadat, Muhammad Anwar al-. *Revolt on the Nile.* New York, 1957.

Safran, Nadav. *Egypt in Search of Political Community.* Cambridge, Mass., 1961.

Steffen, H. von. *Salaam: Geheimkommando zum Nil—1942.* Neckargemünd, 1960.

Subay, Muhammad. *Ayyam wa-ayyam* [Days and Days]. Cairo, 1967.

Yisraeli, David. "The Third Reich and Palestine," *Middle Eastern Studies,* October 1971.

Zayid, Mahmoud Y. *Egypt's Struggle for Independence.* Beirut, 1965.

The Jewish National Home until the Birth of Israel

Bauer, Yehuda. "The Arab Revolt of 1935," *New Outlook,* Summer, 1966.

———. *Flight and Rescue: Bricha.* New York, 1970.

———. *From Diplomacy to Resistance: A History of Jewish Palestine, 1939–1945.* Philadelphia, 1970.

Ben-Gurion, David. *B'Hilachem Yisrael* [While Israel Fights]. Tel Aviv, 1949.

———. *The Peel Report and the Jewish State.* Jerusalem, 1938.

Bullock, Alan. *The Life and Times of Ernest Bevin,* Vol. I. London, 1960.

Cana'an, Haviv. *B'Tzet HaBritim* [On the British Departure]. Tel Aviv, 1958.

Cohen, Aharon. *Israel and the Arab World.* New York, 1970.

Cohn, Michael. *Palestine: Retreat from the Mandate; The Making of British Policy.* New York, 1978.

Elath, Eliahu. *Zionism in the U.N.* Philadelphia, 1976.

Ever-Hadani, Aharon. *Am b'Milchamto* [A People at War]. Tel Aviv, 1948.

Feis, Herbert. *The Birth of Israel: The Tousled Diplomatic Bed.* New York, 1969.

Francis-Williams, Edward. *Ernest Bevin.* London, 1946.

Friedman, Isaiah. *The Question of Palestine, 1914–1918.* New York, 1973.

Gilbert, Martin. *Exile and Return.* New York, 1979.

Halpern, Ben. *The Idea of the Jewish State.* Cambridge, Mass., 1961.

Hilberg, Raoul. *The Destruction of the European Jews.* Chicago, 1961.

Hurewitz, J. C. *The Struggle for Palestine.* New York, 1950.

Kimche, Jon and David. *The Secret Roads: The "Illegal" Migration of a People.* London, 1954.

Krammer, Arnold. *The Forgotten Friendship: Israel and the Soviet Bloc, 1947–53.* Urbana, Ill., 1974.

Landau, Jacob. *The Arabs in Israel.* London, 1969.

Landsborough, T. *HaKomando shel Tobruk* [The Tobruk Commando]. Tel Aviv, 1959.

Laqueur, Walter. *A History of Zionism.* New York, 1972.

Lifschitz, Y., ed. *Safer HaBrigada* [The Book of the Jewish Brigade]. Tel Aviv, 1957.

Naufah, Sayyid. "A Short History of the Arab Opposition to Zionism and Israel," *Islamic Review,* February 1965.

Porath, Yehoshua. *The Emergence of the Palestinian-Arab National Movement, 1918–1939.* London, 1974.

Rabinowitz, Louis. *Soldiers from Judea.* London, 1945.

Sachar, Howard M. *Aliyah: The Peoples of Israel.* Cleveland, 1961.

———. *Europe Leaves the Middle East, 1936–1954.* New York, 1972.

———. *A History of Israel: From the Rise of Zionism to our Time.* New York, 1976.

Sharett, Moshe. *B'Sh'ar HaUmot, 1945–1949* [At the Gate of Nations]. Tel Aviv, 1958.

Stein, Leonard. *The Balfour Declaration.* London, 1961.

Sykes, Christopher. *Crossroads to Israel, 1917–1948.* New York, 1965.

Winer, Gerson. *The Founding Fathers of Israel.* New York, 1971.

Woodward, Sir E. Llewellyn. *British Foreign Policy in the Second World War.* London, 1962.

Zasloff, Joseph H. *Great Britain and Palestine: A Study of the Problem before the United Nations.* New York, 1942.

Egyptian-Zionist Relations until the Birth of Israel. The Jews of Egypt

American Jewish Congress. *The Black Record: Nasser's Persecution of Egyptian Jewry.* New York, 1957.

Ben-Zvi, Yitzchak. *The Exiled and the Redeemed.* Philadelphia, 1957.

Cohen, Aharon. *Israel and the Arab World.* New York, 1970.

Emanuel, Yitzchak M. *Tzahak Yehudei Mitzrayim—Hatzilu!* [Egyptian Jewry's Cry for Help]. Tel Aviv, 1967.

Feinberg, Natan. *Eretz Yisrael bi'l'kufat HaMandat u'M'dinat Yisrael* [The Land of Israel during the Mandate and the State of Israel]. Jerusalem, 1962.

Frank, Gerold. *The Deed.* New York, 1963.

Frischwasser, Ra'anan, H. F. *The Frontiers of a Nation.* London, 1955.

Gordon, Benjamin L. *New Judea: Jewish Life in Modern Palestine and Egypt.* Philadelphia, 1919.

Kaffuri, Mishil. *Al-Sahyuniyah, Nash'atuha wa-Atharuha al-Ijtima'i* [Zionism, Its Origins and Social Impact]. Cairo, 1946.

Landau, Jacob M. *Jews in Nineteenth Century Egypt.* New York, 1969.

Mandel, Neville J. *The Arabs and Zionism before World War I.* Berkeley, 1976.

Pearlman, Moshe. "Chapters of Arab-Jewish Diplomacy, 1918–22," *Jewish Social Studies*, April 1944.

Roi, Ya'akov. "HaEmdah HaTzionit Klapei HaAravim, 1908–1914," [The Zionist Position vis-à-vis the Arabs, 1908–1914], *Keshet*, Nos. 42, 43, 1969.

Rose, Norman. "The Debate on Partition, 1937–38: The Anglo-Zionist Aspect—I: The Proposal," *Middle Eastern Studies*, October 1970; "II: The Withdrawal," *Middle Eastern Studies*, January 1971.

Rubin, Barry. *The Arab States and the Palestine Conflict, 1918–1948.* Unpublished doctoral dissertation, Washington, D.C., 1977.

———. "Egypt and the Palestine Question, 1922–1939," *Wiener Library Bulletin*, Nos. 45, 46, 1978.

Sachar, Howard M. *Europe Leaves the Middle East, 1936–1954.* New York, 1972.

———. *From the Ends of the Earth: The Peoples of Israel.* Cleveland, 1964.

Stillman, Norman A. *The Jews of Arab Lands.* Philadelphia, 1979.

Storrs, Sir Ronald. *Orientations.* London, 1937.

Weisgal, Meyer, and Joel Carmichael, eds. *Chaim Weizmann: A Biography by Several Hands.* New York, 1963.

Weizmann, Chaim. *Trial and Error.* New York, 1949.

Yahudiya, Masriya. *Yehudei Mitzrayim* [The Jews of Egypt]. Ramat Gan, 1974.

The First Palestine War: 1948

Allon, Yigal. *The Making of Israel's Army.* London, 1970.

Avinoam, Reuven, ed. *Such Were Our Fighters.* New York, 1965.

Banai, Ya'akov. *Chayalim Almonim* [Unknown Soldiers]. Tel Aviv, 1958.

Bar-Zohar, Michael. *Ben-Gurion: The Armed Prophet.* Englewood Cliffs, N.J., 1967.

———. *Gesher al HaYam HaTichon* [Bridge across the Mediterranean]. Tel Aviv, 1964.

Bell, J. Bowyer. *The Long War: Israel and the Arabs Since 1946.* Englewood Cliffs, N.J., 1969.

Ben-Gurion, David. *B'Hilachem Yisrael* [While Israel Fights]. Tel Aviv, 1949.

Dupuy, T. N. *Elusive Victory: The Arab-Israeli Wars, 1947–1974.* London, 1978.

Gilad, Zerubavel, ed. *Sefer HaPalmach* [The Book of the Palmach]. 2 vols. Tel Aviv, 1955.

Golan, Aviezer. *Milchemet HaAtzma'ut* [Israel's War of Independence]. Tel Aviv, 1949.

Hawari, Muhammad Nimr al-. *Sirr al-Nakbah* [The Secret of the Disaster]. Beirut, 1955.

Hourani, Albert. "The Decline of the West in the Middle East," *International Affairs*, July 1953.

Jamali, Muhammad Fadil al-. *Mudhakkarat wa-Ibar* [Memoirs and Lessons]. Beirut, 1964.

Khatab, Mahmud al-. *Tariq al-Nasr fi Ma'rakat al-Tha'r* [The Road to Victory in the Battle for Revenge]. Beirut, 1966.

Khatib, Muhammad Nimr al-. *Ahadith Nakbat Filastin* [Events of the Palestinian Catastrophe]. Beirut, 1967.

Krammer, Arnold. *The Forgotten Friendship: Israel and the Soviet Bloc, 1947–53*. Urbana, Ill., 1974.

Lorch, Netanel. *The Edge of the Sword: Israel's War of Independence*. New York, 1961.

Mardor, Munya. *Haganah*. New York, 1966.

Meir, Golda. *My Life*. New York, 1975.

Nasser, Gamal Abd al-. *The Truth About the Palestine War*. Cairo, 1956.

O'Ballance, Edgar. *The Arab-Israeli War, 1948*. London, 1956.

Rifaat Bey, Muhammed. "The Story of el Faluge," *Islamic Review*, June, 1949.

Sachar, Howard M. *Europe Leaves the Middle East, 1936–1954*. New York, 1972.

Sharett, Moshe. *Yoman M'dini* [Political Diary]. Tel Aviv, 1968.

Smolansky, O. M. "Soviet Policy in the Arab East, 1945–47," *Journal of International Affairs*, 1959.

Talmi, Efraim. *Yisrael b'Marachah* [Israel on the Battleline]. Tel Aviv, 1952.

Tuqan, Qadri Hafiz. *Ba'da al-Nakbah* [After the Catastrophe]. Beirut, 1960.

Yakobovits, M. *M'Palmach ad Tzahal* [From Palmach to the Armed Forces of Israel]. Tel Aviv, 1943.

Yasin, Subhi. *Tariq al-Awdah li-Filastin* [The Road of Return to Palestine]. Cairo, 1961.

Beleaguered Israel: From the Rhodes Armistices to the Sinai War of 1956

Azcarate y Flores, Pablo de. *Mission in Palestine, 1948–1952*. Washington, D.C., 1966.

Ben-Asher, A. *Yachsei Chutz shel Yisrael* [Israel's Foreign Policy]. Tel Aviv, 1955.

Bovis, H. Eugene. *The Jerusalem Question, 1917–1968*. Stanford, 1971.

Brecher, Michael. *The Foreign Policy System of Israel*. London, 1972.

Brook, David. *Preface to Peace: The United Nations and the Arab-Israel Armistice System*. Washington, D.C., 1954.

Byford-Jones, W. *Forbidden Frontiers*. London, 1958.

Cohen, Yerucham. *L'Or HaYom u'vaMachshach* [In Daylight and in Darkness]. Tel Aviv, 1969.

Comay, Michael. *U.N. Peace-Keeping in the Israel-Arab Conflict, 1948–1975*. Jerusalem, 1975.

Eban, Abba. *An Autobiography.* New York, 1978.

Eytan, Walter. *The First Ten Years: A Diplomatic History of Israel.* New York, 1958.

Feinberg, Natan. *Eretz Yisrael bi'l'kufat HaMandat u'M'dinat Yisrael* [The Land of Israel during the Mandate and the State of Israel]. Jerusalem, 1962.

Ghazzali, Abd al-Mun'im al-. *Isra'il qa'idah lil-isti'mar walaysut ummah* [Israel Is a Colonial Base, Not a Nation]. Cairo, 1958.

Giniewski, Paul. *Israel devant l'Afrique et l'Asie.* Paris, 1958.

Harkabi, Yehoshafat. *Arab Attitudes to Israel.* Jerusalem, 1972.

Israel. Ministry for Foreign Affairs. *Egypt and the Suez Canal, 1948–1956.* Jerusalem, 1956.

Jabara, Abdeen. *The Armistice in International Law and the Egyptian Search of Israel-Bound Cargoes and Seizure of Contraband under the Egyptian-Israeli General Armistice Agreement.* Beirut, 1966.

Lehrman, Hal. *Israel: The Beginning and Tomorrow.* New York, 1951.

Marwen, Iskander. *The Arab Boycott of Israel.* Beirut, 1966.

Naufah, Sayyid. "A Short History of the Arab Opposition to Zionism and Israel," *Islamic Review,* February 1965.

Patinkin, Don. *The Israel Economy: The First Decade.* Jerusalem, 1963.

Rosenne, Shabtai. *Israel's Armistice Agreements with the Arab States: A Juridical Interpretation.* Tel Aviv, 1951.

Szereszewski, Robert. *Essays on the Structure of the Jewish Economy in Palestine and Israel.* Jerusalem, 1968.

United Arab Republic. Information Department. *Navigation in the Suez Canal: Israeli Pretensions Refuted.* Cairo, 1961.

Vatikiotis, P. J. *Egypt Since the Revolution.* London, 1968.

The Egyptian Revolution and the Emergence of Nasserist Imperialism

Abd Allah, Ismail Sabri. *A Quest for Economic Independence. Case Study: United Arab Republic.* Cairo, 1971.

Abdel-Fadil, Mahmoud. *Development, Income Distribution, and Social Change in Rural Egypt.* New York, 1970.

Awdah, Awdah Butrus. *Abd al-Nasir wa-al-Isti'mar al-Alami* [Nasser and World Imperialism]. Beirut, 1975.

Awdah, Filib, and Sa'ad Kamil. *Qissat al-Suvyit ma'a Misr* [The Story of the Soviets and Egypt]. Beirut, 1975.

Ben-Gurion, David. *Negotiations with Nasser.* Jerusalem, 1973.

Campbell, John. *Defense of the Middle East.* New York, 1960.

Copeland, Miles. *The Game of Nations.* New York, 1969.

Dawisha, A. I. *Egypt in the Arab World.* New York, 1969.

Hopkins, Harry. *Egypt: The Crucible.* London, 1969.

Hurewitz, J. C. *Middle East Politics: The Military Dimension.* New York, 1969.

Hussein, Mahmud. *Class Conflict in Egypt, 1945–1970*. New York, 1973.
Issawi, Charles P. *Egypt in Revolution: An Economic Analysis*. London, 1963.
Mabro, Robert. *The Industrialization of Egypt, 1939–1973*. Oxford, 1973.
Mursi, Ahmad Fuad al-. *Al-Alaqat al-Misriyah al-Suvyitiyah, 1943–1956* [Soviet-Egyptian Relations, 1943–1956). Cairo, 1975.
Perlmutter, Amos. *Egypt: the Praetorian State*. New Brunswick, N.J., 1974.
Ra'anan, Uri. *The USSR Arms the Third World*. Cambridge, Mass., 1969.
Rimawi, Qasim. *The Challenge of Industrialization: Egypt*. Beirut, 1974.
Rubenstein, Alvin. *Red Star on the Nile*. Princeton, 1977.
Vatikiotis, P. J. *Egypt Since the Revolution*. London, 1968.

Egyptian Pan-Arabism and the Second Egyptian-Israeli War, 1956

Abd al-Hamid, Muhammad Kamil. *Marakat Sina wa-Qanat al-Suways* [The Sinai Campaign and the Suez Canal]. Beirut, 1965.
Abd al-Qadir, Lufti. *Fi al-marakah al-fasilah* [The Decisive Campaign]. Cairo, 1966.
Assima, Georges. *Le Crise de Suez 1956*. Lausanne, 1956.
Avneri, Aryeh. *P'shitot HaTagmul* [The Retaliation Forays]. Tel Aviv, 1969.
Barer, Shlomo. *The Weekend War*. Tel Aviv, 1959.
Barker, A. J. *Suez: The Seven Day War*. London, 1964.
Bar-Zohar, Michael. *Suez: ultra-secret*. Paris, 1964.
Beaufré, André. *L'expédition de Suez, 1956*. Paris, 1968.
Bell, J. Bowyer. *The Long War: Israel and the Arabs since 1946*. Englewood Cliffs, N.J., 1969.
Ben-Gurion, David. *Negotiations with Nasser*. Jerusalem, 1973.
Blaland, Gregory. *Egypt and Sinai: Eternal Battleground*. New York, 1968.
Brecher, Michael. *Decisions in Israel's Foreign Policy*. New Haven, 1974.
Chasin, Eliahu, and Don Horowitz. *HaParashah* [The (Lavon) Affair]. Tel Aviv, 1962.
Comay, Michael. *U.N. Peace-Keeping in the Israel-Arab Conflict, 1948–1975*. Jerusalem, 1975.
Dan, Uri, and Y. Ben-Porat. *The Secret War: The Spy Game in the Middle East*. New York, 1970.
Dayan, Moshe. *Diary of the Sinai Campaign*. New York, 1965.
———. *Story of My Life*. London, 1976.
Dupuy, T. N. *Elusive Victory: The Arab-Israeli Wars, 1947–1974*. London, 1978.
Eban, Abba. *An Autobiography*. New York, 1978.
Eden, Anthony (Lord Avon). *Full Circle*. London, 1960.
Eshed, Hagai. *Mi Notan et HaHora'ah?* [Who Gave the Order (for the Spy Mission)?]. Tel Aviv, 1979.
Evron, Yosef. *B'Yom Sagrir* [On a Dreary Day]. Tel Aviv, 1968.
Fahmi, Wafiq Abd al-Aziz. *Al-Udwan al-Thualathi* [The Tripartite Enmity]. Beirut, 1964.

Golan, Aviezer. *Ma'arachet Sinai* [The Sinai Campaign]. Tel Aviv, 1966.
———. *Operation Susannah*. New York, 1978.
Harel, Isser. *Anatomia shel B'gida* [The Anatomy of Treason]. Tel Aviv, 1980.
Hasson, Jaques M. *Suez: Represailles et menottes: journal d'un interné par la police politique de Nasser*. Paris, 1959.
Jumrah, Rabih Lufti. *Sahq al-udwan* [Crushing the Enemy]. Cairo, 1962.
Kagan, Benjamin. *Combat secret pour Israël*. Paris, 1963.
Lartéguy, Jean. *Les murailles d'Israël: Les secrets de l'armée la plus secrète du monde*. Paris, 1970.
Lavergne, Bernard. *Problèmes africains: Afrique noire, Algérie, affaire de Suez*. Paris, 1957.
Marshall, S. L. A. *Sinai Victory*. New York, 1958.
O'Ballance, Edgar. *The Sinai Campaign, 1956*. London, 1960.
Peres, Shimon. *David's Sling*. New York, 1970.
Pineau, Christian. *1956*. Paris, 1976.
Reingold, Uriel. *HaMasah el Sharm es-Sheikh*. [The Trek to Sharm es-Sheikh]. Tel Aviv, 1966.
Robertson, Terence. *Crisis: The Inside Story of the Suez Conspiracy*. New York, 1965.
Safran, Nadav. *From War to War: The Arab-Israeli Confrontation, 1948–1967*. New York, 1969.
———. *Israel: The Embattled Ally*. Cambridge, Mass., 1978.
Talmi, Efraim. *Milchamot Yisrael, 1949–1969* [Israel's Wars, 1949–1969]. Tel Aviv, 1969.
Thomas, Hugh. *The Suez Affair*. London, 1967.
Tournoux, J. R. *Secrets d'État*. Paris, 1960.
Umar, Ali. *Ayyam hazzat al-alam* [Days that Shook the World]. Beirut, 1965.
United Arab Republic. Ministry of National Guidance. *Secrets of the Suez War*. Cairo, 1967.

The Socialization of Egypt. Israel's "Take-Off." A Decade of Oblique Confrontation, 1957–1967

Abdel-Malek, Anowar. *Egypt: Military Society*. New York, 1968.
Bar-Zohar, Michael. *The Avengers*. London, 1968.
———. *Spies in the Promised Land: Iser Harel and the Israeli Secret Service*. Boston, 1971.
Berque, Jacques. *L'Égypte: imperialism et revolution*. Paris, 1967.
Brecher, Michael. *The Foreign Policy System of Israel*. London, 1972.
Chasin, Eliahu, and Don Horowitz. *HaParashah* [The (Lavon) Affair]. Tel Aviv, 1961.
Crosbie, Sylvia K. *A Tacit Alliance: France and Israel from Suez to the Six-Day War*. Princeton, 1974.
Dan, Uri, and Yehoshua Ben-Porat. *The Secret War: The Spy Game in the Middle East*. New York, 1970.

Dawisha, A. *Egypt in the Arab World: The Elements of Foreign Policy*. London, 1976.

Deutschkron, Inge. *Bonn and Jerusalem: The Strange Coalition*. Philadelphia, 1970.

Douek, Raymond Ibrahim. *La voie égyptienne vers le socialisme*. Cairo, 1966.

"Fifteen Years That Changed the Face of Israel," *Jewish Observer and Middle East Report*, Nov. 19, 1965.

Gibbons, Scott. *The Conspirators*. London, 1967.

Giniewski, Paul. *Israël devant l'Afrique et l'Asie*. Paris, 1958.

Goneid, Abd al-Moneim. *La République Arabe Unie "Egypte" dans l'unité arabe et l'unité africaine*. Cairo, 1968.

Halevi, Nadav, and Ruth Klinov-Malul. *The Economic Development of Israel*. New York, 1968.

Horowitz, David. *The Enigma of Economic Growth: A Case Study of Israel*. New York, 1972.

Hussein, Mahmud. *Class Conflict in Egypt, 1945–1970*. New York, 1970.

Ismail, Tariq Y. *The U.A.R. in Africa: Egypt's Policy under Nasser*. Evanston, Ill., 1971.

Kramer, Thomas W. *Deutsche-ägyptische beziehungen in Vergangenheit und Gegenwart*. Tübingen, 1974.

Kreinin, Mordecai. *Israel and Africa*. New York, 1964.

Laufer, Leopold. *Israel and the Developing Countries*. New York, 1967.

Lutz, Wolfgang. *The Champagne Spy*. London, 1972.

Mabro, Robert. *The Egyptian Economy, 1952–1972*. London, 1974.

Mead, Donald C. *Growth and Structural Change in the Egyptian Economy*. Homewood, Ill., 1967.

O'Brien, Patrick K. *The Revolution in Egypt's Economic System*. London, 1966.

Peres, Shimon. *David's Sling*. New York, 1970.

Powell, Ivor. *Disillusion by the Nile: What Nasser Has Done to Egypt*. London, 1967.

Rejwan, Nissim. *Nasserist Ideology: Its Exponents and Critics*. New York, 1974.

Sachar, Howard M. *From the Ends of the Earth: The Peoples of Israel*. Cleveland, 1964.

Safran, Nadav. *From War to War: The Arab-Israeli Confrontation 1948–1967*. New York, 1969.

———. *Israel: The Embattled Ally*. Cambridge, Mass., 1978.

Sager, Peter. *Kairo und Moskau in Arabien*. Bern, 1967.

Sawant, A. "Rivalry Between Egypt and Israel in Africa South of the Sahara, 1956–1974." *International Studies*, April–June 1978.

Sawiris, Salib Butros. *Planning, Economic Development in Underdeveloped Countries with Special Reference to Egypt*. Cairo, 1972.

Segev, Shmuel. *Israël, les Arabes et les grandes puissances, 1963–1968*. Paris, 1968.

Semah, David. *Four Egyptian Literary Critics*. Leiden, 1974.

Sharabi, Hisham B. *Nationalism and Revolution in the Arab World*. Princeton, 1966.

Shinnar, Felix. *B'Ol Korach v'Reg'shut b'Shlichut HaM'dinah: Yachsei Yisrael-Germania 1951 ad 1966* [Under Constraint and Discretion on a State Mission: Israeli-German Relations 1951 to 1966]. Jerusalem, 1967.

Speier, Hans. *Crisis and Catharsis in the Middle East, 1965: A Chapter of German Foreign Policy*. Santa Monica, 1967.

Tahsin, Hassan. *Munazzamat al-Duwal al-Ifriqiyah* [The Organization of African Governments]. Beirut, 1967.

Udah, Abd al-Malik. *Isra'il wa-Afriqiya* [Israel and Africa]. Cairo, 1972.

Uwayni, Muhammad Ali al-. *Siyasat Isra'il al-kharijiyah fi Afriqiya* [Israel's Foreign Policy in Africa]. Cairo, 1972.

Yahya, Jalal. *Misr al-Ifriqiyah* [African Egypt]. Cairo, 1967.

The Six-Day War

Abu-Loghod, Ibrahim, ed. *The Arab-Israeli Confrontation of June 1967: An Arab Perspective*. Evanston, Ill., 1970.

Avneri, Aryeh. *HaYom HaKatzar b'Yotair* [The Shortest Day]. Tel Aviv, 1967.

Bar-Zohar, Michael. *Embassies in Crisis: Diplomats and Demagogues behind the Six-Day War*. Englewood Cliffs, N.J., 1970.

Ben-Shaul, Moshe. *Alufei Yisrael* [Israel's Generals]. Tel Aviv, 1969.

Dagan, Avigdor. *Moscow and Jerusalem: Twenty Years of Relations between Israel and the Soviet Union*. London, 1970.

Dan, Uri. *De Gaulle contre Israël*. Paris, 1969.

Dayan, David. *M'Hermon ad Suets*. [From Mount Hermon to Suez]. Ramat Gan, 1967.

Dayan, Moshe. *Story of My Life*. London, 1976.

Dupuy, T. N. *Elusive Victory: The Arab-Israeli Wars, 1947–1974*. London, 1978.

Eban, Abba. *An Autobiography*. New York, 1978.

Ehrlich, Israel. *B'Ma'alot Giborim* [The Virtues of Heroes]. Tel Aviv, 1969.

Ghitani, Jalal al-. *Al-Misruyun wa-al-Harb* [The Egyptians and the War]. Cairo, 1974.

Haber, Eitan, Eli Landau, and Ze'ev Schiff. *M'Et Katavenu HaTzv'ai* [Report from Our Military Correspondent]. Tel Aviv, 1967.

Hadid, Salah al-Din al-. *Shahid ala harb 67* [A Martyr of the 1967 War]. Beirut, 1974.

Harel, Yehuda. *HaKrav al HaYam* [The War at Sea]. Tel Aviv, 1970.

Hashavia, Aryeh. *A History of the Six-Day War*. Tel Aviv, 1969.

Huwaydi, Amin. *Harub Abd al-Nasir* [The Wars of Nasser]. Beirut, 1977.

Israel. Ministry for Foreign Affairs. *Egypt's Unlawful Blockade of the Gulf of Aqaba*. Jerusalem, 1967.

Khuli, Lufti al-. *Khamsah Yunu, al-haqiqah wa-al-mustaqbal* [The Fifth of June, the Truth, and the Future]. Beirut, 1974.

Kimche, David, and Dan Bavly. *The Sandstorm*. London, 1968.

Kosut, Hal, ed. *Israel and the Arabs: The June 1967 War*. New York, 1967.

Lall, Arthur. *The United Nations and the Middle East Crisis, 1967*. New York, 1968.

Laqueur, Walter. *The Road to War*. London, 1968.

Matar, Fuad. *Rusiya al-Nasiriyah wa-Misr al-Misriyah* [Nasser's Russia and Egyptian Egypt]. Beirut, 1972.

Mezerik, Avraham, ed. *The Arab-Israeli Conflict and the United Nations*. New York, 1969.

Murad, Mahmud. *Muharib li-kull al-usur* [A Warrior for All Ages]. Cairo, 1972.

Nakdimon, Shlomo. *Likrat Sha'at HaEfes* [Towards Zero-Hour]. Tel Aviv, 1968.

Nashashibi, Nasir al-Din al-. *Safir mutajawwil* [A Roving Ambassador]. Beirut, 1970.

O'Ballance, Edgar. *The Third Arab-Israeli War*. Hamden, Conn., 1972.

Perlmutter, Amos. "Assessing the Six-Day War," *Commentary*, Jan. 1970.

Porat, Yeshayahu, and Uri Dan. *Embargo: Mirage neged Mig* [Embargo: Mirage against MiG]. Ramat Gan, 1968.

Prittie, Terence. *Eshkol: The Man and the Nation*. New York, 1969.

Qazan, Fuad. *Al-Thawrah al-Arabiyah wa-Isra'il* [The Arab Revolt and Israel]. Beirut, 1968.

Rabin, Yitzchak. *The Rabin Memoirs*. Jerusalem, 1979.

Rikhye, Indar Jit. *The Sinai Blunder: Withdrawal of the United Nations Emergency Force Leading to the Six Day War, June 1967*. New Delhi, 1978.

Safran, Nadav. *From War to War: The Arab-Israeli Confrontation 1948–1967*. New York, 1969.

———. *Israel: The Embattled Ally*. Cambridge, Mass., 1978.

Segev, Shmuel. *Sadin Adom* ["Red Sheet"]. Tel Aviv, 1967.

Shalabi, Ahmad. *Misr fi harbayn* [Egypt in Two Wars]. Beirut, 1975.

Shihatah, Ali. *Al-Suways wa-harb al-ayyam al-sittah* [The Suez and the Six-Day War]. Beirut, 1969.

Suleiman, Isam Muhammad. *Harb al-ayyam al-sittah* [The Six-Day War]. Amman, 1969.

Talmi, Efraim. *Milchamot Yisrael* [Israel's Wars]. II. Tel Aviv, 1969.

Van Horn, Carl. *Soldiering for Peace*. New York, 1967.

Wagner, A. R. *Crisis Decision-Making: Israel's Experience in 1967 and 1973*. New York, 1974.

The Aftermath of Trauma. The War of Attrition

Arad, Yitzchak, ed. *1000 HaYomim: 12 Yuni 1967–8 August 1970* [The 1,000 Days: June 12, 1967–August 8, 1970]. Tel Aviv, 1972.

Awad, Lewis. *Cultural and Intellectual Developments in Egypt since 1952.* New York, 1968.

Bavly, Dan, and David Farhi. *Israel and the Palestinians.* London, 1970.

Blum, Yahuda Z. *Secure Boundaries and Middle Eastern Peace.* Jerusalem, 1971.

Dawisha, Karen. *Soviet Foreign Policy Towards Egypt.* New York, 1979.

Dayan, Moshe. *Mapah Chadashah* [A New Map]. Tel Aviv, 1969.

———. *Story of My Life.* London, 1976.

Dekmijian, R. *Egypt Under Nasir.* Albany, 1971.

Eban, Abba. *An Autobiography.* New York, 1978.

Ellis, Harry B. *The Dilemma of Israel.* Washington, D.C., 1970.

Glassman, Jon D. *Arms for the Arabs.* Baltimore, 1975.

Heymont, Irving. "The Israeli Defense of the Suez Canal," *Middle East Information Series*, Spring 1971.

Horelick, Arnold L. "Soviet Involvement in the Middle East and the Western Response," *Middle East Information Series*, June 1972.

Kanovsky, Eliahu. *The Economic Impact of the Six-Day War.* New York, 1970.

Kilpatrick, Hilary. *The Modern Egyptian Novel.* London, 1974.

Kissinger, Henry. *The White House Years.* Boston, 1978.

Kochav, David. "Israel's Second Front: How to Pay for Defence," *New Middle East*, Jan., 1970.

Kotler, Yair. *HaKrav al HaTa'alah* [The War on the Canal]. Jerusalem, 1969.

McKalip, Homer D. *Arms Transfer as an Element of American Foreign Policy.* Washington, D.C., 1977.

Meir, Golda. *My Life.* Jerusalem, 1975.

Na'or, Mordechai. *HaMilchamah l'achar HaMilchamah* [The War after the War]. Tel Aviv, 1973.

Reich, B., and E. Conroy. "Peace Plans and Proposals for the Arab-Israeli Conflict: 1947–1977," *Middle East Review*, Winter 1977.

Roi, Ya'akov, and David Ronel. *The Soviet Economic Presence in Egypt.* Jerusalem, 1974.

Rubenstein, Alvin Z. *Red Star on the Nile.* Princeton, 1977.

Sabri, Yusuf. *Wa-Kanat al-bidayah min al-sifr* [It All Began at Zero Hour]. Beirut, 1972.

Schiff, Ze'ev. *K'nafayim m'al Suets* [Wings Over Suez]. Haifa, 1970.

Sheehan, E. R. F. "The Way Egyptians See Israel," *New York Times Magazine*, Sept. 4, 1970.

Stevens, Georgiana. "What Nasser Did," *Atlantic*, Jan. 1971.

Wahba, Magdi. *Cultural Policy in Egypt.* Paris, 1972.

Whetten, Lawrence L. "June 1967 to June 1971: Four Years of Canal War Reconsidered," *New Middle East*, June 1971.

The Emergence of Anwar al-Sadat and the October 1973 War

Adan, Avraham. *Al Shtai G'dot HaSuets* [On Both Sides of the Suez]. Jerusalem, 1979.

Ahdab, Aziz al-. *Dam'at Dayan* [Dayan's Tear]. Beirut, 1974.

An-Nahar Arab Report. *The October War*. Beirut, 1973.

Aruri, Naseer H., ed. *Middle East Crucible: Studies on the Arab-Israeli War of October 1973*. Wilmette, Ill., 1975.

Avneri, Aryeh. *Shamayim Bo'arim* [Burning Skies]. Tel Aviv, 1974.

Badawi, Musa. *Al-Sadat rajul al-harb, rajul al-sal'am* [Sadat As a Man of War, As a Man of Peace]. Cairo, 1978.

Badri, Hasan al-. *Harb Ramadan* [The War of Ramadan]. Beirut, 1974.

Bartov, Hanoch. *Dado* [David Elazar]. Tel Aviv, 1978.

"Bombast for the Unfaithful," *Economist*, May 6, 1972.

Brookings Institution. *Toward Peace in the Middle East*. Washington, D.C., 1975.

Cairo University. *International Symposium on the 1973 October War*. Cairo, 1975.

Darwish, Abd al-Karim. *Harb al-Sa'at al-sitt* [The Six-Hour War]. Cairo, 1974.

Dayan, Moshe. *Story of My Life*. London, 1976.

Eran, Oded, and Jerome Singer. "Exodus from Egypt and the Threat to Kremlin Leadership," *New Middle East*, Nov. 1972.

Farid, Samir. *Harb Uktubir fi al-sinima* [The October War in Cinema]. Cairo, 1974.

Ghitani, Jalal al-. *Al-Misruyun wa-al-Harb*. [The Egyptians and the War]. Beirut, 1974.

Gitelson, Susan A. "Africa's Rupture with Israel," *Midstream*, Feb. 1974.

Golan, Galia. *The Soviet Union and the Arab-Israeli War of October 1973*. Jerusalem, 1974.

Hamdan, Jamal al-Dain Mahmud. *Sittah Uktubir fi al-istiratijiyah al-alamiyah* [October 6 in World Strategy]. Cairo, 1974.

Hashavia, Aryeh. *Milchemet Yom HaKippurim* [The Yom Kippur War]. Tel Aviv, 1974.

Hazim, Husam. *Asrar Harb Uktubir* [The Secrets of the October War]. Beirut, 1974.

Heikal, Mohamed Hassanein. *The Cairo Documents*. New York, 1973.

————. *The Road to Ramadan*. New York, 1975.

Helmensdorfer, Erich. *The Great Crossing*. Neckarsulm, 1975.

"If the Middle East Should Explode Again," *Economist*, Jan. 1, 1972.

International Symposium, Jerusalem, Israel. *Military Aspects of the Arab-Israeli Conflict*. Tel Aviv, 1975.

Kraft, Joseph. "Letter from Cairo." *New Yorker*, Sept. 18, 1971.

Kunayyisi, Hamdi al-. *Al-Yawm al-sabi* [The Seventh Day]. Beirút, 1974.

McKenzie-Smith, R. "Crisis Decision-Making in Israel: The Case of the October 1973 Middle East War," *Naval War College Review*, No. 1, 1976.

Medzini, Meron. "Israel and Africa—What Went Wrong?" *Midstream*, December 1972.

Meir, Golda. *My Life*. New York, 1975.

Mustafa Imam, Sayyid. *Yawmiyat muqatil fi al-Jaysh al-Thalith* [Diary of a Soldier in the Third Army]. Cairo, 1974.

Noor, Mordechai. *Y'mei Oktober* [The Days of October]. Tel Aviv, 1974.

O'Ballance, Edgar. *No Victor, No Vanquished: The Yom Kippur War*. London, 1978.

Owen, David. "Sinai is the Key to Peace," *New Statesman*, Nov. 2, 1973.

Palit, D. K. *Return to Sinai*. New Delhi, 1974.

Quandt, William. "Soviet Policy in the October Middle East War: I," *International Affairs*, July 1977.

Roth, Stanley. *Middle East Balance of Power after the Yom Kippur War*. Cambridge, Mass., 1974.

Rubenstein, Alvin Z. "Egypt Since Nasser," *Current History*, January 1972.

Rugh, A. "Arab Media and Politics During the October War," *Middle East Journal*, Summer 1975.

Rühl, Lothar. *Israels letzer Krieg*. Hamburg, 1974.

Sabri, Musa. *Watha'iq Harb Uktubir* [Documents of the October War]. Cairo, 1974.

Sadat, Anwar al-. *In Search of Identity*, New York, 1977.

———. *Programme of National Action*. Cairo, July 23, 1971.

Shalabi, Ahmad. *Misr fi harbayn* [Egypt in Two Wars]. Cairo, 1975.

Shamir, Shimon. *Mitzrayim B'Hanhagat Sadat* [Egypt under the Leadership of Sadat]. Tel Aviv, 1978.

Sheehan, Edward R. F. "The Real Sadat and the Demythologized Nasser," *New York Times Magazine*, July 18, 1971.

Sheehy, Gail. "The Riddle of Sadat." *Esquire*, Jan. 30, 1979.

Smith, Hedrick. "Where Egypt Stands," *Atlantic*, January 1971.

Suleiman, Michael W. "Attitudes of the Arab Elite Toward Palestine and Israel," *American Political Science Review*, June 1973.

Tantawi, Hassan al-. *Butulat Harb Ramadan* [The Heroism of the War of Ramadan]. Cairo, 1974.

Tawila, Abd al-Sattar al-. *Harb al-sa'at al-sitt wa-ihtimalat al-harb al-khamisah* [The Six-Hour War and the Imminence of the Future War]. Cairo, 1975.

Van Creveld, Martin. *Military Lessons of the Yom Kippur War.* London, 1975.

Weinland, R. "Superpower Naval Diplomacy in the October 1973 Arab-Israeli War," *Washington Papers,* No. 61, 1979.

Whetten, Lawrence A., and M. Johnson. "Military Lessons of the Yom Kippur War," *World Today,* March 1974.

Ziku, Ali Uthman. *Abtal al-tayaran fi ma'rakat Ramadan* [Air Heroes of the Ramadan Campaign]. Cairo, 1974.

Disengagement. Anwar al-Sadat's and Menachem Begin's Quest for Peace.

"After the Peace Treaty: The Military Situation in the Middle East," *Journal of Palestine Studies,* No. 1, 1979.

Ali, M. "Jordan's Stance Toward the Camp David Agreements," *Pakistan Horizon,* No. 31, 1978.

Amit, Meir. "Israel: The Bases of Economic Growth," *Washington Quarterly,* Spring 1979.

Baker, Raymond L. *Egypt's Uncertain Revolution under Nasser and Sadat.* Cambridge, Mass., 1978.

Baumgartel, Elise. *The Cultures of Prehistoric Egypt.* New York, 1963.

Begin, Menachem. *BaMachteret* [In the Underground]. 4 vols. Tel Aviv, 1959–61.

———. *The Revolt.* New York, 1951.

———. *White Nights.* New York, 1957.

Business International, S.A. *Egypt: Business Gateway to the Middle East?* Geneva, 1976.

Chase World Information Corporation. *Agribusiness Potential in the Middle East and North Africa.* New York, 1977.

Dawisha, A. "Syria and the Sadat Initiative," *World Today,* May 1978.

Dayan, Moshe. *Breakthrough to Peace.* London, 1981.

Development Assistance Corporation (Chase National Bank). *Egypt-New York.* New York, 1977.

Dowty, A. "In Defense of Camp David," *Commentary,* April 1980.

Dubberstein, W. "Sinai II: In Retrospect," *Strategic Review,* No. 2, 1977.

Duclos, J. S. "Un essai de rapprochement égypto-israélien," *Maghreb-Machrek,* Jan. 1976.

Gaskill, Gordon. "Mission: Reopen the Suez Canal," *Reader's Digest,* July 1975.

Gilboa, E. "Educating Israeli Officers in the Process of Peacemaking in the Middle East," *Journal of Peace Research,* No. 2, 1979.

Golan, Matti. *The Secret Conversations of Henry Kissinger.* New York, 1976.

Haber, Eitan, Ze'ev Schiff, and Ehud Yaari. *The Year of the Dove.* New York, 1979.

Hareven, Aluph. "Can We Learn to Live Together?" *Jerusalem Quarterly*, No. 4, 1979.

Harris, John R., ed. *The Legacy of Egypt*. London, 1971.

Hussein, Taha. *The Future of Culture in Egypt*. Washington, D.C., 1954.

Jamal, Mustafa al-. *Istiratijiyat Isra'il ba'da Harb Uktubir* [Israel's Strategy after the October War]. Beirut, 1976.

Kalb, Marvin, and Bernard Kalb. *Kissinger*. New York, 1974.

Lapidoth, R. "The Camp David Agreements: Some Legal Aspects," *Jerusalem Quarterly*, No. 19, 1979.

Luttwak, Edward N. "Strategic Implications of the Camp David Accords," *Washington Quarterly*, No. 19, 1979.

Mansour, Anis. "Getting to Know You," *New Outlook*, May–June 1979.

Mark, Clyde R. *Arab-Israeli Peace: Sadat-Begin Negotiations*. Washington, D.C., 1978.

Markus, Yoel. *Camp David: Petach l'Shalom* [Camp David: Gateway to Peace]. Tel Aviv, 1979.

Meyer, Gail E. *Egypt and the United States*. Cranbury, N.J., 1980.

Murray, Margaret A. *The Splendor That Was Egypt*. New York, 1963.

Nes, D. "Egypt Breaks the Deadlock," *Journal of Palestine Studies*, No. 2, 1978.

Neumann, Robert G. "The Middle East after Camp David: Perils and Opportunities," *Washington Quarterly*, No. 19, 1979.

Niv, David. *Ma'arachot HaIrgun HaTzv'ai HaL'eumi.* [Campaigns of the Etzel]. 2 vols. Tel Aviv, 1965.

Nooter, Robert. "American Contributions to Development," *Washington Quarterly*, No. 19, 1979.

Oweis, Ibrahim, and Charles Issawi. "Two Views of Potentials for Economic Development in Egypt," *Washington Quarterly*, No. 19, 1979.

Paxton, E. "Taha Hussein and Hamud Taimur: An Appreciation," *Asian Affairs*, June 1974.

Peres, Shimon. "A Strategy for Peace in the Middle East," *Foreign Affairs*, April 1980.

Razzaq, Asad. *Greater Israel: A Study in Zionist Expansionist Thought*. Beirut, 1970.

"Sadat Is Not the Man," *Economist*, Feb. 12, 1972.

Sayegh, F. "The Camp David Agreement and the Palestine Problem," *Journal of Palestine Studies*, No. 1, 1979.

Sayeh, Hamed el-. "Egypt: The Foundations of the Economy," *Washington Quarterly*, No. 19, 1979.

Schechtman, Joseph B. *Vladimir Jabotinsky*. 2 vols. New York, 1956–61.

Seale, P. "Sadat in Jerusalem," *New Statesman*, Nov. 25, 1977.

Segev, Shmuel. *Sadat, HaDerech l'Shalom* [Sadat, the Road to Peace]. Tel Aviv, 1978.

Sheehan, Edward R. "How Kissinger Did It: Step by Step in the Middle East," *Foreign Policy*, No. 22, Spring 1976.

Shufani, E. "Sadat's Initiative: The Reaction in Israel," *Journal of Palestine Studies*, No. 1, 1979.

Sid-Ahmed, Mohamed. *After the Guns Fall Silent: Peace or Armageddon in the Middle East*. London, 1978.

Tariq, Muhammad al-. *Masirat al-Sadat min Salizburj hatta al-Kinisit* [Sadat's Journey from Salzburg to the Knesset]. Beirut, 1977.

Torgovnik, E. "Accepting Camp David: The Role of Party Factions in Israeli Policy-Making," *Middle East Review*, No. 2, 1978–79.

Waterbury, John. *Egypt: Burdens of the Past, Options for the Future*. Bloomington, Ind., 1978.

Weizman, Ezer. *The Battle for Peace*. New York, 1981.

The Egyptian-Israeli Peace Treaty

TREATY OF PEACE BETWEEN
THE ARAB REPUBLIC OF EGYPT AND THE STATE OF ISRAEL

The Government of the Arab Republic of Egypt and the Government of the State of Israel;

PREAMBLE

Convinced of the urgent necessity of the establishment of a just, comprehensive and lasting peace in the Middle East in accordance with Security Council Resolutions 242 and 338;

Reaffirming their adherence to the ''Framework for Peace in the Middle East Agreed at Camp David,'' dated September 17, 1978;

Noting that the aforementioned Framework as appropriate is intended to constitute a basis for peace not only between Egypt and Israel but also between Israel and each of its other Arab neighbors which is prepared to negotiate peace with it on this basis;

Desiring to bring to an end the state of war between them and to establish a peace in which every state in the area can live in security;

Convinced that the conclusion of a Treaty of Peace between Egypt and Israel is an important step in the search for comprehensive peace in the area and for the attainment of the settlement of the Arab-Israeli conflict in all its aspects;

Inviting the other Arab parties to this dispute to join the peace process with Israel guided by and based on the principles of the aforementioned Framework;

Desiring as well to develop friendly relations and cooperation between themselves in accordance with the United Nations Charter and the principles of international law governing international relations in times of peace;

Agree to the following provisions in the free exercise of their sovereignty, in order to implement the ''Framework for the Conclusion of a Peace Treaty Between Egypt and Israel'':

ARTICLE I

1. The state of war between the Parties will be terminated and peace will be established between them upon the exchange of instruments of ratification of this Treaty.

2. Israel will withdraw all its armed forces and civilians from the Sinai behind the international boundary between Egypt and mandated Palestine, as provided in the annexed protocol (Annex I), and Egypt will resume the exercise of its full sovereignty over the Sinai.

3. Upon completion of the interim withdrawal provided for in Annex I, the Parties will establish normal and friendly relations, in accordance with Article III (3).

ARTICLE II

The permanent boundary between Egypt and Israel is the recognized international boundary between Egypt and the former mandated territory of Palestine, as shown on the map at Annex II, without prejudice to the issue of the status of the Gaza Strip. The Parties recognize this boundary as inviolable. Each will respect the territorial integrity of the other, including their territorial waters and airspace.

ARTICLE III

1. The Parties will apply between them the provisions of the Charter of the United Nations and the

principles of international law governing relations among states in times of peace. In particular:

> a. They recognize and will respect each other's sovereignty, territorial integrity and political independence;
> b. They recognize and will respect each other's right to live in peace within their secure and recognized boundaries;
> c. They will refrain from the threat or use of force, directly or indirectly, against each other and will settle all disputes between them by peaceful means.

2. Each Party undertakes to ensure that acts or threats of belligerency, hostility, or violence do not originate from and are not committed from within its territory, or by any forces subject to its control or by any other forces stationed on its territory, against the population, citizens or property of the other Party. Each Party also undertakes to refrain from organizing, instigating, inciting, assisting or participating in acts or threats of belligerency, hostility, subversion or violence against the other Party, anywhere, and undertakes to ensure that perpetrators of such acts are brought to justice.

3. The Parties agree that the normal relationship established between them will include full recognition, diplomatic, economic and cultural relations, termination of economic boycotts and discriminatory barriers to the free movement of people and goods, and will guarantee the mutual enjoyment by citizens of the due process of law. The process by which they undertake to achieve such a relationship parallel to the implementation of other provisions of this Treaty is set out in the annexed protocol (Annex III).

ARTICLE IV

1. In order to provide maximum security for both Parties on the basis of reciprocity, agreed security arrangements will be established including limited force zones in Egyptian and Israeli territory, and United Nations forces and observers, described in detail as to nature and timing in Annex I, and other security arrangements the Parties may agree upon.

2. The Parties agree to the stationing of United Nations personnel in areas described in Annex I. The Parties agree not to request withdrawal of the United Nations personnel and that these personnel will not be removed unless such removal is approved by the Security Council of the United Nations, with the affirmative vote of the five Permanent Members, unless the Parties otherwise agree.

3. A Joint Commission will be established to facilitate the implementation of the Treaty, as provided for in Annex I.

4. The security arrangements provided for in paragraphs 1 and 2 of this Article may at the request of either party be reviewed and amended by mutual agreement of the Parties.

ARTICLE V

1. Ships of Israel, and cargoes destined for or coming from Israel, shall enjoy the right of free passage through the Suez Canal and its approaches through the Gulf of Suez and the Mediterranean Sea on the basis of the Constantinople Convention of 1888, applying to all nations. Israeli nationals, vessels and cargoes, as well as persons, vessels and cargoes destined for or coming from Israel, shall be accorded non-discriminatory treatment in all matters connected with usage of the canal.

2. The Parties consider the Strait of Tiran and the Gulf of Aqaba to be international waterways open to all nations for unimpeded and non-suspendable freedom of navigation and overflight. The Parties will respect each other's right to navigation and overflight for access to either country through the Strait of Tiran and the Gulf of Aqaba.

ARTICLE VI

1. This Treaty does not affect and shall not be interpreted as affecting in any way the rights and obligations of the Parties under the Charter of the United Nations.

2. The Parties undertake to fulfill in good faith their obligations under this Treaty, without regard to action or inaction of any other party and independently of any instrument external to this Treaty.

3. They further undertake to take all the necessary measures for the application in their relations of the provisions of the multilateral conventions to which they are parties, including the submission of appropriate notification to the Secretary General of the United Nations and other depositaries of such conventions.

4. The Parties undertake not to enter into any obligation in conflict with this Treaty.

5. Subject to Article 103 of the United Nations Charter, in the event of a conflict between the obligations of the Parties under the present Treaty and any of their other obligations, the obligations under this Treaty will be binding and implemented.

ARTICLE VII

1. Disputes arising out of the application or interpretation of this Treaty shall be resolved by negotiations.

2. Any such disputes which cannot be settled by negotiations shall be resolved by conciliation or submitted to arbitration.

ARTICLE VIII

The Parties agree to establish a claims commission for the mutual settlement of all financial claims.

ARTICLE IX

1. This Treaty shall enter into force upon exchange of instruments of ratification.

2. This Treaty supersedes the Agreement between Egypt and Israel of September, 1975.

3. All protocols, annexes, and maps attached to this Treaty shall be regarded as an integral part hereof.

4. The Treaty shall be communicated to the Secretary General of the United Nations for registration in accordance with the provisions of Article 102 of the Charter of the United Nations.

DONE at Washington, D.C. this 26th day of March, 1979, in triplicate in the English, Arabic, and Hebrew languages, each text being equally authentic. In case of any divergence of interpretation, the English text shall prevail.

حررت فى واشنطن دى • سى • فى ٢٦ مارس ١٩٧٩م ، ٢٧ ربيع الاول ١٣٩٩ هـ
من ثلاث نسخ باللغات الانجليزية والعربية والعبرية وتعتبر جميعها متساوية
الحجية ، وفى حالة الخلاف حول التفسير فيكون النص الانجليزى هو الذى يعتد به •

נעשה בוושינגטון, די.סי. ביום זה כ"ז באדר לשנת תשל"ט, 26 במרץ 1979, בשלושה
עותקים בשפות האנגלית, הערבית והעברית וכל נוסח אמין במידה שווה. במקרה של הבדלי
פרשנות, יכריע הנוסח האנגלי .

For the Government of the   For the Government
Arab Republic of Egypt: of Israel:

عن حكومـة   عن حكومـة
جمهورية مصــر العربيــة :   اسرائيـــــــل :

בשם ממשלת הרפובליקה הערבית   בשם ממשלת ישראל :
של מצרים :

Witnessed by:
شهد التوقيـــع :
הועד על-ידי :

Jimmy Carter, President
of the United States of America

جيمى كارتـــــر ، رئيـــــــس
الولايات المتحــــــدة الامريكيـــة

ג'ימי קארטר, נשיא
ארצות הברית של אמריקה

PROTOCOL CONCERNING ISRAELI
WITHDRAWAL AND SECURITY ARRANGEMENTS

Article I
Concept of Withdrawal

1. Israel will complete withdrawal of all its armed forces and civilians from the Sinai not later than three years from the date of exchange of instruments of ratification of this Treaty.

2. To ensure the mutual security of the Parties, the implementation of phased withdrawal will be accompanied by the military measures and establishment of zones set out in this Annex and in Map I, hereinafter referred to as "the Zones."

3. The withdrawal from the Sinai will be accomplished in two phases:

    a. The interim withdrawal behind the line from east of El Arish to Ras Muhammed as delineated on Map 2 within nine months from the date of exchange of instruments of ratification of this Treaty.

    b. The final withdrawal from the Sinai behind the international boundary not later than three years from the date of exchange of instruments of ratification of this Treaty.

4. A Joint Commission will be formed immediately after the exchange of instruments of ratification of this Treaty in order to supervise and coordinate movements and schedules during the withdrawal, and to adjust plans and timetables as necessary within the limits established by paragraph 3, above. Details relating to the Joint Commission are set out in Article IV of the attached Appendix. The Joint Commission will be dissolved upon completion of final Israeli withdrawal from the Sinai.

Article II
Determination of Final Lines and Zones

1. In order to provide maximum security for both Parties after the final withdrawal, the lines and the Zones delineated on Map I are to be established and organized as follows:

a. Zone A

(1) Zone A is bounded on the east by line A (red line) and on the west by the Suez Canal and the east coast of the Gulf of Suez, as shown on Map I.

(2) An Egyptian armed force of one mechanized infantry division and its military installations, and field fortifications, will be in this Zone.

(3) The main elements of that Division will consist of:

    (a) Three mechanized infantry brigades.

    (b) One armored brigade.

    (c) Seven field artillery battalions including up to 126 artillery pieces.

    (d) Seven anti-aircraft artillery battalions including individual surface-to-air missiles and up to 126 anti-aircraft guns of 37 mm and above.

    (e) Up to 230 tanks.

    (f) Up to 480 armored personnel vehicles of all types.

    (g) Up to a total of twenty-two thousand personnel.

b. Zone B

(1) Zone B is bounded by line B (green-line) on the east and by line A (red line) on the west, as shown on Map I.

(2) Egyptian border units of four battalions equipped with light weapons and wheeled vehicles will provide security and supplement the civil police in maintaining order in Zone B. The main elements of the four Border Battalions will consist of up to a total of four thousand personnel.

(3) Land based, short range, low power, coastal warning points of the border patrol units may be established on the coast of this Zone.

(4) There will be in Zone B field fortifications and military installations for the four border battalions.

c. Zone C

(1) Zone C is bounded by line B (green line) on the west and the International Boundary and the Gulf of Aqaba on the east, as shown on Map 1.

(2) Only United Nations forces and Egyptian civil police will be stationed in Zone C.

(3) The Egyptian civil police armed with light weapons will perform normal police functions within this Zone.

(4) The United Nations Force will be deployed within Zone C and perform its functions as defined in Article VI of this Annex.

(5) The United Nations Force will be stationed mainly in camps located within the following stationing areas shown on Map 1, and will establish its precise locations after consultations with Egypt:

(a) In that part of the area in the Sinai lying within about 20 Km. of the Mediterranean Sea and adjacent to the International Boundary.

(b) In the Sharm el Sheikh area.

d. Zone D

(1) Zone D is bounded by line D (blue line) on the east and the international boundary on the west, as shown on Map 1.

(2) In this Zone there will be an Israeli limited force of four infantry battalions, their military installations, and field fortifications, and United Nations observers.

(3) The Israeli forces in Zone D will not include tanks, artillery and anti-aircraft missiles except individual surface-to-air missiles.

(4) The main elements of the four Israeli infantry battalions will consist of up to 180 armored personnel vehicles of all types and up to a total of four thousand personnel.

2. Access across the international boundary shall only be permitted through entry check points designated by each Party and under its control. Such access shall be in accordance with laws and regulations of each country.

3. Only those field fortifications, military installations, forces, and weapons specifically permitted by this Annex shall be in the Zones.

Article III
Aerial Military Regime

1. Flights of combat aircraft and reconnaisance flights of Egypt and Israel shall take place only over Zones A and D, respectively.

2. Only unarmed, non-combat aircraft of Egypt and Israel will be stationed in Zones A and D, respectively.

3. Only Egyptian unarmed transport aircraft will take off and land in Zone B and up to eight such aircraft may maintained in Zone B. The Egyptian border units may be equipped with unarmed helicopters to perform their functions in Zone B.

4. The Egyptian civil police may be equipped with unarmed police helicopters to perform normal police functions in Zone C.

5. Only civilian airfields may be built in the Zones.

6. Without prejudice to the provisions of this Treaty, only those military aerial activities specifically permitted by this Annex shall be allowed in the Zones and the airspace above their territorial waters.

Article IV
Naval Regime

1. Egypt and Israel may base and operate naval vessels along the coasts of Zones A and D, respectively.

2. Egyptian coast guard boats, lightly armed, may be stationed and operate in the territorial waters of Zone B to assist the border units in performing their functions in this Zone.

3. Egyptian civil police equipped with light boats, lightly armed, shall perform normal police functions within the territorial waters of Zone C.

4. Nothing in this Annex shall be considered as derogating from the right of innocent passage of the naval vessels of either party.

5. Only civilian maritime ports and installations may be built in the Zones.

6. Without prejudice to the provisions of this Treaty, only those naval activities specifically permitted by this Annex shall be allowed in the Zones and in their territorial waters.

Article V
Early Warning Systems

Egypt and Israel may establish and operate early warning systems only in Zones A and D respectively.

Article VI
United Nations Operations

1. The Parties will request the United Nations to provide forces and observers to supervise the implementation of this Annex and employ their best efforts to prevent any violation of its terms.

2. With respect to these United Nations forces and observers, as appropriate, the Parties agree to request the following arrangements:

> a. Operation of check points, reconnaissance patrols, and observation posts along the international boundary and line B, and within Zone C.
> b. Periodic verification of the implementation of the provisions of this Annex will be carried out not less than twice a month unless otherwise agreed by the Parties.
> c. Additional verifications within 48 hours after the receipt of a request from either Party.
> d. Ensuring the freedom of navigation through the Strait of Tiran in accordance with Article V of the Treaty of Peace.

3. The arrangements described in this article for each zone will be implemented in Zones A, B, and C by the United Nations Force and in Zone D by the United Nations Observers.

4. United Nations verification teams shall be accompanied by liaison officers of the respective Party.

5. The United Nations Force and observers will report their findings to both Parties.

6. The United Nations Force and Observers operating in the Zones will enjoy freedom of movement and other facilities necessary for the performance of their tasks.

7. The United Nations Force and Observers are not empowered to authorize the crossing of the international boundary.

8. The Parties shall agree on the nations from which the United Nations Force and Observers will be drawn. They will be drawn from nations other than those which are permanent members of the United Nations Security Council.

9. The Parties agree that the United Nations should make those command arrangements that will best assure the effective implementation of its responsibilities.

Article VII
Liaison System

1. Upon dissolution of the Joint Commission, a liaison system between the Parties will be established. This liaison system is intended to provide an effective method to assess progress in the implementation of obligations under the present Annex and to resolve any problem that may arise in the course of implementation, and refer other unresolved matters to the higher military authorities of the two countries respectively for consideration. It is also intended to prevent situations resulting from errors or misinterpretation on the part of either Party.

2. An Egyptian liaison office will be established in the city of El-Arish and an Israeli liaison office will be established in the city of Beer-Sheba. Each office will be headed by an officer of the respective country, and assisted by a number of officers.

3. A direct telephone link between the two offices will be set up and also direct telephone lines with the United Nations command will be maintained by both offices.

Article VIII
Respect for War Memorials

Each Party undertakes to preserve in good condition the War Memorials erected in the memory of soldiers of the other Party, namely those erected by Israel in the Sinai and those to be erected by Egypt in Israel, and shall permit access to such monuments.

Article IX
Interim Arrangements

The withdrawal of Israeli armed forces and civilians behind the interim withdrawal line, and the conduct of the forces of the Parties and the United Nations prior to the final withdrawal, will be governed by the attached Appendix and Maps 2 and 3.

APPENDIX TO ANNEX I
ORGANIZATION OF MOVEMENTS IN THE SINAI

Article I
Principles of Withdrawal

1. The withdrawal of Israeli armed forces and civilians from the Sinai will be accomplished in two phases as described in Article I of Annex I. The description and timing of the withdrawal are included in this Appendix. The Joint Commission will develop and present to the Chief Coordinator of the United Nations forces in the Middle East the details of these phases not later than one month before the initiation of each phase of withdrawal.

2. Both Parties agree on the following principles for the sequence of military movements.

a. Notwithstanding the provisions of Article IX, paragraph 2, of this Treaty, until Israeli armed forces complete withdrawal from the current J and M Lines established by the Egyptian-Israeli Agreement of September 1975, hereinafter referred to as the 1975 Agreement, up to the interim withdrawal line, all military arrangements existing under that Agreement will remain in effect, except those military arrangements otherwise provided for in this Appendix.

b. As Israeli armed forces withdraw, United Nations forces will immediately enter the evacuated areas to establish interim and temporary buffer zones as shown on Maps 2 and 3, respectively, for the purpose of maintaining a separation of forces. United Nations forces' deployment will precede the movement of any other personnel into these areas.

c. Within a period of seven days after Israeli armed forces have evacuated any area located in Zone A, units of Egyptian armed forces shall deploy in accordance with the provisions of Article II of this Appendix.

d. Within a period of seven days after Israeli armed forces have evacuated any area located in Zones A or B, Egyptian border units shall deploy in accordance with the provisions of Article II of this Appendix, and will function in accordance with the provisions of Article II of Annex I.

e. Egyptian civil police will enter evacuated areas immediately after the United Nations forces to perform normal police functions.

f. Egyptian naval units shall deploy in the Gulf of Suez in accordance with the provisions of Article II of this Appendix.

g. Except those movements mentioned above, deployments of Egyptian armed forces and the activities covered in Annex I will be effected in the evacuated areas when Israeli armed forces have completed their withdrawal behind the interim withdrawal line.

Article II
Subphases of the Withdrawal to the Interim Withdrawal Line

1. The withdrawal to the interim withdrawal line will be accomplished in subphases as described in this Article and as shown on Map 3. Each subphase will be completed within the indicated number of months from the date of the ex-

change of instruments of ratification of this Treaty.

    a. First subphase: within two months, Israeli armed forces will withdraw from the area of El Arish, including the town of El Arish and its airfield, shown as Area I on Map 3.

    b. Second subphase: within three months, Israeli armed forces will withdraw from the area between line M of the 1975 Agreement and line A, shown as Area II on Map 3.

    c. Third subphase: within five months, Israeli armed forces will withdraw from the areas east and south of Area II, shown as Area III on Map 3.

    d. Fourth subphase: within seven months, Israeli armed forces will withdraw from the area of El Tor–Ras El Kenisa, shown as Area IV on Map 3.

    e. Fifth subphase: Within nine months, Israeli armed forces will withdraw from the remaining areas west of the interim withdrawal line, including the areas of Santa Katrina and the areas east of the Giddi and Mitla passes, shown as Area V on Map 3, thereby completing Israeli withrawal behind the interim withdrawal line.

2. Egyptian forces will deploy in the areas evacuated by Israeli armed forces as follows:

    a. Up to one-third of the Egyptian armed forces in the Sinai in accordance with the 1975 Agreement will deploy in the portions of Zone A lying within Area I, until the completion of interim withdrawal. Thereafter, Egyptian armed forces as described in Article II of Annex I will be deployed in Zone A up to the limits of the interim buffer zone.

    b. The Egyptian naval activity in accordance with Article IV of Annex I will commence along the coasts of Areas II, III, and IV, upon completion of the second, third, and fourth subphases, respectively.

    c. Of the Egyptian border units described in Article II of Annex I, upon completion of the first subphase one battalion will be deployed in Area I. A second battalion will be deployed in Area II upon completion of the second subphase. A third battalion will be deployed in Area III upon completion of the third subphase. The second and third

battalions mentioned above may also be deployed in any of the subsequently evacuated areas of the southern Sinai.

3. United Nations forces in Buffer Zone I of the 1975 Agreement will redeploy to enable the deployment of Egyptian forces described above upon the completion of the first subphase, but will otherwise continue to function in accordance with the provisions of that Agreement in the remainder of that zone until the completion of interim withdrawal, as indicated in Article I of this Appendix.

4. Israeli convoys may use the roads south and east of the main road junction east of El Arish to evacuate Israeli forces and equipment up to the completion of interim withdrawal. These convoys will proceed in daylight upon four hours notice to the Egyptian liaison group and United Nations forces, will be escorted by United Nations forces, and will be in accordance with schedules coordinated by the Joint Commission. An Egyptian liaison officer will accompany convoys to assure uninterrupted movement. The Joint Commission may approve other arrangements for convoys.

Article III
United Nations Forces

1. The Parties shall request that United Nations forces be deployed as necessary to perform the functions described in this Appendix up to the time of completion of final Israeli withdrawal. For that purpose, the Parties agree to the redeployment of the United Nations Emergency Force.

2. United Nations forces will supervise the implementation of this Appendix and will employ their best efforts to prevent any violation of its terms.

3. When United Nations forces deploy in accordance with the provisions of Articles I and II of this Appendix, they will perform the functions of verification in limited force zones in accordance with Article VI of Annex I, and will establish check points, reconnaissance patrols, and observation posts in the temporary buffer zones described in Article II above. Other functions of the United Nations forces which concern the interim buffer zone are described in Article V of this Appendix.

Article IV
Joint Commission and Liaison

1. The Joint Commission referred to in Article IV of this Treaty will function from the date of exchange of instruments of ratification of this Treaty up to the date of completion of final Israeli withdrawal from the Sinai.

2. The Joint Commission will be composed of representatives of each Party headed by senior officers. This Commission shall invite a representative of the United Nations when discussing subjects concerning the United Nations, or when either Party requests United Nations presence. Decisions of the Joint Commission will be reached by agreement of Egypt and Israel.

3. The Joint Commission will supervise the implementation of the arrangements described in Annex I and this Appendix. To this end, and by agreement of both Parties, it will:

   a. coordinate military movements described in this Appendix and supervise their implementation;
   b. address and seek to resolve any problem arising out of the implementation of Annex I and this Appendix, and discuss any violations reported by the United Nations Force and Observers and refer to the Governments of Egypt and Israel any unresolved problems;
   c. assist the United Nations Force and Observers in the execution of their mandates, and deal with the timetables of the periodic verifications when referred to it by the Parties as provided for in Annex I and in this Appendix;
   d. organize the demarcation of the international boundary and all lines and zones described in Annex I and this Appendix;
   e. supervise the handing over of the main installations in the Sinai from Israel to Egypt;
   f. agree on necessary arrangements for finding and returning missing bodies of Egyptian and Israeli soldiers;
   g. organize the setting up and operation of entry check points along the El Arish–Ras Muhammed line in accordance with the provisions of Article 4 of Annex III;
   h. conduct its operations through the use of joint liaison teams consisting of one Israeli representative and one Egyptian representative, provided from a standing Liaison Group, which will conduct activities as directed by the Joint Commission;
   i. provide liaison and coordination to the United Nations command implementing provisions of the Treaty, and, through the joint liaison teams, maintain local coordination and cooperation with the United Nations Force stationed in specific areas or United Nations Observers monitoring specific areas for any assistance as needed;
   j. discuss any other matters which the Parties by agreement may place before it.

4. Meetings of the Joint Commission shall be held at least once a month. In the event that either Party or the Command of the United Nations Force requests a special meeting, it will be convened within 24 hours.

5. The Joint Commission will meet in the buffer zone until the completion of the interim withdrawal and in El Arish and Beer-Sheba alternately afterwards. The first meeting will be held not later than two weeks after the entry into force of this Treaty.

Article V
Definition of the Interim Buffer Zone and Its Activities

1. An interim buffer zone, by which the United Nations Force will effect a separation of Egyptian and Israeli elements, will be established west of and adjacent to the interim withdrawal line as shown on Map 2 after implementation of Israeli withdrawal and deployment behind the interim withdrawal line. Egyptian civil police equipped with light weapons will perform normal police functions within this zone.

2. The United Nations Force will operate check points, reconnaissance patrols, and observation posts within the interim buffer zone in order to ensure compliance with the terms of this Article.

3. In accordance with arrangements agreed upon by both Parties and to be coordinated by the Joint Commission, Israeli personnel will operate

military technical installations at four specific locations shown on Map 2 and designated as T1 (map central coordinate 57163940), T2 (map central coordinate 59351541), T3 (map central coordinate 59331527), and T4 (map central coordinate 61130979) under the following principles:

a. The technical installations shall be manned by technical and administrative personnel equipped with small arms required for their protection (revolvers, rifles, sub-machine guns, light machine guns, hand grenades, and ammunition), as follows:

T1–up to 150 personnel
T2 and T3–up to 350 personnel
T4–up to 200 personnel.

b. Israeli personnel will not carry weapons outside the sites, except officers who may carry personal weapons.

c. Only a third party agreed to by Egypt and Israel will enter and conduct inspections within the perimeters of technical installations in the buffer zone. The third party will conduct inspections in a random manner at least once a month. The inspections will verify the nature of the operation of the installations and the weapons and personnel therein. The third party will immediately report to the Parties any divergence from an installation's visual and electronic surveillance or communications role.

d. Supply of the installations, visits for technical and administrative purposes, and replacement of personnel and equipment situated in the sites, may occur uninterruptedly from the United Nations check points to the perimeter of the technical installations, after checking and being escorted by only the United Nations forces.

e. Israel will be permitted to introduce into its technical installations items required for the proper functioning of the installations and personnel.

f. As determined by the Joint Commission, Israel will be permitted to:

(1) Maintain in its installations firefighting and general maintenance equipment as well as wheeled administrative vehicles and mobile engineering equipment necessary for the maintenance of the sites. All vehicles shall be unarmed.

(2) Within the sites and in the buffer zone, maintain roads, water lines, and communications cables which serve the sites. At each of the three installation locations (T1, T2 and T3, and T4), this maintenance may be performed with up to two unarmed wheeled vehicles and by up to twelve unarmed personnel with only necessary equipment, including heavy engineering equipment if needed. This maintenance may be performed three times a week, except for special problems, and only after giving the United Nations four hours notice. The teams will be escorted by the United Nations.

g. Movement to and from the technical installations will take place only during daylight hours. Access to, and exit from, the technical installations shall be as follows:

(1) T1: through a United Nations check point, and via the road between Abu Aweigila and the intersection of the Abu Aweigila road and the Gebel Libni road (at Km. 161), as shown on Map 2.

(2) T2 and T3: through a United Nations checkpoint and via the road constructed across the buffer zone to Gebel Katrina, as shown on Map 2.

(3) T2, T3, and T4: via helicopters flying within a corridor at the times, and according to a flight profile, agreed to by the Joint Commission. The helicopters will be checked by the United Nations Force at landing sites outside the perimeter of the installations.

h. Israel will inform the United Nations Force at least one hour in advance of each intended movement to and from the installations.

i. Israel shall be entitled to evacuate sick and wounded and summon medical experts and medical teams at any time after giving immediate notice to the United Nations Force.

4. The details of the above principles and all other matters in this Article requiring coordination by the Parties will be handled by the Joint Commission.

5. These technical installations will be withdrawn when Israeli forces withdraw from the interim withdrawal line, or at a time agreed by the Parties.

Article VI
Disposition of Installations and Military Barriers

Disposition of installations and military barriers will be determined by the Parties in accordance with the following guidelines:

1. Up to three weeks before Israeli withdrawal from any area, the Joint Commission will arrange for Israeli and Egyptian liaison and technical teams to conduct a joint inspection of all appropriate installations to agree upon condition of structures and articles which will be transferred to Egyptian control and to arrange for such transfer. Israel will declare, at that time, its plans for disposition of installations and articles within the installations.

2. Israel undertakes to transfer to Egypt all agreed infrastructure, utilities, and installations intact, inter alia, airfields, roads, pumping stations, and ports. Israel will present to Egypt the information necessary for the maintenance and operation of these facilities. Egyptian technical teams will be permitted to observe and familiarize themselves with the operation of these facilities for a period of up to two weeks prior to transfer.

3. When Israel relinquishes Israeli military water points near El Arish and El Tor, Egyptian technical teams will assume control of those installations and ancillary equipment in accordance with an orderly transfer process arranged beforehand by the Joint Commission. Egypt undertakes to continue to make available at all water supply points the normal quantity of currently available water up to the time Israel withdraws behind the international boundary, unless otherwise agreed in the Joint Commission.

4. Israel will make its best effort to remove or destroy all military barriers, including obstacles and minefields, in the areas and adjacent waters from which it withdraws, according to the following concept:

    a. Military barriers will be cleared first from areas near populations, roads, and major installations and utilities.

    b. For those obstacles and minefields which cannot be removed or destroyed prior to Israeli withdrawal, Israel will provide detailed maps to Egypt and the United Nations through the Joint Commission not later than 15 days before entry of United Nations forces into the affected areas.

    c. Egyptian military engineers will enter those areas after United Nations forces enter to conduct barrier clearance operations in accordance with Egyptian plans to be submitted prior to implementation.

Article VII
Surveillance Activities

1. Aerial surveillance activities during the withdrawal will be carried out as follows:

    a. Both Parties request the United States to continue airborne surveillance flights in accordance with previous agreements until the completion of final Israeli withdrawal.

    b. Flight profiles will cover the Limited Forces Zones to monitor the limitations on forces and armaments, and to determine that Israeli armed forces have withdrawn from the areas described in Article II of Annex I, Article II of this Appendix, and Maps 2 and 3, and that these forces thereafter remain behind their lines. Special inspection flights may be flown at the request of either Party or of the United Nations.

    c. Only the main elements in the military organizations of each Party, as described in Annex I and in this Appendix, will be reported.

2. Both Parties request the United States operated Sinai Field Mission to continue its operations in accordance with previous agreements until completion of the Israeli withdrawal from the area east of the Giddi and Mitla Passes. Thereafter, the Mission will be terminated.

Article VIII
Exercise of Egyptian Sovereignty

Egypt will resume the exercise of its full sovereignty over evacuated parts of the Sinai upon Israeli withdrawal as provided for in Article I of this Treaty.

PROTOCOL CONCERNING RELATIONS
OF THE PARTIES

Article 1
Diplomatic and Consular Relations

The Parties agree to establish diplomatic and consular relations and to exchange ambassadors upon completion of the interim withdrawal.

Article 2
Economic and Trade Relations

1. The Parties agree to remove all discriminatory barriers to normal economic relations and to terminate economic boycotts of each other upon completion of the interim withdrawal.

2. As soon as possible, and not later than six months after the completion of the interim withdrawal, the Parties will enter negotiations with a view to concluding an agreement on trade and commerce for the purpose of promoting beneficial economic relations.

Article 3
Cultural Relations

1. The Parties agree to establish normal cultural relations following completion of the interim withdrawal.

2. They agree on the desirability of cultural exchanges in all fields, and shall, as soon as possible and not later than six months after completion of the interim withdrawal, enter into negotiations with a view to concluding a cultural agreement for this purpose.

Article 4
Freedom of Movement

1. Upon completion of the interim withdrawal, each Party will permit the free movement of the nationals and vehicles of the other into and within its territory according to the general rules applicable to nationals and vehicles of other states. Neither Party will impose discriminatory restrictions on the free movement of persons and vehicles from its territory to the territory of the other.

2. Mutual unimpeded access to places of religious and historical significance will be provided on a nondiscriminatory basis.

Article 5
Cooperation for Development and
Good Neighborly Relations

1. The Parties recognize a mutuality of interest in good neighborly relations and agree to consider means to promote such relations.

2. The Parties will cooperate in promoting peace, stability and development in their region. Each agrees to consider proposals the other may wish to make to this end.

3. The Parties shall seek to foster mutual understanding and tolerance and will, accordingly, abstain from hostile propaganda against each other.

Article 6
Transportation and Telecommunications

1. The Parties recognize as applicable to each other the rights, privileges and obligations provided for by the aviation agreements to which they are both party, particularly by the Convention on International Civil Aviation, 1944 ("The Chicago Convention") and the International Air Services Transit Agreement, 1944.

2. Upon completion of the interim withdrawal any declaration of national emergency by a party under Article 89 of the Chicago Convention will not be applied to the other party on a discriminatory basis.

3. Egypt agrees that the use of airfields left by Israel near El Arish, Rafah, Ras El Nagb and Sharm El Sheikh shall be for civilian purposes only, including possible commercial use by all nations.

4. As soon as possible and not later than six months after the completion of the interim withdrawal, the Parties shall enter into negotiations for the purpose of concluding a civil aviation agreement.

5. The Parties will reopen and maintain roads and railways between their countries and will consider further road and rail links. The Parties further agree that a highway will be constructed and maintained between Egypt, Israel and Jordan near Eilat with guaranteed free and peaceful passage of persons, vehicles and goods between Egypt and Jordan, without prejudice to their sovereignty over that part of the highway which falls within their respective territory.

6. Upon completion of the interim withdrawal, normal postal, telephone, telex, data facsimile, wireless and cable communications and television relay services by cable, radio and satellite shall be established between the two Parties in accordance with all relevant international conventions and regulations.

7. Upon completion of the interim withdrawal, each Party shall grant normal access to its ports for vessels and cargoes of the other, as well as vessels and cargoes destined for or coming from the other.

Such access shall be granted on the same conditions generally applicable to vessels and cargoes of other nations. Article 5 of the Treaty of Peace will be implemented upon the exchange of instruments of ratification of the aforementioned Treaty.

Article 7
Enjoyment of Human Rights

The Parties affirm their commitment to respect and observe human rights and fundamental freedoms for all, and they will promote these rights and freedoms in accordance with the United Nations Charter.

Article 8
Territorial Seas

Without prejudice to the provisions of Article 5 of the Treaty of Peace each Party recognizes the right of the vessels of the other Party to innocent passage through its territorial sea in accordance with the rules of international law.

AGREED MINUTES
TO ARTICLES I, IV, V AND VI AND ANNEXES I AND III
OF TREATY OF PEACE

ARTICLE I

Egypt's resumption of the exercise of full sovereignty over the Sinai provided for in paragraph 2 of Article I shall occur with regard to each area upon Israel's withdrawal from that area.

ARTICLE IV

It is agreed between the parties that the review provided for in Article IV(4) will be undertaken when requested by either party, commencing within three months of such a request, but that any amendment can be made only with the mutual agreement of both parties.

ARTICLE V

The second sentence of paragraph 2 of Article V shall not be construed as limiting the first sentence of that paragraph. The foregoing is not to be construed as contravening the second sentence of paragraph 2 of Article V, which reads as follows:

"The parties will respect each other's right to navigation and overflight for access to either country through the Strait of Tiran and the Gulf of Aqaba."

ARTICLE VI(2)

The provisions of Article VI shall not be construed in contradiction to the provisions of the framework for peace in the Middle East agreed at Camp David. The foregoing is not to be construed as contravening the provisions of Article VI(2) of the Treaty, which reads as follows:

"The Parties undertake to fulfill in good faith their obligations under this Treaty, without regard to action or inaction of any other party and independently of any instrument external to this Treaty."

ARTICLE VI(5)

It is agreed by the Parties that there is no assertion that this Treaty prevails over other Treaties or agreements or that other Treaties or agreements prevail over this Treaty. The foregoing is not to be construed as contravening the provisions of Article VI(5) of the Treaty, which reads as follows:

"Subject to Article 103 of the United Nations Charter, in the event of a conflict between the obligations of the Parties under the present Treaty and any of their other obligations, the obligations under this Treaty will be binding and implemented."

ANNEX I

Article VI, Paragraph 8, of Annex I provides as follows:

"The Parties shall agree on the nations from which the United Nations force and observers will be drawn. They will be drawn from nations other than those which are permanent members of the United Nations Security Council."

The Parties have agreed as follows:

"With respect to the provisions of paragraph 8, Article VI, of Annex I, if no agreement is reached between the Parties, they will accept or support a U.S. proposal concerning the composition of the United Nations force and observers."

ANNEX III

The Treaty of Peace and Annex III thereto provide for establishing normal economic relations between the Parties. In accordance therewith, it is agreed that such relations will include normal commercial sales of oil by Egypt to Israel, and that Israel shall be fully entitled to make bids for

Egyptian-origin oil not needed for Egyptian domestic oil consumption, and Egypt and its oil concessionaires will entertain bids made by Israel, on the same basis and terms as apply to other bidders for such oil.

Witnessed by:

For the Government of Israel:

M. BEGIN

For the Government of the Arab Republic of Egypt:

A. SADAT

JIMMY CARTER

Jimmy Carter, President of the United States of America

JOINT LETTER TO PRESIDENT CARTER FROM
PRESIDENT SADAT AND PRIME MINISTER BEGIN

March 26, 1979

Dear Mr. President:

This letter confirms that Egypt and Israel have agreed as follows:

The Governments of Egypt and Israel recall that they concluded at Camp David and signed at the White House on September 17, 1978, the annexed documents entitled "A Framework for Peace in the Middle East Agreed at Camp David" and "Framework for the conclusion of a Peace Treaty between Egypt and Israel."

For the purpose of achieving a comprehensive peace settlement in accordance with the above-mentioned Frameworks, Egypt and Israel will proceed with the implementation of those provisions relating to the West Bank and the Gaza Strip. They have agreed to start negotiations within a month after the exchange of the instruments of ratification of the Peace Treaty. In accordance with the "Framework for Peace in the Middle East," the Hashemite Kingdom of Jordan is invited to join the negotiations. The Delegations of Egypt and Jordan may include Palestinians from the West Bank and Gaza Strip or other Palestinians as mutually agreed. The purpose of the negotiation shall be to agree, prior to the elections, on the modalities for establishing the elected self-governing authority (administrative council), define its powers and responsibilities, and agree upon other related issues. In the event Jordan decides not to take part in the negotiations, the negotiations will be held by Egypt and Israel.

The two Governments agree to negotiate continuously and in good faith to conclude these negotiations at the earliest possible date. They also agree that the objective of the negotiations is the establishment of the self-governing authority in the West Bank and Gaza in order to provide full autonomy to the inhabitants.

Egypt and Israel set for themselves the goal of completing the negotiations within one year so that elections will be held as expeditiously as possible after agreement has been reached between the parties. The self-governing authority referred to in the "Framework for Peace in the Middle East" will be established and inaugurated within one month after it has been elected, at which time the transitional period of five years will begin. The Israeli military government and its civilian administration will be withdrawn, to be replaced by the self-governing authority, as specified in the "Framework for Peace in the Middle East." A withdrawal of Israeli armed forces will then take place and there will be a redeployment of the remaining Israeli forces into specified security locations.

This letter also confirms our understanding that the United States Government will participate fully in all stages of negotiations.

Sincerely yours,

For the Government of Israel:	For the Government of the Arab Republic of Egypt:
M. BEGIN	A. SADAT
Menachem Begin	Mohamed Anwar El-Sadat

The President,
The White House

Explanatory Note

President Carter, upon receipt of the Joint Letter to him from President Sadat and Prime Minister Begin, has added to the American and Israeli copies the notation: "I have been informed that the expression 'West Bank' is understood by the Government of Israel to mean 'Judea and Samaria'." This notation is in accordance with similar procedures established at Camp David.

LETTERS REGARDING EXCHANGE OF AMBASSADORS

March 26, 1979

Dear Mr. President:

In response to your request, I can confirm that, within one month after the completion of Israel's withdrawal to the interim line as provided for in the Treaty of Peace between Egypt and Israel, Egypt will send a resident ambassador to Israel and will receive a resident Israeli ambassador in Egypt.

Sincerely,

A. SADAT

Mohamed Anwar El-Sadat

The President,
The White House

March 26, 1979

Dear Mr. Prime Minister:

I have received a letter from President Sadat that, within one month after Israel completes its withdrawal to the interim line in Sinai, as provided for in the Treaty of Peace between Egypt and Israel, Egypt will send a resident ambassador to Israel and will receive in Egypt a resident Israeli ambassador.

I would be grateful if you will confirm that this procedure will be agreeable to the Government of Israel.

Sincerely,

JIMMY CARTER

Jimmy Carter

His Excellency
Menachem Begin,
*Prime Minister of the
State of Israel*

March 26, 1979

Dear Mr. President:

I am pleased to be able to confirm that the Government of Israel is agreeable to the procedure set out in your letter of March 26, 1979 in which you state:

"I have recieved a letter from President Sadat that, within one month after Israel completes its withdrawal to the interim line in Sinai, as provided for in the Treaty of Peace between Egypt and Israel, Egypt will send a resident ambassador to Israel and will receive in Egypt a resident Israeli ambassador."

Sincerely,

M. BEGIN

Manachem Begin

The President,
The White House

LETTERS FROM PRESIDENT CARTER TO PRESIDENT
SADAT AND PRIME MINISTER BEGIN

March 26, 1979

Dear Mr. President:

I wish to confirm to you that subject to United States Constitutional processes:

In the event of an actual or threatened violation of the Treaty of Peace between Egypt and Israel, the United States will, on request of one or both of the Parties, consult with the Parties with respect thereto and will take such other action as it may deem appropriate and helpful to achieve compliance with the Treaty.

The United States will conduct aerial monitoring as requested by the Parties pursuant to Annex I of the Treaty.

The United States believes the Treaty provision for permanent stationing of United Nations personnel in the designated limited force zone can and should be implemented by the United Nations Security Council. The United States will exert its utmost efforts to obtain the requisite action by the Security Council. If the Security Council fails to establish and maintain the arrangements called for in the Treaty, the President will be prepared to take those steps necessary to ensure the establishment and maintenance of an acceptable alternative multinational force.

Sincerely,

JIMMY CARTER
Jimmy Carter

His Excellency
   Mohamed Anwar El-Sadat,
      President of the Arab
      Republic of Egypt

March 26, 1979

Dear Mr. Prime Minister:

I wish to confirm to you that subject to United States Constitutional processes:

In the event of an actual or threatened violation of the Treaty of Peace between Israel and Egypt, the United States will, on request of one or both of the Parties, consult with the Parties with respect thereto and will take such other action as it may deem appropriate and helpful to achieve compliance with the Treaty.

The United States will conduct aerial monitoring as requested by the Parties pursuant to Annex I of the Treaty.

The United States believes the Treaty provision for permanent stationing of United Nations personnel in the designated limited force zone can and should be implemented by the United Nations Security Council. The United States will exert its utmost efforts to obtain the requisite action by the Security Council. If the Security Council fails to establish and maintain the arrangements called for in the Treaty, the President will be prepared to take those steps necessary to ensure the establishment and maintenance of an acceptable alternative multinational force.

Sincerely,

JIMMY CARTER
Jimmy Carter

His Excellency
   Menachem Begin,
      Prime Minister of the
      State of Israel

EXCHANGE OF REMARKS
AMONG
THE PRESIDENT OF THE UNITED STATES,
ANWAR AL-SADAT, PRESIDENT OF EGYPT,
AND
MENACHEM BEGIN, PRIME MINISTER OF ISRAEL
UPON SIGNING OF THE
PEACE TREATY BETWEEN EGYPT AND ISRAEL

President Carter

During the past 30 years, Israel and Egypt have waged war. But for the past 16 months, these same two great nations have waged peace. Today we celebrate a victory—not of a bloody military campaign, but of an inspiring peace campaign. Two leaders who will loom large in the history of nations—President Anwar Al-Sadat and Prime Minister Menachem Begin—have conducted this campaign with all the courage, tenacity, brilliance and inspiration of any generals who have ever led men and machines onto the field of battle.

At the end of this campaign the soil of the two lands is not drenched with young blood. (Applause) The countrysides of both lands are free from the litter and the carnage of a wasteful war. Mothers in Egypt and Israel are not weeping today for their children fallen in senseless battle. The dedication and determination of these two world statesmen have borne fruit. Peace has come to Israel and to Egypt. (Applause)

I honor these two leaders and their government officials who have hammered out this peace treaty which we have just signed. But most of all, I honor the people of these two lands whose yearning for peace kept alive the negotiations which today culminate in this glorious event.

We have won at last the first step of peace, a first step on a long and difficult road. We must not minimize the obstacles which still lie ahead. Differences still separate the signatories to this treaty from one another, and also from some of their neighbors who fear what they have just done. To overcome these differences, to dispel these fears, we must rededicate ourselves to the goal of a broader peace with justice for all who have lived in a state of conflict in the Middle East.

We have no illusions—we have hopes, dreams, prayers, yes—but no illusions.

There now remains the rest of the Arab world whose support and whose cooperation in the peace process is needed and honestly sought.

I am convinced that other Arab people need and want peace. But some of their leaders are not yet willing to honor these needs and desires for peace. We must now demonstrate the advantages of peace, and expand its benefits to encompass all those who have suffered so much in the Middle East.

Obviously, time and understanding will be necessary for people, hitherto enemies, to become neighbors in the best sense of the word.

Just because a paper is signed, all the problems will not automatically go away. Future days will require the best from us to give reality to these lofty aspirations.

Let those who would shatter peace—who would callously spill more blood—be aware that we three and all others who may join us will vigorously wage peace.(Applause)

So let history record that deep and ancient antagonism can be settled without bloodshed and without staggering waste of precious lives, without rapacious destruction of the land.

It has been said, and I quote, "Peace has one thing in common with its enemy, with the fiend it battles, with war; peace is active, not passive; peace is doing, not waiting; peace is aggressive—attacking; peace plans its strategy and encircles the enemy; peace marshals its forces and storms the gates; peace gathers its weapons and pierces the defense; peace, like war, is waged."

It is true that we cannot enforce trust and cooperation between nations, but we can use all our strength to see that nations do not again go to war. (Applause)

All our religious doctrines give us hope. In the Koran, we read: "But if the enemy incline towards peace, do thou also incline towards peace, and trust in God: for He is the One that heareth and knoweth all things.''

And the prophet Isaiah said: "Nations shall beat their swords into plowshares and their spears into pruninghooks: nation shall not lift up sword against nation, neither shall they learn war any more."

So let us now lay aside war. Let us now reward all the children of Abraham who hunger for a comprehensive peace in the Middle East. Let us now enjoy the adventure of becoming fully human, fully neighbors, even brothers and sisters. We pray God, we pray God together that these dreams will come true. I believe they will. Thank you very much. (Applause)

President Sadat

President Carter, dear friends:

This is certainly one of the happiest moments in my life. (Applause) It is a historic turning point of great significance for all peace-loving nations. Those among us who are endowed with vision cannot fail to comprehend the dimensions of our sacred mission. The Egyptian people, with their heritage and unique awareness of history, have realized from the very beginning the meaning and value of this endeavor.

In all the steps I took, I was not performing a personal mission. I was merely expressing the will of a nation. I am proud of my people and of belonging to them. (Applause)

Today, a new dawn is emerging out of the darkness of the past. A new chapter is being opened in the history of coexistence among nations, one that is worthy of our spiritual values and civilization. Never before had men encountered such a complex dispute, which is highly charged with emotions. Never before did men need that much courage and imagination to confront a single challenge. Never before had any cause generated that much interest in all four corners of the globe.

Men and women of good will have labored day and night to bring about this happy moment. Egyptians and Israelis alike pursued this sacred goal undeterred by difficulties and complications. Hundreds of dedicated individuals on both sides have given generously of their thought and effort to translate the cherished dream into a living reality.

But the man who performed the miracle was President Carter. (Applause) Without any exag-

geration, what he did constitutes one of the greatest achievements of our time. He devoted his skill, hard work, and above all his firm belief in the ultimate triumph of good against evil to ensure the success of our mission. (Applause)

To me he has been the best companion and partner along the road to peace. With his deep sense of justice and genuine commitment to human rights, we were able to surmount the most difficult obstacles.

There came certain moments when hope was eroding and retreating in the face of crisis. However, President Carter remained unshaken in his confidence and determination. He is a man of faith and compassion. Before anything else, the signing of the peace treaty and the exchanged letter is a tribute to the spirit and ability of Jimmy Carter. (Applause)

Happily, he was armed with the blessing of God and the support of his people. For that we are grateful to each and every American who contributed in his own way to the success of our endeavor.

We are also heartened by the understanding of hundreds of thousands of Israelis who remained unwavering in their commitment to peace. The continuation of this spirit is vital to the coronation of our effort. We realize that difficult times lay ahead. The signing of these documents marks only the beginning of peace. But it is an indispensable start. Other steps remain to be taken without delay or procrastination. Much will depend on the success of these steps.

We are all committed to pursue our efforts until the fruits of the comprehensive settlement we agreed upon are shared by all parties to the conflict.

President Carter once said that the United States is committed without reservation to seeing the peace process through until all parties to the Arab-Israeli conflict are at peace. We value such a pledge from a leader who raised the banner of morality and ethics as a substitute for power politics and opportunism. The steps we took in the recent past will serve Arab vital interests. The liberation of Arab land and the reinstitution of Arab authority in the West Bank and Gaza would certainly enhance our common strategic interests.

While we take the initiative to protect these interests, we remain faithful to our Arab commitment. To us, this is a matter of destiny. Pursuing peace is the only avenue which is compatible with our culture and creed.

Let there be no more wars or bloodshed between Arabs and Israelis. (Applause) Let there be no more wars or bloodshed between Arabs and the Israelis. Let there be no more suffering or denial of rights. Let there be no more despair or loss of faith. Let no mother lament the loss of her child. Let no young man waste his life on a conflict from which no one benefits. Let us work together until the day comes when they beat their swords into plowshares and their spears into pruninghooks. And God does call to the abode of peace, He does guide whom He pleases to His way. (President Sadat spoke briefly in Egyptian.) (Applause)

Prime Minister Begin

Mr. President of the United States of America, Mr. President of the Arab Republic of Egypt, Mr. Vice President, Mr. Speaker of the House of Representatives, Mr. Speaker of the Knesset, Members of the Cabinets of the United States, of Egypt and Israel; Members of the Congress and the Knesset; Your Excellencies; Chairman of the Board of Governors of the Jewish Agency; Chairman of the Executive of the Zionist Organization; Mrs. Gruber, the mother of the sons, distinguished guests, ladies and gentlemen: I have come from the land of Israel, the land of Zion and Jerusalem and here I am in humility and with pride as a son of the Jewish people, as one of the generation of the Holocaust and redemption.

The ancient Jewish people gave the world a vision of eternal peace, of universal disarmament, of abolishing the teaching and the learning of war.

Two prophets, Yishayahu Benamotz and Micah Hamorashti, having foreseen the spiritual unity of man under God, with these words coming forth from Jerusalem, gave the nations of the world the following vision—expressed in identical terms— "And they shall beat the swords into plowshares and their spears into pruninghooks: nation shall not lift up sword against nation, neither shall they learn war any more."

Despite the tragedies and disappointments of the past, we must never forsake that vision, that human dream, that unshakable faith.

Peace is the beauty of life. It is sunshine. It is the smile of a child, the love of a mother, the joy of a father, the togetherness of a family. It is the advancement of man, the victory of a just cause, the triumph of truth.

Peace is all of these and more, and more.

These are words I uttered in Oslo on December 10th, 1978, while receiving the second half of the Nobel Peace Prize. The first half went, rightly so, to President Sadat. (Applause) And I took the liberty to repeat them here on this momentous, historic occasion.

It is a great day in the annals of two ancient nations, Egypt and Israel, whose sons met in battle five times in one generation, fighting and falling.

Let us turn our hearts to our heroes and pay tribute to their eternal memory. It is thanks to them, to our fallen heroes, that we could have reached this day.

However, let us not forget that in ancient times, our two nations met also in alliance. Now we make peace, the cornerstone of cooperation and friendship. (Applause) It is a great day in your life, Mr. President of the United States. You have worked so hard, so insistently, so consistently, to achieve this goal. And your labors and your devotion bore God-blessed fruit. (Applause)

Our friend, President Sadat, said that you are the unknown soldier of the peace-making effort. I agree, but as usual, with an amendment. (Laughter) A soldier in the service of peace, you are. You are, Mr. President even, *mirabile dictu*, an intransigent fighter for peace. (Applause)

But, Jimmy Carter, the President of the United States, is not completely unknown. (Laughter) And so it is his efforts which will be remembered and recorded by generations to come. (Applause)

It is, of course, a great day in your life, Mr. President of the Arab Republic of Egypt. In the face of adversity and hostility, you have demonstrated the human value that can change history— civil courage. (Applause)

A great field commander once said, "Civil courage is sometimes more difficult to show than military courage." You showed both, Mr. President. (Applause) But now it is time for all of us to show civil courage in order to proclaim to our peoples and to others: no more war, no more bloodshed, no more bereavement; peace unto you. Shalom, Salaam forever. (Applause)

And it is, ladies and gentlemen, the third greatest day in my life. The first was May 14th, 1948, when our flag was hoisted. Our independence in our ancestors' land was proclaimed after 1,878 years of dispersion, persecution, humiliation and ultimately, physical destruction.

We fought for our liberation alone, and with God's help, we won the day. (Applause) That was spring. Such a spring we can never have again.

The second day was when Jerusalem became

one city and our brave, perhaps most hardened soldiers, the parachutists, embraced with tears and kissed the ancient stones of the remnants of the wall destined to protect the chosen place of God's glory. Our hearts wept with them in remembrance. (Prime Minister Begin spoke briefly in Hebrew.) (Applause)

This is the third day in my life. I have signed a treaty of peace with our great neighbor, with Egypt. The heart is full and overflowing. God gave me the strength to persevere, to survive the horrors of nazism, and of the Stalinite concentration camp, and some other dangers, to endure, not to waver in, nor flinch from my duty, to accept abuse from foreigners, and what is more painful, from my own people, and even from my close friends. This effort, too, bore some fruit.

Therefore, it is the proper place and the appropriate time to bring back to memory the song and prayer of thanksgiving I learned as a child in the home of father and mother that doesn't exist anymore, because they were among the 6 million people, men, women and children, who sanctified the Lord's name with the sacred blood which reddened the rivers of Europe from the Rhine to the Danube, from the Bug to the Volga, because, only because they were born Jews, and because they didn't have a country of their own, and neither a valiant Jewish army to defend them; and because nobody, nobody came to their rescue, although they cried out, "Save us, save us"—*de profundis,* from the depths of the pits, and agony. That is the Song of Degrees, written 2 millenni and 500 years ago when our forefathers returned from their first exile to Jerusalem and Zion. (Prime Minister Begin spoke briefly in Hebrew.)

I will not translate. Every man, whether Jew or Christian or Moslem can read it in his own language in the Book of the Books. It is just Psalm 126. (Applause)

Index

Abaza, Fiqri, 65

Abdullah, of Transjordan: expected to occupy Arab sector of Palestine, 45; Farouk fears ambitions of, in Palestine, 47; favors intervention, territorial aggrandizement, in Palestine, 48, 50; appoints himself commander-in-chief, 50; lays siege to Jerusalem, 51; seeks Arab Palestine for dynasty, 52; loses interest in war, 54; execrated by Nasser, in conversation with Yerucham Cohen, 57; rejects Egyptian-backed government for Palestine, 57; occupies Old City of Jerusalem, confers Hashemite citizenship, 66-7; secretly formulates treaty with Israel, 69; assassinated, 69; fate of, preys on Nasser, 94

Abu Agheila, 58, 106, 109, 149, 151, 152

Abu Rudeis, 231, 238, 240, 250

Abu Saada, General Hassan, 204, 244

Abu Thaleb, Sufi Hassan, 244, 246

Adabiye, 219, 222

Adan, General Avraham, 212, 213, 214, 215, 219, 244

Aden, 141

Adenauer, Konrad, 127, 128

Afghanistan, 91

Africa: Cairo largest city in, 20; Strait of Tiran blockade imperils Israel's trade with, 71; co-sponsors Bandung Conference, 91; Egypt erodes Britain's influence in, 92; nations of, demand Israeli withdrawal from Sinai, in 1956, 117; controls heavy voting bloc in UN General Assembly, 117; post-Sinai immigration to Israel from, 120; Israel

develops trade with, from Eilat, 121; Egypt seeks to establish satellites in, 132-3; Egypt blocks Israel's gateway to, in 1967, 144; Nasser makes Egypt preeminent industrial state of, 179; nations of, sever relations with Israel during 1973 war, 227; Tohami seeks Israel's help against Soviet penetration of, 261; Badawi fears Soviet penetration of, 287; Egyptian-Israeli intelligence cooperation in, 307; *see also* individual African nations

Afro-Asian Institute for Labor Studies and Cooperation, 134

Ahmad, Atef Mitlawi, 253

al-Ahram (newspaper), 33, 73, 126, 178, 183, 199, 272, 288

al-Alamein, 213, 252

al-Aqsa Mosque, 158, 266

al-Arish, 19, 21, 32-3, 106, 109, 115, 183, 258, 268, 275, 283, 291, 299, 302, 310, 312

al-Auja, 56, 58, 61, 69

al-Azhar University, 33, 34, 49, 57, 286, 287

Albania, 138

Alexandria, 31, 166, 187, 188, 201, 248

al-Faluja, 56, 57, 60, 68, 75

Algeria, 92, 98, 99, 126, 140, 143, 145, 148, 260

al-Goumhariyya (newspaper), 180

Ali, General Gamal, 194

al-Isdam (newspaper), 33

al-Kitab (journal), 178

Allenby, General Sir Edmund, 23, 32

Alliance France-Israël, 145

Allon, Yigal, 56, 57, 58, 60, 192, 235, 236

feared by Israel, 80; Israeli spy plot envisages violence against, 82; imminent departure of, enhances Nasser's prestige, 85, 86; role of, in Baghdad Pact viewed as threat by Nasser, 87; Israel equated with, as Egyptian *bête noire*, 87; Egypt fails to acquire weapons from, 91; USSR wishes to break Middle Eastern influence of, 91; presses Israel for territorial concessions, 96; Dayan had served, in invasion of Lebanon, 97; France would disregard, in supplying Israel, 99; frustrated in efforts to contain Nasser's pan-Arabism, 99; had promised loan for Aswan Dam, 99; cancels Aswan loan, 100; reacts to nationalization of Suez Canal, 100; prepares joint invasion plans with France, 100-1; France invites Israel to join, in tripartite attack on Egypt, 102; in strained relations with Israel, dislikes scheme for military collaboration, 102-3; reaches tripartite accord at Sèvres, 104; Egypt's main forces at Suez, to guard against, 106; issues ultimatum to Egypt, Israel, 107-8; Nasser rejects acquiescence to, 108; bombards Egyptian airfields, 108; condemned by UN, US, 112; in abortive paratroop operation at Canal, 113-14; urges Israel's maritime rights, 117; drops further territorial pressure on Israel, 119; attack of, on Suez, ensures Nasser's political survival, 119, 124; owns main businesses in Egypt, 122; airlifts troops to Jordan, 124; plans to evacuate Aden, 141; in 1956, had barred unilateral UNEF evacuation from Gaza, 143; prefers to handle 1967 Sinai crisis within UN, 144; displays support for Israel's position, 146; consults with US on Middle East crisis, 146; admits helplessness, 147; accused of aiding Israel's 1967 offensive, 153; helps formulate UN Resolution 242, 159-60; releases Palestinians for hijacked passengers, 176; Sadat's wartime plotting against, 180; calls for cease-fire in 1973 war, 209; imposes embargo on Israel during 1973 war, 222; refuses US landing rights at Cyprus, 227;

crippled by Arab oil embargo, 228; Jabotinsky rejects collaboration with, 255; arranges to receive Anders army in Palestine, 255; Begin leads underground campaign against, 255-6; Hussein meets with Dayan in, 264; Sadat appeals to, after visit to Jerusalem, 271; Egyptian, Israeli diplomats meet at Leeds Castle, 275-6
Greece, Greeks, 21, 31, 80, 122, 140, 227, 287, 288, 307
Gretchko, Marshal Andrei, 141
Guinea, 136

Habashi, Saba, 248
Had, Major Muhammed al-, 311
Hadi, Ibrahim Abd al-, 64,72
Hadassah Hospital, 68
Hafnawi, Mustafa al-, 100
Haganah, 27, 29, 39-40, 44, 46, 50, 51, 97
Haifa, 27,32, 50, 69, 94, 120, 149, 307
Hakim, Eliahu, 40
Halpern, Ilan, 21, 310
Hammarskjöld, Dag, 95,117, 118, 143
Harel, Isser, 132
Hassan II, of Morocco, 148, 260, 261, 262, 285
Hassan Ali, General Kamal, 260, 288, 310
Heath, Edward, 227
Hebrew University, 62, 68
Hebron, 52, 158
Herzl, Theodor, 22, 32
Heykal, Muhammad Husseinein, 64, 87, 126, 178, 183, 186, 187, 188
Higazi, Abd al-Aziz, 248
Hilali, Naguib, 73
Hilmi, Ahmad Abd al-Aziz, 133
Hitler, Adolf, 27, 36, 39, 131
Hod, General Mordechai, 208
Horev, Colonel Amos, 68
Huleiqat, 56
Hungary, 105, 109, 113, 116
Hussein, of Jordan: forced to abstain from Baghdad Pact, 92; exiles General Glubb, 99; joins Nasser's "United Command" in 1967 crisis, 148; misled on Egyptian "victories," attacks Israel, 157-8; loses half his kingdom, 158; unable to make peace with Israel,